LAW ENFORCEMENT
CLOSE QUARTERS BATTLE

URBAN TACTICS FOR INDIVIDUALS, TEAMS AND TACTICAL UNITS

Special Tactics, LLC

Special Tactics and the Special Tactics Logo are registered trademarks of Special Tactics, LLC

© 2017 by Special Tactics, LLC

ISBN 978-1-945137-04-4

Except as permitted under U.S. Copyright Law, no part of this book may be reprinted, reproduced, transmitted, or utilized in any form by any electronic, mechanical, or other means, now known or hereafter invented, including photocopying, microfilming, and recording, or in any information storage or retrieval system, without written permission from Special Tactics, LLC.

Table of Contents

COURSE OVERVIEW: Urban Tactics For Law Enforcement 1
Manual Structure and Applications   1
An Important Note on Classification, Security and Safety   2

INTRODUCTION: The "Four Pillars" of Survival 3
Proper Mindset   3
Situational Awareness   3
Skill Proficiency   4
Physical Fitness   4

CLOSE QUARTERS BATTLE: Concepts and Fundamentals 5
The Three Principles of Close Quarters Battle   5
Immediate Entry vs. Delayed Entry   6
Deep Entry vs. Shallow Entry   6
Deliberate Clearing vs. Emergency Clearing   7
Technique Combinations, TTP/SOP Development and Training   7
The 8-Steps of Room Entry   7

SECTION 1: TACTICAL TEAM OPERATIONS

Initial Entry and Tactical Stack 11
Tight Stack on an Open Door   13
Tight Stack on a Closed Door   23
Loose Stack   27
Stacking on Interior Doors   28

Single Room Immediate Entry 29
Center-Fed Open Door   30
Center-Fed Closed Door   43
Corner-Fed Open Door   49
Corner-Fed Closed Door   59

Single Room Delayed Entry 61

    Center-Fed Open Door   62
    Center-Fed Closed Door   70
    Corner-Fed Open Door   74
    Corner-Fed Closed Door   79

Multiple Room Immediate Entry 83

    Open Door on the Far Wall   84
    Open Door on the Side Wall   88
    Closed Door on the Far Wall   89
    Closed Door on the Side Wall   92
    Open Door in the Near Corner: Bypass   93
    Open Door in the Near Corner: Hold   95
    Multiple Doors   97
    Back Clear   98
    Clear and Hold   99
    Clear on the Move   100

Multiple Room Delayed Entry 101

    Open Door   102
    Closed Door   103

Hallways Immediate Entry 105

    Hallway Movement   106
    Entering an Open Door from the Hallway   109
    Entering a Closed Door from the Hallway   112
    Entering Opposing Open Doors   115
    Moving From a Room Into the Hallway   117
    Moving Across a Hallway Into Another Room   119
    L-Shape Intersection: High-Low Technique   121
    L-Shape Intersection: Near-Far Technique   125
    T-Shape Intersection   129
    X-Shape Intersection   132
    Intersections with Uneven Corners   135
    Clearing Intersections on the Move   136
    Hallway Joined to an Open Area   137

Hallways Delayed Entry 139

    L-Shape Intersection   140
    T-Shape or X-Shape Intersection   141

Stairwells 143

    Commercial Stairwell   144
    Open Stairwell   149

Complex Configurations and Obstacles 151

    Large Obstacle Along the Near Wall   152
    Large Obstacle Deep in the Room   155
    Half Walls   159
    Confined Areas with Multiple Openings   162
    Cubicle Configurations   165
    Controlling Unarmed Civilians   168

SECION 2: TWO-PERSON OPERATIONS

Single-Room Immediate Entry 173

    Center-Fed Open Door   174
    Center-Fed Closed Door   183
    Corner-Fed Open Door   186
    Corner-Fed Closed Door   195

Single-Room Delayed Entry 197

    Center-Fed Open Door   198
    Center-Fed Closed Door   203
    Corner-Fed Open Door   206
    Corner-Fed Closed Door   209

Multiple Room Immediate Entry 211

    Open Doors   212
    Closed Doors   215
    Multiple Doors   216

Multiple Room Delayed Entry 217

Delayed Entry: Open Doors — 218
Delayed Entry: Closed Doors — 222
Delayed Entry: Multiple Doors — 223

Hallways Immediate Entry 225

Hallway Movement — 226
Entering an Open Door From the Hallway — 229
Entering a Closed Door From the Hallway — 231
Entering Opposing Open Doors — 234
Moving From a Room Into the Hallway — 236
Moving Across a Hallway Into Another Room — 239
L-Shape Intersection: High-Low Technique — 240
L-Shape Intersection: Near-Far Technique — 244
T-Shape Intersection — 248
X-Shape Intersection — 251
Intersections with Uneven Corners — 254
Clearing Intersections on the Move — 255

Hallways Delayed Entry 257

L-Shape Intersections — 258

Stairwells 259

Commercial Stairwell — 260
Open Stairwell — 265

Complex Configurations and Obstacles 267

Large Obstacle Deep in the Room — 268
Confined Areas with Multiple Openings — 271
Cubicle Configurations — 274

SECTION 3: ONE-PERSON OPERATIONS

Single-Room Clearing Without Entry 279

    Center-Fed Open Door   280
    Center-Fed Closed Door   287
    Corner-Fed Open Door   291
    Corner-Fed Closed Door   293
    Quick Clear   294

Single-Room Shallow Entry 297

    Center-Fed Open Door   298
    Center-Fed Closed Door   302
    Corner-Fed Open Door   303
    Corner-Fed Closed Door   306

Single-Room Deep Entry 307

    Center-Fed Open Door   308
    Center-Fed Closed Door   317
    Corner-Fed Open Door   320
    Corner-Fed Closed Door   327

Multiple Rooms 329

    Open Door on the Far Wall   330
    Open Door on the Side Wall   334
    Closed Doors   338
    Multiple Doors   339

Hallways 341

    Hallway Movement   342
    L-Shape Intersection   346
    T-Shape Intersection   347
    X-Shape Intersection   351
    Opposing Open Doors   355

Stairwells 359

Complex Configurations 361

    Confined Areas with Multiple Openings   362
    Cubicle Configurations   365

SECTION 4: MULTIPLE TEAM OPERATIONS

Entry and Movement 375

    Initial Entry   376
    Movement: Leapfrog   380
    Movement: Trail in Direct Support   384
    Simultaneous Entry   388
    Hallway Movement   392
    Intersections   396
    Stairwells   398
    Confined Areas with Multiple Openings   399

SECTION 5: SPECIAL EQUIPMENT

Shotgun, Flashbang, Shield and Mirror 405

    Shotgun Employment   406
    Flashbang Employment: Open Door   410
    Flashbang Employment: Closed Door   416
    Ballistic Shield: Employment Considerations   422
    Ballistic Shield: Corner Clearing   425
    Tactical Mirror   428

SECTION 6: EXTERIOR MOVEMENT

Streets, Alleys and Windows 435

    Moving Down Streets   436
    Crossing Alleys or Narrow Streets   438
    Crossing Wide Streets   441
    Crossing Windows   444

SECTION 7: TACTICAL CONTINGENCIES

Prisoner Handling... 451
    Controlling Subjects in a Room   452
    Using an Arrest Team for Prisoner Handling   456

Casualty Evacuation and Carry.. 459
    Evacuating a Casualty Under Fire   460
    Casualty Carry Techniques   463

FURTHER TRAINING: Courses and Resources 465

Dedicated to the law enforcement officers who have made the ultimate sacrifice in the line of duty

COURSE OVERVIEW
Urban Tactics For Law Enforcement

This manual provides common sense ideas, tactics, techniques and procedures to help law enforcement officers increase their survivability and effectiveness. This manual is designed to be useful to all law enforcement personnel from the patrol officer who faces threats every day on the street, to the first responder who must confront a terrorist or deadly attacker, to the tactical teams that respond to high-threat situations.

All of the TTPs (Tactics, Techniques and Procedures) in this manual are battle-tested and are the product of many decades of lessons learned in high-risk operations. Therefore, the reader can rest assured that everything in this manual is based on sound tactical principles and common sense. However, that does not mean every officer or law enforcement organization will agree with the information presented in this manual.

Officers and organizations are the best judge of their own threat environments and requirements. Officers and organizations should develop their own TTPs, customized for their own particular needs. The goal of this manual is to support this process by providing a wide selection of options to choose from. Some organizations might accept and adopt all the techniques in this manual. Other organizations might choose to adopt some techniques and not others. Either way, the manual is best used as a reference or guide to help law enforcement organizations develop and refine their own TTPs for Close Quarters Battle (CQB) in an urban environment.

The manual may also spark new ideas, challenge assumptions or encourage discussion on tactical themes. Regardless of who "wins" a tactical argument, the process of open-mindedly discussing, questioning and challenging tactical concepts is always beneficial. If this book can encourage this sort of thinking, questioning and discussion, it will have a very positive impact on readiness and tactical performance across the law enforcement community.

Manual Structure and Applications

The manual is divided into chapters that are designed to be somewhat self-contained. Some officers might only be interested in two-person tactics. Others might only employ delayed entry techniques. These officers should be able to read those sections only and be able to follow the text and understand the instructions without reading the entire manual. This also means that some chapters might have repetitive information.

However, making every chapter completely self-contained would cause the manual to be too long and too repetitive. Therefore, readers might have to reference other sections at times to achieve the best understanding of the material. If readers want to get the most comprehensive coverage of the subject matter it is best to read the entire book from start to finish. Even if some chapters seem less useful or relevant, they might contain concepts and information that are universally helpful.

The manual focuses exclusively on CQB tactics and does not go into higher-level planning considerations for specific scenarios and operations like high-risk warrants or hostage rescue. The manual also does not go into detail on specialized sub-skills like breaching and casualty care but instead covers these topics in a more general way. More detailed coverage of all of these subjects (like high-risk warrant, breaching and sniper employment) is available in additional Special Tactics manuals and courses both current and in development.

This manual is not only for SWAT teams and tactical units but instead is designed to be useful to all law enforcement personnel from the most elite tactical units to young officers still going through training. In particular, the sections on single-person and two-person operations might prove useful to officers who are not serving on tactical teams but often have to face overwhelming odds either alone or with a single partner.

This manual can be used as a textbook or learning supplement for police academies and training schools. It can serve as a guide for helping units develop and refine their TTPs. This manual can be a valuable addition to an officer's personal library of professional development materials. This manual is designed for **tacticians**, for officers who are driven to improve their skills, who strive to be the best and possess a deep resolve to protect their community and the American way of life.

An Important Note on Classification, Security and Safety

Nothing in this manual is classified. In addition, all of the information in this manual can be found in other open-source channels. However, because criminals and terrorists study law enforcement and military tactics, it would not be wise to release this manual in digital format to the global audience. While not classified, the information in this manual is sensitive in nature. That is why Special Tactics only provides this manual in hard copy format to law enforcement of verified U.S. government organizations and established training schools that provide training to government clients.

Special Tactics is prepared to work closely with law enforcement organizations and take legal action if necessary to prevent the spread of information in this manual outside the law enforcement community. Making law enforcement tactics available to the global audience could present a serious risk to officers. Special tactics provides a variety of other training resources, available on the open market, that effectively serve the needs of non-government personnel without revealing tactics or information that might put officers at risk.

The techniques described in this manual are dangerous. Officers should not practice these techniques without authorization from the law enforcement organization they serve. In addition, officers should use all available safety measures and training aids (including rehearsals, dry fire training, tabletop exercises etc.) to ensure a firm understanding of tactical concepts prior to live training. This is the smartest and safest approach to training. Improper application of these techniques can cause death or serious injury.

INTRODUCTION
The "Four Pillars" of Survival

The "four pillars" of survival are proper mindset, situational awareness, skill proficiency and physical fitness. These pillars form the basis for mission success and improve split-second decisionmaking in direct combat situations. This manual is not intended only to teach specific techniques but rather to increase the reader's actual chances of survival and success in a real-life emergency. An expert marksman who is not mentally prepared for the stress of combat and not ready to employ lethal force can lose to an untrained adversary. Lack of situational awareness, even for a moment, can cause experienced military and law enforcement professionals to fall victim to unskilled enemies. Therefore, any combat training program must rest on the following four pillars.

Proper Mindset

Proper mindset is the most critical of the four pillars. In the simplest terms, people with the proper mindset devote a large volume of time and energy to prepare for the worst-case scenario. Many people will learn to shoot a pistol or study a martial art but their skills decline quickly because they fail to practice every day. Having the proper mindset means being tough, determined, never cutting corners and taking every precaution to ensure survival. Officers with the proper mindset set aside time ever day to train and maintain their personal equipment. In a combat situation, having the proper mindset means being prepared to employ lethal force without hesitation and never quitting during the fight regardless of fear or pain. The training suggestions in this manual can help develop the proper mindset.

Situational Awareness

Lack of situational awareness is one of the leading causes of failure or death in a deadly force encounter. In modern society, most people's situational awareness is very low. They generally spend their day wrapped up in their own thoughts and problems, paying little attention to what is going on around them. People who live in relatively secure environments often fall into even deeper levels of complacency and unpreparedness. Most victims of crime, terrorism and other deadly attacks lived their lives thinking, "it can't happen to me." Of course, this mindset can be extremely dangerous and may end up leading to catastrophic results.

People with the proper mindset described earlier understand the importance of situational awareness and make disciplined efforts to cultivate it. Situational awareness begins with awareness of the threat and awareness that bad things can happen to anyone. Situational awareness involves trying to remain alert at all times without being paranoid. Situational awareness also involves keeping up with local news, studying trends in violent crime and knowing which neighborhoods and streets to avoid. Those committed to protecting their families might also conduct research to identify registered sex offenders in their area. The best way to improve your situational awareness is to make a conscious effort to continually cultivate and improve it.

Skill Proficiency

Once you have the proper mindset and maintain good situational awareness, the next step is to ensure you have the proper skills or "tools" to protect yourself in a combat situation. When striving to improve skill proficiency it is important to choose the best skills and techniques that are simple, effective, easy to perform and can realistically apply to a real-life scenario. Then you must practice these techniques repeatedly until they become second nature. This will maximize the chances that you will respond immediately in a high-stress situation. The central focus of this manual is to help you build skill proficiency.

Physical Fitness

Even skilled fighters with the proper mindset and high levels of situational awareness can lose a fight simply because they run out of energy. In order to maintain adequate levels of combat fitness, it is not necessary to achieve the same fitness level as a professional or Olympic athlete. Rather, the key is merely to stay healthy, maintain a decent level of cardiovascular endurance, running speed, functional strength and coordination. Popular commercial fitness programs don't always focus on the most useful abilities needed for combat. For example, many people jog but how many also run sprints to build speed? Simply being able to run fast without falling is one of the most critical survival skills in a gunfight or emergency situation, yet most people rarely practice sprinting.

CLOSE QUARTERS BATTLE
Concepts and Fundamentals

The four pillars of proper mindset, situational awareness, skill proficiency and physical fitness establish the foundation for success in any tactical engagement. Building upon that foundation, there are critical concepts and fundamentals that apply specifically to close-quarters battle (CQB). First, there are the three principles of CQB: surprise, speed and controlled aggressive action. There are also different categories of entry techniques. Entry can be immediate or delayed. Entry can also be shallow or deep. Finally, there are two different types of clearing techniques: deliberate and emergency.

The Three Principles of Close Quarters Battle

The three principles of surprise, speed and controlled aggressive action are critical for success and apply to all types of urban operations and close-quarters engagements. Even if officers choose to slow down, operate more cautiously or establish a more defensive posture in specific situations, the principles still apply. For example, the principle of speed does not dictate that officers always move as fast as they can, only fast enough to maintain the initiative and minimize their exposure.

Surprise

Surprise is a critical element for successful tactical entry and can be achieved through rapid execution, deception, and shock. When entering a building or room, officers should use the element of surprise to instill maximum fear and confusion in the mind of the adversary. Surprise is particularly important for initial phase of the entry process because it helps officers gain the initiative in the first critical seconds of the operation and overwhelm the adversaries before they have a chance to respond.

Speed

Speed helps officers capture the initiative and then maintain the initiative by outpacing the adversary. Still, the principle of speed does not dictate that officers always move as fast as they can. If officers move too fast and operate in a reckless manner, catastrophic failure can result. Moving quickly in a controlled manner (sometimes referred to as "careful hurry") will prove most effective in a high-stress situation. Officers only need to move fast enough to outpace the adversary, maintain the initiative, minimize their exposure and avoid becoming bogged down.

Controlled Aggressive Action

Controlled aggressive action means overwhelming the adversary with the maximum level of shock, while still maintaining control of the situation. Many adversaries that officers will confront are extremely committed, violent and aggressive. This is particularly the case with terrorists and extremists. The adversary is often not intimidated by an officer's badge or status. Adversaries will not care whether the officer is highly trained, well-armed or part of an elite tactical unit. The adversary will attack ruthlessly and aggressively and therefore a high level of controlled aggressive action can be required to overwhelm and subdue the adversary. However, aggressive action still must be applied in a controlled and methodical manner. Officers should only use the level of force necessary to resolve the situation and must make every effort to avoid harming innocent civilians and bystanders.

Immediate Entry vs. Delayed Entry

CQB entry techniques can be divided into "immediate entry" and "delayed entry." Immediate entry methods call for offensive, aggressive movement and were developed by military special operations forces for hostage rescue situations. Law enforcement officers may use immediate entry techniques when innocent lives are at stake or when it is critical to quickly overwhelm and dominate the adversary. Immediate entry calls for using surprise and speed to enter and penetrate the room immediately without taking the time to first evaluate the room from the outside. While sometimes necessary, immediate entry is generally more dangerous than delayed entry.

Delayed entry techniques are designed to minimize an officer's exposure and maximize the benefits of cover and concealment. For one-person or two-person operations, delayed entry is generally a safer option than immediate entry. If officers are operating as part of a team, it is easier for them to aggressively rush through the door and dominate the room. However, if officers are operating alone or with only a single partner and have no additional support, it can be dangerous to rush into a fight when the odds might not be in the officer's favor. Teams may also choose to employ delayed entry, especially in high-risk situations.

Delayed entry tactics call for clearing as much of a room or hallway as possible from the outside, before actually making entry. Delayed entry tactics are also a good option for situations where time is on the officer's side and there is no need to move in quickly.

Deep Entry vs. Shallow Entry

Most of the immediate entry tactics developed by the military for hostage situations call for deep entry. Deep entry involves penetrating fully into the room in order to achieve complete domination and clear all danger areas or "dead-space" as quickly as possible. Deep entry was also primarily designed for team-level operations in situations where significant firepower and supporting assets were available.

For one-person operations, shallow entry is often a better option. Because a single officer is more vulnerable, the officer might not want to rush too deep into the room but will instead choose to stay close to the door. This gives the officer the option to quickly retreat or exit the room should he/she encounter stiff opposition. However, there are some situations where a single officer will have no choice but to conduct a deep entry in order to clear behind large pieces of furniture or to secure a room for use as a defensive position or safe area.

Deliberate Clearing vs. Emergency Clearing

CQB clearing techniques can also be divided into "deliberate" clearing and "emergency" clearing. The difference has less to do with speed and more to do with the level of care and attention applied to the clearing process. It is possible to execute deliberate tactics very quickly, as long as officers are careful to clear each room and danger area completely. Essentially, when conducting a deliberate clear, officers will not take any shortcuts.

Emergency tactics are the opposite of deliberate tactics. In an emergency situation, officers may need to take shortcuts and not clear every room or danger area completely. This increases the level of risk. However, in an emergency situation where time is critical or there is imminent danger to innocent people, officers might choose to assume a greater level of risk. Deliberate clearing is generally the best option for single-person and two-person operations due to the increased level of risk. However, officers might end up facing an emergency situation alone and will have no choice but to move at maximum speed. This type of scenario is extremely dangerous and as an individual, there is little an officer can do to reduce the risk. Therefore, the officer may decide to move as quickly as possible and use speed as security, hoping that adversaries will not react fast enough to engage.

Technique Combinations, TTP/SOP Development and Training

Officers do not have to choose only one of the techniques just described. Rather, officers can employ the techniques in various combinations to fit the needs of the unique tactical situation. Officers might initially move into a building cautiously, employing delayed entry and deliberate clearing techniques. If the officers discover hostages in the building or shots are fired, the officers might rapidly shift to using immediate entry and emergency clearing techniques.

Individual law enforcement offices and tactical teams should also develop unique TTPs (Tactics, Techniques and Procedures) and SOPs (Standard Operating Procedures) that fit the particular preferences and needs of the organization. This manual is only a reference for providing suggestions and ideas. Ultimately, each unit or organization should establish its own, customized TTPs and SOPs and collect them in a binder. That binder should be continually updated and evaluated over time to reflect lessons learned in the field and in training. Techniques should emphasize safety, control and team integrity while attempting to achieve manpower and firepower superiority in each engagement.

It is also critical that officers practice techniques frequently under realistic conditions. If sophisticated training facilities are not available, officers can still create realistic scenarios using marked-ground training (engineer tape tied to stakes in the ground to depict room configurations) or even tabletop exercises. Officers must remain highly disciplined and adhere rigidly to an effective training regimen. Officers must also spend as much time at the range as possible to hone their shooting skills and target discrimination ability. This will prove particularly important in a situation when an officer may be required to take an aimed shot when there are numerous civilians in close proximity.

The 8-Steps of Room Entry

The following 8 steps are the foundation of room entry tactics and are worth committing to memory. While the specific procedures depend on the situation or the clearing technique, the general concept behind the eight steps is relevant to all types of room entry. The eight steps are: clear the doorway (immediate area), clear the corners, dominate the room, control occupants, secure the room, report status, back clear, cover and evacuate.

1) Clear the doorway (immediate area) – The lead officer should clear the doorway and the immediate area around the doorway before entering the room. If the doorway is not clear, there is a chance that the entire team will be bottled up in the "fatal funnel" where they will be the focus of hostile fire. The doorway must remain clear for the team to quickly enter the room.

2) Clear the corners – The corners of the room are often the most dangerous places where adversaries can hide. This is because an adversary hiding in the corner can shoot the entire team as the team enters the room. Therefore, the team must clear the corners of the room as quickly as possible.

3) Dominate the room – Even if officers must conduct a "shallow entry" (also called limited penetration) the concept of dominating still applies. Officers must establish their points of domination in places where they can see behind furniture and objects in the room and engage the enemy with interlocking fields of fire.

4) Control occupants – Until the occupants in the room are controlled, the room cannot be secured. Officers control the occupants in the room by applying three principles: dominating presence, verbal commands and physical contact.

5) Secure the room – Securing the room means taking steps to ensure that the room is clear of threats. This includes restraining and searching any occupants in the room and looking behind furniture or opening closets to ensure no adversaries are hiding inside. It is the team leader's decision to declare the room secure. Once the room is secure, the team should "mark" the room using a chemlight. This is so that, in the chaos and confusion of combat, the team will know that a room has been secured. However, when re-entering a secured room, officers should always be prepared to deal with adversaries who have entered the room since the team left. If time is critical, officers may choose to mark the room after the initial clearance and keep moving without checking every closet or cabinet.

6) Report status – Officers do not need to report status after clearing each room. However, officers should report to higher headquarters when the premises are secured, whenever they discover critical information, identify threats, complete specified tasks or suffer casualties.

7) Back clear (secondary sweep) – This step will only apply once the team has moved to the limit of its advance and is ready to exit the building. Back clear means the team will move back to the entry point and prepare to cover and evacuate. This step is particularly important if the team needs to evacuate subjects or hostages. At least one element will back clear to establish a safe route for evacuation.

8) Cover and evacuate – Once the team has back cleared to the entry point, they must be ready to safely exit the structure with any subjects or hostages. In addition, officers should account for any property damage prior to leaving. If officers arrest any suspects, they will need to provide information and contact procedures for any family members left on the premises.

SECTION 1

TACTICAL TEAM OPERATIONS

TEAM OPERATIONS

TEAM OPERATIONS
Initial Entry and Tactical Stack

While many officers might have to operate alone or only with a single partner, a firm grasp of team-level CQB forms the foundation of higher-level CQB mastery. It is always preferable to bring more guns to the fight and officers should always attempt to achieve manpower superiority if additional officers are available. Therefore, officers must know how to work as a team to maximize their effectiveness and avoid accidents. A team is generally defined as three or more officers. If manpower is available, officers should try to remain in groups of three or more. This maximizes security and safety in the entry process and makes casualty evacuation much easier.

The current trend in deadly attacks and terrorist incidents makes knowledge of team operations even more important. Several officers from different departments or jurisdictions may find themselves having to work together as the first responders to a crisis. Some level of standardized team tactics could prove extremely helpful in this type of situation. While teams that specialize in CQB may choose to have their own unique TTPs, this book might prove useful as a standardized reference for officers who do not specialize in CQB but may have to work across organizational boundaries in a crisis.

The first thing a tactical team must do is "stack" at the initial entry point. There are two types of stack configurations, tight stack (closed stack) and loose stack (dispersed stack). Employing a tight stack makes officers more vulnerable but can sometimes be necessary for ensuring quick entry into a room, particularly when operating with a team that has had little time to practice together. The loose stack is generally the preferred technique since it greatly reduces the team's vulnerability to hostile fire, particularly automatic fire. However, if a tactical team does not practice entering a room using the loose stack there is a possibility that there will be dangerous gaps between team members as they enter, which could leave officers' backs exposed.

Some teams may choose to execute a "ready signal" prior to entering a room. Teams that have not spent as much time working together might choose to use a more deliberate signal for greater control. More experienced teams might use simpler signals or even no signal at all.

Whether a door is opened or closed can change the configuration of officers in the stack. In most cases, when faced with a closed door, one officer should move across to the opposite side of the door to act as the breacher.

TEAM OPERATIONS: INITIAL ENTRY AND TACTICAL STACK

TIGHT STACK ON AN OPEN DOOR

STEP 1 - Occupy the Initial Entry Point

The team must remain as quiet as possible to avoid compromise when occupying the initial entry point. Avoiding detection allows the team to maintain the element of surprise and gives the officers time to assess the situation before making entry. The team must also maintain communication and coordinate effectively with any command and control elements. This will help officers maintain the pace of operations, retain the initiative and expedite searches while minimizing the chances of civilian casualties or friendly fire.
NOTE: Color coded shirts, arrows and scan arcs are designed to help the reader keep track of different team members.

TIGHT STACK ON AN OPEN DOOR

STEP 2 - Maintain Correct Spacing

For the tight stack technique, officers should remain close to each other to facilitate control and allow fast and fluid movement into the room. However, officers should still try to maintain some degree of spacing since a tightly packed formation is an easy target for one burst of automatic fire. Also, if officers are so close together that they are in physical contact, there is the chance that they will snag on each other's gear or trip over each other in a high-stress situation.

TIGHT STACK ON AN OPEN DOOR

STEP 3 - Execute the Ready Signal

To ensure the team is ready, it is useful to employ a hand signal. There are several possible signal options. The most deliberate is the "thumb-back, squeeze forward." For this option the second officer in the stack extends a thumb back over the shoulder. The next officer in the stack squeezes the thumb and then extends his/her thumb back to repeat the process until the signal reaches the last officer in the stack. At this point, the last officer will pass a firm squeeze forward. Each officer will pass the squeeze forward until it reaches the first officer. At this point the team is ready for entry. When conducting the squeeze, it is important to use a firm squeeze on the fleshy part of the arm or shoulder. In a high-stress situation, an officer might not feel a squeeze through thick layers of gear or body armor. It is also important to execute a squeeze and not a "tap" or "leg bump." In a high-stress situation, an officer might mistake incidental contact or an accidental bump for the ready signal and move out when the team is not actually ready. Using a firm, positive squeeze makes it impossible to mistake incidental contact for the ready signal. Finally, depending on the situation and the experience level of the officers, some teams might want to simplify the ready signal. For example, it is possible to eliminate the thumb back and only use the squeeze forward. Once the initial entry is complete and the team is inside the building, it is preferable to simplify the ready signal even further. After the initial entry, the second officer can control all movement. The second officer will look around to ensure the team is ready, then pass a squeeze to the first officer, making movement quicker and easier. Experienced teams that train together frequently may be able to flow from room to room without using a signal.

TIGHT STACK ON AN OPEN DOOR

STEP 4 - Team-Member Positioning

It is preferable not to predetermine the order of officers in the stack. As the team moves from room to room it will become increasingly difficult to shuffle officers around into the correct order and attempting to do so will slow movement considerably. Instead it is best to allow stacking order to remain as flexible as possible. However, it is good to apply some general rules to stacking order. For example, it is preferable for the team leader not to be the first or second person to enter the room. If there is a dedicated shotgun breacher on the team, the breacher might want to remain last in the stack or second in the stack depending on unit SOPs. For tactical teams, it can be useful to have two designated shotgun breachers per team. That way, if one shotgun goes down, the other breacher can step forward with no delay.

TIGHT STACK ON AN OPEN DOOR

STEP 5 - Lead Officer Positioning

The lead officer's main responsibility is to provide security on the door. The lead officer should maintain some distance from the door to avoid indiscriminate fire. Adversaries tend to spray bullets in the direction of the door so it is advisable to stay slightly back. Remember, that most interior walls are not bulletproof and the chances of getting shot through a wall are very high. Also, if an officer gets too close to the door, his/her shadow can extend across the opening and compromise the team. The lead officer should also avoid touching or bumping into the wall because doing so will make noise and might also increase the chances of getting shot, since bullets tend to travel along walls. Keeping away from the wall also gives the lead officer a good angle to see into the room. Whether the door is open or closed, standing at a slight angle to see into the room can help prevent the adversary from surprising the team or spraying bullets around the corner.

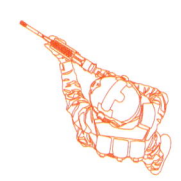

TIGHT STACK ON AN OPEN DOOR

STEP 6 - Second Officer Positioning

The second officer will be positioned slightly to the outside of the lead officer, in a position to provide additional coverage on the door. It is always preferable to have two guns on the door. If the first officer goes down, the second officer can return fire immediately. While the second officer might choose to provide cover to the front, he/she should at least be capable of pivoting to engage the door without bumping into the first officer.

TEAM OPERATIONS: INITIAL ENTRY AND TACTICAL STACK

TIGHT STACK ON AN OPEN DOOR

STEP 7 - Third Officer Positioning

The third officer, who is normally the team leader, will be positioned behind the second officer. The tactical team leader should avoid being first or second into the room. Instead, the team leader should go into the room as number three or four in the stack. If for any reason the team has to split into two-person elements, the team leader should still avoid being first into the room. The third officer will provide cover in whatever directions are not covered by the rest of the team. This might mean providing cover to the front, outward, rear or upward towards upper story windows.

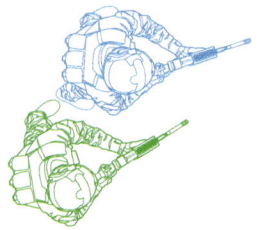

TIGHT STACK ON AN OPEN DOOR

STEP 8 - Last Officer Positioning

The last officer will provide rear security for the team. It is important that the last officer avoid turning his/her back to the team completely. Instead, the last officer should angle his/her body to be able to see the stack with peripheral vision and reduce the chances of being left behind. This is particularly important when operating in the dark. In general, the officer should not be too concerned with orienting his/her armor plate in a particular direction, since hostile fire can come unexpectedly from any angle. Instead, moving naturally in an athletic, fighter's stance will prove more beneficial than constantly attempting to "square off" to every potential threat.

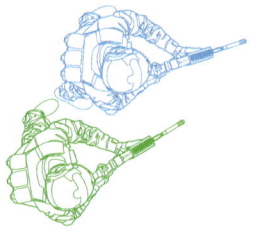

TIGHT STACK ON AN OPEN DOOR

STEP 9 - Positioning for Additional/Fewer Officers

If there are more than four officers on the team, the additional officers assume a similar role and position as the third officer and distribute their cover to protect the team from all angles. If there are only three officers on the team, the roles of the first two officers will remain the same but the third officer will have to cover additional angles and also provide rear security for the team.

TIGHT STACK ON AN OPEN DOOR

STEP 10 - Stacking With Heavy Side and Light Side

It is also possible for additional team members to stack on the opposite side of the door. However, it is ideal for the number of officers on each side of the door to be uneven. When there are an uneven number of officers on each side of the door this will mean there is a "heavy side" and "light side." Having a heavy side and light side helps coordinate the entry process since all of the officers on the heavy side will enter first and then the officers on the light side will follow. While it is possible to enter with equal number of officers on each side of the door, this can create confusion about which side will enter the room first.

TEAM OPERATIONS: INITIAL ENTRY AND TACTICAL STACK

TIGHT STACK ON A CLOSED DOOR

Team-Member Positioning

If the door is closed, the general positioning of officers will remain the same. However, one officer will generally have to move to the opposite side of the door to act as a breacher. Depending on the situation and the team's SOPs, this can either be the last officer, the second officer or the first officer. The positioning of the doorknob and whether the door opens in or out is not of critical importance. While some teams might have preferences about the best place to position the stack in relation to the doorknob, being overly rigid in such preferences can cause confusion in a high-stress situation and slow the team's movement speed. Generally it is best to be able to enter the room quickly and aggressively without worrying too much about the positioning of the doorknob.

TIGHT STACK ON A CLOSED DOOR

OPTION 1 - Last Officer Opens the Door

In some cases the last officer will be the breacher. The team leader has the option of calling the breacher forward to open a door. This is particularly the case for an exterior door or any other door the team leader expects might be locked or barricaded. When the breacher is called, the breacher will move around the team to the opposite side of the door to open it for the team. In this case, the third officer will become the last officer and must pick up rear security. In some situations, another officer may want to cover the breacher's back.

TEAM OPERATIONS: INITIAL ENTRY AND TACTICAL STACK

TIGHT STACK ON A CLOSED DOOR

OPTION 2 - Second Officer Opens the Door

Some teams might have two breachers. If this is the case, it is a good option for the alternate breacher to position himself/herself second in the stack. In other cases, if the door is not locked, the second officer might decide to move across to act as the breacher and open the door. In these cases, the first officer will stop short of the door and provide coverage, focusing all attention on the door in case an adversary opens it. The second officer will then move around the first officer to the opposite side of the door and open the door for the team.

1

2

TIGHT STACK ON A CLOSED DOOR

OPTION 3 - Lead Officer Opens the Door

If the door is closed but not locked, one of the quickest ways to enter the room is for the lead officer to immediately move past the door to the other side to act as the breacher. In these cases, the second officer will immediately assume the lead officer's role and provide coverage on the door in case an adversary opens it. The two previous options of either the lead officer or second officer opening the door are interchangeable. Using the "free-flow" concept, the lead officer and second officer can base their actions off of each other. Therefore, if the first officer stops to cover the door, the second officer can automatically move around to act as the breacher. If the first officer moves across the door to breach, the second officer can automatically assume the lead officer's position. Also, there are some cases when the lead officer will not be able to move to the other side of the door and will have to "self-breach."

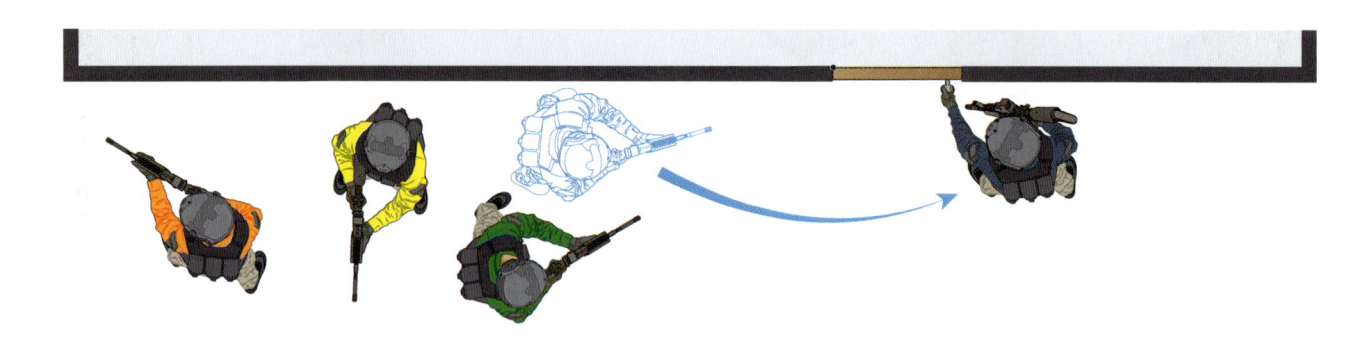

1

2

LOOSE STACK

Team-Member Positioning

While it is useful to understand the close stack when learning the fundamentals of CQB, the loose stack is generally the preferred technique. In a loose stack the roles and positioning of the first two officers remain the same. However, the remaining officers will spread out and assume good firing positions behind cover or concealment if possible. Spreading out minimizes risk to the team and makes it harder for a single burst of automatic fire or a single grenade to incapacitate the entire team. However, while the loose stack is safer, it is also more difficult to execute and requires precise coordination and timing. Once the first two officers enter the room, the remaining team members must converge on the door and enter in sequence. There is no fixed order for entering the room after the first two officers. Whichever officer arrives at the door first will enter first. So, it can be difficult to ensure the remaining officers enter smoothly. If a team does not practice the loose stack often, there can be large gaps between officers as they enter the room or in some cases, officers that are not alert might even be left behind.

STACKING ON INTERIOR DOORS

Team-Member Positioning

Once the team has made entry, the process for stacking on interior doors is similar to the process for stacking on exterior doors. One key difference is that because interior doors are often unlocked, it is not always necessary to send a dedicated breacher around to open every door. Rather, the lead or second officer can quickly move across the door and open it for the team. A second critical point is that the team should attempt to stack on the "long wall" in each room. The long wall offers better cover and concealment and the most space for officers to spread out. In situations where the team has to stack on both sides of the door, the heavy side should generally be on the long wall and the light side should be on the short wall.

TEAM OPERATIONS
Single Room Immediate Entry

The "free flow" method helps teams maintain the initiative and minimize confusion in high-stress situations. When using the free flow method, as little as possible should be scripted or predetermined. For example, officers will not predetermine whether the first officer goes left or right into the room. Instead, all other officers react to the first officer's decision. Each officer follows the principle: "move in the opposite direction of the officer in front of you." This helps officers stay outwardly focused on the situation instead of inwardly focused on a set checklist or procedure.

This same free flow concept applies to all aspects of CQB. If the first officer picks up coverage on an open door, the second officer will flow past. If instead the first officer moves past, the second officer sees the vulnerable angle and picks up coverage on the door. If there are two danger areas, the first officer will pick one and cover it. The next officer will naturally pick up the remaining danger area. Minimal communication or discussion is needed. Team members simply react to each other's actions and keep moving. Even when officers make mistakes (which is inevitable) they should keep moving and maintain momentum.

Immediate entry (as opposed to delayed entry) is useful for situations where officers need to move through a building quickly or enter and clear a room without hesitation. The most common example of this type of scenario is a hostage situation. When innocent lives are at stake, officers may choose to assume greater risk and execute an immediate entry. However, if there is no reason to rush into a room, the team may choose to use delayed entry instead of immediate entry to minimize exposure and reduce risk.

The critical point to remember is that the immediate and delayed entry techniques described in this manual are interchangeable. Therefore, a team can seamlessly transition between immediate entry and delayed entry depending on the situation. The team can also use distraction devices (flashbangs) to minimize the risks of immediate entry.

When conducting an immediate entry, the first two officers will clear the doorway, immediate area, corners, and then move to their domination points within the room. These two team members will maintain good visual contact with each other once they reach their domination points. The third and fourth officers will clear the doorway, immediate area, the center area of the room and check behind the door. Whoever is the last team member to enter the room will position near the door and provide rear security for the team.

IMMEDIATE ENTRY: CENTER-FED OPEN DOOR

Overview

Rooms generally fall into two categories: center-fed and corner-fed. A center-fed room is a room where the door is in the center of the wall, allowing the officer to move either left or right when entering the room. When faced with a center-fed, open door, the team will stack using one of the methods already discussed. Once again, the loose stack is preferred to maximize officer safety. The following pages will describe the actions of each officer in sequence. However, note that in actual application, all officers will attempt to enter the room as quickly as possible. For example, the second officer will enter the room and begin clearing immediately following the lead officer. **NOTE: A room where the door is very close to the corner but is not completely flush with the corner (see bottom example) is still considered a corner-fed room.**

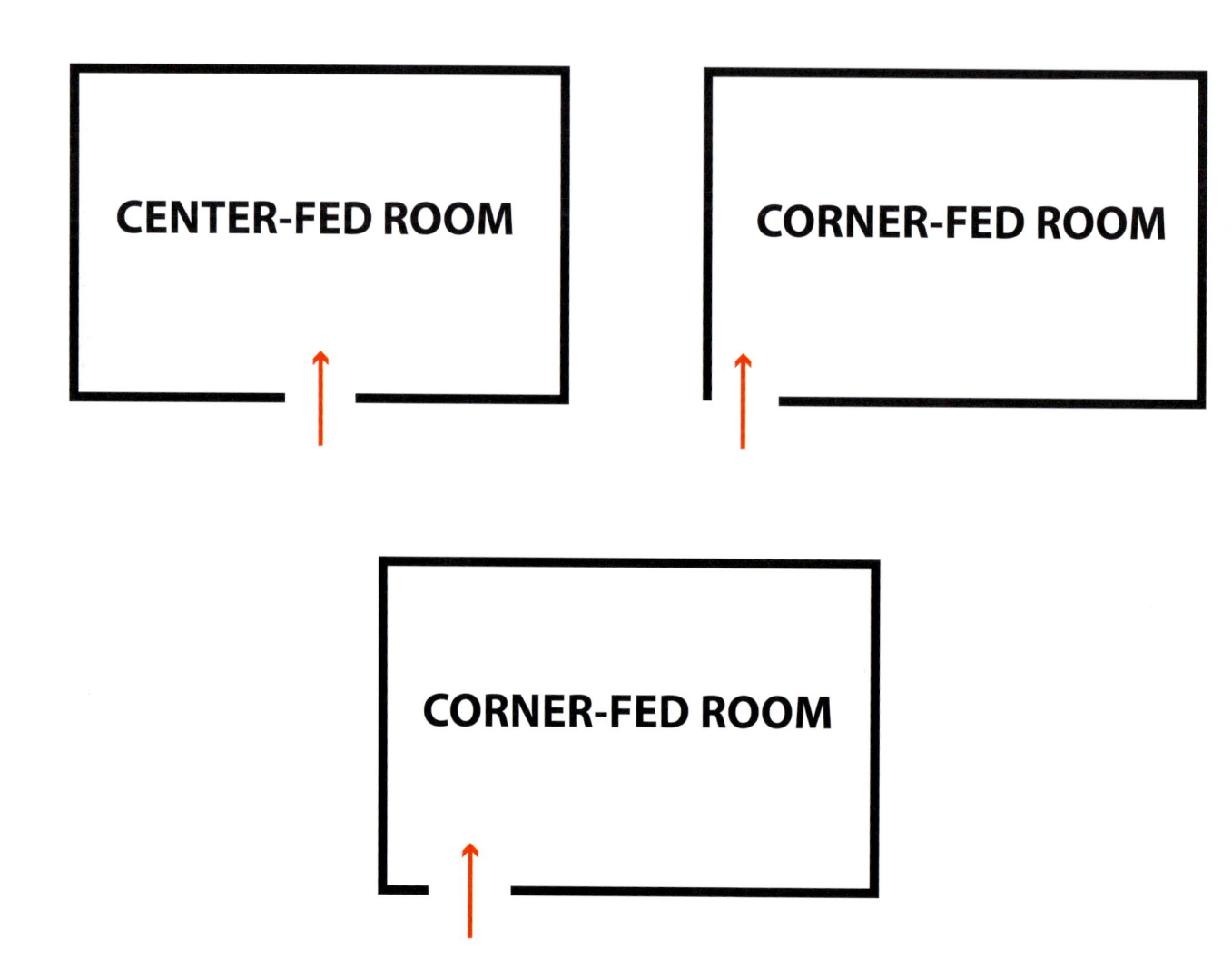

CENTER-FED ROOM

CORNER-FED ROOM

CORNER-FED ROOM

Team Operations: Single-Room Immediate Entry   31

IMMEDIATE ENTRY: CENTER-FED OPEN DOOR

LEAD OFFICER STEP 1 - Clear the Doorway

The lead officer steps outward slightly to have a better angle of vision into the room while ensuring that the doorway is clear. The lead officer can also take this opportunity to engage deep threats in the center of the room. If the officer does not clear the doorway and the immediate area around the doorway but instead moves directly towards the corner, it is possible that the officer will fail to see an adversary near the doorway until it is too late. This adversary can then block the whole team's entry into the room. Therefore, if the first officer steps out slightly before entering and takes a moment to clear the doorway and the area around it, the officer will be able to engage any immediate threats **before** entering the room. This helps the officer avoid being shot by an adversary hiding in the corner.

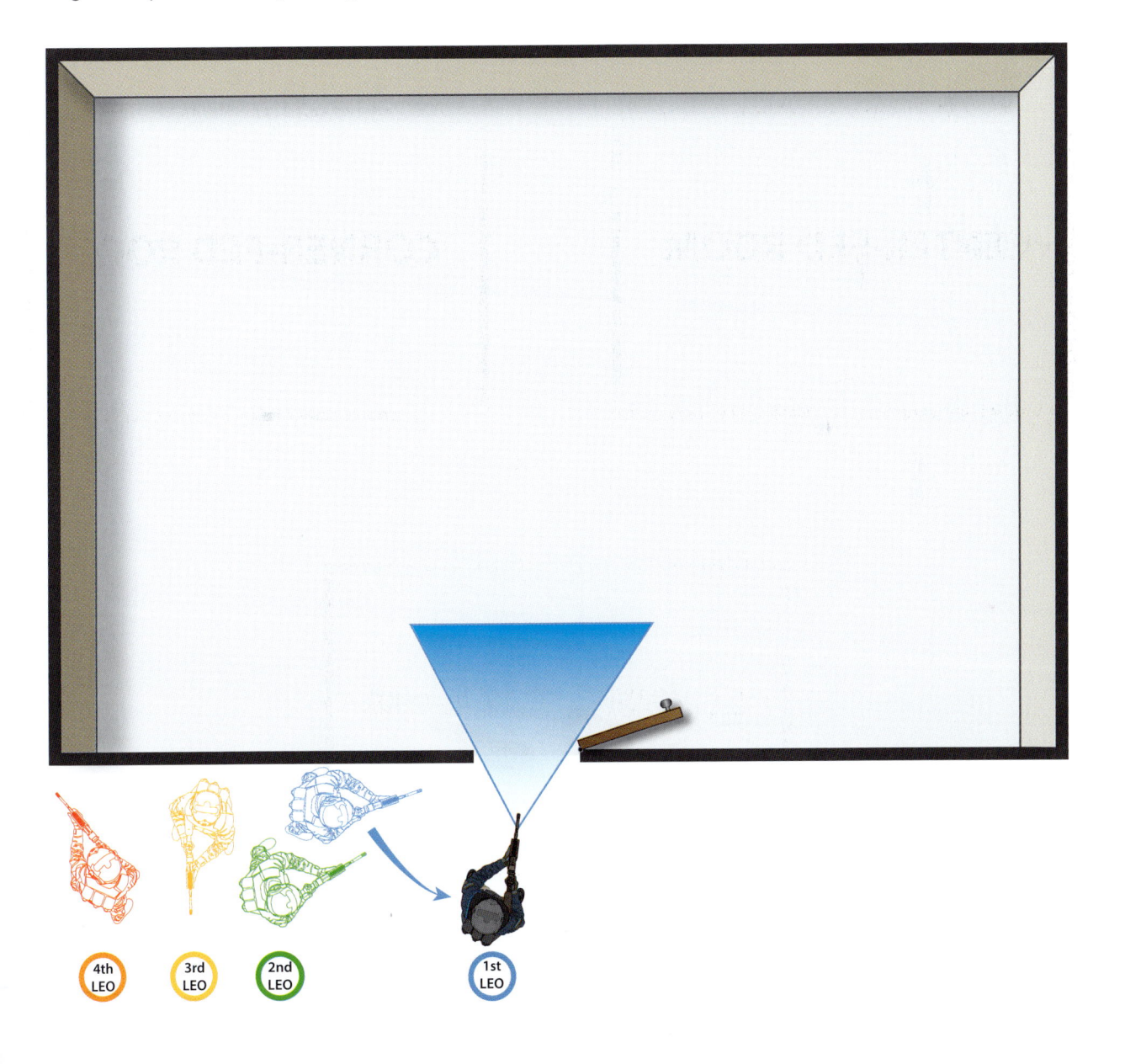

IMMEDIATE ENTRY: CENTER-FED OPEN DOOR

LEAD OFFICER STEP 2 - Clear the Corner

Clearing the doorway from outside the room will allow the lead officer to turn immediately to the corner once inside the room. The lead officer should not predetermine which direction to turn. In general, the lead officer should turn to address the greatest threat first. For example, if the officer hears movement to the left, he/she might want to clear the left corner. However, in the end, the decision of which way to turn is up to the first officer. Once the lead officer makes the turn, he/she will clear the corner and engage any threats in the corner until they are neutralized.

IMMEDIATE ENTRY: CENTER-FED OPEN DOOR

LEAD OFFICER STEP 3 - Move to the Domination Point

Once the corner is clear, the lead officer should not stay focused on the corner but should instead immediately begin to scan inward while moving along the wall. The officer continues to scan and move towards his/her domination point. The domination point (depicted below) is slightly forward of the corner. Moving slightly forward in this way will give the lead officer a better angle to see behind furniture and obstacles in the room. The lead officer will continue to scan inward until the scan reaches a point three feet off the second officer's muzzle. At this point the lead officer will scan back and forth across his/her full sector several times to ensure the sector is clear and to identify potential danger areas. Experienced teams can shorten this deliberate scanning process and may also break each officer's sector into primary and secondary sectors.

IMMEDIATE ENTRY: CENTER-FED OPEN DOOR

SECOND OFFICER STEP 1 - Clear the Corner

The second officer will turn in the opposite direction of the lead officer. Once again, the lead officer can choose to turn either way. The second officer must remain alert and turn in the opposite direction. It is also critical that the second officer uses a tighter and more direct approach angle in order to enter the room as close as possible behind the lead officer. This is to ensure the lead officer's back is not left exposed. The lead officer clears one corner but his/her back will be exposed to any adversary standing in the other corner. Therefore, the second officer must clear the other corner as quickly as possible to cover the lead officer's back. Once the second officer makes the turn, he/she will clear the corner and engage any threats in the corner until they are neutralized.

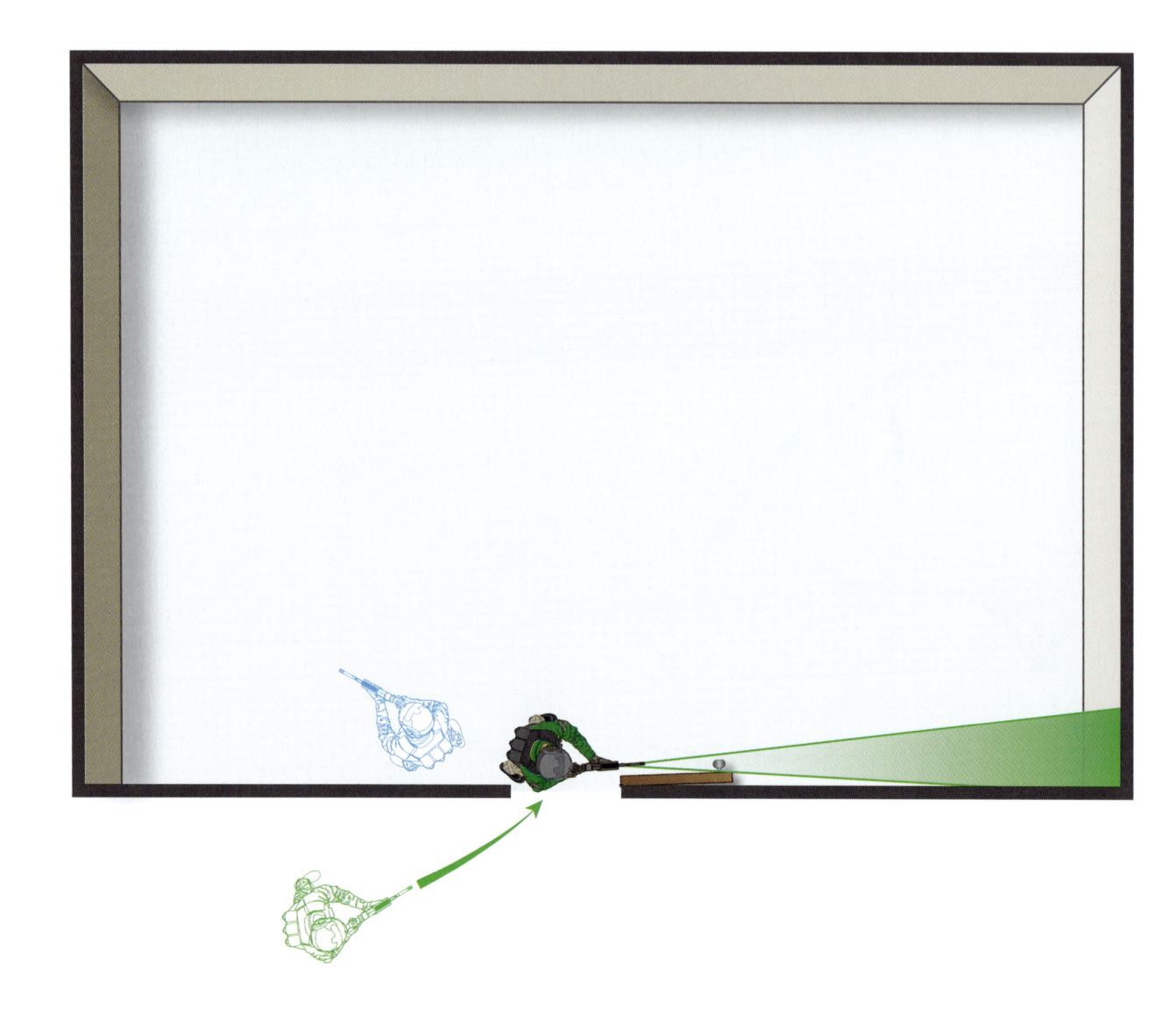

IMMEDIATE ENTRY: CENTER-FED OPEN DOOR

SECOND OFFICER STEP 2 - Move to the Domination Point

Once the corner is clear, the second officer should not stay focused on the corner but should instead immediately begin to scan inward while moving along the wall. The officer continues to scan and move towards his/her domination point. The domination point (depicted below) is slightly forward of the corner. The second officer will continue to scan inward until the scan reaches a point three feet off the lead officer's muzzle. At this point the second officer will scan back and forth across his/her full sector several times to ensure the sector is clear and to identify potential danger areas. Experienced teams can shorten this deliberate scanning process.

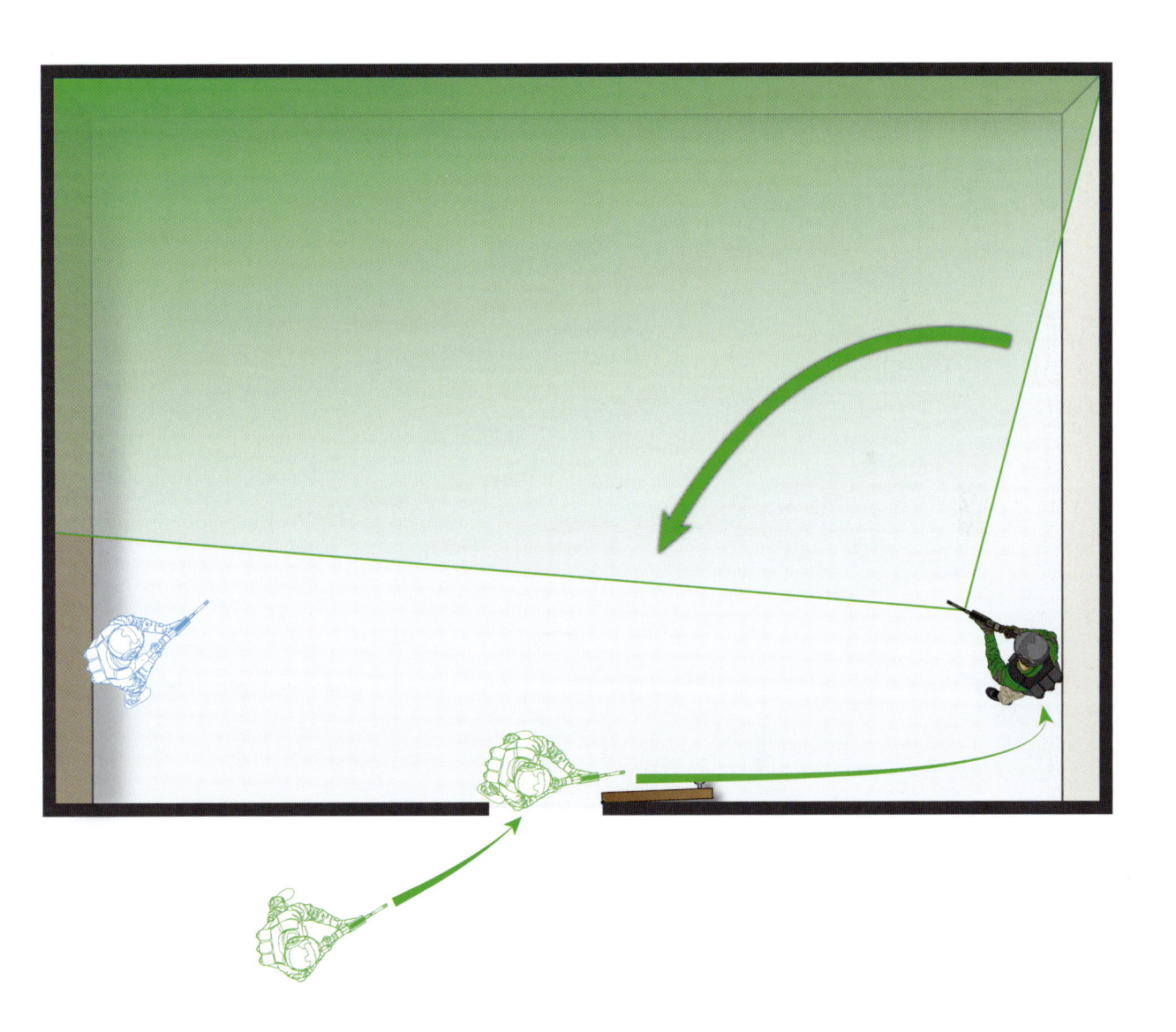

IMMEDIATE ENTRY: CENTER-FED OPEN DOOR

THIRD OFFICER - Clear the Center of the Room and Scan

The third officer will enter the room, moving in the opposite direction of the second officer. Once again, the rule is "move in the opposite direction of the officer in front of you." As the third officer enters the room, he/she will identify the center of the room and start to scan in the direction of movement. For example, if the third officer enters the room and moves to the left, he/she will scan from right to left, in the same direction as the entry movement. The third officer should also start the scan slightly behind the center point of the room. For example if the officer moves left, the scan will start to the right of the center point of the room. See the illustration below for further clarification. While scanning, the third officer will move to a domination point just to the side of the door. The third officer will continue the initial scan in the direction of movement until it reaches a point three feet off the lead officer. The third officer will then scan back in the other direction to a point three feet off the second officer. At this point the third officer will scan back and forth across his/her full sector several times to ensure the sector is clear and to identify potential danger areas.

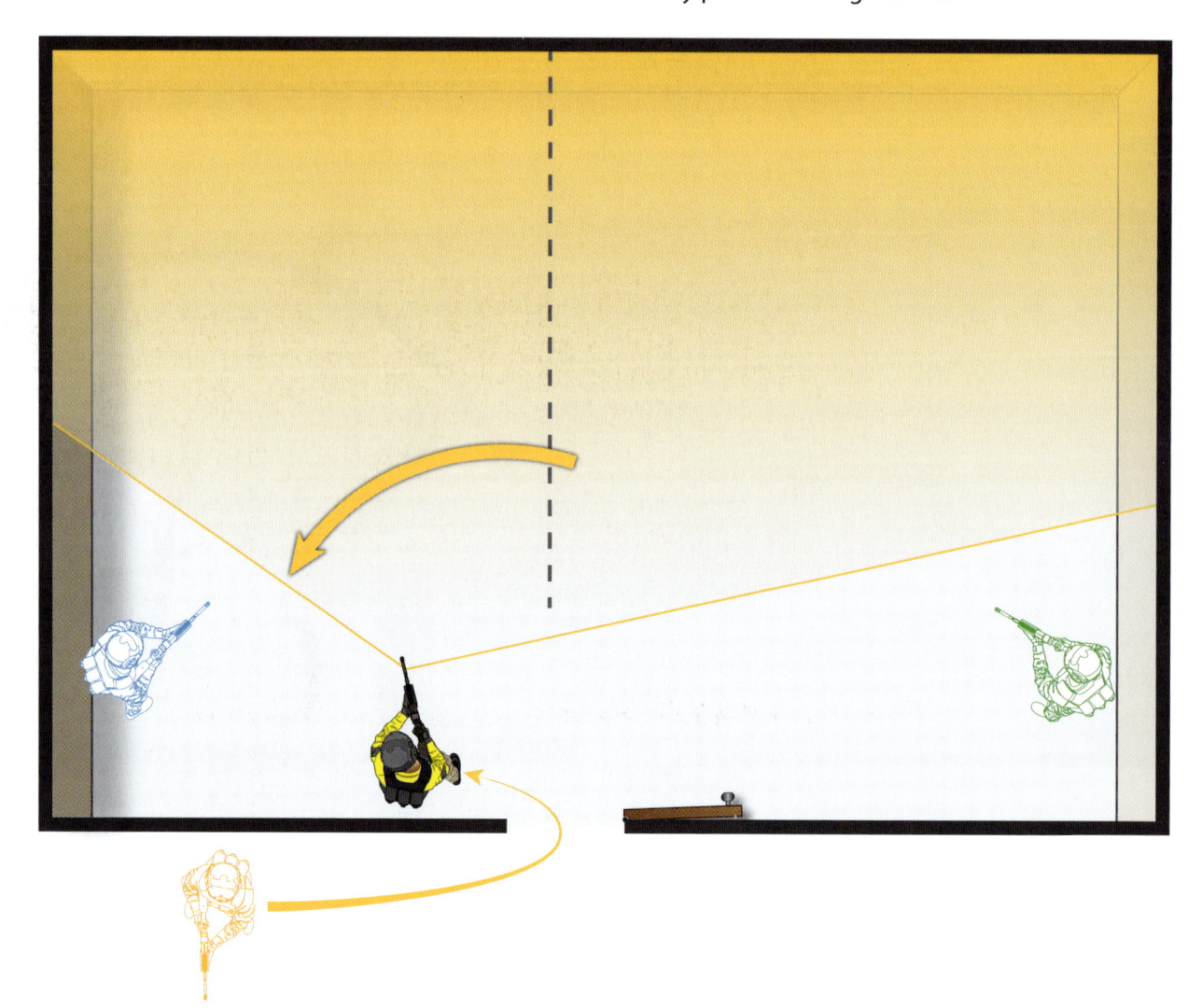

Team Operations: Single-Room Immediate Entry   37

IMMEDIATE ENTRY: CENTER-FED OPEN DOOR

FOURTH OFFICER STEP 1 - Clear the Center and Scan

The fourth officer will enter the room, moving in the opposite direction of the third officer. Once again, the rule is "move in the opposite direction of the officer in front of you." As the fourth officer enters the room, he/she will identify the center of the room and start to scan in the direction of movement. The fourth officer should also start the scan slightly behind the center point of the room. While scanning, the fourth officer will move to a domination point just to the side of the door. The fourth officer will continue the initial scan in the direction of movement until it reaches a point three feet off the second officer. The third officer will then scan back in the other direction to a point three feet off the lead officer. At this point the third officer will scan back and forth across his/her full sector several times to ensure the sector is clear and to identify danger areas.

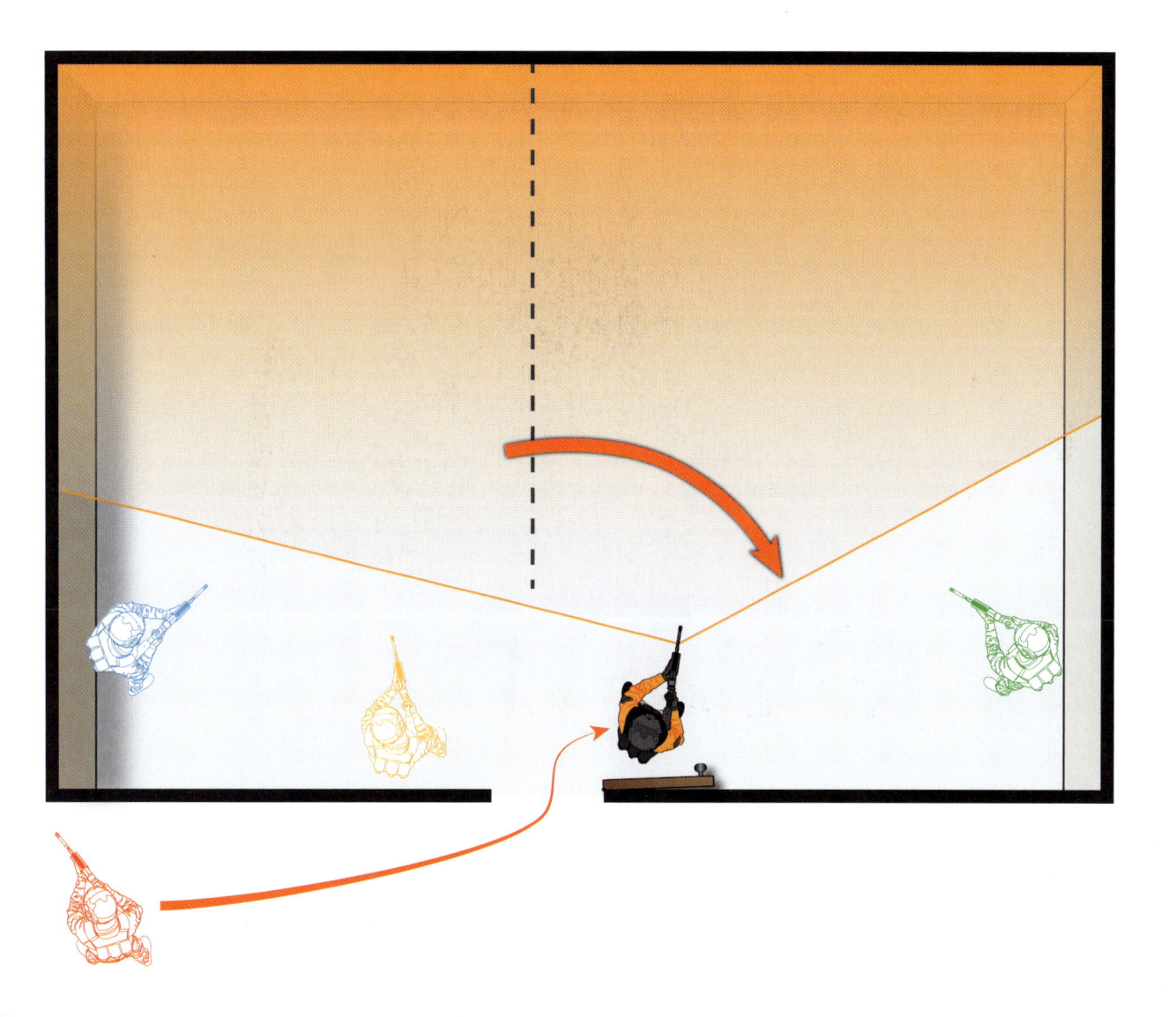

IMMEDIATE ENTRY: CENTER-FED OPEN DOOR

FOURTH OFFICER STEP 2 - Check Behind the Door

Once the fourth officer finishes clearing his/her sectors, the fourth officer will turn quickly to check that no one is hiding behind the door. In some cases, if an officer detects a threat behind the door, he/she might need to address that threat immediately to protect the team. Either way, clearing behind the door is only necessary if the door opens inward. Also, if the door is completely flush with the wall and there is no way to hide behind it, the fourth officer might skip this step if time is critical. However, it is possible for smaller adversaries to flatten themselves tightly to the wall behind the door. In other cases, buildings are designed in a way that leaves a small space or indentation behind the door. Finally, in a high-stress situation, officers may think the door is flush against the wall when it actually is not. Because of these factors it is always preferable to check behind the door. When checking behind the door, the officer should step back to ensure a hiding adversary cannot surge forward and grab the officer's weapon. The officer should also step directly back (90-degree angle with the wall) to achieve a "tactical-L" in case other officers need to engage the threat. Finally, depending on the room/door configuration, the third officer might be the one who checks behind the door.

IMMEDIATE ENTRY: CENTER-FED OPEN DOOR

FOURTH OFFICER STEP 3 - Provide Rear Security

Once the fourth officer finishes clearing his/her sectors and checks behind the door, the fourth officer will turn around to provide rear security for the team. It is critical that the fourth officer not exit the room to provide rear security. There are many reasons for this. Officers have better cover and concealment when they remain in the room. Also, if the rear security officer goes down, fellow officers will not have to exit the room to drag the officer to safety. The fourth officer can reposition as needed to provide cover in either direction or peek his/her head and weapon out the door as necessary, but the fourth officer should remain in the room with the team. Finally, depending on the room/door configuration, the third officer might be the one who turns to provide rear security instead of the fourth officer.

IMMEDIATE ENTRY: CENTER-FED OPEN DOOR

COMPLETE SEQUENCE 1 - First and Second Officers Enter

Once again, while each officer's actions were explained individually above, in real execution all officers will move simultaneously and enter the room as quickly as possible, one behind the other. It is optimal to have as little gap as possible between officers as they enter the room since a gap in the entry process can leave sectors momentarily uncovered. Viewed as a complete sequence, the lead officer will clear the immediate area, turn to clear one of the two corners and start scanning inward while moving to the domination point. The second officer will be right behind the lead officer and move in the opposite direction of the lead officer, covering the lead officer's back and clearing the opposite corner.

IMMEDIATE ENTRY: CENTER-FED OPEN DOOR

COMPLETE SEQUENCE 2 - Third and Fourth Officers Enter

As the first two officers move to their domination points, the third and fourth officers will enter right behind, each moving in the opposite direction of the officer in front and clearing the center of the room. The third and fourth officers will move to domination points just inside the door.

IMMEDIATE ENTRY: CENTER-FED OPEN DOOR

COMPLETE SEQUENCE 3 - Scan and Cover the Rear

As all officers scan their sectors, it is also important that they look up to check for threats hiding in the ceiling. Either the third or fourth officer will check behind the door. The third or fourth officer will also turn to provide rear security for the team while remaining inside the room. As shown in the sector diagram below, once all officers are at their domination points, they will be in a "shallow horseshoe" configuration. It is important that the team is positioned in this way. If they simply line up along the wall (sometimes known as a "strong wall" technique) the first two officers will not have as good angles of observation behind furniture in the room. On the other hand, if officers penetrate too deep into the room they run the risk of being accidentally shot by a fellow officer.

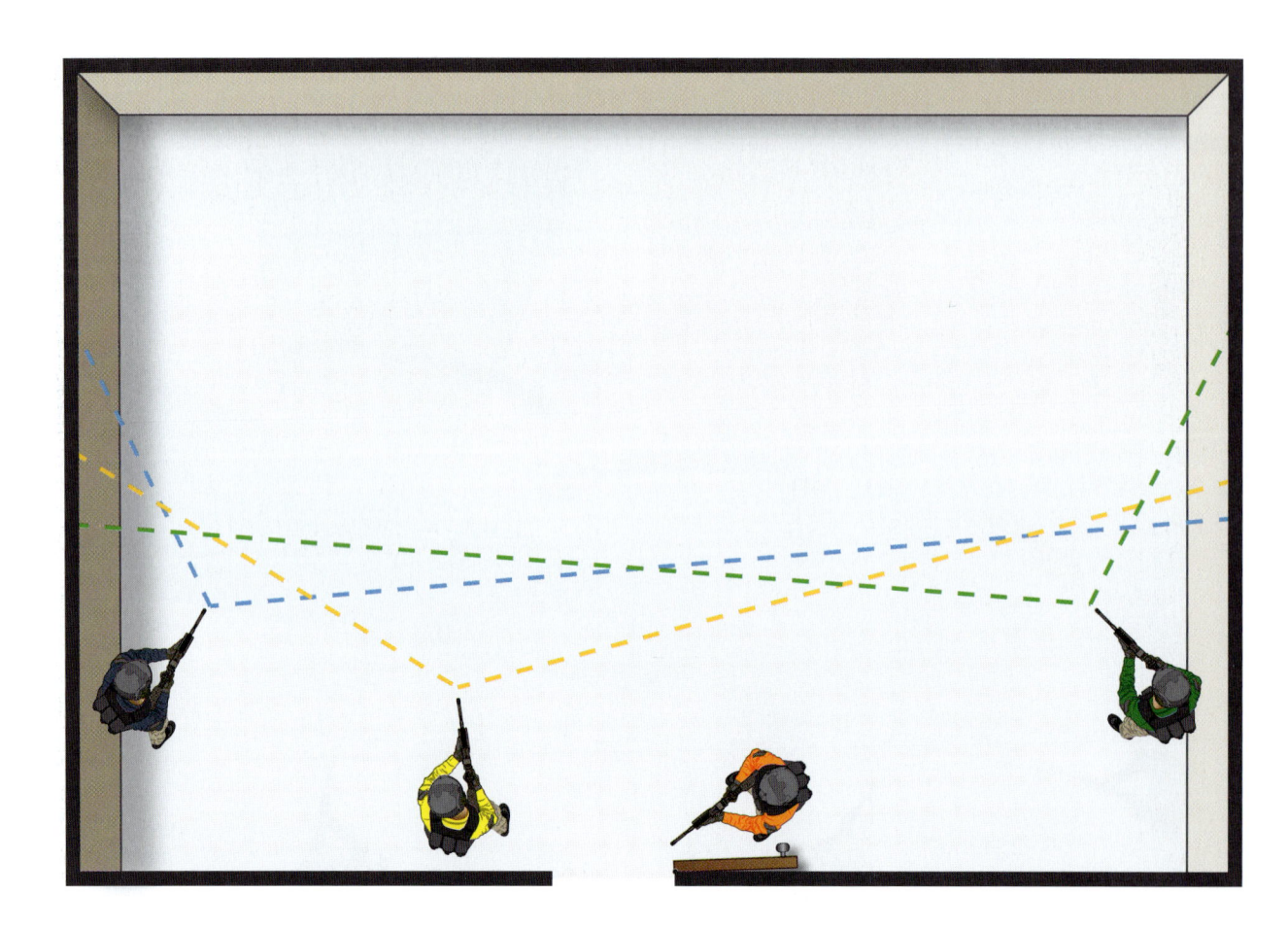

IMMEDIATE ENTRY: CENTER-FED CLOSED DOOR

Team-Member Positioning

When faced with a center-fed, closed door, the team will stack using one of the methods already discussed. Once again, the loose stack is preferred to maximize officer safety. However, one officer will have to move to the opposite side of the door to act as the breacher. The following pages will describe the actions of each officer in sequence. However, note that in actual application, all officers will attempt to enter the room as quickly as possible. For example, the second officer will enter the room and begin clearing immediately following the lead officer.

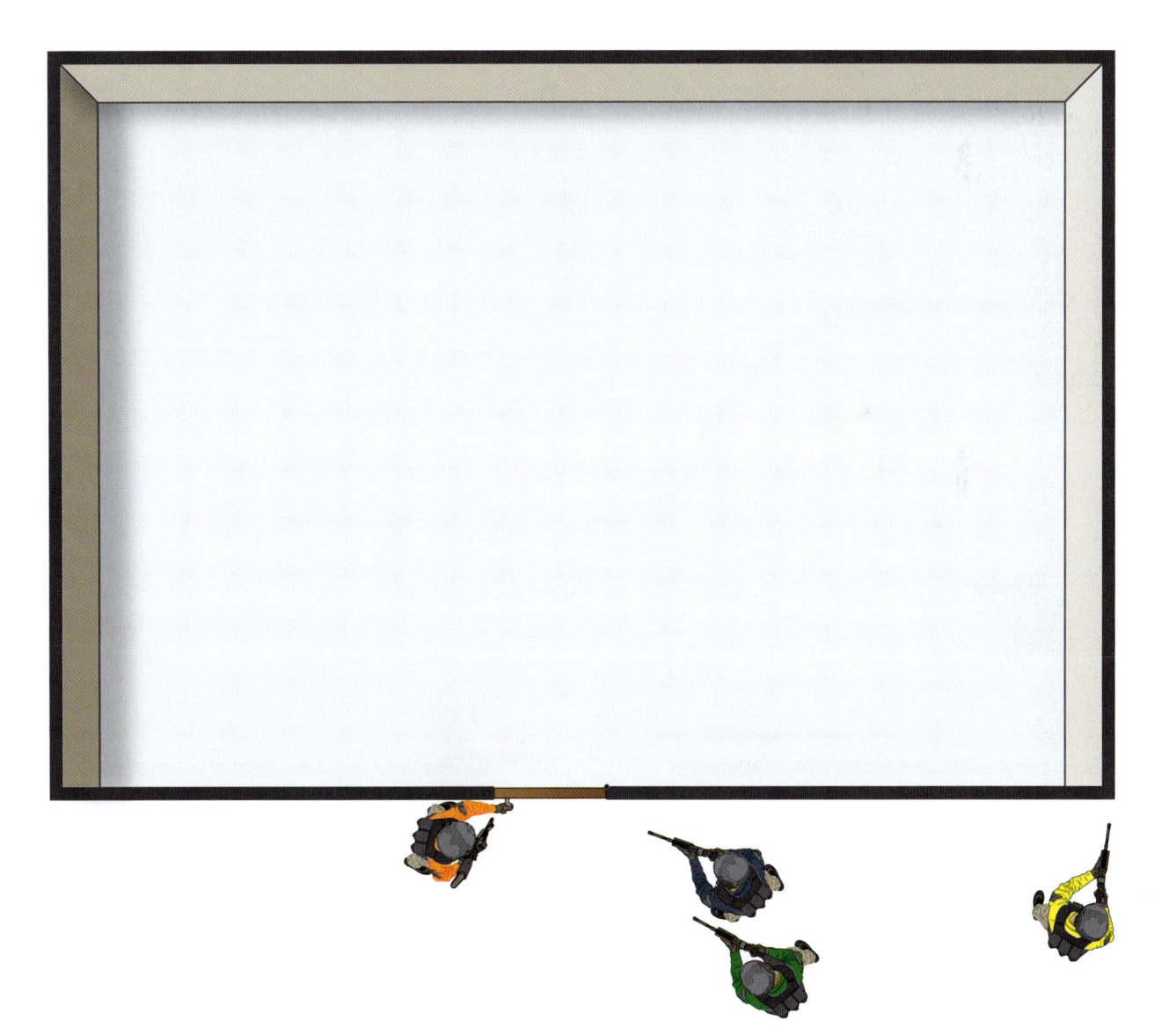

IMMEDIATE ENTRY: CENTER-FED CLOSED DOOR

LEAD OFFICER - Doorway, Corner and Domination Point

After the ready signal is complete, the first officer nods his/her head to signal the breacher to open the door. Once the door is open, the clearing process is the same as for an open door. The lead officer steps outward slightly to have a better angle of vision into the room while ensuring that the doorway is clear. The lead officer will take the opportunity to engage any deep threats in the center of the room before crossing the threshold. The lead officer then clears the corner and scans inward while moving to the domination point. The lead officer will continue to scan inward until the scan reaches a point three feet off the second officer's point of domination.

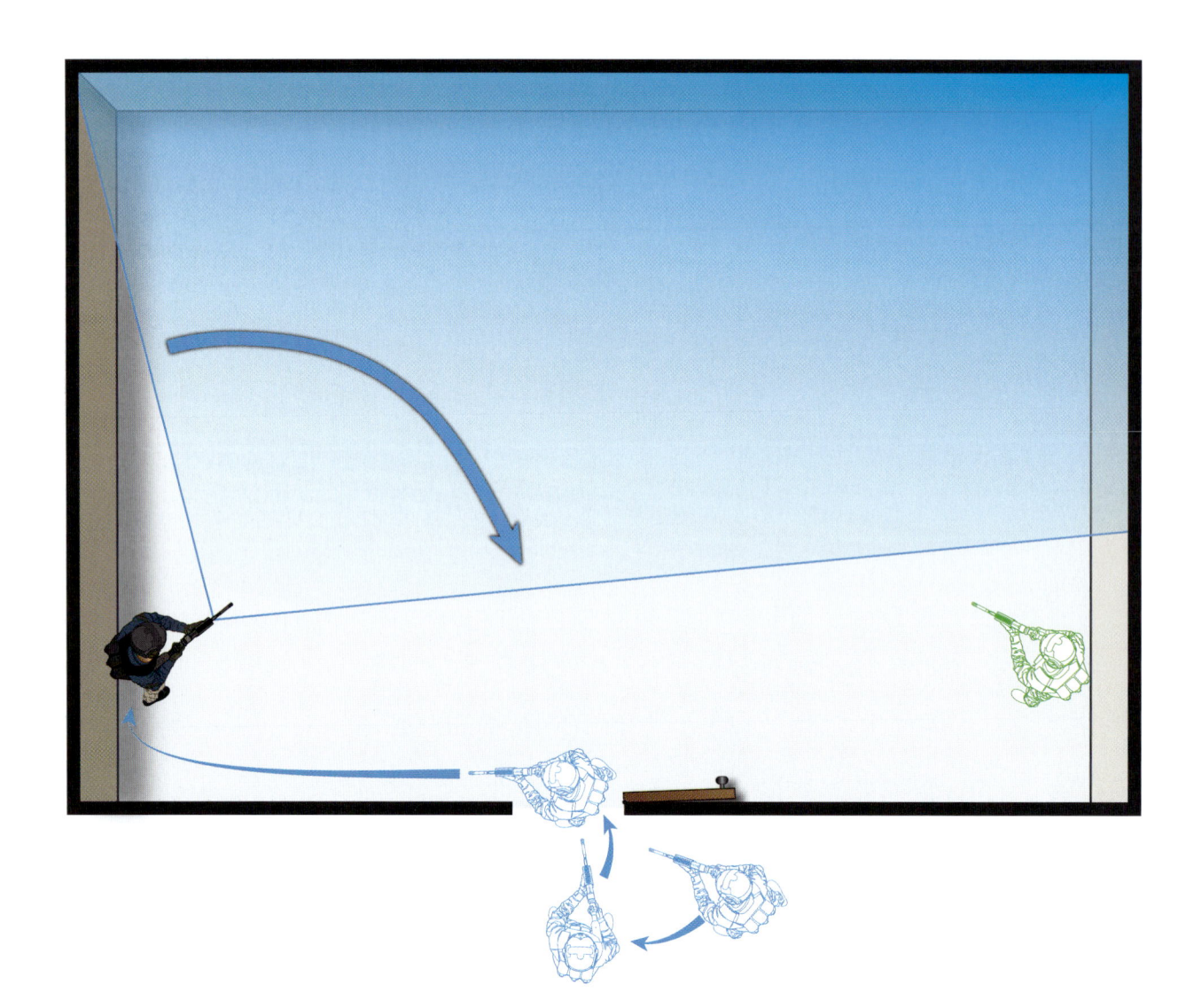

IMMEDIATE ENTRY: CENTER-FED CLOSED DOOR

SECOND OFFICER - Corner and Domination Point

The second officer will turn in the opposite direction of the lead officer. Once again, the lead officer can choose to turn either way. The second officer must remain alert and turn in the opposite direction. It is also critical that the second officer enter the room as close as possible behind the lead officer. This is to ensure the lead officer's back is not left exposed. Once the second officer makes the turn, he/she will clear the corner and engage any threats in the corner until they are neutralized. The second officer will then scan inward and move to the domination point.

IMMEDIATE ENTRY: CENTER-FED CLOSED DOOR

THIRD OFFICER - Clear the Center of the Room and Scan

The third officer will enter the room, moving in the opposite direction of the second officer. Once again, the rule is "move in the opposite direction of the officer in front of you." As the third officer enters the room, he/she will identify the center of the room and start to scan in the direction of movement. The third officer should also start the scan slightly behind the center point of the room. See the illustration below for further clarification. While scanning, the third officer will move to a domination point just to the side of the door.

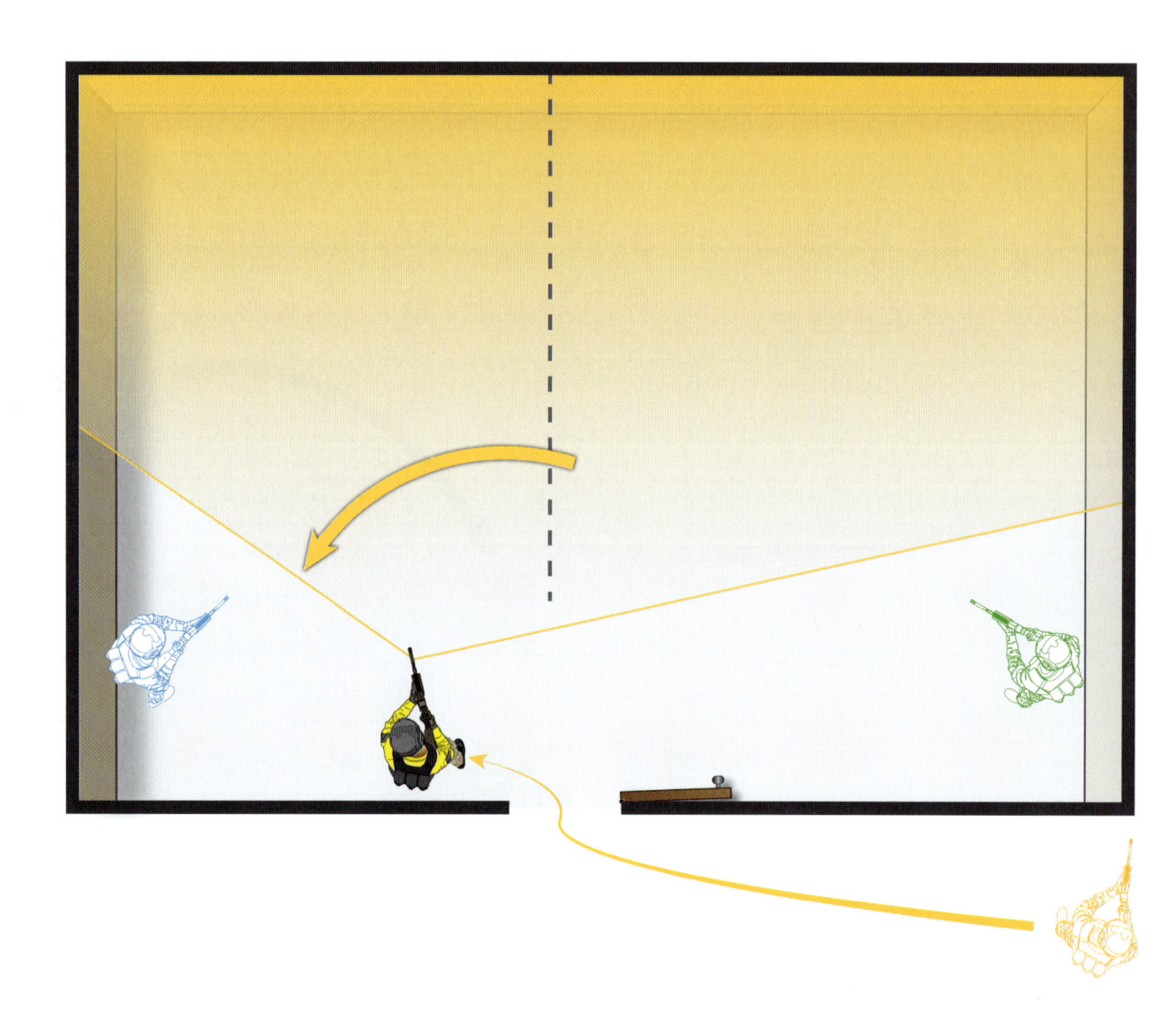

TEAM OPERATIONS: SINGLE-ROOM IMMEDIATE ENTRY   47

IMMEDIATE ENTRY: CENTER-FED CLOSED DOOR

FOURTH OFFICER - Clear, Check the Door and Cover Rear

The fourth officer will enter the room, moving in the opposite direction of the third officer. As the fourth officer enters the room, he/she will identify the center of the room and start to scan in the direction of movement. The fourth officer should also start the scan slightly behind the center point of the room. While scanning, the fourth officer will move to a domination point just to the side of the door. Once the fourth officer finishes clearing his/her sectors, the fourth officer will turn quickly to check that no one is hiding behind the door. After checking behind the door, the fourth officer will turn around to provide rear security for the team from inside the room. Depending on the room/door configuration, the third officer might be the one who checks behind the door or turns to provide rear security.

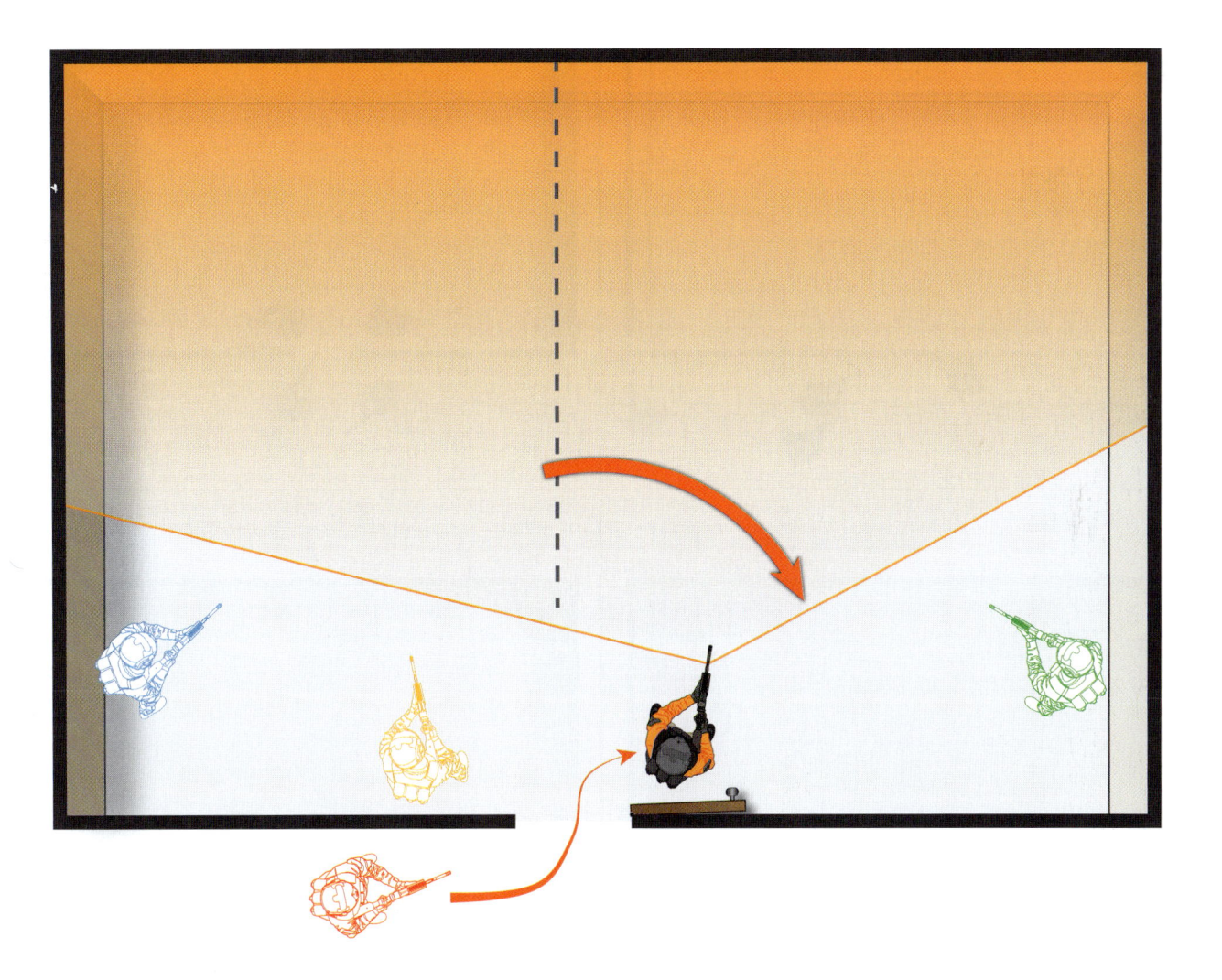

IMMEDIATE ENTRY: CENTER-FED CLOSED DOOR

COMPLETE SEQUENCE

The lead officer will nod to signal the breacher to open the door, then clear the immediate area, clear the corner and move to the domination point. The second officer will move in the opposite direction of the lead officer. The third and fourth officers will enter right behind, each moving in the opposite direction of the officer in front and clearing the center of the room. Either the third or fourth officer will check behind the door. The third or fourth officer will also turn to provide rear security.

TEAM OPERATIONS: SINGLE-ROOM IMMEDIATE ENTRY

IMMEDIATE ENTRY: CORNER-FED OPEN DOOR

Team-Member Positioning

A corner-fed room is a room where the door is flush with the corner of the room, allowing an officer to turn only one direction when entering the room. Entering through a corner-fed, open door is similar to entering through a center-fed door but there are several changes to the procedure. The team will stack using one of the methods already discussed. Once again, the loose stack is preferred to maximize officer safety.

IMMEDIATE ENTRY: CORNER-FED OPEN DOOR

LEAD OFFICER STEP 1 - Clear the Doorway

The lead officer will step outward slightly to have a better angle of vision into the room while ensuring that the doorway is clear. The lead officer will take the opportunity to engage any deep threats in the center of the room before crossing the threshold.

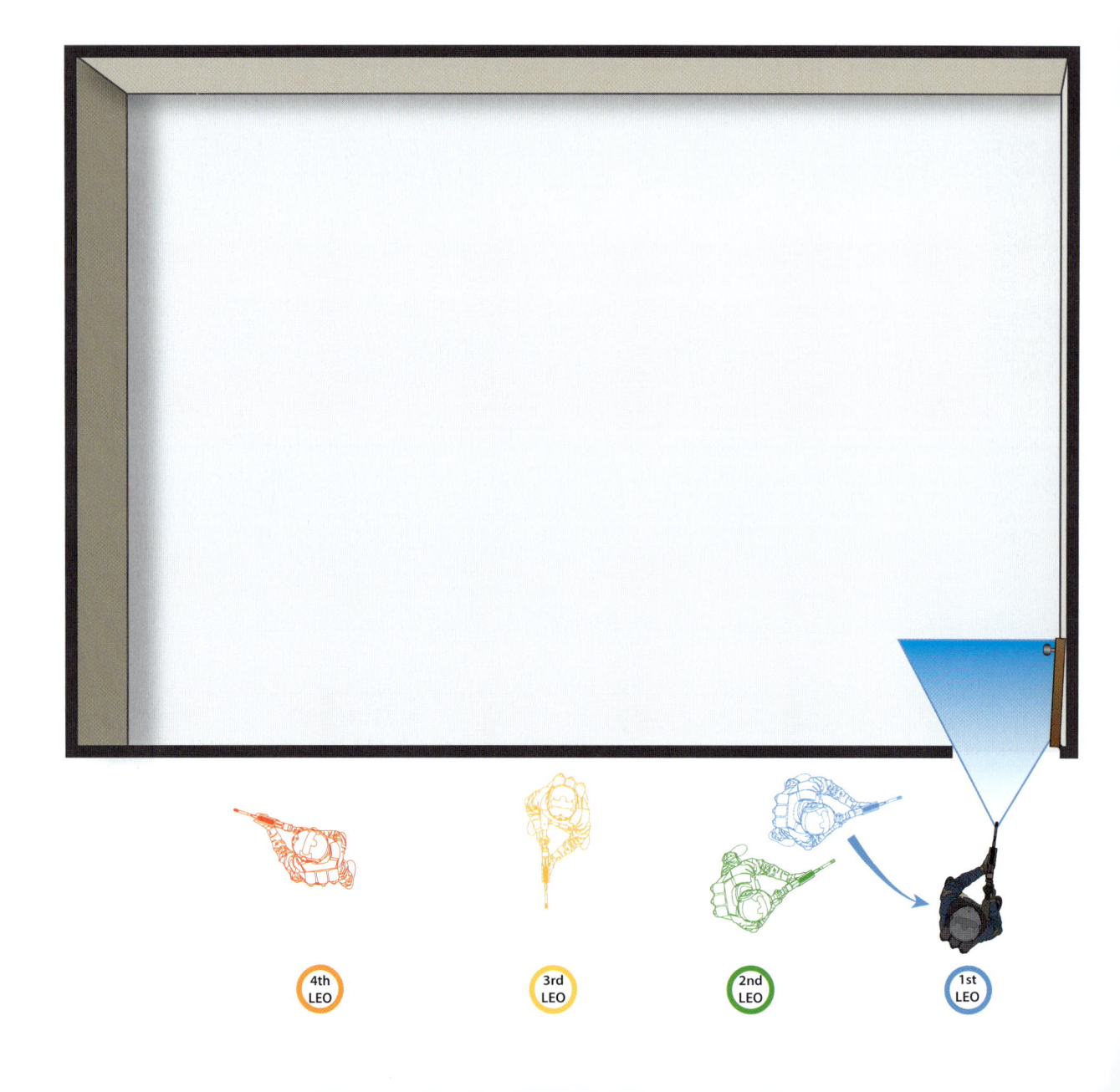

4th LEO

3rd LEO

2nd LEO

1st LEO

IMMEDIATE ENTRY: CORNER-FED OPEN DOOR

LEAD OFFICER STEP 2 - Clear the Corner

Clearing the doorway from outside the room will allow the lead officer to turn immediately to the corner once inside the room. The lead officer should not predetermine which direction to turn. In general, the lead officer should turn to address the greatest threat first. Once the lead officer makes the turn, he/she will clear the corner and engage any threats in the corner until they are neutralized.

IMMEDIATE ENTRY: CORNER-FED OPEN DOOR

LEAD OFFICER STEP 3 - Move to the Domination Point

Once the corner is clear, the lead officer should not stay focused on the corner but should instead immediately begin to scan inward while moving along the wall. The officer continues to scan and move towards his/her domination point. The domination point (depicted below) is slightly forward of the corner. The lead officer will continue to scan inward until the scan reaches a point three feet off the second officer's point of domination. At this point the lead officer will scan back and forth across his/her full sector several times to ensure the sector is clear and to identify potential danger areas. Experienced teams can shorten this deliberate scanning process and might also break each team member's sectors into primary and secondary sectors.

TEAM OPERATIONS: SINGLE-ROOM IMMEDIATE ENTRY 53

IMMEDIATE ENTRY: CORNER-FED OPEN DOOR

SECOND OFFICER STEP 1 - Clear the Corner

The second officer will move in the opposite direction of the lead officer. It is also critical that the second officer enter the room as close as possible behind the lead officer. This is to ensure the lead officer's back is not left exposed.

IMMEDIATE ENTRY: CORNER-FED OPEN DOOR

SECOND OFFICER STEP 2 - Move to the Domination Point

Once the corner is clear, the second officer should not stay focused on the corner but should instead immediately begin to scan inward while moving along the wall. The officer continues to scan and move towards his/her domination point. The domination point (depicted below) is slightly forward of the corner. The second officer will continue to scan inward until the scan reaches a point three feet off the lead officer's point of domination. At this point the second officer will scan back and forth across his/her full sector several times to ensure the sector is clear and to identify potential danger areas.

Team Operations: Single-Room Immediate Entry 55

IMMEDIATE ENTRY: CORNER-FED OPEN DOOR

THIRD OFFICER - Clear the Center of the Room and Scan

The third officer will enter the room, moving in the opposite direction of the second officer. Once again, the rule is "move in the opposite direction of the officer in front of you." As the third officer enters the room, he/she will identify the center of the room (marked with the dashed grey line in the picture below) and start to scan in the direction of movement. The third officer should also start the scan slightly behind the center point of the room. While scanning, the third officer will move to a domination point just to the side of the door.

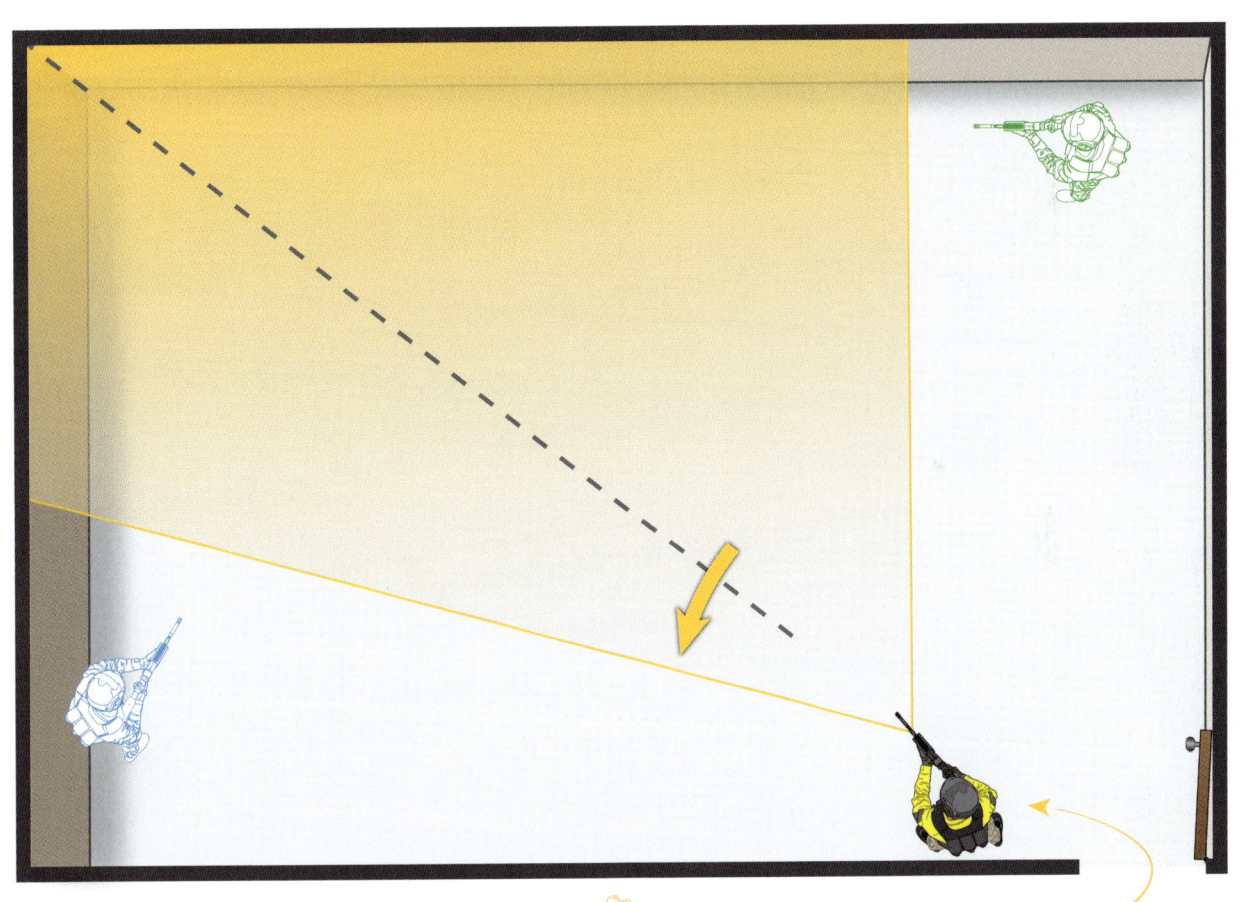

IMMEDIATE ENTRY: CORNER-FED OPEN DOOR

FOURTH OFFICER STEP 1 - Clear the Center and Scan

The fourth officer will enter the room, moving in the opposite direction of the third officer. As the fourth officer enters the room, he/she will identify the center of the room and start to scan in the direction of movement. The fourth officer should also start the scan slightly behind the center point of the room. While scanning, the fourth officer will move to a domination point just to the side of the door.

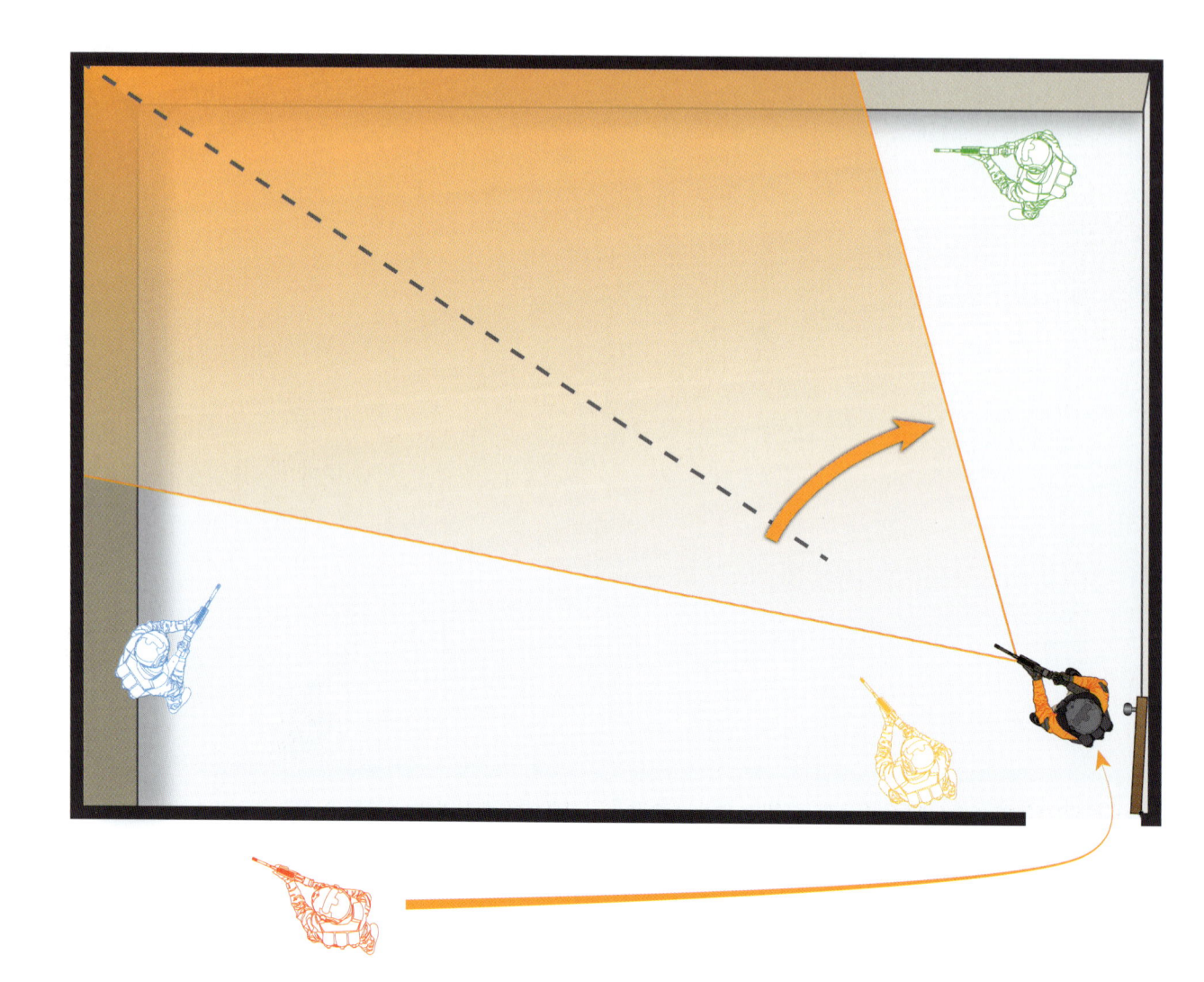

IMMEDIATE ENTRY: CORNER-FED OPEN DOOR

FOURTH OFFICER STEP 2 - Check the Door and Cover Rear

Once the fourth officer finishes clearing his/her sectors, the fourth officer will turn quickly to check that no one is hiding behind the door. After checking behind the door, the fourth officer will turn around to provide rear security for the team from inside the room. Depending on the room/door configuration, the third officer might be the one who checks behind the door or turns to provide rear security.

IMMEDIATE ENTRY: CORNER-FED OPEN DOOR

COMPLETE SEQUENCE

The lead officer will clear the immediate area, turn to clear one of the two corners and start scanning inward while moving to the domination point. The second officer will move in the opposite direction of the lead officer. The third and fourth officers will enter right behind, clearing the center of the room. Either the third or fourth officer will check behind the door and turn to provide rear security. In a corner-fed room, the team will assume more of an "L-shape" configuration rather than a "horseshoe."

IMMEDIATE ENTRY: CORNER-FED CLOSED DOOR

COMPLETE SEQUENCE

The method for clearing a corner-fed room with a closed door is the same as the method for clearing an open door except that a team member or breacher will have to open to door prior to entry. In some cases, a team member or breacher will be able to move to the opposite side of the door as described in the "center-fed closed door" section. However, in other cases, if the door is up against the wall, the lead officer might have to open the door himself/herself (self-breach) to avoid congestion or unnecessary exposure at the doorway.

TEAM OPERATIONS
Single Room Delayed Entry

For team operations, delayed entry is similar to immediate entry but the initial steps are different. Officers may choose to use delayed entry tactics when time is not critical or when extra caution is advisable. Delayed entry tactics are designed to allow officers to clear as much of a room or hallway as possible from the outside, before actually making entry.

In most situations, delayed entry is safer than immediate entry. For that reason, some officers or tactical teams may choose to use delayed entry as their primary clearing technique. In general, if there is no reason to rush into a room, it is a better option to use delayed entry. However, it is still useful to practice immediate entry so the team is ready to respond in a scenario where speed is critical, such as a hostage situation.

It is also important to note that the delayed and immediate entry techniques described in this manual are interchangeable. Therefore, officers can switch back and fourth between delayed entry and immediate entry depending on the situation. For example, a team might begin to clear a house using delayed entry techniques but then switch to immediate entry when they hear a hostage screaming down the hall.

When conducting a delayed entry, the majority of the team will remain away from the door and only one officer will move forward to conduct an initial sweep of the target room. This minimizes the exposure of the team as a whole. However, it is important that the lead officer not move too far away from the team to the point where all officers are not able to provide mutual support and casualty evacuation in an emergency.

The officer should conduct the sweep (also known as slicing-the-pie) in one, smooth movement. Once completing the initial sweep, the officer may conduct more sweeps as needed. In some situations, the room configuration or furniture might make it impossible to conduct a full sweep. In these cases the officer might conduct a half sweep or conduct the sweep with a shallower arc.

Once the lead officer has conducted a sweep of the room, the first officer will lead the way during the entry process and the remaining officers will follow, clearing their respective sectors just as they did in the immediate entry process already described. However, when conducting a delayed entry, the team might decide not to enter the room at all. If the lead officer detects or engages a threat while conducting the sweep, the team might decide to hold position or pull back. The team can then "call out" the adversary or wait for a better time and place to make entry.

DELAYED ENTRY: CENTER-FED OPEN DOOR

LEAD OFFICER STEP 1 - Approach the Door

The lead officer approaches the open door from the outside of the room, positioned close to the wall, several yards from the doorway. The lead officer should avoid touching or bumping into the wall because doing so will make noise and might also increase the chances of getting shot, since bullets tend to travel along walls.

APPROX 10 DEGREES

Team Operations: Single-Room Delayed Entry | 63

DELAYED ENTRY: CENTER-FED OPEN DOOR

LEAD OFFICER STEP 2 - Avoid Indiscriminate Fire

Staying away from the doorway is also important. Many adversaries, especially terrorists with automatic weapons, will not fire single, aimed shots but will rather spray bullets indiscriminately in the direction of any noise or potential threat. This spray of bullets will generally form an arc several yards wide. If the lead officer stays close to a door, he/she might get hit with a barrage of bullets coming through the doorway and the walls surrounding the doorway. Remember, that most interior walls are not bulletproof and the chances of getting shot through a wall are very high. By staying a few yards back from the door, officers minimize the chances of getting hit by indiscriminate fire.

DELAYED ENTRY: CENTER-FED OPEN DOOR

LEAD OFFICER STEP 3 - Watch for Exposed Shadow

Staying back from the door also helps minimize the chances of detection, especially in terms of shadows created by interior lights. Most buildings have multiple light sources in each room or hallway. This means that when officers come close to an open door, someone standing inside the room can most likely see the shadow moving across the floor behind the opening. Officers should keep their distance from the door and try to remain aware of their shadows as they move.

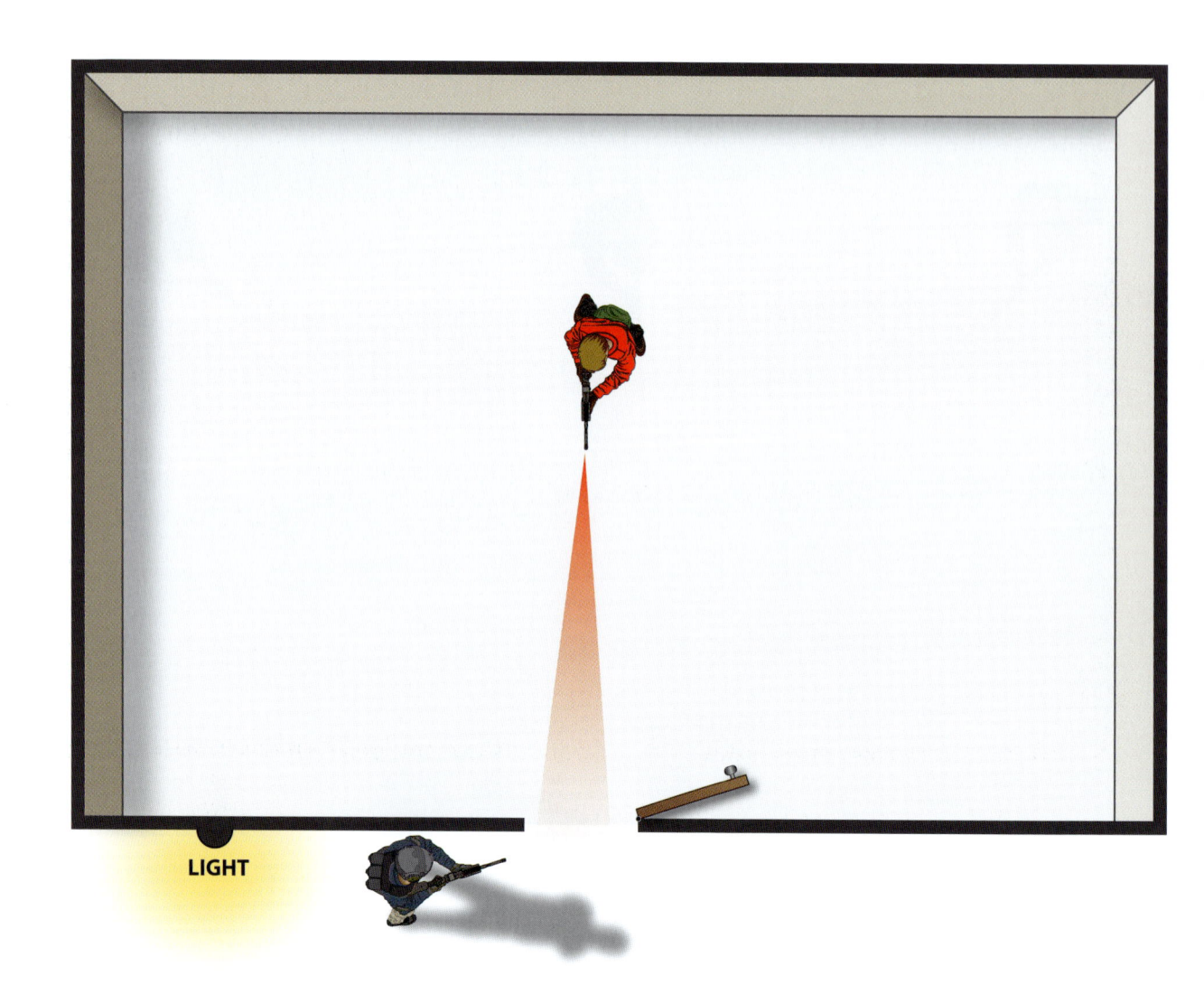

LIGHT

DELAYED ENTRY: CENTER-FED OPEN DOOR

LEAD OFFICER STEP 4 - Conduct "Sweep" Movement

Next, the lead officer will sweep out in a wide arc, keeping his/her weapon focused on the doorway and moving all the way across to a position close to the wall on the opposite side of the door. The purpose of the sweep is to visually clear the room as quickly as possible to identify any threats inside and possibly draw those threats out of the room. When executing the sweep, officers should move in an arc as fast as possible while keeping the weapon relatively steady and taking care not to trip. It is sometimes necessary to sacrifice some weapon accuracy in order to minimize exposure and vulnerability through speed. Moving quickly along the arc makes it difficult for an adversary to engage effectively and will leave officers exposed for only a fraction of a second. After completing the initial sweep, the lead officer can conduct additional sweeps if needed to check the room more carefully.

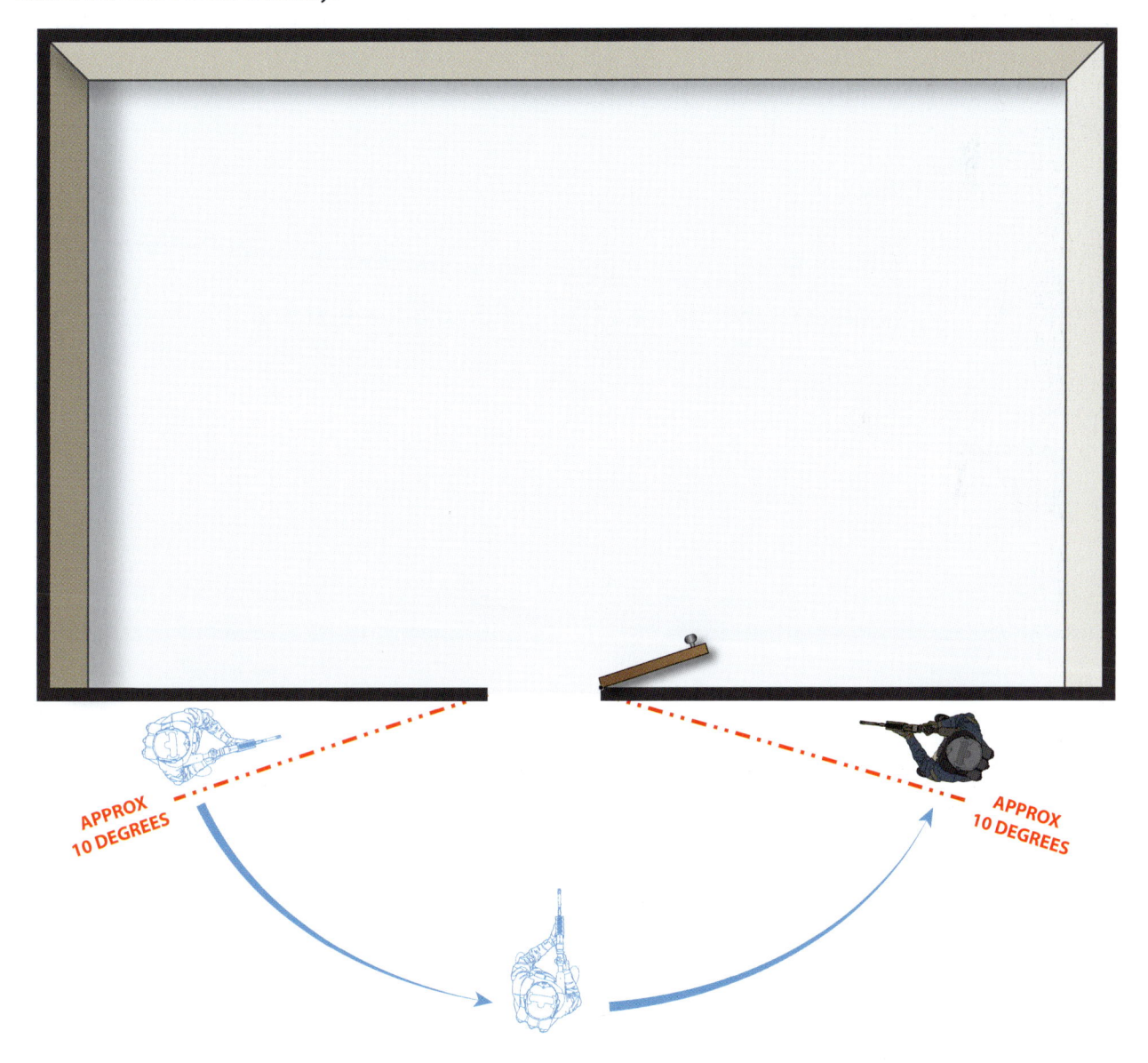

APPROX 10 DEGREES

APPROX 10 DEGREES

DELAYED ENTRY: CENTER-FED OPEN DOOR

LEAD OFFICER STEP 5 - Reverse Sweep and Entry

Once completing the initial sweep, if the team decides to enter the room, the lead officer will sweep along the arc in the opposite direction until he/she is facing directly towards the door. The lead officer will then move towards the door remaining alert for deep threats in the center of the room. Once reaching the threshold, the lead officer then clears the corner and scans inward while moving to the domination point.

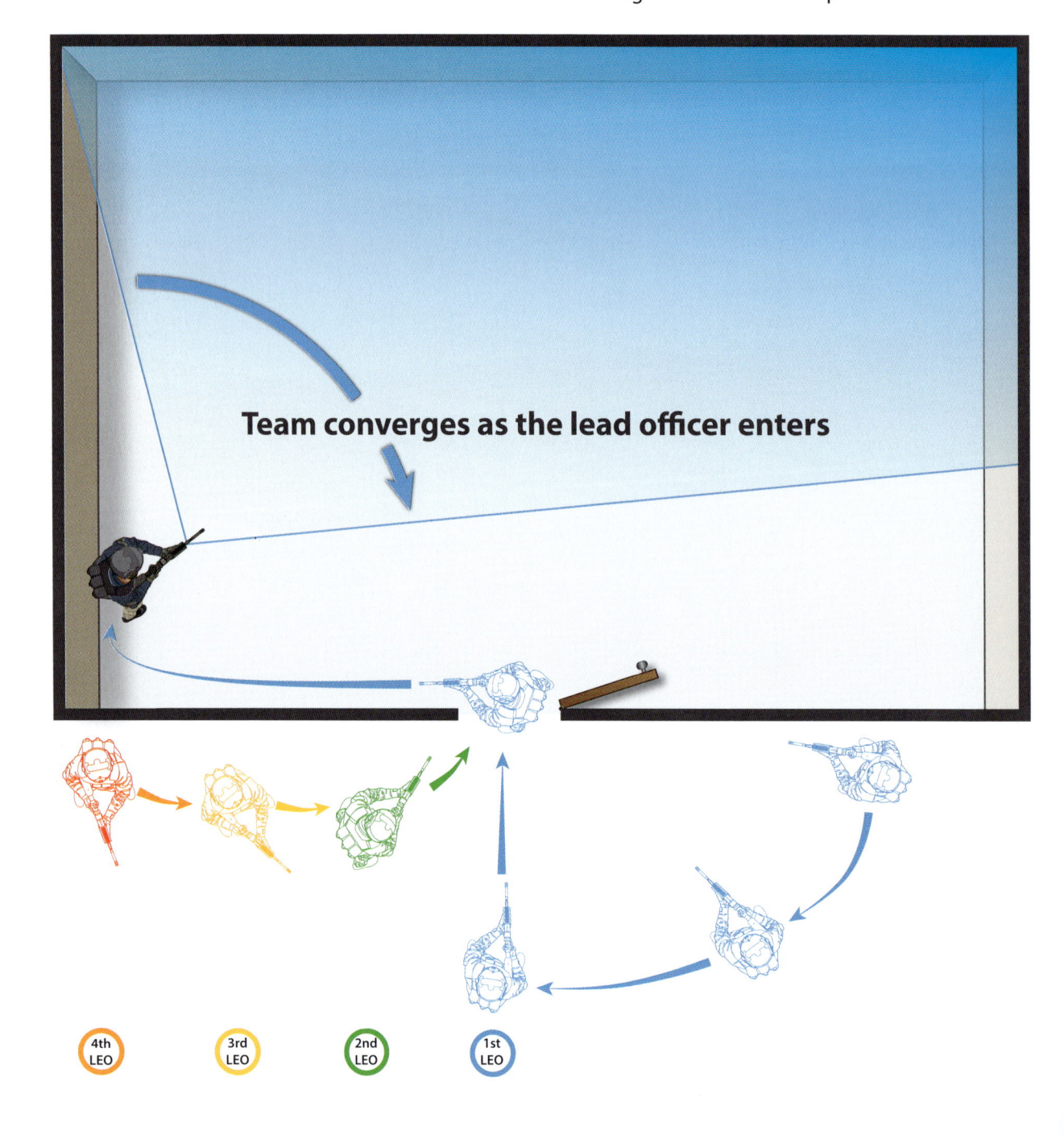

Team converges as the lead officer enters

4th LEO   3rd LEO   2nd LEO   1st LEO

DELAYED ENTRY: CENTER-FED OPEN DOOR

SECOND OFFICER – Clear the Corner and Dominate

The second officer will initially keep some distance from the door along with the rest of the team and allow the lead officer time and space to conduct the initial sweep. If the team decides to enter the room, the second officer will wait until the lead officer completes the reverse sweep and is moving head-on towards the door. At this point, the second team member will also begin to approach the door, timing his/her entry to cover the back of the lead officer. Upon reaching the door, the second officer will turn in the opposite direction of the lead officer. The second officer will have to choose a good approach angle and use good timing in order to enter the room as close as possible behind the lead officer. There is no universal formula for how to do this. It just takes practice and situational awareness. Once the second officer enters the room and makes the turn, he/she will clear the corner and engage any threats in the corner until they are neutralized. The second officer will then scan inward and move to the domination point just as in the immediate entry technique.

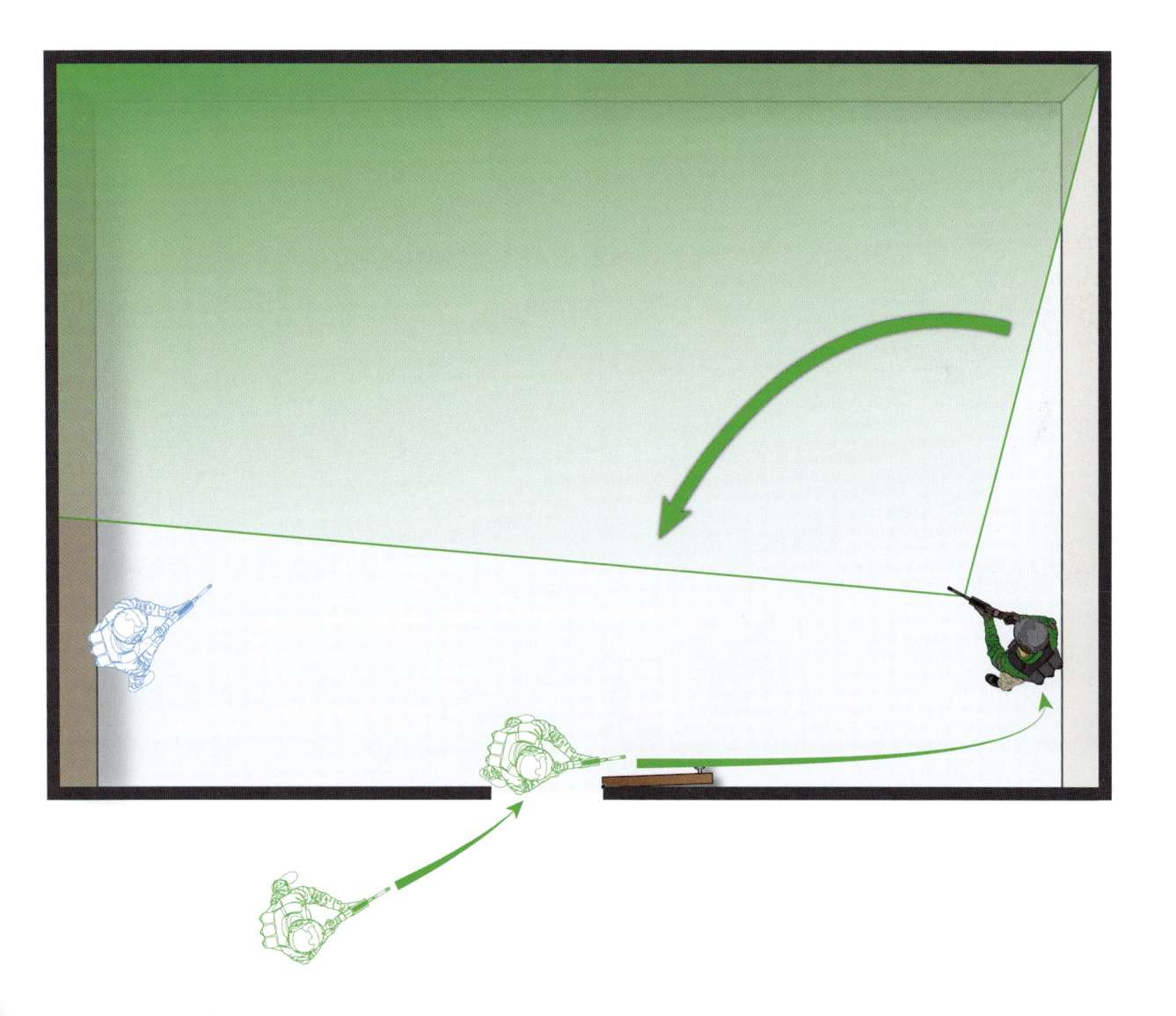

DELAYED ENTRY: CENTER-FED OPEN DOOR

THIRD AND FOURTH OFFICER - Clear Center, Cover Rear

The procedures for the third and fourth officers in delayed entry are no different from immediate entry. The third and fourth officers will follow close behind the second officer. As the first two officers move to their domination points, the third and fourth officers will enter right behind, each moving in the opposite direction of the officer in front and clearing the center of the room. The third and fourth officers will move to domination points just inside the door. Either the third or fourth officer will check behind the door. The third or fourth officer will also turn to provide rear security for the team while remaining inside the room. As shown in the sector diagram below, once all officers are at their domination points, they will be in a "shallow horseshoe" configuration.

DELAYED ENTRY: CENTER-FED OPEN DOOR

COMPLETE SEQUENCE

For team operations, delayed entry is similar to immediate entry but the initial steps are different. The majority of the team will remain away from the door and only the lead officer will move forward to conduct an initial sweep of the target room. Once the sweep is complete, the lead officer will move back in the opposite direction and then move straight towards the door. At this point the second officer will begin to move towards the door to enter the room right behind the lead officer. The remaining officers will also move towards the door to follow behind into the room with as little gap between officers as possible.

DELAYED ENTRY: CENTER-FED CLOSED DOOR

LEAD OFFICER STEP 1 - Open the Door

The technique for a center-fed closed door is almost the same as the technique for clearing the open door with a few minor adjustments. The first difference is that because the door is closed, the team must first open the door before conducting the sweep. To open the door, the lead officer will position close to the wall and away from the door with weapon at the ready and oriented towards the door just in case the door opens and an adversary walks out. The lead officer will move towards the door quickly, grasp the doorknob with the non-firing hand and swing the door open. The lead officer will then back away just in case an adversary fires towards the door.

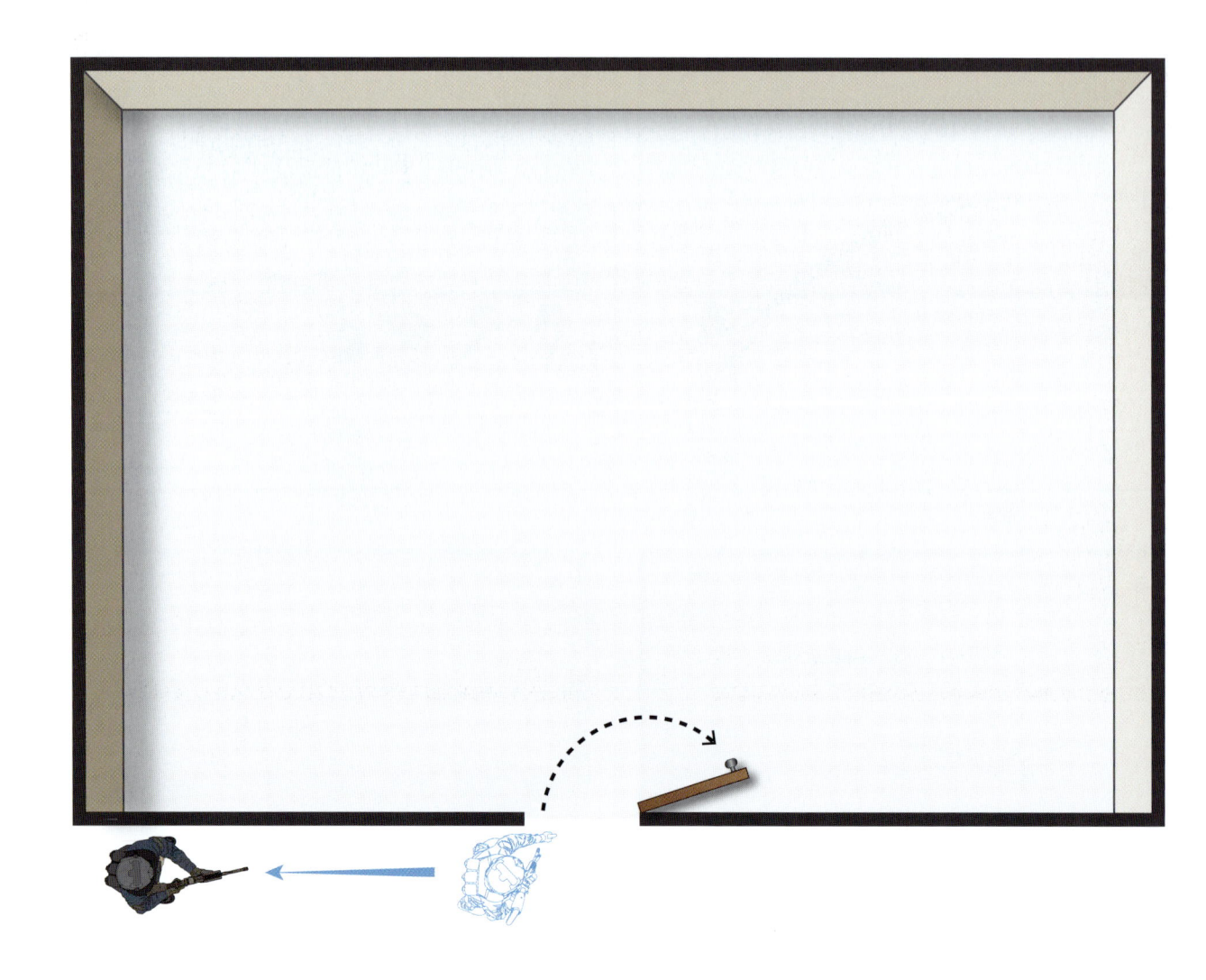

DELAYED ENTRY: CENTER-FED CLOSED DOOR

LEAD OFFICER STEP 2 - Conduct Sweep and Enter

Once the door is open, the clearing technique is the same as for a closed door. The lead officer will conduct a sweep across the door, then sweep back in the opposite direction and enter the room. The lead officer will clear the corner and scan inward while moving to the domination point.

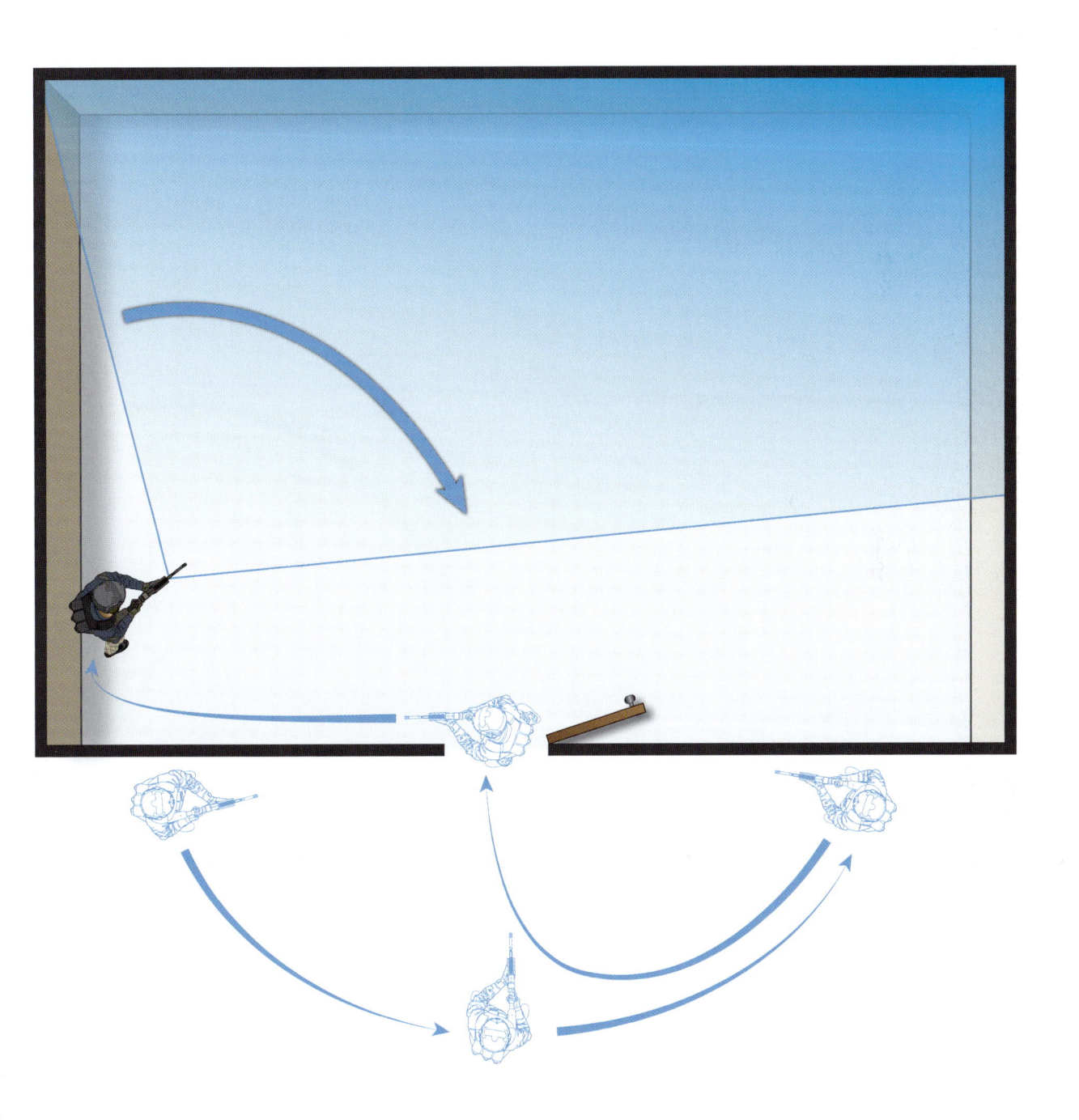

DELAYED ENTRY: CENTER-FED CLOSED DOOR

SECOND OFFICER - Clear the Corner and Dominate

The second officer will initially keep some distance from the door along with the rest of the team and allow the lead officer time to open the door and space to conduct the initial sweep. The second officer will wait until the lead officer completes the reverse sweep and is moving head-on towards the door. At this point, the second team member will also begin to approach the door, timing his/her entry to cover the back of the lead officer. Upon reaching the door, the second officer will turn in the opposite direction of the lead officer. Once the second officer enters the room and makes the turn, he/she will clear the corner and engage any threats in the corner until they are neutralized. The second officer will then scan inward and move to the domination point just as in the immediate entry technique.

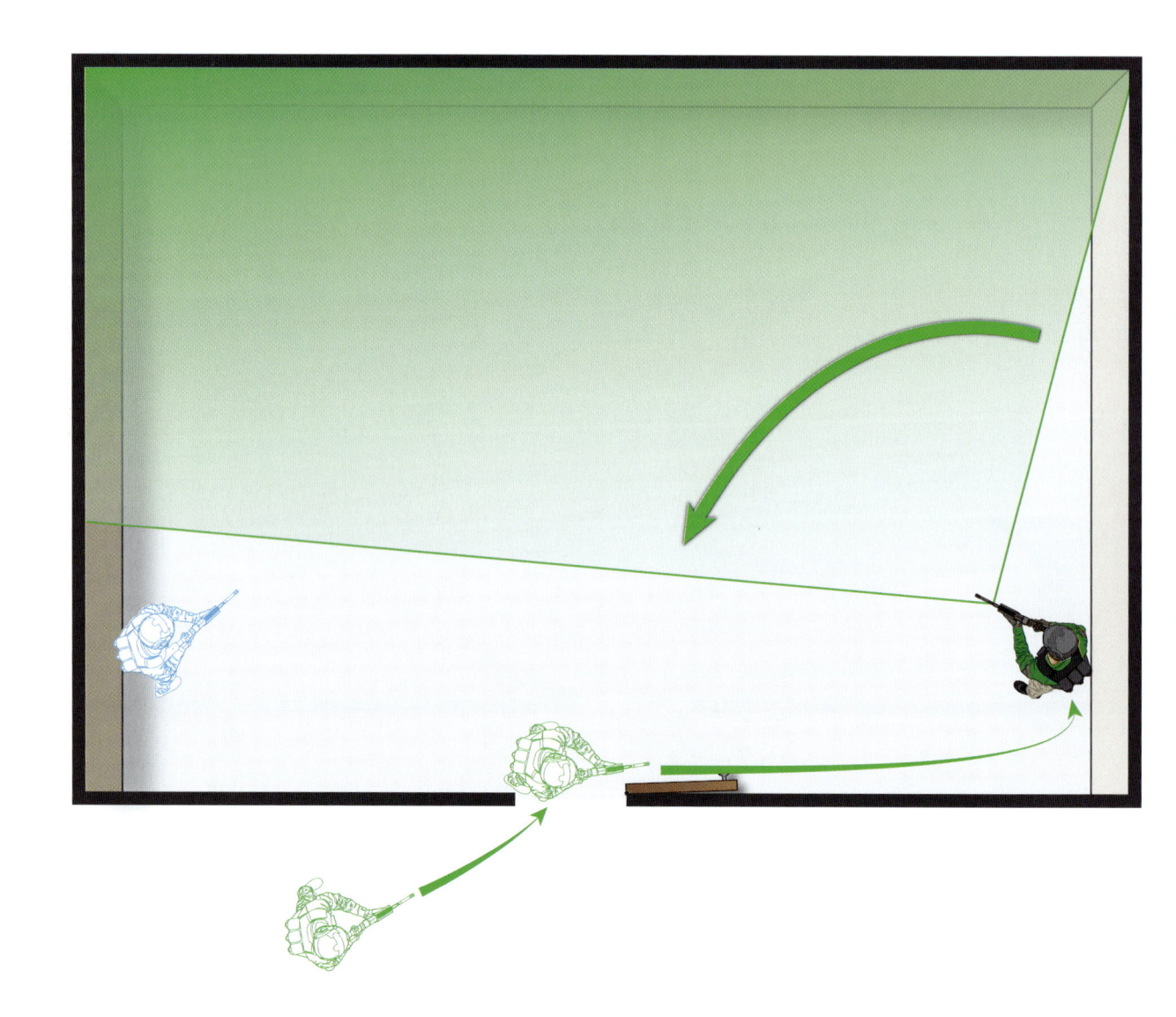

DELAYED ENTRY: CENTER-FED CLOSED DOOR

THIRD AND FOURTH OFFICERS - Clear Center, Cover Rear

The procedures for the third and fourth officer in delayed entry are no different from immediate entry. The third and fourth officers will follow close behind the second officer. As the first two officers move to their domination points, the third and fourth officers will enter right behind, each moving in the opposite direction of the officer in front and clearing the center of the room. The third and fourth officers will move to domination points just inside the door. Either the third or fourth officer will check behind the door. The third or fourth officer will also turn to provide rear security for the team while remaining inside the room. As shown in the sector diagram below, once all officers are at their domination points, they will be in a "shallow horseshoe" configuration.

DELAYED ENTRY: CORNER-FED OPEN DOOR

LEAD OFFICER STEP 1 - Conduct Half Sweep

Clearing a corner-fed open door is similar to clearing a center-fed open door. When conducting a delayed entry, the term "corner-fed" or "center-fed" refers to the room the team starts in as well as the room the team is clearing. In some cases, when clearing a corner-fed door the lead officer will only be able to approach from one side and conduct only a "half sweep." The lead officer will position close to the wall while staying several yards away from the door. The lead officer will then sweep out in a quick but smooth arc, maintaining distance from the doorway while clearing the interior of the room.

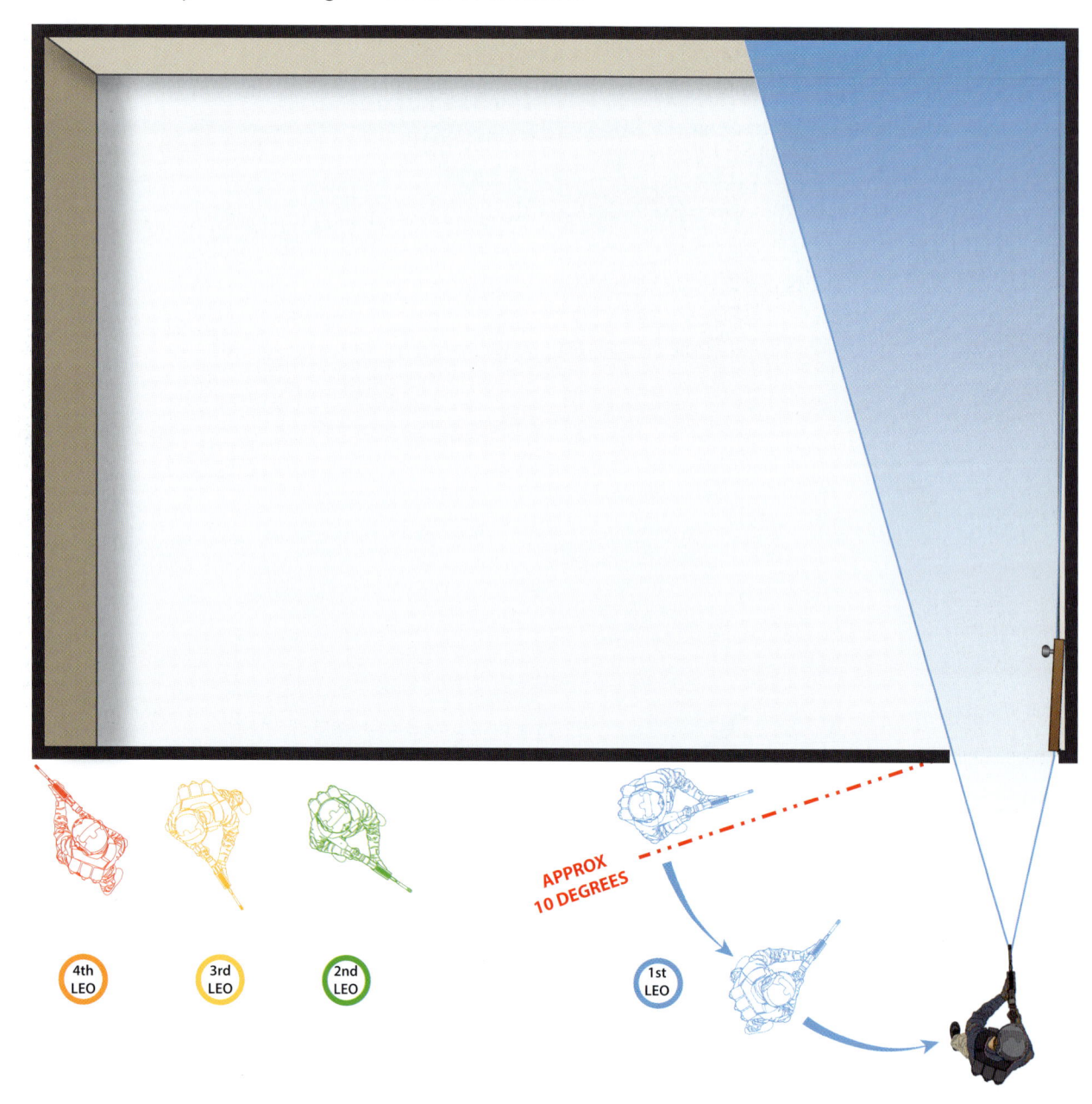

APPROX 10 DEGREES

4th LEO
3rd LEO
2nd LEO
1st LEO

DELAYED ENTRY: CORNER-FED OPEN DOOR

LEAD OFFICER STEP 2 - Approach the Door and Enter

After completing the initial half sweep, if the team decides to enter the room, the lead officer will move towards the door remaining alert for deep threats in the room. When reaching the threshold, the lead officer then clears the corner and scans inward while moving to the domination point just as in the immediate entry technique.

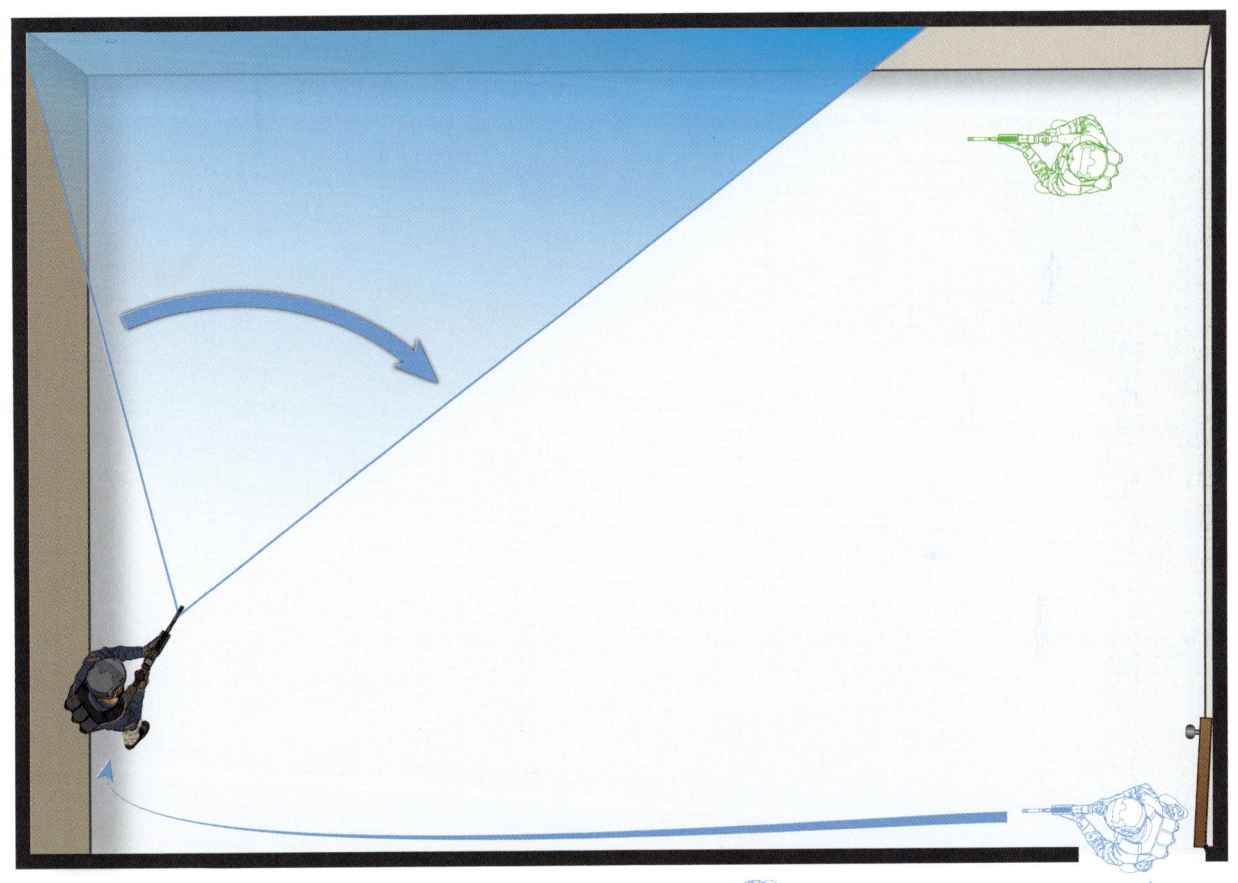

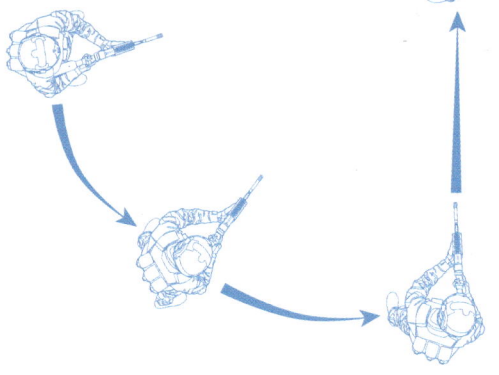

DELAYED ENTRY: CORNER-FED OPEN DOOR

SECOND OFFICER - Clear the Corner and Dominate

The second officer will initially keep some distance from the door along with the rest of the team and allow the lead officer time and space to conduct the sweep. If the team decides to enter the room, the second officer will wait until the lead officer completes the reverse sweep and is moving head-on towards the door. At this point, the second team member will also approach the door and enter right behind the lead officer. Once the second officer enters the room and turns in the opposite direction of the lead officer, he/she will clear the corner and engage any threats in the corner until they are neutralized. The second officer will then scan inward and move to the domination point just as in the immediate entry technique.

DELAYED ENTRY: CORNER-FED OPEN DOOR

THIRD AND FOURTH OFFICER - Clear Center, Cover Rear

The procedures for the third and fourth officer in delayed entry are no different from immediate entry. The third and fourth officer will follow close behind the second officer. As the first two officers move to their domination points, the third and fourth officers will enter right behind, each moving in the opposite direction of the officer in front and clearing the center of the room. The third and fourth officers will move to domination points just inside the door. Either the third or fourth officer will check behind the door. The third or fourth officer will also turn to provide rear security for the team while remaining inside the room. As shown in the sector diagram below, a key difference between the corner-fed and center-fed clearing technique is that in a corner-fed room, the team will assume more of an "L-shape" configuration than a "horseshoe."

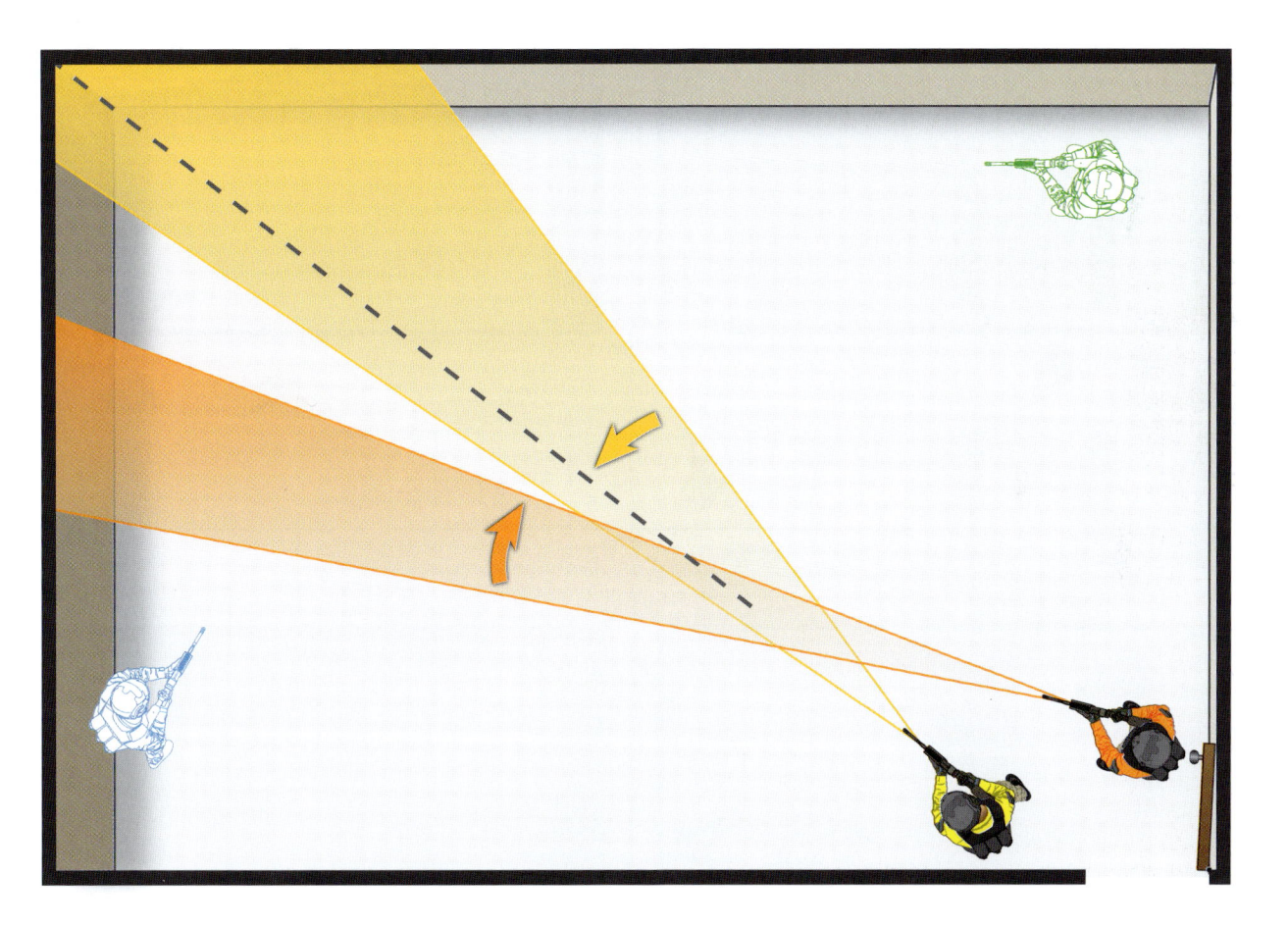

DELAYED ENTRY: CORNER-FED OPEN DOOR

COMPLETE SEQUENCE

The majority of the team will remain away from the door and only the lead officer will move forward to conduct an initial half sweep of the target room. Once the sweep is complete, the lead officer will move straight towards the door. At this point the second officer will begin to move towards the door to enter the room right behind the lead officer. The remaining officers will also move towards the door to follow behind into the room.

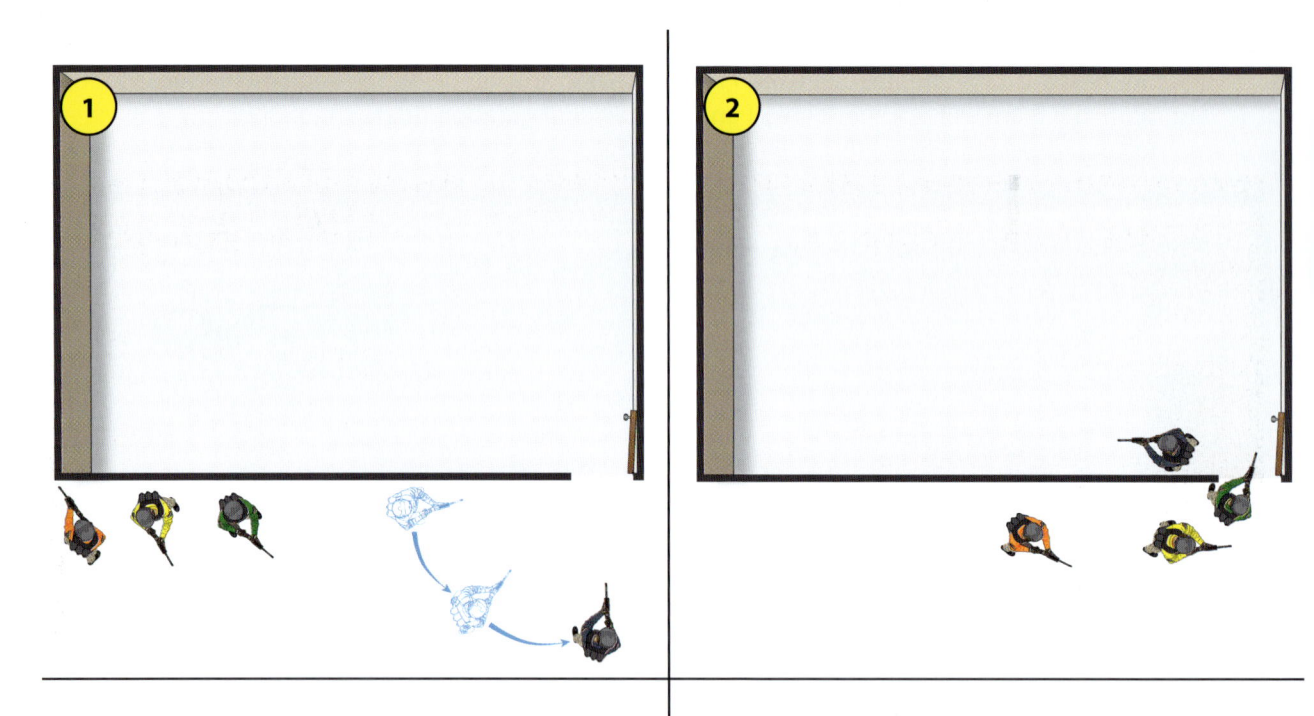

TEAM OPERATIONS: SINGLE-ROOM DELAYED ENTRY   79

DELAYED ENTRY: CORNER-FED CLOSED DOOR

LEAD OFFICER STEP 1 - Open the Door

The technique for a corner-fed closed door is almost the same as the technique for clearing the open door with a few minor adjustments. The first difference is that because the door is closed, the team must first open the door before conducting the sweep. To open the door, the lead officer will position close to the wall and away from the door with weapon at the ready and oriented towards the door just in case the door opens and an adversary walks out. The lead officer will move towards the door quickly, grasp the doorknob with the non-firing hand and swing the door open. The lead officer will then back away just in case an adversary fires towards the door.

4th LEO   3rd LEO   2nd LEO   1st LEO

DELAYED ENTRY: CORNER-FED CLOSED DOOR

LEAD OFFICER STEP 2 - Conduct Sweep and Enter

Once the door is open, the clearing technique is the same as for a closed door. The lead officer will conduct a half sweep across the door, then move towards the door and enter the room. The lead officer will clear the corner and scan inward while moving to the domination point.

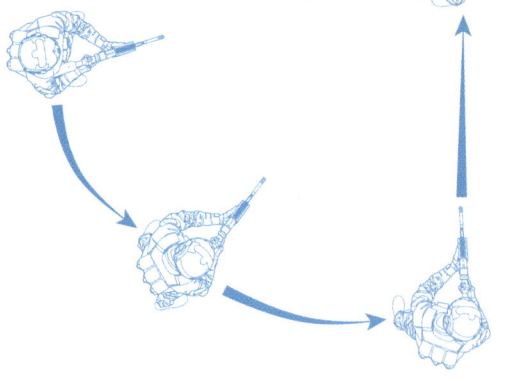

Team Operations: Single-Room Delayed Entry

DELAYED ENTRY: CORNER-FED CLOSED DOOR

SECOND OFFICER - Clear the Corner and Dominate

The second officer will initially keep some distance from the door along with the rest of the team and allow the lead officer time to open the door and space to conduct the initial sweep. The second officer will wait until the lead officer is moving head-on towards the door. At this point, the second officer will also approach the door and enter right behind the lead officer. Once the second officer enters the room and turns in the opposite direction of the lead officer, he/she will clear the corner and engage any threats in the corner until they are neutralized. The second officer will then scan inward and move to the domination point just as in the immediate entry technique.

DELAYED ENTRY: CORNER-FED CLOSED DOOR

THIRD AND FOURTH OFFICERS - Clear Center, Cover Rear

The procedures for the third and fourth officer in delayed entry are no different from immediate entry. The third and fourth officer will follow close behind the second officer. As the first two officers move to their domination points, the third and fourth officers will enter right behind, each moving in the opposite direction of the officer in front and clearing the center of the room. The third and fourth officers will move to domination points just inside the door. Either the third or fourth officer will check behind the door. The third or fourth officer will also turn to provide rear security for the team while remaining inside the room. As shown in the sector diagram below, a key difference between the corner-fed and center-fed clearing technique is that in a corner-fed room, the team will assume more of an "L-shape" configuration than a "horseshoe."

TEAM OPERATIONS
Multiple Room Immediate Entry

The techniques for moving from one room to the next depend on the positioning of the doors in the room and whether the doors are open or closed. When the team enters a room and encounters an open door, one officer will generally have a better angle of observation into that room. That officer will hold coverage on the open door while the rest of the team collapses to stack on the door.

If the team encounters a closed door, there will be no need to hold long coverage on the door. Instead, the team will collapse and stack on the door but at least one officer will move to the opposite side of the door from the rest of the team to act as the breacher. When stacking on both sides of a door, it is generally best for the heavy side to stack on the long wall and the light side to stack on the short wall.

One of the most challenging configurations is multiple open doors in one room. In this type of situation, it is particularly difficult to apply any predetermined or fixed formula. Instead, officers must use their common sense and judgment to deal with the situation in the safest way possible. This will generally call for officers to cover each open door while the team leader directs the team to stack on one of the doors. The team will attempt to maintain coverage on all openings until they move into the next room.

Another frequently used technique when moving through multiple rooms is the "back clear." The back clear is simply clearing a room a second time using the same techniques. A team may use the back clear if they enter a room with no doors and they must move back to clear another area of the building. A team might also use the back clear technique to conduct a second, more deliberate clearance of a building to ensure there are no adversaries hiding in concealed locations.

If officers want to move through a room quickly without clearing it, they can use the "clear and hold" technique. The clear and hold technique calls for officers to peel off and momentarily stop to cover doors or danger areas while the rest of the team flows past. Once the team passes, the holding officers will rejoin the rear of the formation. The clear and hold technique is faster but is more dangerous for the team.

If speed is critical, officers might choose to use the "clear on the move" technique. When clearing on the move, officers will remain in formation and clear all danger areas without stopping. The clear on the move technique is the fastest technique but it is also the most dangerous for the team. Therefore, it is generally best to use the clear on the move only when time is critical or when there is imminent danger to innocent people.

OPEN DOOR ON THE FAR WALL

STEP 1 - Dominate the First Room

The team will enter and dominate the first room using one of the methods already described. Once the officers are at their domination points, each officer will have a different angle of observation through the open door into the next room. While at least one officer will turn around to provide rear security, the remaining officers will focus their attention on the open doors leading to adjacent rooms. At this point the team leader will determine the direction of travel. The team leader will choose a door, point to it with his/her non-firing hand and call out "stack…stack…stack." For experienced teams, the team leader can also just point without saying anything. This tells the team which door to stack on next.

OPEN DOOR ON THE FAR WALL

STEP 2 - Maintain Long Coverage

Once the team knows where to stack, depending on the positioning of the open door, one officer will have a better angle of observation into the next room than the other officers. The officer with the best observation angle will remain in place and maintain "long coverage" on the door. There are no formulas or fixed rules for how to best emplace long coverage. For example, the officer covering long may choose to move closer to the door, step farther from the door or shuffle to the left or right to get the best observation angle into the room. In general, when conducting an immediate entry, officers should not "give up" angles of observation that they already have. If the officer providing long coverage has to take a shot through the door, he/she may choose to alert the officers stacked on the door if there is time to do so.

OPEN DOOR ON THE FAR WALL

STEP 3 - Converge on the Door

Once long coverage is established, the remaining officers will converge on the door in either a tight stack or loose stack. The loose stack is the preferred technique for experienced teams. Once again, there are no formulas or set rules for how to position the various team members when converging on the door. Officers should avoid crossing in front of the open door as much as possible. Therefore, officers whose domination points are on the right side of the door should generally stay on the right and vice versa. In some cases officers will have no choice but to cross in front of an open door. In these cases, officers should move quickly in an arc movement while maintaining coverage on the door.

OPEN DOOR ON THE FAR WALL

STEP 4 - Stack and Enter

After converging on the door the team will position itself in a stack, ready to enter the next room. The order of officers in the stack is not important when using the free-flow method. Officers just converge on the door in whatever order they arrive. However, it is generally a good idea for the team leader not to be the first or second officer into the room. This is very easy to accomplish. If the team leader ends up in the lead, he/she can simply slow down and let other officers cut in front. One officer will be maintaining long coverage and at least one officer should maintain rear security. Once the team is ready to enter the next room, the second officer in the stack will look around to make sure the team is ready to enter. If the team is ready the second officer will deliver the ready signal (firm squeeze) to the first officer to initiate movement. The lead officer will then lead the way into the next room.

OPEN DOOR ON THE SIDE WALL

COMPLETE SEQUENCE

The process for entering through an open door on a side wall is exactly the same as for an open door on the far wall. However, the location of the door will affect the positioning of officers inside the room. Once again, there are no formulas or fixed rules for how to maintain long coverage and stack on the door. However, the officer farthest from the door will generally pick up long coverage and the remaining officers will converge to stack on the door. **NOTE: The illustration below shows only one example of how to handle this configuration.**

Team Operations: Multiple Room Immediate Entry

CLOSED DOOR ON THE FAR WALL

STEP 1 - Dominate the First Room

The team will enter and dominate the first room using one of the methods already described. Unlike an open door, a closed door provides less of an immediate threat to the officers in the room. However, officers should still maintain coverage on the door in case an adversary walks through it. At least one officer will turn around to provide rear security. At this point the team leader will determine the direction of travel. The team leader will choose a door, point to it with his/her non-firing hand and call out "stack…stack…stack." For experienced teams, the team leader can also just point without saying anything.

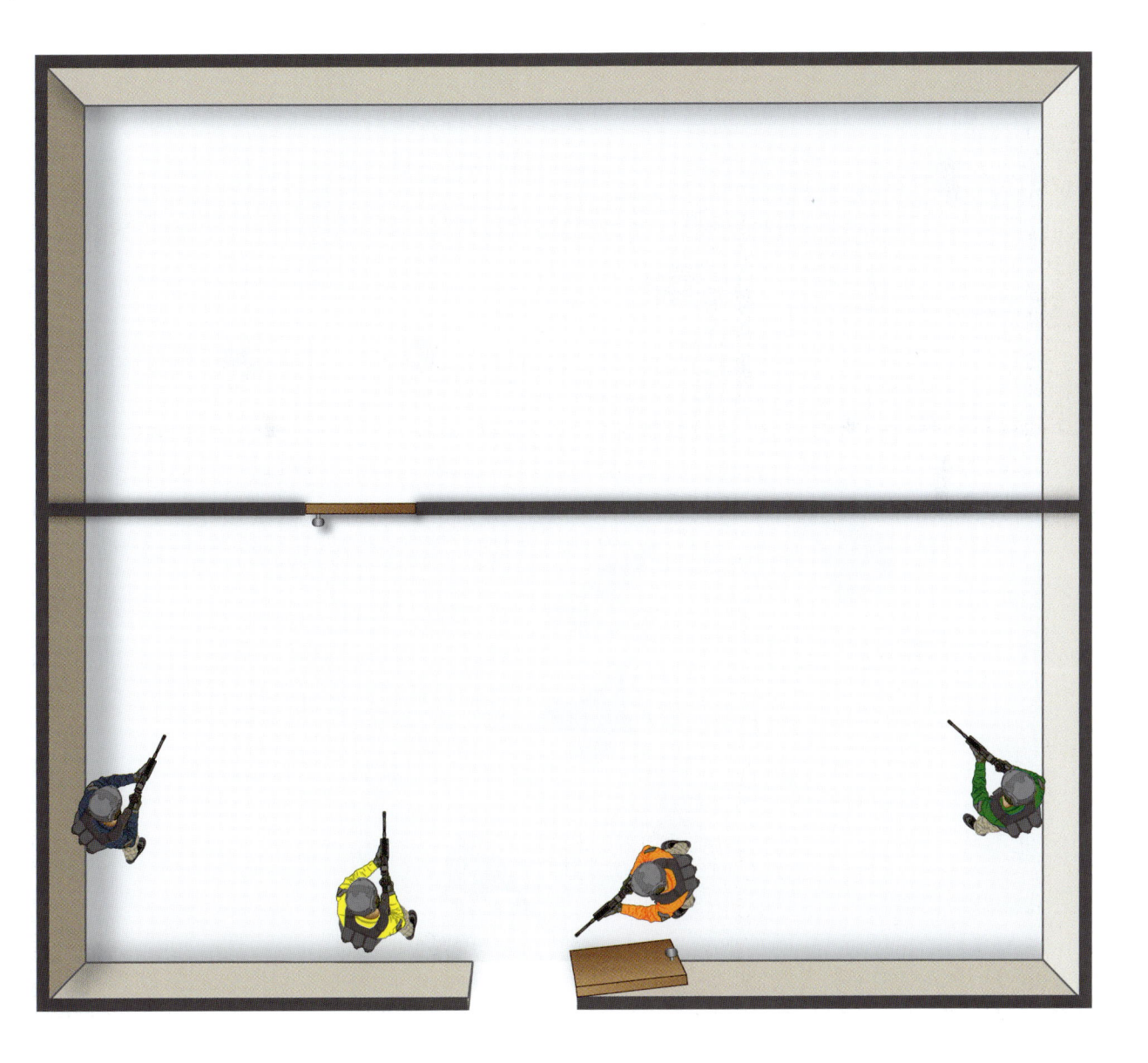

CLOSED DOOR ON THE FAR WALL

STEP 2 - Converge on the Door

When converging on a closed door, there is no need to maintain long coverage. However, one officer will need to move to the opposite side of the door to act as the breacher. There are no formulas or set rules for determining which officer becomes the breacher. The more a team practices, the easier it will be for them to quickly converge on the door with the entry team on one side and the breacher on the other. Since most interior doors are unlocked, it is usually possible for any officer in the team to act as the breacher. However, if the team encounters a locked door, team members may need to shuffle positions to get the officer with the shotgun or breaching tools into position to bypass the locked door.

CLOSED DOOR ON THE FAR WALL

STEP 3 - Stack and Enter

After converging on the door the team will position itself in a stack, ready to enter the next room. The order of officers in the stack is not important when using the free-flow method. However, it is generally a good idea for the team leader not to be the first or second officer into the room. One officer will be positioned on the opposite side of the door as the breacher and at least one officer should maintain rear security. Once the team is ready to enter the next room, the second officer in the stack will look around to make sure the team is ready to enter. If the team is ready the second officer will deliver the ready signal (firm squeeze) to the first officer to initiate movement. The first officer will nod without looking away from the door. This nod will signal the breacher to open the door. Once the door is open, the team will enter and the breacher will follow the team into the room as the last officer.

CLOSED DOOR ON THE SIDE WALL

COMPLETE SEQUENCE

The process for entering through a closed door on a side wall is exactly the same as for a closed door on the far wall. However, the location of the door will affect the positioning of officers in the room. Once again, there are no formulas or fixed rules for how to position the breacher and stack on the door. **NOTE: The illustration below shows only one example of how to handle this configuration.**

TEAM OPERATIONS: MULTIPLE ROOM IMMEDIATE ENTRY

OPEN DOOR IN THE NEAR CORNER: BYPASS

STEP 1 - Bypass the Door

A common tactical problem is for the team to encounter an open door in the near corner of a room. This presents a danger for the team since there will be an opening exposing the team's flank once they have dominated the room. The first option for dealing with this problem is for the first or second officer (whichever is responsible for clearing the corner with the open door) to bypass the open door. As the officer enters the room, he/she will clear the corner as usual, however, because of the open door, the "corner" will extend into the visible portion of the next room. Once the corner is clear, the officer will continue to move to the domination point and push forward, out of the way of the open door.

OPEN DOOR IN THE NEAR CORNER: BYPASS

STEP 2 - Reorient on the Door

Once the room is clear, the team will be vulnerable to adversaries coming from the next room. Therefore, the team must quickly reposition to converge on the open door and prepare for entry. The officer who bypassed the door will quickly turn around and become the lead officer in the stack. One officer will maintain long coverage while the rest of the officers swing around to stack on the door. Once the team is in position, the second officer will check to make sure the team is ready to enter, then deliver the squeeze to the first officer. The team will then enter and clear the room. **NOTE: The illustration below shows only one example of how to handle this configuration.**

OPEN DOOR IN THE NEAR CORNER: HOLD

STEP 1 - Hold on the Door

The second option for dealing with an open door in the near corner is for the first or second officer (whichever is responsible for clearing the corner with the open door) to stop and hold on the open door. An officer might choose this method if he/she identifies a possible threat in the next room and wants to maintain coverage. As the officer enters the room, he/she will clear the corner as usual, however, because of the open door, the "corner" will extend into the visible portion of the next room. The officer will then stop and hold coverage on the open door. The next officer moving in that direction (the third or fourth officer) will have to remain alert and bypass the officer who is holding on the door and assume that officer's domination point and clearing responsibilities.

OPEN DOOR IN THE NEAR CORNER: HOLD

STEP 2 - Reorient on the Door

Once the room is clear, the team will be vulnerable to adversaries coming from the next room. Therefore, the team must quickly reposition to converge on the open door and prepare for entry. The officer holding on the door will remain in place and provide long coverage. The remaining officers will swing around to stack on the door. Once the team is in position, the second officer will check to make sure the team is ready to enter, then deliver the squeeze to the first officer. The team will then enter and clear the room. In the example below, if the yellow officer is the team leader, he/she might want to shuffle back to the third position in the stack. **NOTE: The illustration below shows one example of how to handle this configuration.**

MULTIPLE DOORS

COMPLETE SEQUENCE

The team might enter a room that contains multiple doors leading to other rooms. The basic procedures for clearing this type of configuration remain the same. Once the team dominates the room, officers will cover all the doors in the room, especially open doors. The team leader will then decide which door to enter next and communicate this to the team. Generally, the team will enter the room that presents the greatest threat first. Another general rule is to enter and clear through open doors first before moving on to closed doors. However, the greatest threat takes precedence whether the door is open or closed. As the team moves to stack on the next door, officers will need to remain alert to ensure they maintain rear security and also cover additional doors in the room. In some cases, it is impossible to cover every angle and trying to do so will just slow the team down and disrupt the flow into the next room. **NOTE: The illustration below shows one example of how to handle this configuration.**

BACK CLEAR

COMPLETE SEQUENCE

There are some situations where a team will be clearing from room to room and run into a dead end, a room that has no other doors besides the door that the team entered through. At this point, the team will have to "back clear" or move back through a room they already cleared. The back clear is the safest and most deliberate way for a team to retrace its steps. The technique for conducting a back clear is no different from the technique for clearing a new room. A team might also use the back clear technique to conduct a second, more deliberate clearance of a building to ensure there are no adversaries hiding in concealed locations.

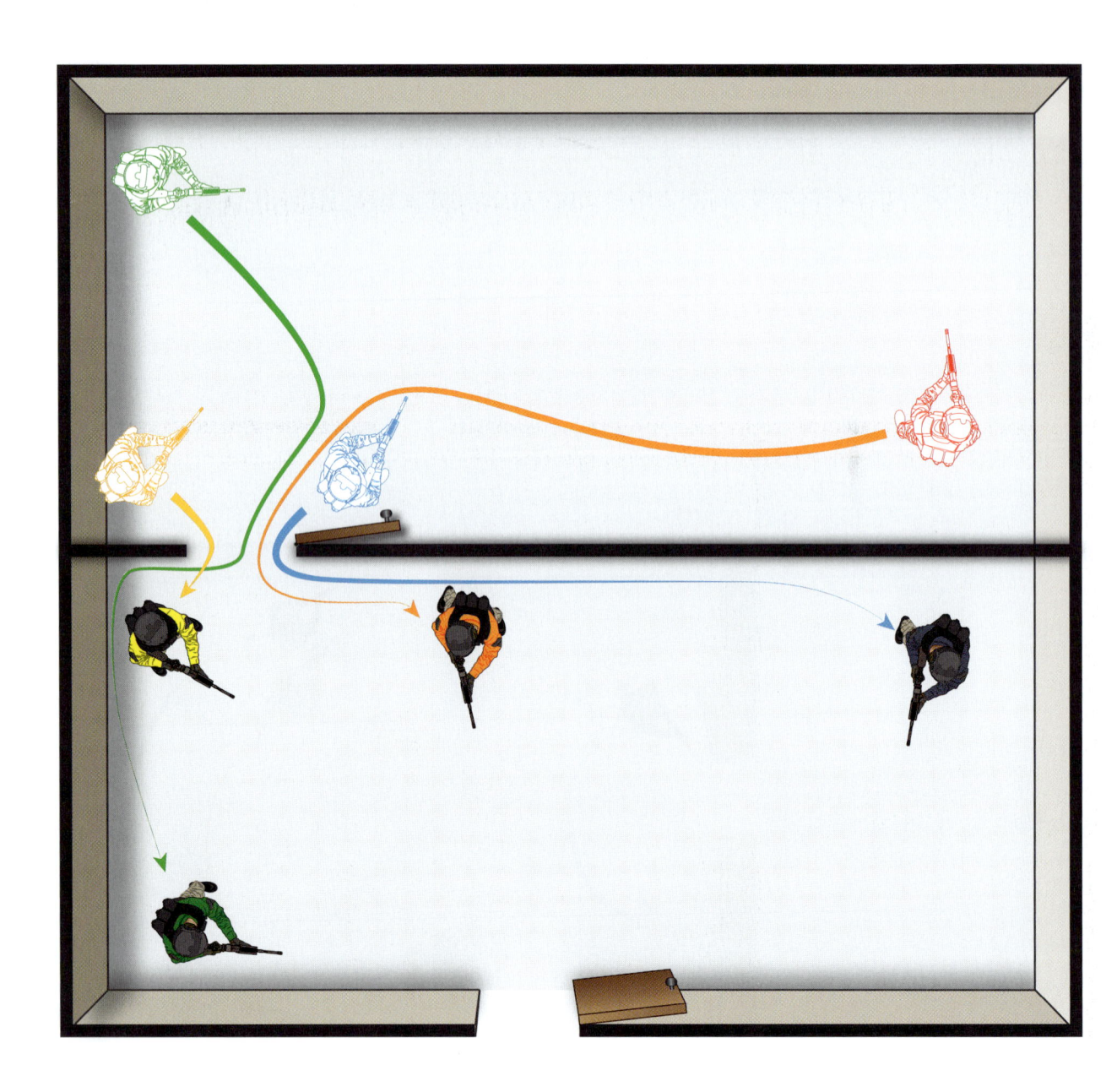

CLEAR AND HOLD

COMPLETE SEQUENCE

There are some situations where the team will want to move back through a room that was already cleared but will not want to take the time to "back clear" the room all over again. In these cases, the team can move through the cleared room and stack directly on the next door. The team leader will give a "clear and hold" command and then direct the team where to stack by pointing at the desired door with the non-firing hand and calling out "stack" if necessary. The team will then move into the room and one officer will hold coverage on the danger area while the rest of the team stacks. Generally, the first officer will hold but the second officer can also pick up the holding responsibility if the first officer bypasses it. If there are multiple danger areas to cover, officers will cover them as needed without waiting for specific instructions. This is an example of the "free flow" method. Once in the stack, the team will then enter the next room and the holding officer will become the last officer into the room.

CLEAR ON THE MOVE

COMPLETE SEQUENCE

There are some situations where the team will want to move back through a room that was already cleared as quickly as possible. In these cases, the team can move through the cleared room using the "clear on the move" technique and stack directly on the next door. The team leader will give the "clear on the move" command and direct the team which door to stack on next. In other cases, the team might choose to move through the next door without stacking. When clearing on the move, the team will move directly to the next location without any officers stopping to hold on doors or danger areas. Clearing on the move simply means that officers will move quickly and clear any danger areas they pass without stopping. Clearing on the move is a faster but more dangerous technique and therefore is generally used only for "emergency" clearing as opposed to deliberate clearing.

TEAM OPERATIONS
Multiple Room Delayed Entry

If a team must move from room to room in a situation where time is not critical, officers may choose to employ the delayed entry technique in order to minimize exposure and risk to the team. The delayed entry technique is also particularly useful in situations where the team aims to locate and "call out" a subject without committing too far into a house or building.

To move from room to room using delayed entry, the team will first conduct a sweep of the first room and then enter, with each officer moving to his/her domination point. When the team identifies an open or closed door in the room, one officer is usually in a better position to conduct a sweep of the next room. As with previous techniques, there are no formulas or set rules for who should conduct the sweep and officers must use their common sense based on the situation.

For an open door, the officer conducting the sweep will move to a position close to the wall, offering observation as far into the next room's corner as possible. The officer will then sweep around in the same, smooth arc movement described in the single-room delayed entry section. The officer will conduct additional sweeps as needed to check the next room for threats. In other situations, because of the room configuration or the positioning of furniture, the officer might only be able to conduct a partial sweep of the next room.

The procedures for a closed door are the same, except the officer will need to first approach the door, open the door, back away and then conduct the sweep. Once the lead officer opens the door, all officers on the team should remain alert in case an adversary emerges from the door.

Whether the door is open or closed, while the first officer conducts the sweep, the other officers in the team should position themselves away from the door to minimize exposure. The point of having only one officer conduct the sweep is to keep the majority of the team away from danger and hostile fire. Therefore, when conducting delayed entry, officers may give up angles of observation into the next room for the sake of minimizing exposure. This differs from immediate entry where officers try not to give up angles of observation into the next room.

Another reason why the rest of the team should move away from the door is to give the lead officer room to conduct the sweep and avoid a situation where the sweeping officer is passing in front of other officers' lines of fire. When moving away from the door, the team should still try not to bunch up and maintain as much dispersion as possible.

OPEN DOOR

COMPLETE SEQUENCE

Once the team knows where to stack, depending on the positioning of the open door, one officer will have a better angle of observation into the next room than the other officers. The officer with the best observation angle will usually be the best officer to conduct the sweep for the delayed entry. The rest of the team will move away from the door to give the sweeping officer space to conduct the sweep. There is no set formula for how officers should adjust position in the room but at least one officer should provide rear security. It is also ideal if the sweeping officer does not pass through other officers' lines of fire. **NOTE: The illustration below shows one example of how to handle this configuration.**

Team Operations: Multiple Room Delayed Entry 103

CLOSED DOOR

COMPLETE SEQUENCE

When confronted with a closed door, one officer can use the delayed entry techniques already described while the rest of the team moves back away from the door. The first officer will open the door, then step back and conduct a sweep. Once the sweep is complete, if the team wants to enter the next room they will do so using the same techniques described in the delayed entry section.

TEAM OPERATIONS
Hallways Immediate Entry

Hallways are considered danger areas for several key reasons. First of all, the shape of the hallway forces the team to bunch up or "canalize" so that a single burst of fire from down the hall can rip through the entire team. Even if the team is wearing body armor or employing a ballistic shield, bullets can still pass through the legs of multiple officers before running out of energy. Multiple gunshot wounds below the waist, particularly to the pelvic girdle, can prove as lethal as wounds to the vital organs. Therefore, a team that is bunched up, moving down a hallway is particularly vulnerable.

Hallways are also more dangerous because they generally have many doors running along their length. An adversary could emerge from any one of these doors without warning. More importantly, an adversary could simply extend his/her weapon around the corner and spray indiscriminately. Because of the shape of the hallway, there is a greater chance that this type of indiscriminate fire will hit the team.

For these reasons, the team should move through the hallway quickly, maintaining dispersion. The objective should be to get out of the hallway and into a room that offers better protection. Officers should avoid moving in a single file formation and should instead try to have as many guns pointing down the hallway as possible. Officers should also maintain "cross coverage" while moving and use the "clear and hold" or "clear on the move" techniques as needed when passing open doors.

When moving from a hallway into a room, or moving from a room into the hallway, the team must remain alert for potential threats coming from either direction. If the team must send a breacher to the opposite side of the entry door, another officer might want to move around with the breacher to cover his/her back.

Probably the most dangerous hallway configurations a team will encounter are hallway intersections. Intersections are danger areas for all of the same reasons as a single hallway. However, when the team passes though an intersection, officers will be exposed from multiple directions instead of just two, increasing the level of risk and presenting more angles for officers to cover. Therefore, officers should try to move through intersections as quickly as possible to get away from the intersection to a safer location.

There are many different intersection configurations but the most common are the L-shape intersection, T-shape intersection and the X-shape intersection. There are also intersections with uneven hallways.

HALLWAY MOVEMENT

Cross Coverage

When a team moves down a hallway, the lead two officers will position themselves even with each other on each side of the hallway. They will provide "cross coverage" which means that the officer on the right will cover to the left and the officer on the left will cover to the right. This is because officers have a better angle of observation through doors and openings across the hall than they do on the same side of the hall. If the hall is wide enough, the third officer can stand between the lead officers and provide cover to the front. Additional officers will provide rear security. The formation ends up taking the shape of a "shallow-Y." In narrow hallways, there might not be room for the third officer to cover the front. In extremely narrow hallways there might not even be enough room for cross coverage. In these cases, officers should just stagger their formation and cover the front and rear as they move.

HALLWAY MOVEMENT

Moving Past Doors - Clear and Hold

As the team approaches an open door, the two lead officers will maintain cross coverage until they reach the door. On the approach, the officer across the hall will have the best angle of vision through the open door. However, this officer will have to momentarily give up cross coverage as the team reaches the door. The lead officer on the same side as the door will quickly turn and provide coverage as the team passes. The covering officer can adjust as needed to achieve the best angle to cover the team and minimize exposure. Once the last officer passes the covering officer, the last officer will squeeze the covering officer and call out "last man." At this point the covering officer will fall into the rear of the formation as the last officer. The process is the same for passing two opposing open doors except both lead officers will hold and provide coverage as the team passes through.

HALLWAY MOVEMENT

Moving Past Doors - Clear on the Move

The clear on the move technique is less secure but it is faster and easier to execute. Conducting the clear on the move is simple. Officers will still maintain cross coverage as they move down the hall. However, as an officer reaches an open door, he/she will momentarily pivot to clear the doorway while moving. If there are multiple officers following in trail, each officer will repeat the clearing process as he/she passes the open door.

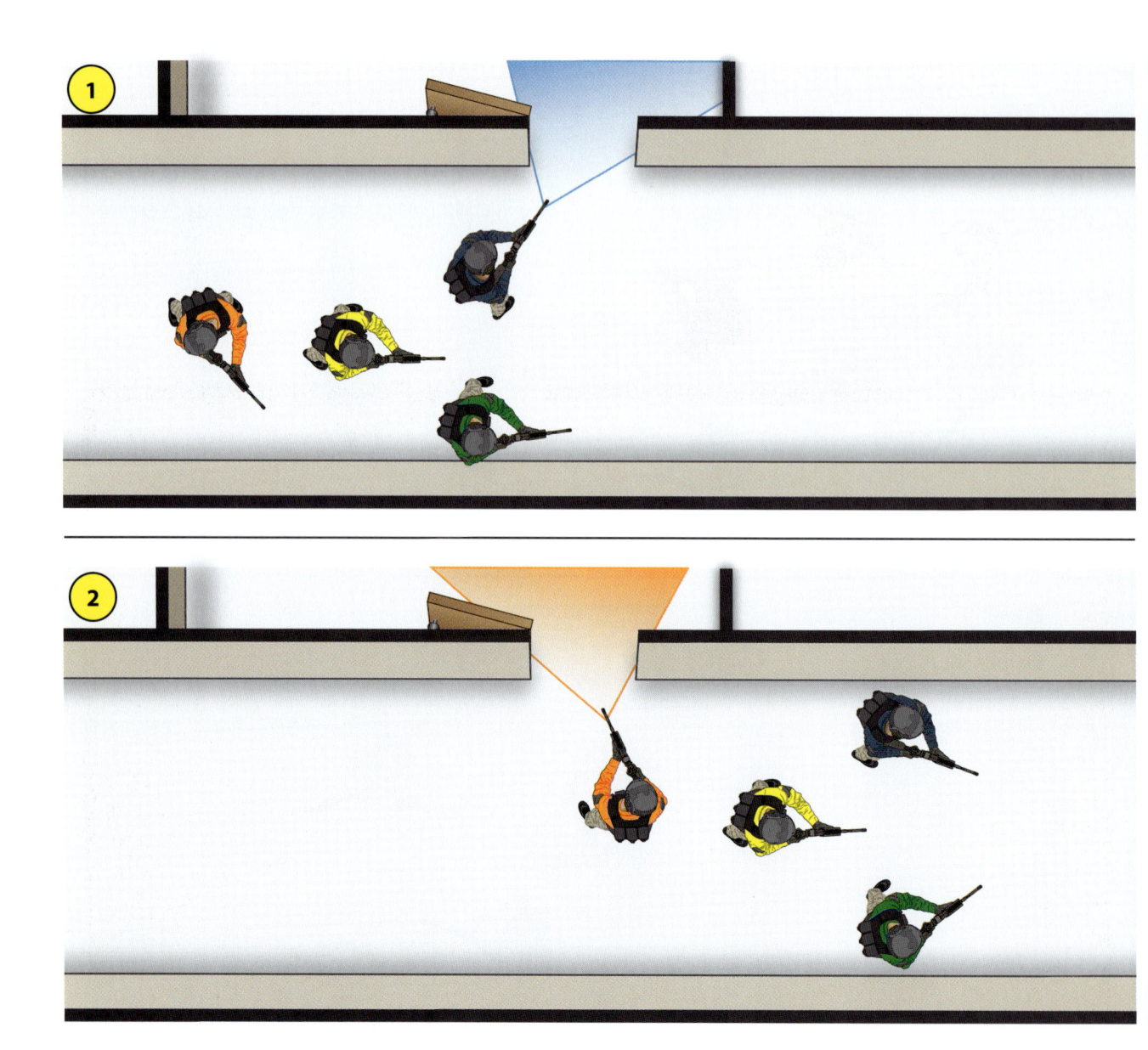

TEAM OPERATIONS: HALLWAYS IMMEDIATE ENTRY   109

ENTERING AN OPEN DOOR FROM THE HALLWAY

STEP 1 - Approach the Door

As the team moves down the hallway with the lead two officers providing cross coverage, one of the officers will identify the open door. It is the team leader's decision whether to enter the room or bypass it. Once the team leader decides to enter the room, the two lead officers will maintain cross coverage as the team approaches the open door.

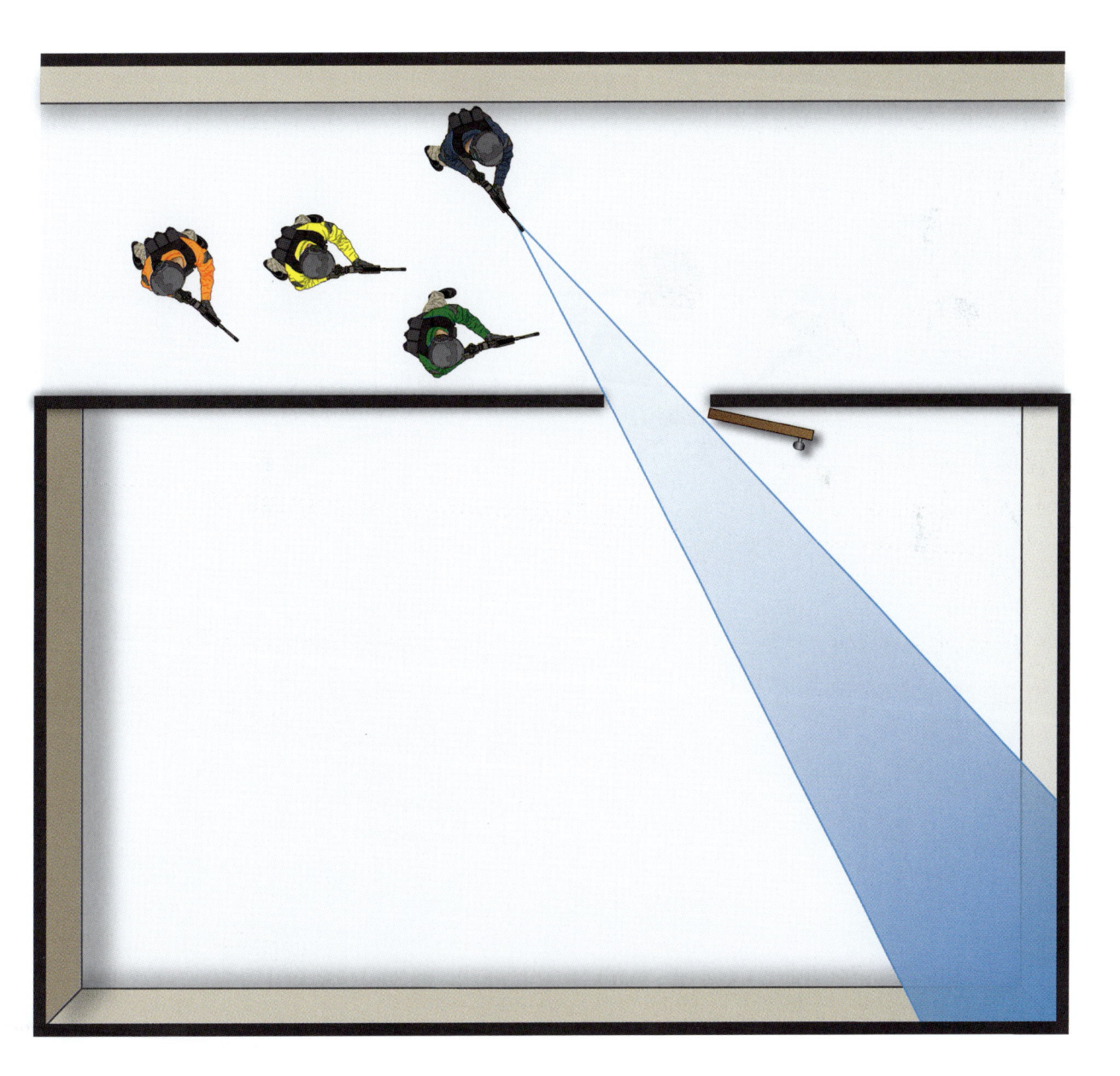

ENTERING AN OPEN DOOR FROM THE HALLWAY

STEP 2 - Stack on the Door

The officer opposite the side of the open door will move into position to provide long coverage while the remainder of the team stacks behind the other lead officer. The rear officer will continue to provide rear security and the remaining team members will cover exposed angles up and down the hall. In the example below, the team leader has shuffled the stack to avoid being second into the room.

ENTERING AN OPEN DOOR FROM THE HALLWAY

STEP 3 - Enter and Clear

Once the team is stacked on the door and the officer on the far side of the hall is providing long coverage, the second officer in the stack will look around to make sure the team is ready to enter. Once the first officer receives the squeeze, the first officer will lead the team into the room. The officer providing long coverage will become the last officer into the room. The team will clear the room using any of the techniques previously described.

ENTERING A CLOSED DOOR FROM THE HALLWAY

STEP 1 - Approach the Door

The team will move down the hallway with the lead two officers providing cross coverage. When an officer identifies the closed door, it will be the team leader's decision whether to enter the room or bypass it. Once the team leader decides to enter the room, the team will have to position itself to breach the door and enter the room.

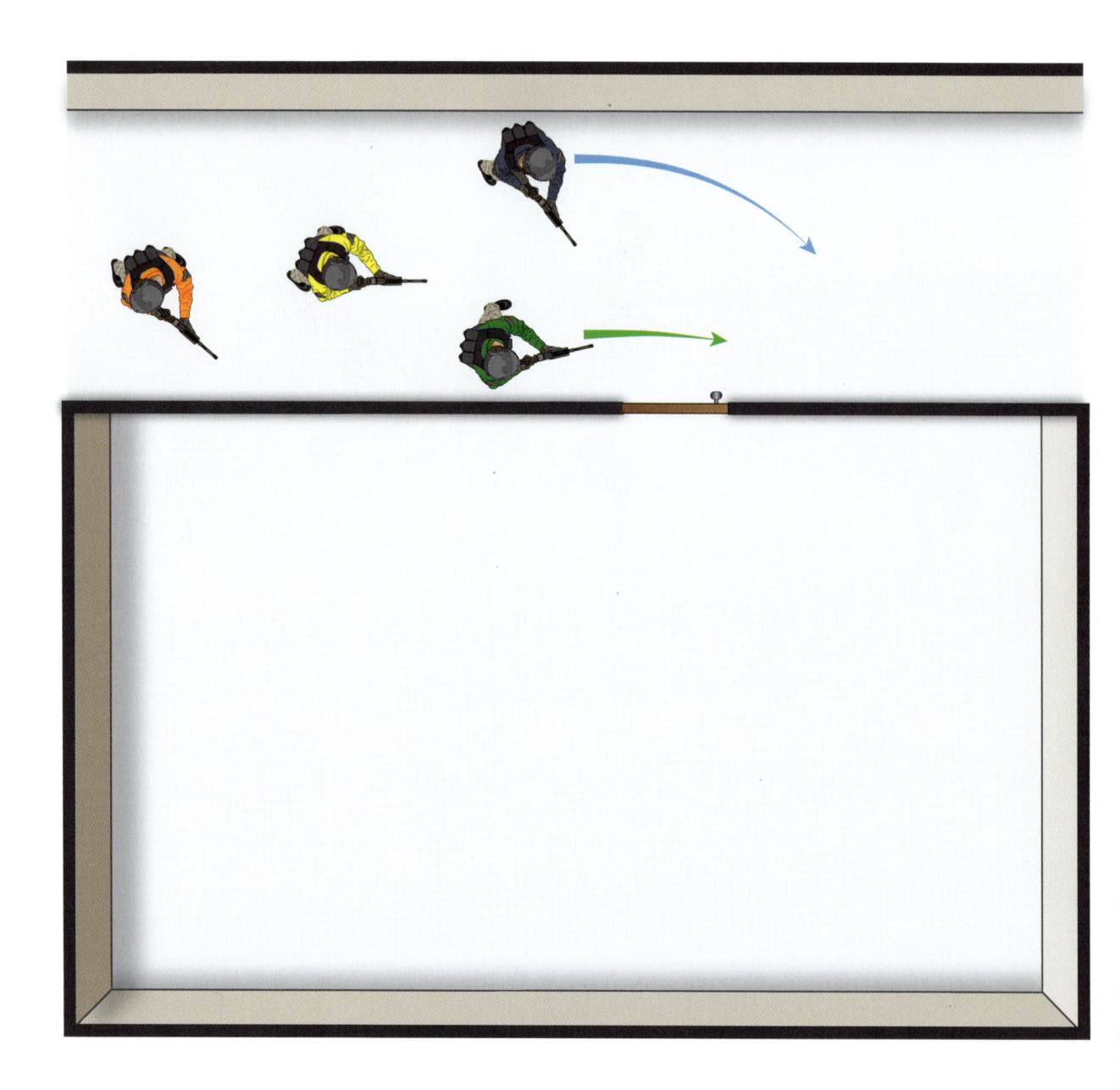

ENTERING A CLOSED DOOR FROM THE HALLWAY

STEP 2 - Stack on the Door

There is no fixed formula for deciding which officer will position to breach the door for the rest of the team. However, it is important to try to maintain coverage both to the front and rear down the hallway. The lead officer across the hall from the door can maintain coverage to the front while the lead officer on the same side as the door pushes past to become the breacher. Or, the officer on the same side as the door can push past the door to provide coverage to the front and the breacher can also move past the door. Once again, there is no fixed formula.

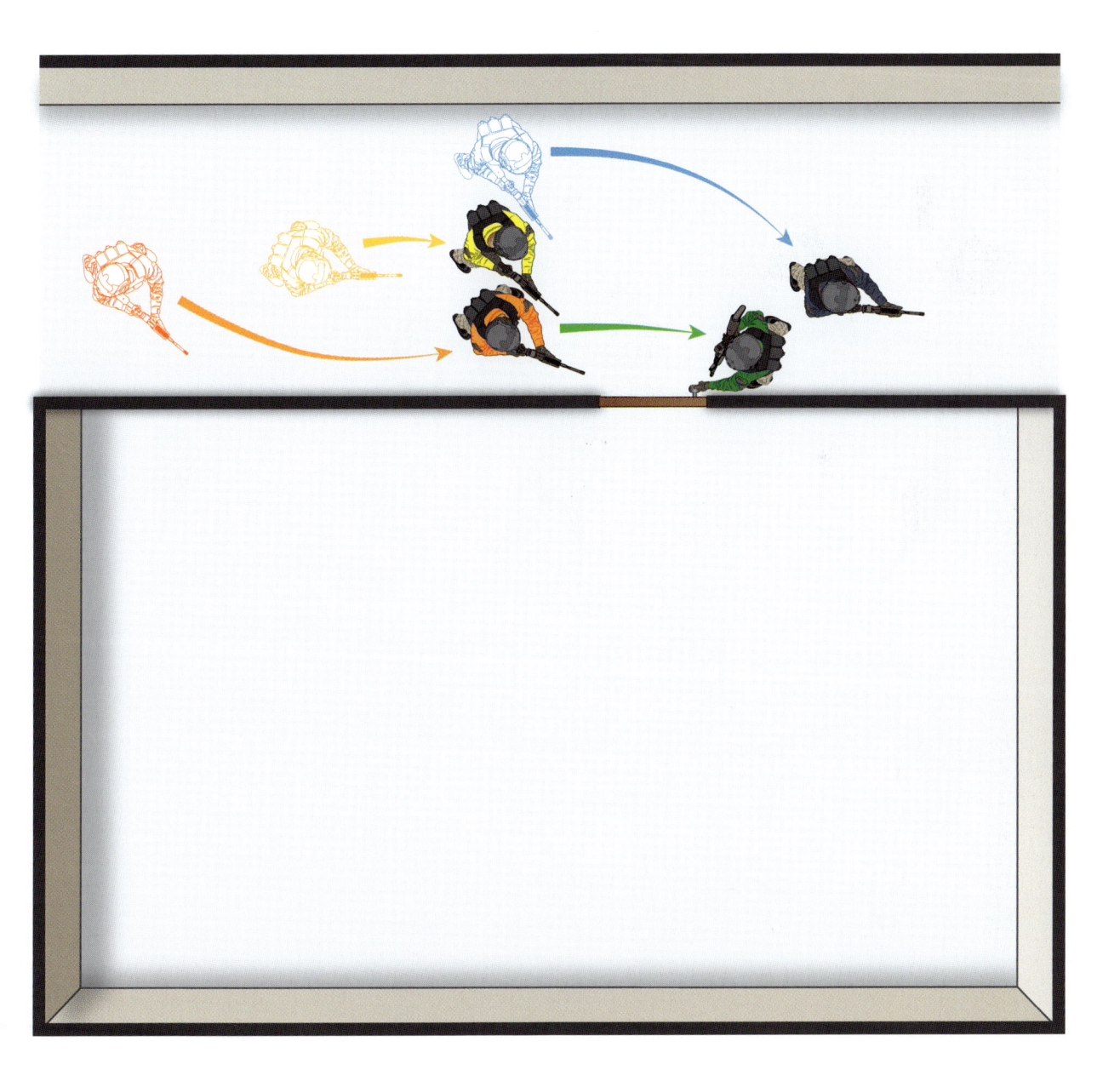

ENTERING A CLOSED DOOR FROM THE HALLWAY

STEP 3 - Breach and Clear

Once the team is stacked on the door and the breacher is in position, the second officer in the stack will look around to make sure the team is ready to enter. Once the first officer receives the squeeze, the first officer will nod, signaling the breacher to open the door. Once the door is open, the team will flow into the room using any of the techniques already described.

TEAM OPERATIONS: HALLWAYS IMMEDIATE ENTRY — 115

ENTERING OPPOSING OPEN DOORS

STEP 1 - Approach the Door

Opposing open doors (two open doors facing each other across the hallway) are one of the more difficult configurations a team can encounter. This is because the team cannot enter one door without exposing its back to the other. It is possible for the team to split and clear both doors simultaneously. This will be covered in the multiple teams section. If the team wants to remain together, the lead two officers will maintain cross coverage as they approach the opposing doors. The team leader will decide which door to enter and provide directions to the team.

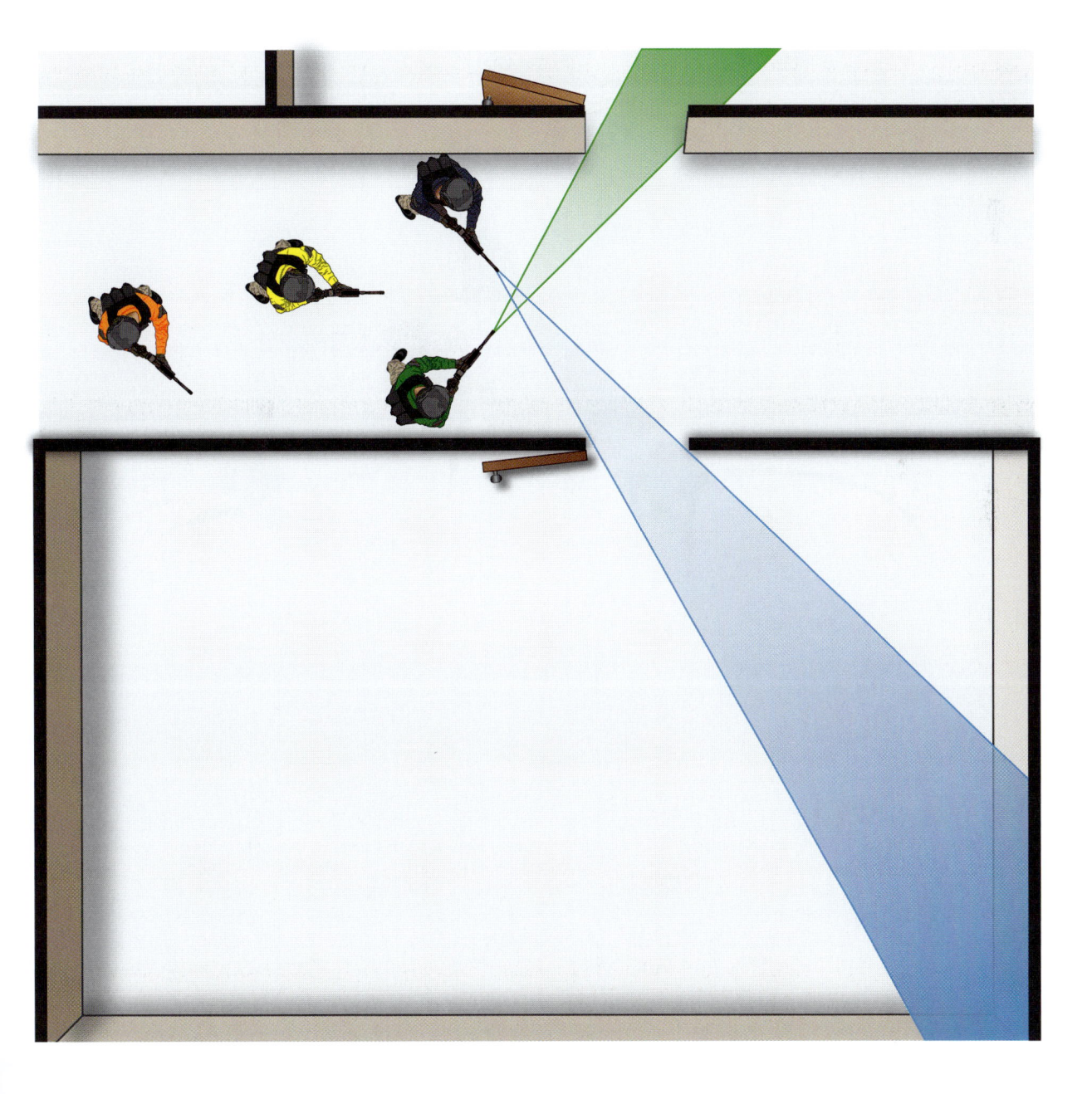

ENTERING OPPOSING OPEN DOORS

STEP 2 - Hold on the Opposing Door and Enter

As the two officers maintaining cross coverage reach the open doors, the officer on the entry side will lead the team into the room while the officer on the opposite side steps out to momentarily cover the team's back as it enters the room. The covering officer will become the last officer into the room. It is possible to stop, stack, squeeze and enter but, given the threat presented by the opposing door, it is often best to move into the room as quickly as possible, "stacking" only for an instant to ensure there is no spacing between officers as they enter the room. This minimizes the team's exposure as it enters.

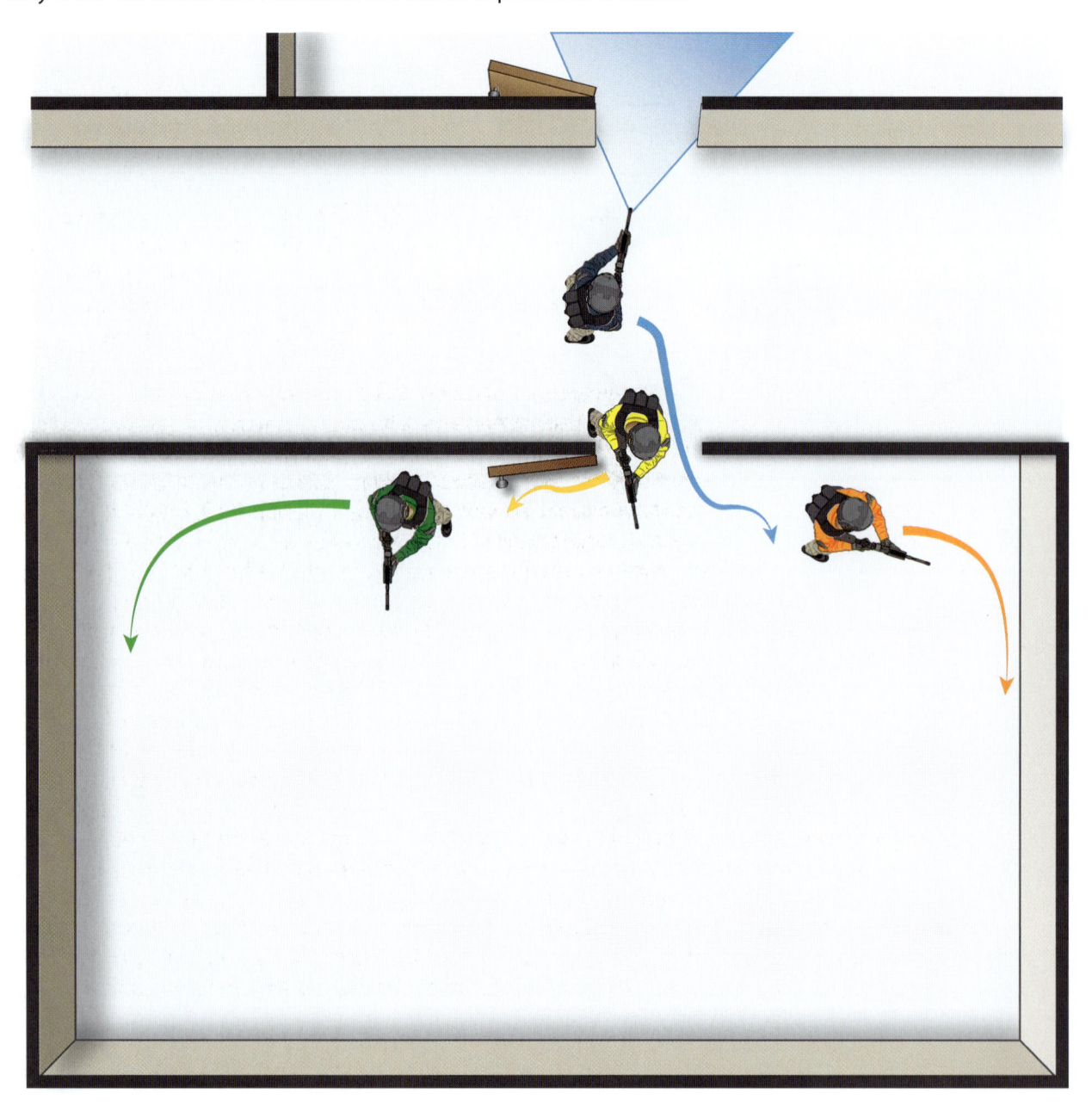

MOVING FROM A ROOM INTO THE HALLWAY

STEP 1 - Stack on the Door

When the team clears a room and then wants to move back into the hallway, the team leader will first tell the team to stack on the door. The team leader then must decide which direction the team should move using the "clear and hold" technique. For example, the team leader might say "hold left… go right." More experienced teams can shorten this command by leaving out the "hold" command and simply saying "go right…go right."

MOVING FROM A ROOM INTO THE HALLWAY

STEP 2 - Hold and Move

Once the team knows which direction to move, the officers will re-enter the hallway. Generally, the first officer will hold in the opposite direction of movement and the other officers will flow past. However, if the first officer does not hold, the second officer can pick up the holding responsibility. This is similar to the free-flow method of room entry where the second officer will pick up the coverage direction opposite the first officer. Whichever officer holds, the rest of the officers will flow past in the direction of travel. When the last officer passes the holding officer, he/she will deliver a squeeze and call out "last man" to ensure the holding officer is not left behind.

MOVING ACROSS A HALLWAY INTO ANOTHER ROOM

STEP 1 - Stack on the Door

When the team clears a room and then wants to move back across the hallway into another room, the team leader must first tell the team to stack on the door. The team leader will then call out "hold left and right… go straight across." More experienced teams can shorten this command by leaving out the "hold" commands and simply saying "straight across… straight across."

MOVING ACROSS A HALLWAY INTO ANOTHER ROOM

STEP 2 - Hold and Move

Once the team knows which direction to move, the officers will re-enter the hallway. Generally, the first two officers will hold to the left and right down the hall and the other officers will flow past into the room. When deciding which officer holds in which direction, the team will use the free-flow method, the first officer will make a decision to go left or right and the second officer will pick up the coverage direction opposite the first officer. When the last officer passes across the hall, he/she will call out "last man" to ensure the holding officers are not left behind and follow quickly into the room.

L-SHAPE INTERSECTION: HIGH-LOW TECHNIQUE

STEP 1 - Lead Officer Kneels

The high-low technique is used to clear a hallway when the lead officer perceives danger around the corner. Essentially, the high-low can be useful if officers want to maximize the cover and concealment provided by the corner and don't want to overly expose themselves in the hallway. The lead officer will kneel on one knee (the inside knee nearest to the wall) while maintaining front security. The lead officer should orient his/her weapon at about a 45-degree angle off the corner and be sure not to let the weapon extend past the corner where adversaries might see it. When moving close to the corner, officers should also make sure their shadows do not extend into the hall.

L-SHAPE INTERSECTION: HIGH-LOW TECHNIQUE

STEP 2 - Second Officer Provides Support

The second officer will assume a position at a slight angle away from the lead team officer and provide additional cover on the corner. The lead two officers will be covering the corner and the rest of the team will be positioned behind, covering any additional angles or danger areas.

L-SHAPE INTERSECTION: HIGH-LOW TECHNIQUE

STEP 3 - Corner Clear

Once in position, the second officer will look around to ensure that the team is ready to move. The second officer will then give the ready signal (shoulder or arm squeeze) to the lead officer to initiate the corner clearing process. The lead officer will pause briefly to allow the second officer to reset and bring his/her hand back to the weapon. When ready, both officers will shift position outward around the corner and clear the hallway while still taking advantage of the cover/concealment provided by the corner and exposing themselves as little as possible.

L-SHAPE INTERSECTION: HIGH-LOW TECHNIQUE

STEP 4 - Pick-up and Move

After clearing the corner, the team will continue its movement and proceed down the hallway. To initiate movement, the second officer will reach down with the non-firing hand and "pick-up" the lead officer. The lead officer must remain in place and remain kneeling until another officer comes and picks him/her up. This is important because of the increased risk that can come if a kneeling officer unexpectedly stands up into the line of fire of the other officers. Once the lead officer is picked up, the team will resume movement down the hallway.

L-SHAPE INTERSECTION: NEAR-FAR TECHNIQUE

STEP 1 - Lead Officer Prepares to Clear

This technique is similar to the high-low technique but it is faster and easier to execute. For the near-far, the lead officer will not assume a kneeling position, but will instead clear from the standing position. As the team reaches the corner, the lead officer will cover the corner and provide front security. The lead officer should orient his/her weapon at about a 45-degree angle off the corner and be sure not to let the weapon extend past the corner where adversaries might see it. When moving close to the corner, officers should also make sure their shadows do not extend into the hall.

L-SHAPE INTERSECTION: NEAR-FAR TECHNIQUE

STEP 2 - Second Officer Provides Support

The second officer will assume a position at a slight angle away from the lead team officer and provide additional cover on the corner. The lead two officers will be covering the corner and the rest of the team will be positioned behind, covering any additional angles or danger areas.

L-SHAPE INTERSECTION: NEAR-FAR TECHNIQUE

STEP 3 - Corner Clear

Once in position, the second officer will look around to ensure that the team is ready to move. The second officer will then give the ready signal (shoulder or arm squeeze) to the lead officer to initiate the corner clearing process. The lead officer will pause briefly to allow the second officer to reset and bring his/her hand back to the weapon. When ready, both officers will swing around the corner and clear the hallway. The lead officer will stay close to the corner, taking advantage of cover/concealment. The second officer will push across to the opposite side of the hallway, maintaining good spacing from the lead officer.

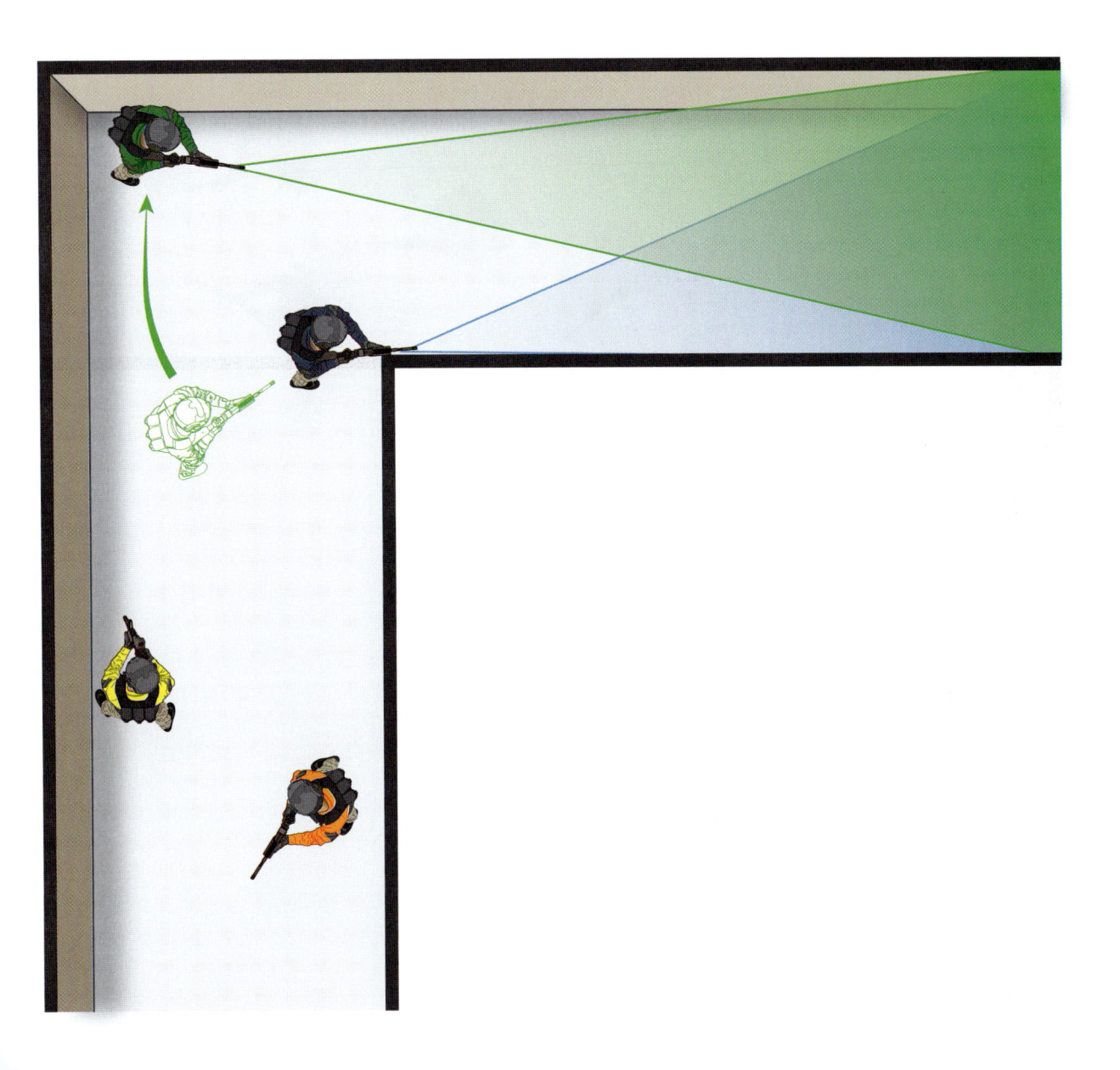

L-SHAPE INTERSECTION: NEAR-FAR TECHNIQUE

STEP 4 - Continue Movement

After clearing the corner, the team will continue its movement and proceed down the hallway. The lead and second officers will already be in position on either side of the hallway to conduct cross coverage and the rest of the team will fall in behind.

T-SHAPE INTERSECTION

STEP 1 - Approach the Intersection

As the team approaches the intersection, the two lead officers will maintain cross coverage. The team leader must tell the team which direction to turn at the intersection. The two lead officers will continue to maintain cross coverage until they reach their respective corners. When moving close to the corner, officers should also make sure their shadows do not extend into the hall.

T-SHAPE INTERSECTION

STEP 2 - Clear the Intersection

Once the lead officers reach their corners they will give up their cross coverage, switch to same-side coverage and clear their corners simultaneously. Teams that have less practice working together, may want to use the squeeze signal to synchronize the switch from cross coverage to same-side coverage and then another squeeze to initiate the simultaneous clear. Officers behind the lead officers will position themselves and coordinate to deliver the squeeze at exactly the same time. More experienced teams can proceed without the squeeze.

T-SHAPE INTERSECTION

STEP 3 - Move Down the Hall

Once the intersection is clear, the team will make the turn and move down the hallway in the desired direction of movement. The officer providing coverage opposite the direction of movement will join the rear of the formation as the last officer. It is helpful for the passing team to call out "last man" (or deliver an arm squeeze) to ensure the covering officer is not left behind.

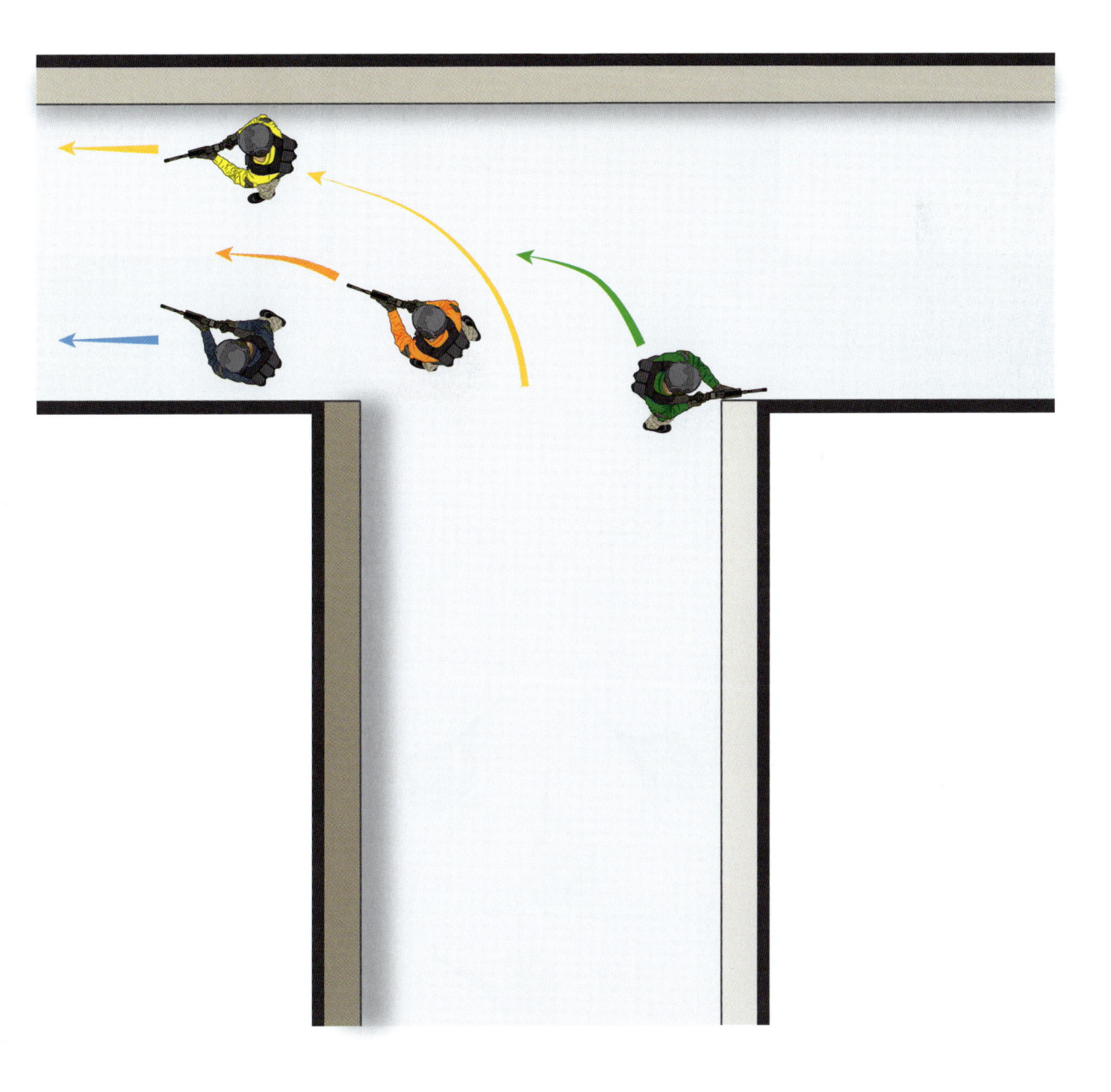

X-SHAPE INTERSECTION

STEP 1 - Approach the Intersection

Clearing an X-shape intersection is similar to clearing a T-shape intersection except there is an additional possible direction of travel and additional angles to cover. As the team approaches the intersection, the two lead officers will maintain cross coverage. If there is room, the third officer will maintain front coverage down the hall. The team leader must tell the team which direction to move once reaching the intersection. The two lead officers will continue to maintain cross coverage until they reach their respective corners. When moving close to the corner, officers should also make sure their shadows do not extend into the hall.

X-SHAPE INTERSECTION

STEP 2 - Clear the Intersection

Once the lead officers reach their corners they will give up their cross coverage, switch to same-side coverage and clear their corners simultaneously. Teams that have less practice working together, may want to use the squeeze signal to synchronize the switch from cross coverage to same-side coverage and then another squeeze to initiate the simultaneous clear. More experienced teams can proceed without the squeeze.

X-SHAPE INTERSECTION

STEP 3 - Move Down the Hall

Once the intersection is clear, the team will either make a turn and move down the hallway or continue moving straight ahead. If the team decides to move straight ahead, the two covering officers will remain in place until the team passes though the intersection. If the team decides to turn left or right, one officer can push forward to cover to the front until the team clears the intersection. All officers providing coverage will join the rear of the formation as the team passes by.

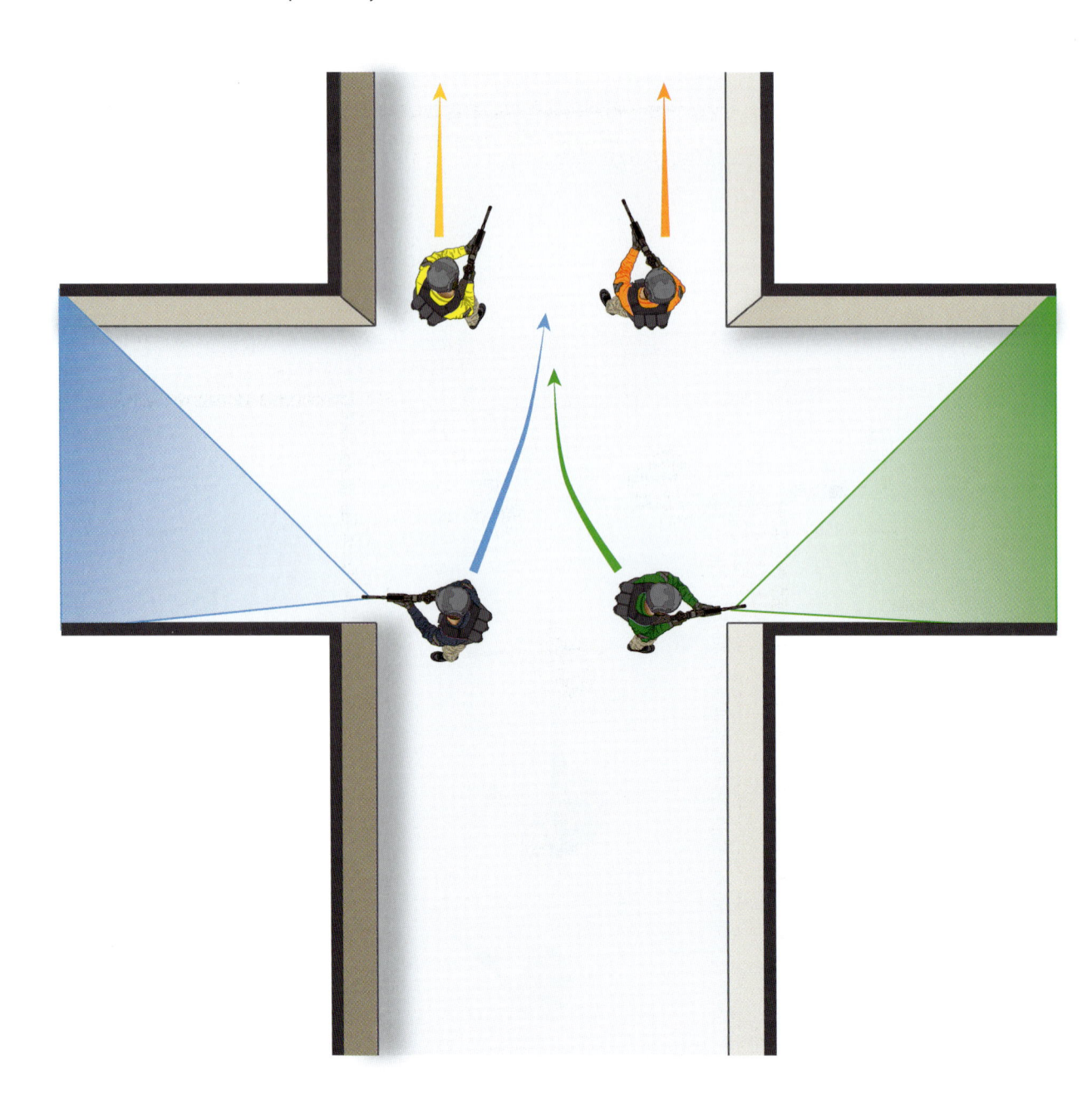

INTERSECTIONS WITH UNEVEN CORNERS

COMPLETE SEQUENCE

In some situations, a team may encounter a T-intersection or X-intersection with uneven corners. The clearing process for uneven corners is very similar to the process for even corners. The main difference is that with uneven corners, the team should clear the near corner slightly before they clear the far corner. If the team cleared the corners simultaneously, the officer clearing the far corner would be exposing his/her back to the opposing hallway.

CLEARING INTERSECTIONS ON THE MOVE

COMPLETE SEQUENCE

In an emergency clearing situation, where time is critical, the team might choose to use the "clear on the move" method. Conducting the clear on the move is simple. Officers maintain their general formation and cross coverage and individually clear danger areas as the team passes. For example, to cross an X-shape intersection, the team would maintain formation but each officer would clear down the hallway on his/her side as the team passed through the intersection. The aim is to minimize the time that the team is exposed from multiple directions. The team should get out of the intersection as quickly as possible.

HALLWAY JOINED TO AN OPEN AREA

COMPLETE SEQUENCE

In some cases, a hallway will open directly into a large room or open area. In these cases the team will flow directly into the open area just as they would flow into a room. Depending on the configuration of the open area, it is critically important that the team maintain rear security since officers' backs might be exposed to other hallways. In some cases an officer might want to turn around or move to a position to cover the rear, as long as he/she does not break visual contact with the team.

TEAM OPERATIONS
Hallways Delayed Entry

If the team is approaching a hallway intersection and detects a potential threat around the corner, the team might want to slow down and employ a delayed clearing technique. However, whenever a team slows down or stops in a hallway, the officers must consider the fact that they will be vulnerable to unexpected attacks from the rear or from adversaries emerging from doorways. Therefore, the team should generally employ delayed hallway clearing techniques only when the threat to the front is more serious than the threat from the rear or other directions. An example of this is if the team hears shots fired from around a corner. In that situation, the team will probably not want to rush towards the intersection and move around the corner, unless there are innocent lives at stake.

If the team decides to employ a delayed hallway clearing technique, one or two officers will move forward towards the intersection while the remaining officers stay back at a safe distance. The clearing officer(s) will move forward cautiously and may choose to use some of the single-person clearing techniques described later in this book. It is critical that the clearing officer(s) make as little noise as possible and avoid letting shadows extend into the intersection.

For clearing an L-shape intersection it is generally best to use one officer. To clear a T-shape or X-shape intersection, two officers will find it easier to clear multiple danger areas simultaneously. However, it is still possible for an experienced single officer to clear a T-shape or X-shape intersection alone.

Once the intersection is clear, the rest of the team can move forward to continue down the hallway in the desired direction of movement. In other cases, if the clearing officer encounters hostile fire, he/she may choose to fall back to the rest of the team. At this point it is the team leader's decision whether to attempt to clear the intersection or to fall back to a room or a safer location.

One of the most critical factors to consider is that the clearing officer(s) should not advance so far that the rest of the team will not be able to provide casualty evacuation in the event of a downed officer. All officers should remain in visual contact and position themselves to be mutually supporting.

When executing delayed clearing techniques, the clearing officers can also employ special equipment like mirrors or cameras to clear the intersection. However, if one officer is using a mirror, another officer should be close by in support. Techniques for using special equipment will be covered later.

L-SHAPE INTERSECTION

COMPLETE SEQUENCE

Clearing an L-shape intersection using the delayed technique is very similar to the immediate technique. However, the main difference with delayed intersection clearing is that the team stays back from the intersection to minimize exposure while one or two officers move up to clear the intersection. The officer(s) can clear the corner from either the standing or kneeling position. Another important difference is that with delayed clearing, once the lead officers clear around the corner, they might not call the rest of the team forward. Instead the whole team might fall back down the hallway or establish security in a nearby room. It is also important that the team is close enough to drag the lead officer to safety if the lead officer is shot.

T-SHAPE OR X-SHAPE INTERSECTION

COMPLETE SEQUENCE

Clearing a T-shape or X-shape intersection using the delayed technique is similar to the immediate technique but the team will stay back while one or two officers move up to clear the intersection. The two lead officers will maintain cross coverage until they reach their corners, then turn to clear both corners simultaneously. One officer can also move up quickly to check both corners. Another important difference is that with delayed clearing, once the lead officers clear around their corners, they might not call the rest of the team forward. Instead the whole team might fall back.

TEAM OPERATIONS
Stairwells

Stairwells are even more dangerous than hallways for several reasons. First of all, in commercial or industrial buildings, stairwells typically consist of sturdy metal and concrete construction with steel beams, which makes bullets more likely to ricochet off the solid walls. Adversaries can also toss grenades down the stairs without exposing themselves.

Because the team is so tightly bunched up in the stairwell, officers are particularly vulnerable to these sorts of indiscriminate attacks. The team will also find it difficult to move quickly up or down stairs without tripping, particularly in the dark. For all these reasons, the team is particularly at risk in a stairwell and will find it more difficult to evade hostile fire or grenades.

Therefore, the team should move up or down stairwells as quickly as possible in order to get out of the stairwell to a safer location. While it is critical for the team to move fast, officers must not move so fast that they trip or fall down the stairs. This can be a very real danger, particularly in high-stress situations or when under fire. It is also critical that officers not walk backwards up or down stairs since this makes the chances of tripping even more likely.

The following techniques are the same whether officers are moving up or down the stairwell. The officers will first occupy the stairwell's landing or entryway just as they would an ordinary room. At this point the officers will begin to move up or down the stairs, staying as close to the outer railing as possible. This allows the officers to have the best angles of observation around bends in the stairs.

Each time the lead officer in the team reaches a landing, he/she will quickly turn and cover the shaft of the stairwell in the direction that the team is moving to protect the front of the team. As the team passes around the covering officer, the covering officer will switch his/her coverage (up or down) to protect the rear of the team as it passes. Once the team passes, the covering officer will rejoin the rear of the formation. If the team encounters a landing with a door, one officer will peel off from the formation to cover the stairwell shaft and another officer will peel off to cover the door.

Officers may also encounter "open stairwells," particularly in residential structures. When clearing an open stairwell, two officers will need to move up the stairs to clear the upper floor. When conducting this movement, it is critical that officers not walk backwards up the stairs. Instead, they should walk forward up the stairs, pausing or turning as necessary to check various angles of the upper floor.

COMMERCIAL STAIRWELL

STEP 1 - Enter the First Landing

Before the team can move up or down the stairs, they must enter and clear the stairwell landing just as they would clear a room. Each officer will enter and turn opposite the officer in front, clearing the corners, scanning the landing and checking behind the door.

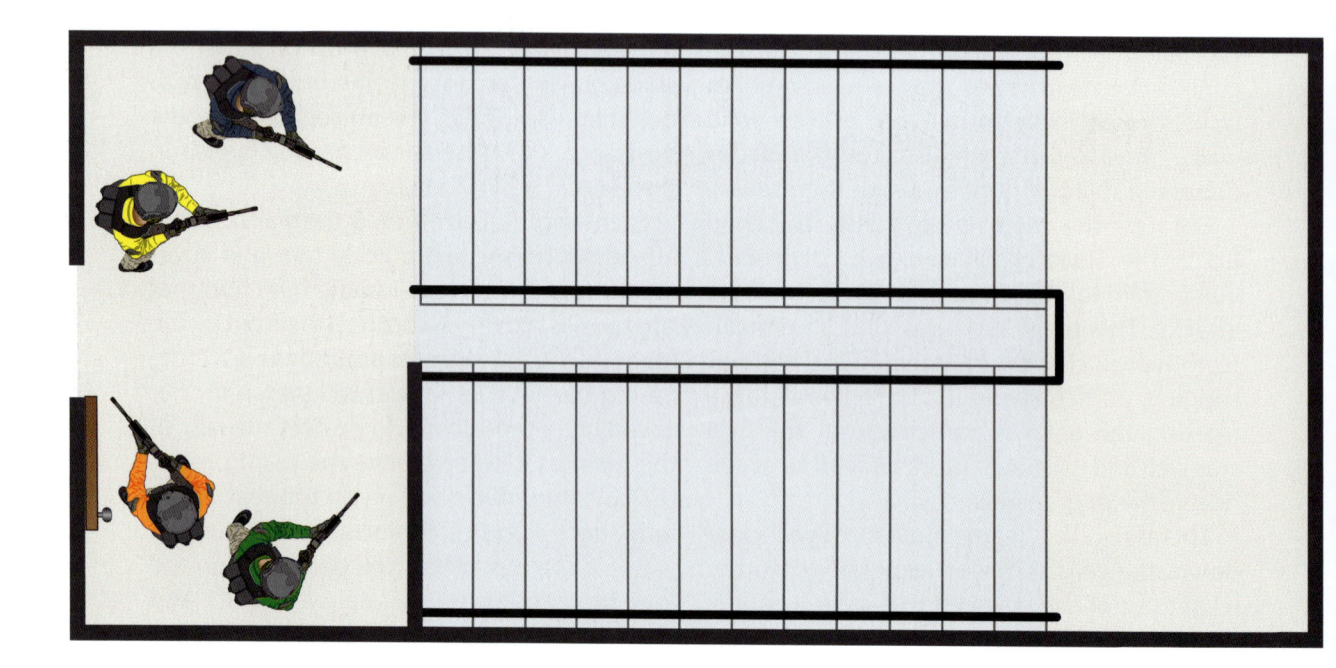

COMMERCIAL STAIRWELL

STEP 2 - Move Up/Down the Stairs

Once the landing is dominated, the officer closest to the stairs will start moving up or down the stairwell. The rest of the team will follow behind. When moving on stairs, officers should orient their weapons in the direction of travel (up or down) and keep as close as possible to the wall, away from the center banister. This will offer the best angle to see around the bend in the stairs. Officers should turn towards the bend in the stairwell as they move, being careful not to trip. This way officers will be ready to engage any adversaries waiting around the bend in the stairs as soon as they emerge.

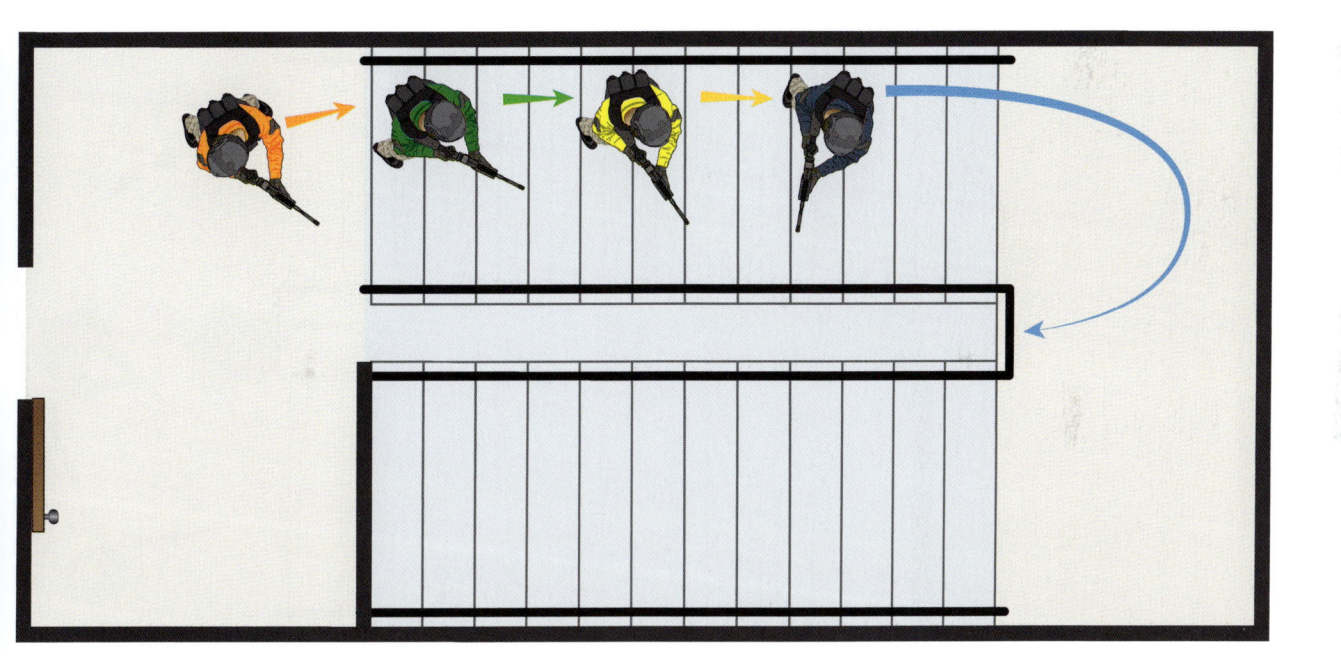

COMMERCIAL STAIRWELL

STEP 3 - Cover the Shaft

When the lead officer reaches the next landing his/her weapon should already be oriented pointing up/down the shaft of the stairwell. The officer will stop at this point and cover the team from a static position. As the team moves around behind the covering officer and continues up/down the stairs, the lead officer will shift coverage to cover the team's rear. For example if the team is moving up the stairs, the covering officer will start out oriented up the shaft to cover the team's front. As the team passes the covering officer, the officer will drop coverage to look down the shaft and cover the team's rear. The last officer will call out "last man" as he/she passes the covering officer and supplement this call with a squeeze if necessary to ensure the covering officer does not get left behind.

TEAM OPERATIONS: STAIRWELLS   147

COMMERCIAL STAIRWELL

STEP 4 - Cover the Door

If there is a door on the landing, either open or closed, one officer will break off from the formation to cover the door. This means that on a landing with a door, one officer will be covering the shaft of the stairwell and another officer will be covering the door. As the team passes these two covering officers, the last team member will call out "last man" and supplement this call with a squeeze if necessary to ensure the covering officers do not get left behind. It is also important that the officer covering the shaft rejoins the formation first and the officer covering the door is the last to give up coverage and join the team.

COMMERCIAL STAIRWELL

STEP 5 - Exit the Stairwell

Once the team reaches the desired floor, they will stack on the door and exit the stairwell just as they would exit a normal room.

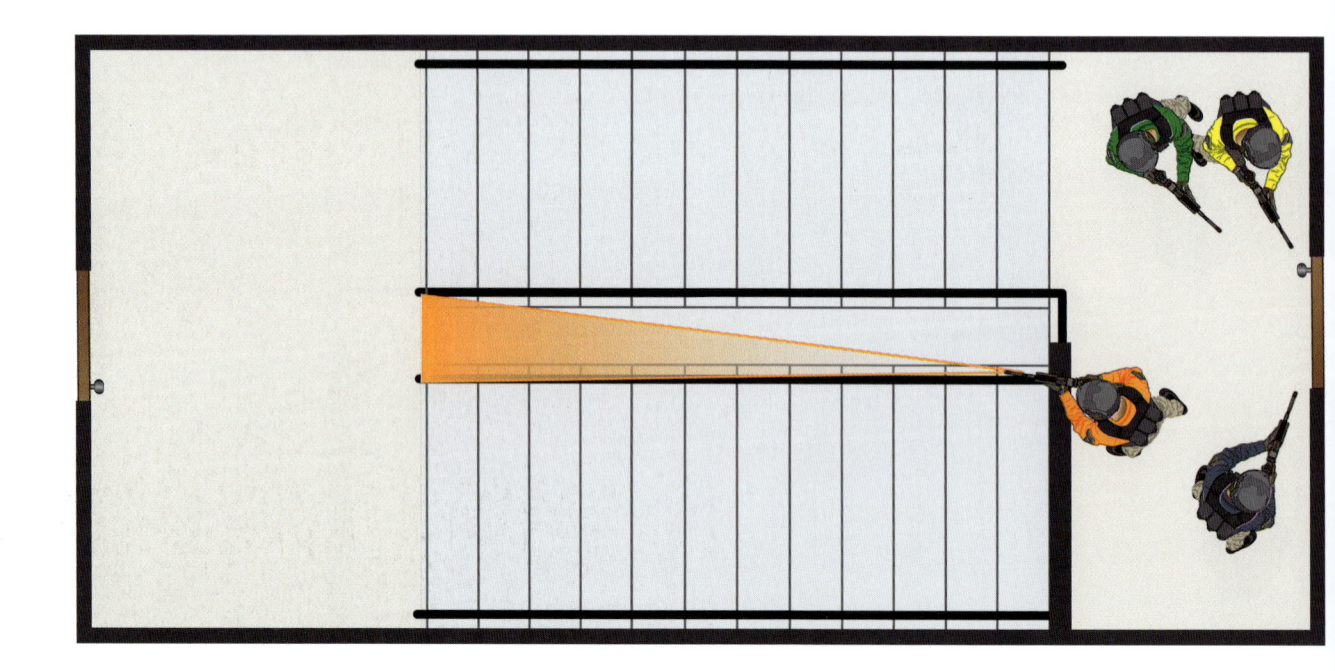

TEAM OPERATIONS: STAIRWELLS   149

OPEN STAIRWELL

STEP 1 - Check the Upper Floor

Open stairwells open directly into a room or hallway and are common in residential architecture. Open stairwells are particularly dangerous because adversaries have a perfect vantage point from the upper floor to shoot officers as they move up the stairs. Therefore, officers should move more carefully to ensure the upper floor is secure before moving too far up the stairs. Once reaching the stairwell, at least two officers will lead the way. The lead officer will cover forward up the stairs. The second officer will turn 180-degrees (or as far as needed) and look up to check the upper floor.

OPEN STAIRWELL

STEP 2 - Move Up the Stairs

If the upper floor appears clear, both officers can move farther up the stairs. It is important that the second officer not walk backwards since doing so can be hazardous. Instead the second officer should walk forwards but pause if necessary to turn 180-degrees and recheck the upper floor landing. It is necessary to recheck to ensure an adversary is not crouching or lying in wait. The second officer can pause when needed to ensure the area is clear. At a certain point, when the second officer has moved up far enough to ensure there are no adversaries hiding on the upper floor, both officers can move more quickly to get past the stairwell. The rest of the team will follow close behind.

TEAM OPERATIONS
Complex Configurations and Obstacles

When officers clear houses and buildings in a real-life scenario, they will encounter many different combinations of furniture, obstacles and complex room configurations. This next section provides some basic principles for dealing with these types of tactical problems.

Furniture is the most common obstacle officers will encounter in a room. Furniture is often positioned along walls, which naturally interferes with officers' movement towards their domination points. Officers must be prepared to quickly move around obstacles to prevent the team from losing momentum. Furniture deep in the room can also provide covered positions for enemies to hide. Officers must be able to move deeper into the room to check behind furniture.

"Half walls" are another common architectural configuration that can be confusing for an entry team. When a half wall is long enough, it will effectively separate a space into two separate rooms that must be cleared individually. Officers must remain alert and avoid pushing past the half wall before the rest of the team is prepared to follow.

Confined areas with multiple openings (such as foyers, entryways or vestibules) are also very common in modern architecture and present a difficult tactical problem for the team. Rather than try to dominate these danger areas, the team should quickly move past them into a room that offers better protection.

Another common configuration, found in commercial structures, are larger rooms filled with cubicles. Cubicles are particularly dangerous since they must each be cleared individually and offer many hiding places for adversaries. When the team must clear multiple cubicles, it is usually best to break into smaller elements and clear cubicles simultaneously on both sides of an aisle.

Civilians and unarmed adversaries can also become obstacles for a team trying to quickly enter and clear a room. While the team's ultimate objective is to protect innocent civilians, it is necessary to treat all occupants of a room as potentially hostile until they can be properly searched and questioned.

To control occupants in a room, officers can use three elements: dominating presence, verbal commands and physical contact. Officers must not be afraid to use aggressive physical force to move panicked civilians away from danger. In a high-stress situations, civilians might be unresponsive or noncompliant. Adversaries who drop their weapons can also continue to resist arrest. The team must be prepared to rapidly impose control on a chaotic situation.

LARGE OBSTACLE ALONG THE NEAR WALL

STEP 1 - Clear Up To the Obstacle

If the lead or second officer enters a room and encounters a large obstacle or piece of furniture on the near wall, the officer must continue to clear past the obstacle to clear the corner of the room. The officer should not stop short of the obstacle since this could impede flow into the room and there could also be an adversary hiding behind the obstacle, in the corner, who could then jump out and surprise the team.

LARGE OBSTACLE ALONG THE NEAR WALL

STEP 2 - Move Past the Obstacle and Clear the Corner

The officer should move around the obstacle and then clear all the way into the corner, ensuring there are no adversaries hiding there.

LARGE OBSTACLE ALONG THE NEAR WALL

STEP 3 - Continue Scan from Adjusted Domination Point

Once the officer clears the corner, the officer will establish a domination point in a position where he/she can see the rest of the team. The only requirement is that the officer adjust the domination point to be sure that the obstacle is not blocking the officer's view of the rest of the team. From this adjusted domination point the officer will conduct the scan just as in previous techniques.

TEAM OPERATIONS: COMPLEX CONFIGURATIONS AND OBSTACLES 155

LARGE OBSTACLE DEEP IN THE ROOM

STEP 1 - Dominate the Room

In some cases, the team will dominate a room but there will still be large obstacles or pieces of furniture deep in the room where an adversary might be hiding. In these cases, the team will first dominate the room as they usually would, watching carefully in case adversaries pop out from behind furniture deep in the room.

LARGE OBSTACLE DEEP IN THE ROOM

STEP 2 - Officer Calls "Going Deep"

At this point, one officer (usually the lead or second officer into the room) will identify the obstacle and prepare to move to clear behind it. The officer will call out "going deep" to notify the officers that he/she will be moving deep into the room. The officer will begin to move in an arc to clear behind the obstacle or furniture.

Team Operations: Complex Configurations and Obstacles

LARGE OBSTACLE DEEP IN THE ROOM

STEP 3 - Second Officer Follows in Support

Once the lead officer starts moving, whichever officer is the closest or in best position to support should move with the lead officer to provide support if needed. It is always better to clear an obstacle or danger area with two officers. In some cases the officers will establish a "tactical L" to clear the obstacle from two angles. In other cases, like a large cabinet or closet, one officer might have to open the door while the other officer covers the opening. Once the danger area is clear, the clearing officer will call out "clear" to notify the team that it is safe to proceed.

LARGE OBSTACLE DEEP IN THE ROOM

STEP 4 - Team Adjusts Domination Points as Needed

When the two officers go deep, the team might need to adjust domination points to reduce the risk of friendly fire. In general, this will mean the entire team shifting to the left or right to be more on-line with the officers going deep.

HALF WALLS

STEP 1 - Dominate the Room

In some cases, the team will encounter "half walls" that are too large to be considered obstacles but instead end up creating two different rooms. In these cases it is sometimes better for the team to dominate the first room or area, not penetrating past the half wall, then re-stacking to clear the second area beyond the half wall. The team will dominate the first area but team members will be careful not to penetrate too far, exposing themselves to the second area.

HALF WALLS

STEP 2 - Re-stack on the Next Area

The team will treat the next area like a separate room, with one officer holding long coverage as the other officers stack on the corner.

TEAM OPERATIONS: COMPLEX CONFIGURATIONS AND OBSTACLES

HALF WALLS

STEP 3 - Enter and Clear

The team will enter and clear the next area just as they would clear a normal room.

CONFINED AREAS WITH MULTIPLE OPENINGS

STEP 1 - Team Enters and Commits to One Opening

Confined areas with multiple openings are very common in architectural designs. These types of configurations can be found in the entryway or foyer of many residential homes. When the team enters, it will find itself bunched up in a very vulnerable position with multiple openings and danger areas all around. Therefore, the team will not want to "dominate" this area since it will not really be dominating anything. Instead, the team leader will make a fast decision to commit to one of the openings. The team leader will call out "go right… go right" or "go left… go left."

CONFINED AREAS WITH MULTIPLE OPENINGS

STEP 2 - Hold and Enter

One officer (usually the lead officer or second officer) will hold and provide security in the opposite direction while the rest of the team passes though into the opening. The holding officer will become the last officer into the room.

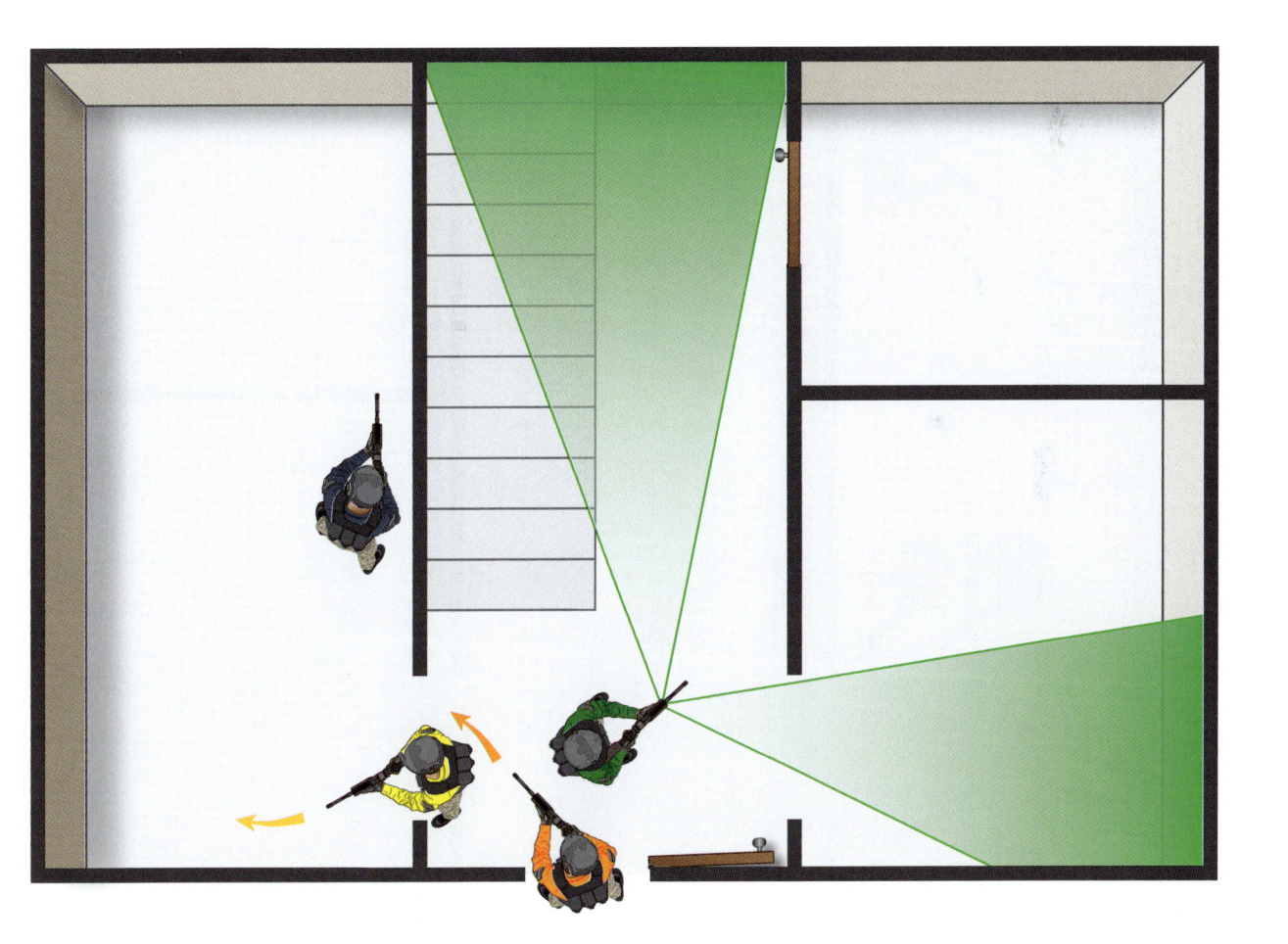

CONFINED AREAS WITH MULTIPLE OPENINGS

STEP 3 - Prepare for Next Movement

Once the team has dominated a real room and is out of the confined area, the team will be in a safer position to look and listen for threats and plan the next move, which could call for moving quickly back across the confined area or moving into other rooms.

TEAM OPERATIONS: COMPLEX CONFIGURATIONS AND OBSTACLES 165

CUBICLE CONFIGURATIONS

STEP 1 - Team Dominates the Entire Room

If the team enters a room filled with cubicles, the first step is to enter and dominate the room just like a normal room. Depending on the height of the cubicle walls, the officers may be able to see into some cubicles and clear some danger areas from the initial points of domination. Officers must remain alert since adversaries might emerge from any cubicle without warning. Once the room is dominated officers will prepare to adjust formation to clear each cubicle individually.

CUBICLE CONFIGURATIONS

STEP 2 - Break Into Two-Person Teams

For clearing very small areas like a cubicle, only two officers are needed. Usually, there will be a single aisle running down the center of the room with cubicles branching off to each side. Once the room is dominated, the team will reconsolidate near the center aisle and break into two-person elements, one to clear the left row and one to clear the right row. If the aisle is narrow, officers should spend as little time bunched together in the aisle as possible. Alternatively, only two officers can move down the aisle with one officer clearing cubicles on the right and one officer clearing cubicles on the left.

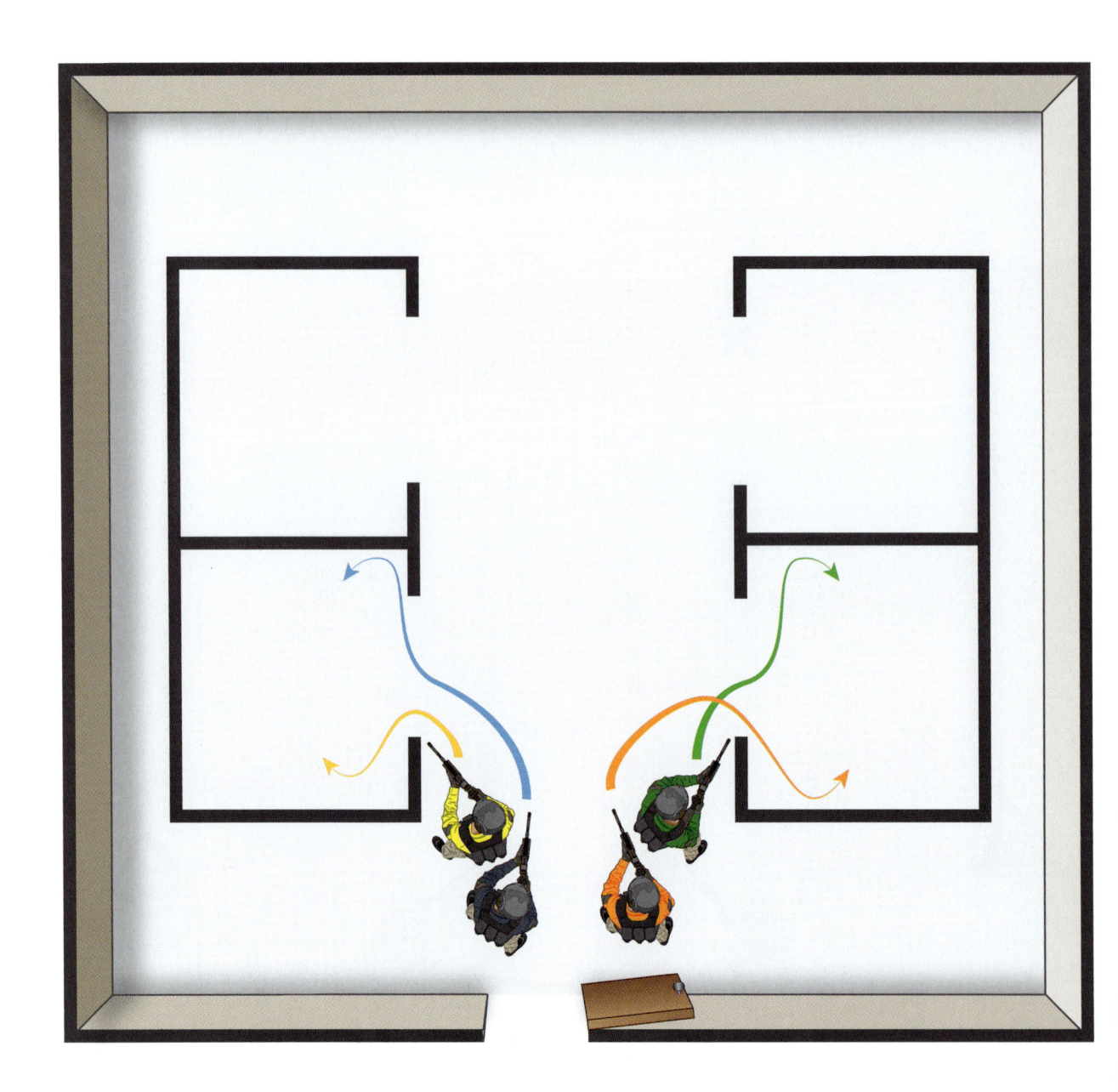

CUBICLE CONFIGURATIONS

STEP 3 - Clear Cubicles Simultaneously

The two elements will move down the aisle, maintaining cross coverage. As the two teams reach the cubicles, they will peel off to clear the two opposing cubicles simultaneously. Once both cubicles are clear, the two teams will exit and move to clear the next set of cubicles. When entering each cubicle, officers can choose to turn right or left, just like in a normal room.

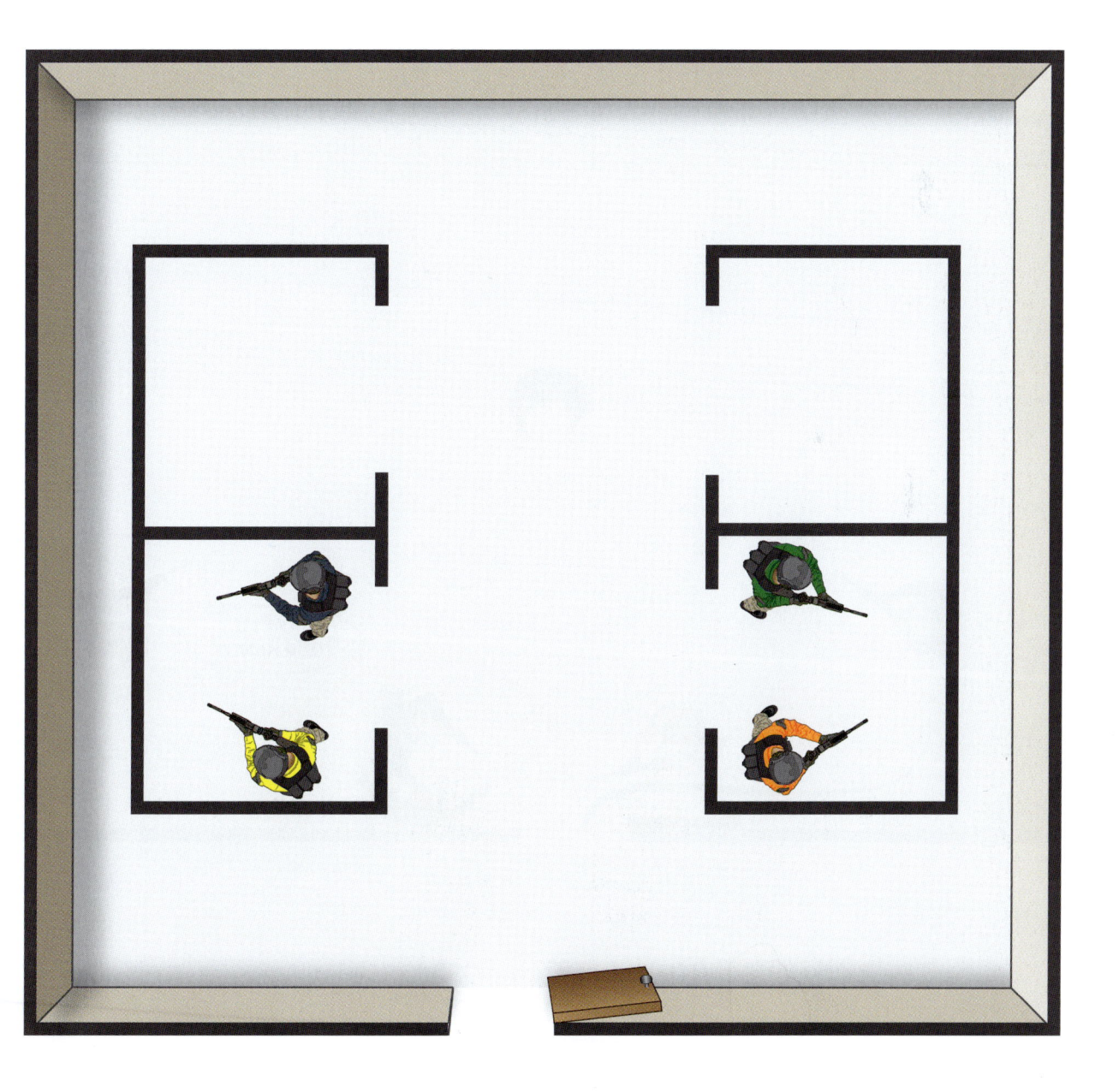

CONTROLLING UNARMED INDIVIDUALS

Elements of Control

In some cases, the team will run into human obstacles. These might include panicked civilians who charge the team or refuse to move out of the way. In other cases, these people might be unarmed adversaries. If officers cannot be completely certain whether someone is a threat, the officers will need to use techniques to control that person. To control occupants in a room, officers can use three elements: dominating presence, verbal commands and physical contact. This will be discussed in more detail in the prisoner handling chapter.

CONTROLLING UNARMED INDIVIDUALS

Person Blocking the Door

If there is a unarmed person blocking the door, that can be very dangerous for the team. If the team gets bottled up in the doorway, they will be very vulnerable to hostile fire. Therefore, the team must continue movement into the room. This of course only applies for an immediate entry. If there is a person blocking the door, the lead officer will momentarily lower the weapon and use his/her non-firing hand to aggressively "stiff arm" (push) the person back into the center of the room. The officer will then put both hands back on the weapon and continue clearing. It is best not to "muzzle punch" or strike using the weapon since this can kill an innocent person or allow an unarmed adversary to grab the weapon. The "stiff arm" technique is the quickest, safest way to push the person out of the way. If there is an armed adversary blocking the door, the officer can simply shoot the adversary at close range.

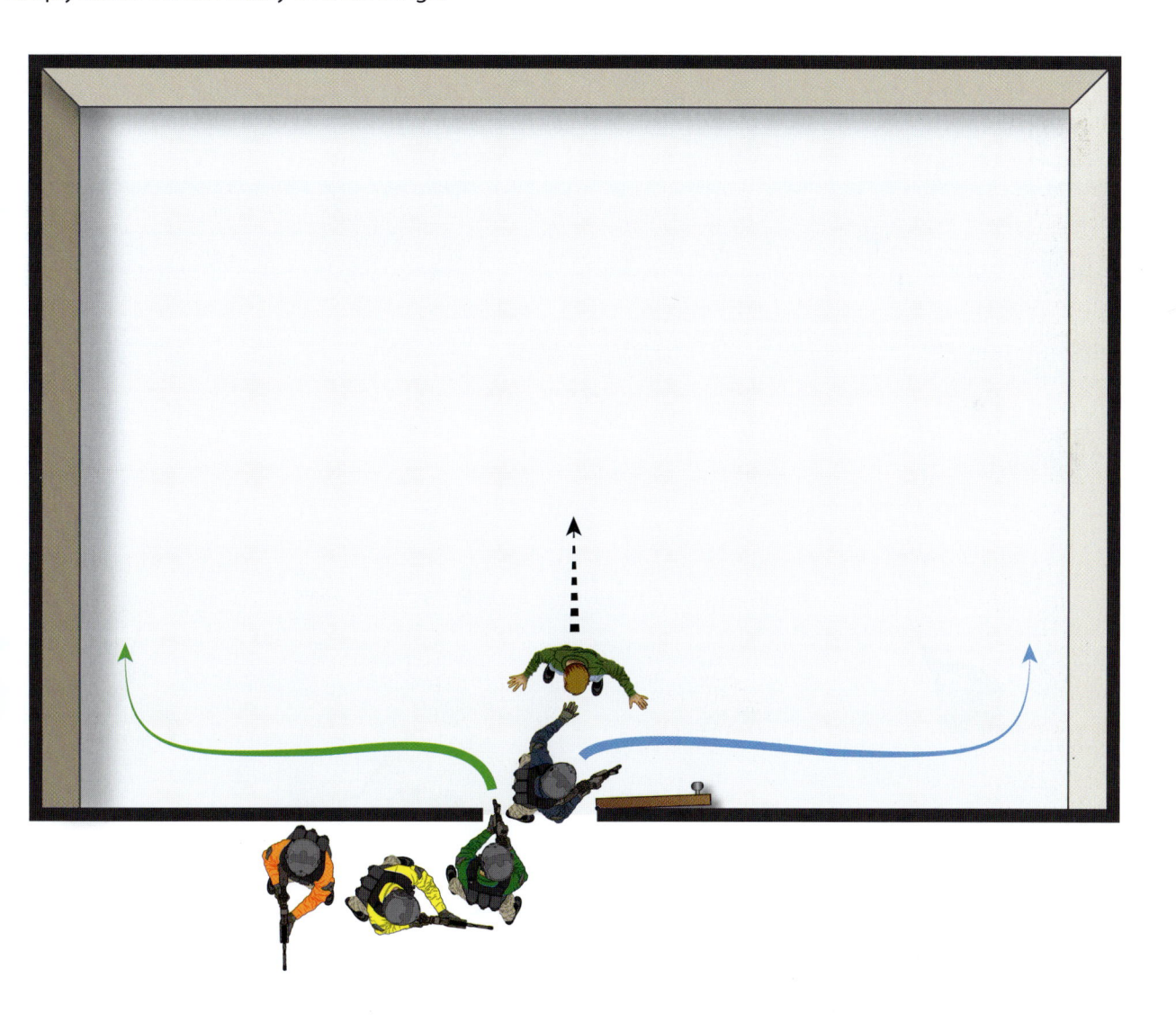

CONTROLLING UNARMED INDIVIDUALS

Person Along the Wall

If an officer encounters a unarmed person along the wall, the officer will need to stop and pin the person in place. The next officer following behind will see this and bypass the pinning officer and assume responsibility for any uncleared sectors in the room. While pinning the person, the officer should be aggressive and put the person on the ground if needed. The officer can never be certain if the pinned individual is innocent or an adversary. Officers must treat every person in the room as potentially hostile until there is time for a detailed search.

SECTION 2

TWO-PERSON OPERATIONS

FEAR NOT

TWO-PERSON OPERATIONS
Single-Room Immediate Entry

Most dedicated tactical teams usually possess clear manpower superiority and firepower superiority in every engagement. They also have a variety of supporting assets such as sniper teams and helicopters. However, patrol officers often have to respond to a crisis alone or with a single partner. This section provides techniques for officers who are working together as a two-person team.

Executing an immediate entry with only two officers is similar to an immediate entry with a full team. However, because of the lack of manpower, officers will have to be especially alert and shoot accurately when entering the room. Each officer will also have to cover a larger area inside the room since there are not as many guns in the fight.

Also, instead of scanning from the corner to the center of the room, officers will scan from the center of the room outward to the corner as they enter. This allows officers to clear the room as it becomes visible around the edge of the door. If the two officers turned directly to the corners, they would be vulnerable to threats in the center of the room since there are no additional backup officers to clear the center of the room and the two officers might not be able to scan back to the center of the room in time to engage the threats. It is possible to clear the corners first as a two-person team but this move requires officers to be extremely fast. The safer option is to scan outward from the center of the room.

Aside from these differences, the actual clearing steps for two officers are the same as for a full-sized team unless the door swings inward. If the door opens inward, the first officer to enter the room should move in the opposite direction of the door if possible. The second officer (who moves in the direction of the door) should control the door immediately upon entry and clear the room while continuing to control the door. This is to ensure that someone hiding behind the door cannot shoot the officer in the back.

If the second officer has to bypass the door, he/she must still readdress the door as soon as possible during the room clearing process. If the door is completely flush with the wall and there is no way to hide behind it, officers may choose not to clear behind the door if time is critical. However, it is possible for smaller adversaries to flatten themselves tightly to the wall behind the door. In other cases, buildings are designed in a way that leaves a small space or indentation behind the door. Finally, in a high-stress situation, officers may think the door is flush against the wall when it actually is not. Because of these factors it is always preferable to check behind the door.

IMMEDIATE ENTRY: CENTER-FED OPEN DOOR

Team-Member Positioning

If the door is open, the lead officer will face the door and the second officer will stand behind, providing rear-security. It is important however that the second officer use a bladed stance to avoid turning his/her back to the lead officer. This will ensure no officer is left behind, especially in the dark. The second officer can also adjust position depending on the room configuration.

IMMEDIATE ENTRY: CENTER-FED OPEN DOOR

LEAD OFFICER STEP 1 - Clear the Doorway and the Center

The lead officer steps outward slightly to have a better angle of vision into the room while ensuring that the doorway is clear. If the first officer steps out slightly before entering and takes a moment to clear the doorway and the area around it, he/she will be able to engage any immediate threats or threats in the center of the room before entering the room.

IMMEDIATE ENTRY: CENTER-FED OPEN DOOR

LEAD OFFICER STEP 2 - Scan Outward

After clearing the center of the room, instead of immediately turning to clear the corner, the lead officer will scan from inside to out while moving into the room. This is because there will not be a third and fourth officer coming into the room to clear the center of the room. Two officers will have to clear the center of the room as well as the corners. Clearing the center of the room and scanning outward lets the officer use his/her approach angle to take advantage of cover and concealment provided by the wall while moving into the room. This movement is similar to a "sweep" or "slice the pie" but is faster and the arc is tighter. The lead officer should not predetermine which direction to turn. Instead, the "lead officer is always correct," no matter which direction he/she decides to turn. However, in two-person operations, if the door opens inward the lead officer should try to move in the opposite direction that the door opens.

IMMEDIATE ENTRY: CENTER-FED OPEN DOOR

LEAD OFFICER STEP 3 - Clear the Corner

By the time the lead officer comes through the doorway, he/she should already have finished the outward scan and be clearing the corner engaging any threats in the corner until they are neutralized.

IMMEDIATE ENTRY: CENTER-FED OPEN DOOR

LEAD OFFICER STEP 4 - Move to the Domination Point

Once the corner is clear, the lead officer should not stay focused on the corner but should instead immediately begin to re-scan the room in an inward direction while moving along the wall. The officer continues to scan and move towards his/her domination point. The domination point (depicted below) is slightly forward of the corner. Moving slightly forward in this way will give the lead officer a better angle to see behind furniture and obstacles in the room. The lead officer will continue to scan inward until the scan reaches a point three feet off the second officer's point of domination. At this point the lead officer will scan back and forth across his/her full sector several times to ensure the sector is clear and to identify potential danger areas. Experienced teams can shorten this deliberate scanning process and might also break each team member's sectors into primary and secondary sectors.

IMMEDIATE ENTRY: CENTER-FED OPEN DOOR

SECOND OFFICER STEP 1 - Clear Doorway and Center

The second officer will turn in the opposite direction of the lead officer. Once again, the lead officer can choose to turn either way. The second officer must remain alert and turn in the opposite direction. It is also critical that the second officer uses a tighter and more direct approach angle in order to enter the room as close as possible behind the lead officer. This is to ensure the lead officer's back is not left exposed. The second officer will begin by clearing the center before crossing the threshold and be ready to scan outward quickly to cover the lead officer's back.

IMMEDIATE ENTRY: CENTER-FED OPEN DOOR

SECOND OFFICER STEP 2 - Scan Outward

After clearing the center of the room the second officer will scan from inside to out while moving into the room. Clearing the center of the room and scanning outward lets the officer use his/her approach angle to take advantage of cover and concealment provided by the wall while moving into the room. This movement is similar to a "sweep" or "slice the pie" but is faster and the arc is tighter.

IMMEDIATE ENTRY: CENTER-FED OPEN DOOR

SECOND OFFICER STEP 3 - Clear Corner, Control the Door

By the time the second officer comes through the doorway, he/she should already have finished the outward scan and be clearing the corner engaging any threats in the corner until they are neutralized. It is also critical that the second officer clears the corner as quickly as possible in order to cover the lead officer's back. If the door opens inward, the second officer will also need to control the door in case an adversary is hiding behind it. If the second officer is sure that no one is hiding behind the door, he/she can bypass it. However, it is always safer to assume that an adversary is hiding behind the door.

IMMEDIATE ENTRY: CENTER-FED OPEN DOOR

SECOND OFFICER STEP 4 - Check Behind the Door

Once both officers have completed their scans, the second officer will still be controlling the door. If the second officer detects an adversary or any kind of resistance behind the door, the second officer may have to step back and clear behind the door immediately. Otherwise, the second officer will finish scanning the room first, then turn around and check behind the door. It is critical that the second officer step back when checking behind the door to ensure that an adversary is not close enough to jump out and grab the officer's weapon.

IMMEDIATE ENTRY: CENTER-FED CLOSED DOOR

Team-Member Positioning

If the door is closed, the officers will most likely position on either side of the door with one officer acting as the breacher and the other officer leading the way into the room. In this situation, officers must be especially alert since there is no dedicated rear-security element. In other situations, both officers will position themselves on one side of the door and the lead officer will have to open the door himself/herself.

IMMEDIATE ENTRY: CENTER-FED CLOSED DOOR

LEAD OFFICER

Once the lead officer is ready to enter, he/she will nod to signal the second officer to open the door. If the lead officer must open the door, he/she will quickly reach out with the non-firing hand, open the door and prepare for entry. Once the door is open, the lead officer will conduct the clearing process in the same way as for an open door, clearing the center of the room, scanning outward to the corner and scanning back inward while moving to the domination point.

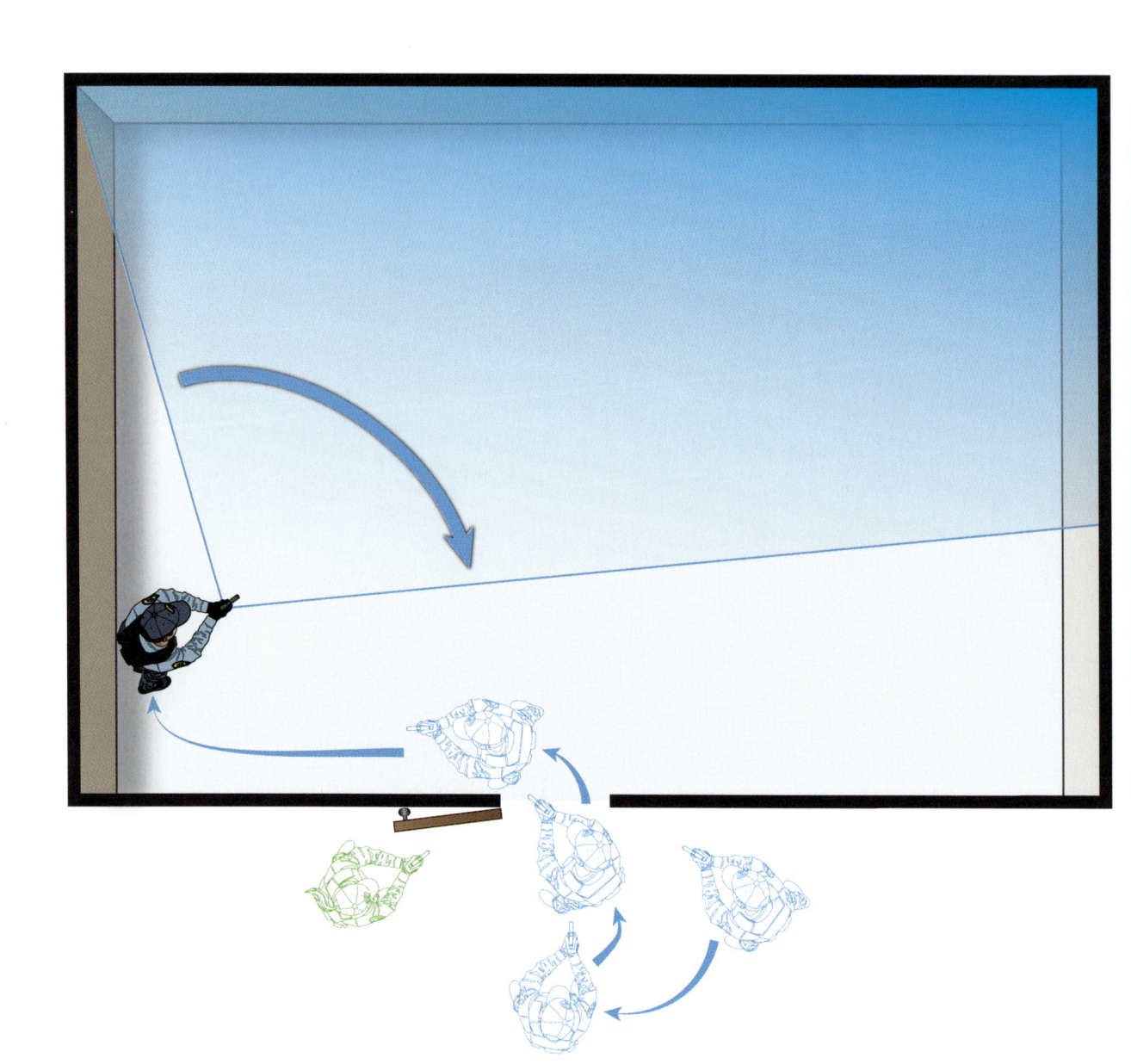

IMMEDIATE ENTRY: CENTER-FED CLOSED DOOR

SECOND OFFICER

The second officer will watch for the nod from the lead officer and then open the door. Once the door is open the second officer should step back and bring both hands back onto the weapon, preparing to enter the room as closely as possible behind the lead officer to cover the lead officer's back. The second officer will step out to clear the center of the room, then scan outward to clear the corner. If the door opens inward, the second officer will control the door while continuing to scan the room. Once the room is clear the second officer will turn around quickly to clear behind the door. If the door opens outward (like in the example below) the second officer can establish a domination point near the corner, or choose a shallower domination point near the door to provide rear security.

IMMEDIATE ENTRY: CORNER-FED OPEN DOOR

LEAD OFFICER STEP 1 - Clear Doorway and Deep Corner

Clearing a corner-fed room with two officers is similar to clearing a center fed room with a few minor changes. The lead officer will still step outward slightly to have a better angle of vision into the room while ensuring that the doorway is clear. For a corner-fed door, as the lead officer steps out he/she will have good observation straight ahead to the deep corner of the room. The officer should engage any threats in this deep corner before crossing the threshold of the doorway.

IMMEDIATE ENTRY: CORNER-FED OPEN DOOR

LEAD OFFICER STEP 2 - Scan Outward

After clearing deep, instead of immediately turning to clear the other corner, the lead officer will scan from inside to out while moving into the room. Clearing the center of the room and scanning outward lets the officer use his/her approach angle to take advantage of cover and concealment provided by the wall while moving into the room. This movement is similar to a "sweep" or "slice the pie" but is faster and the arc is tighter. If the door opens inward the lead officer should try to move in the opposite direction that the door opens.

IMMEDIATE ENTRY: CORNER-FED OPEN DOOR

LEAD OFFICER STEP 3 - Clear the Corner

By the time the lead officer comes through the doorway, he/she should already have finished the outward scan and be clearing the corner engaging any threats in the corner until they are neutralized.

Two-Person Operations: Single-Room Immediate Entry — 189

IMMEDIATE ENTRY: CORNER-FED OPEN DOOR

LEAD OFFICER STEP 4 - Move to the Domination Point

Once the corner is clear, the lead officer should not stay focused on the corner but should instead immediately begin to rescan the room in an inward direction while moving along the wall. The officer continues to scan and move towards his/her domination point.

IMMEDIATE ENTRY: CORNER-FED OPEN DOOR

SECOND OFFICER STEP 1 - Clear Doorway and Center

The second officer will move into the room in the opposite direction of the lead officer. For a corner-fed door the second officer will focus first on a point near the middle of the far wall and then scan outward to the corner. This is to ensure the sectors of fire of the lead officer and second officer overlap in the most effective way.

IMMEDIATE ENTRY: CORNER-FED OPEN DOOR

SECOND OFFICER STEP 2 - Scan Outward

After clearing the center of the room, the second officer will scan from inside to out towards the deep corner while moving into the room. The deep corner will have already been cleared by the lead officer but officers should still scan all areas of the room multiple times to ensure there are no adversaries hiding behind furniture etc.

IMMEDIATE ENTRY: CORNER-FED OPEN DOOR

SECOND OFFICER STEP 3 - Control the Door

If the door opens inward, the second officer will also need to control the door in case an adversary is hiding behind it. If the second officer is sure that no one is hiding behind the door he/she can bypass it. However, it is always safer to assume that an adversary is hiding behind the door.

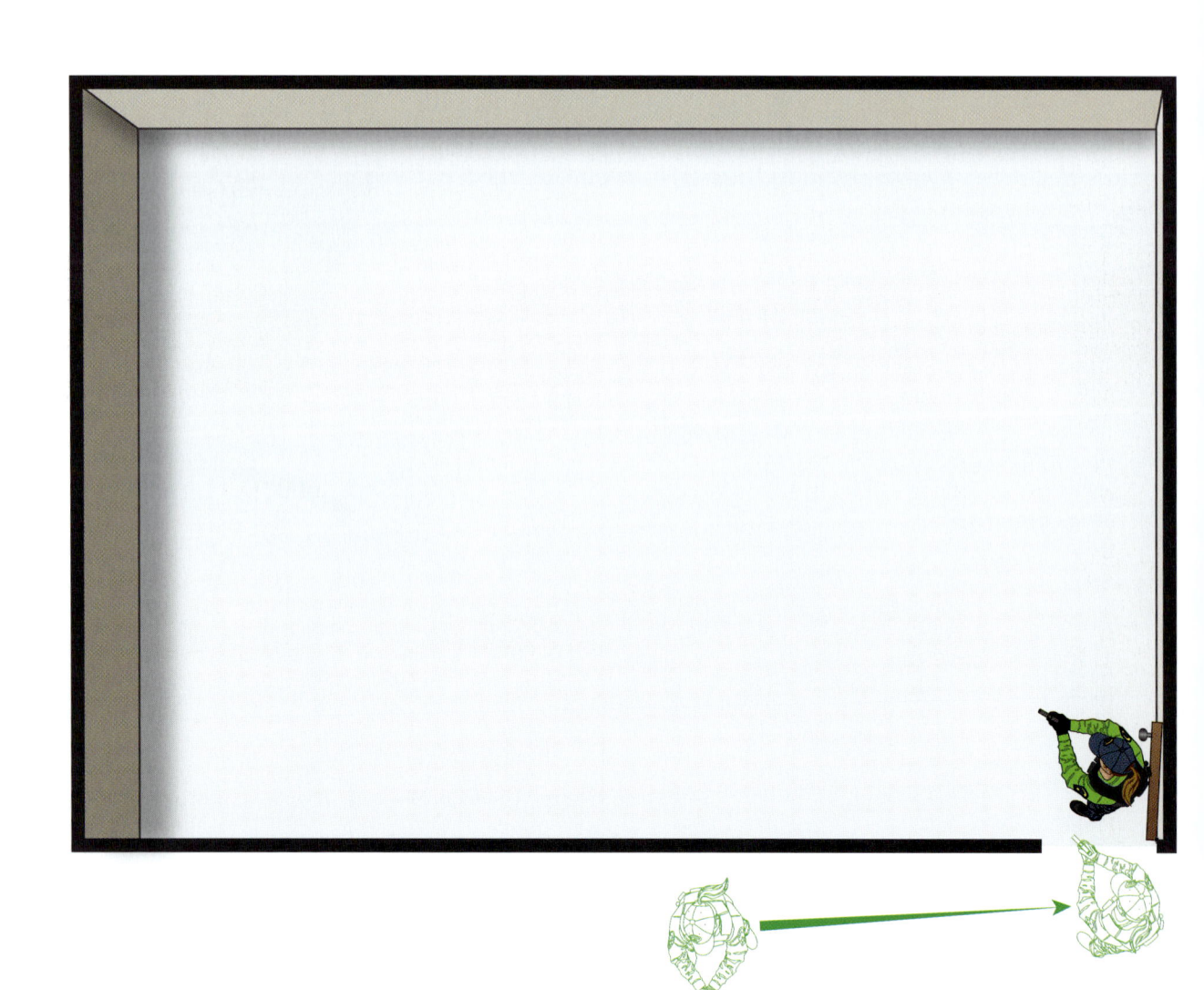

IMMEDIATE ENTRY: CORNER-FED OPEN DOOR

SECOND OFFICER STEP 4 - Check Behind the Door

Once both officers have completed their scans, the second officer will still be controlling the door. If the second officer detects an adversary or any kind of resistance behind the door, the second officer may have to step back and clear behind the door immediately. Otherwise, the second officer will finish scanning the room first, then turn around and check behind the door. It is critical that the second officer step back when checking behind the door to ensure that an adversary is not close enough to jump out and grab the officer's weapon.

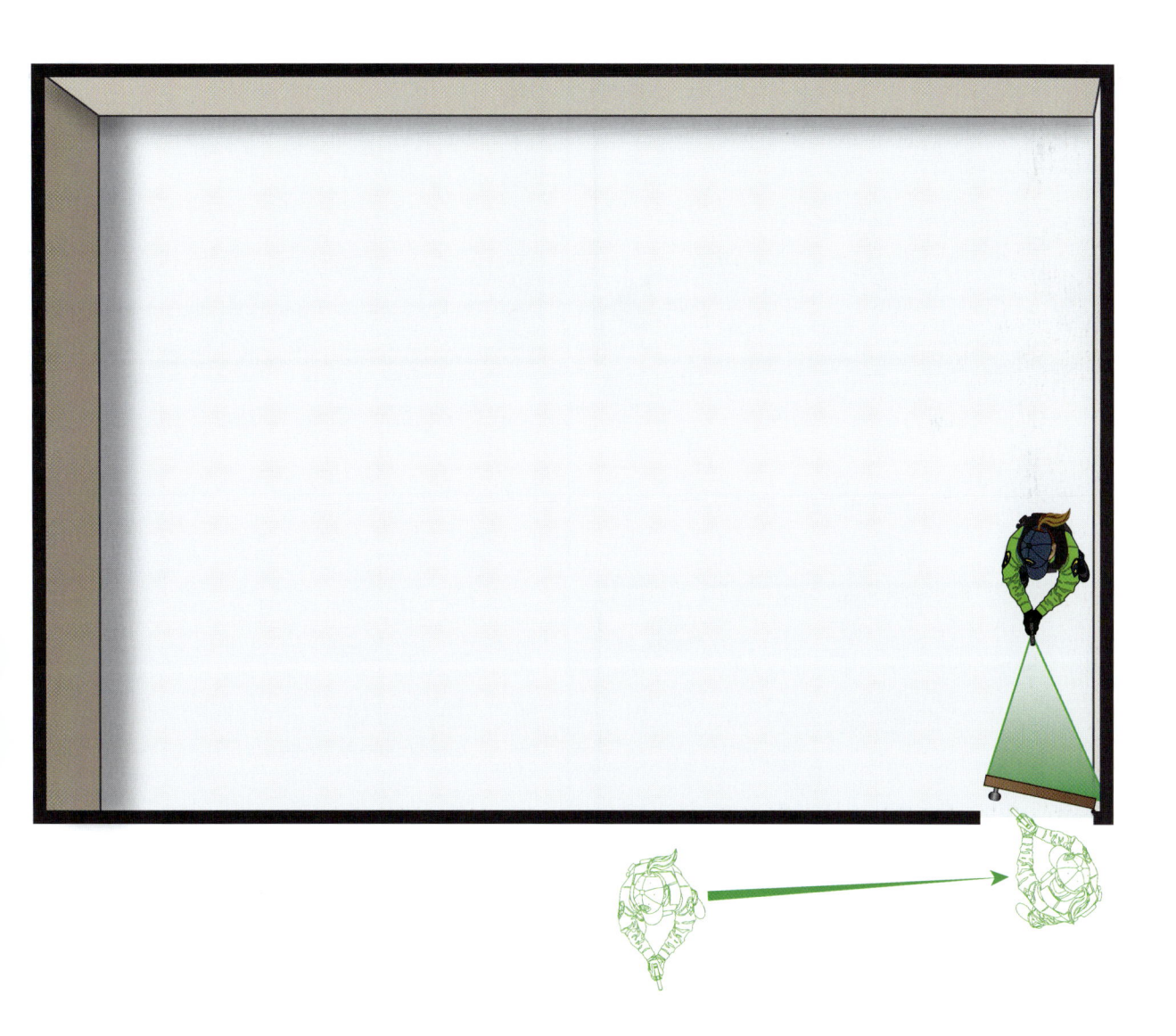

IMMEDIATE ENTRY: CORNER-FED OPEN DOOR

Different Door Configurations

If a corner-fed door opens inward, it can affect the positioning of officers in the room. There are no formulas or fixed rules to determine the officer positioning, however, below are some examples of how officers might position themselves in a room based on the door configuration. It is also possible for the first officer to control the door while the second officer moves into the room. If the door swings out, both officers can dominate deep in the room, or one officer can stay at a shallow domination point.

IMMEDIATE ENTRY: CORNER-FED CLOSED DOOR

LEAD OFFICER

Clearing a corner-fed closed door is similar to clearing a center-fed closed door, except in most cases the lead officer will have to open the door because there will be no room to stand on the other side of the door. Once the door is open, the lead officer will conduct the clearing process in the same way as for an open door, clearing the center of the room, scanning outward to the corner and scanning back inward while moving to the domination point.

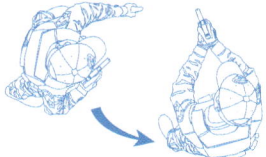

IMMEDIATE ENTRY: CORNER-FED CLOSED DOOR

SECOND OFFICER

The second officer will step out to clear the center of the room, then scan outward to clear the corner. If the door opens inward, the second officer will control the door while continuing to scan the room. Once the room is clear the second officer will turn around quickly to clear behind the door.

TWO-PERSON OPERATIONS
Single-Room Delayed Entry

Delayed entry techniques are particularly useful in two-person operations. Two officers operating without the support of an entire team are particularly vulnerable, especially to adversaries operating in larger groups with automatic weapons. For this reason, it is often a good idea for two-person teams to use delayed entry tactics to minimize their exposure and reduce the level of risk they face in a tactical situation.

It is also important to note that the delayed and immediate entry techniques described in this manual are interchangeable. Therefore, officers can switch back and fourth between delayed entry and immediate entry depending on the situation. For example, a team might begin to clear a house using delayed entry techniques but then switch to immediate entry when they hear a hostage screaming down the hall.

For two-person operations, delayed entry is similar to immediate entry but the initial steps are different. Officers may choose to use delayed entry tactics when time is not critical or when extra caution is advisable. Delayed entry tactics are designed to allow officers to clear as much of a room or hallway as possible from the outside, before actually making entry. When conducting a delayed entry, one officer will remain away from the door while the other officer moves forward to conduct an initial sweep (also known as slicing-the-pie) of the target room.

Once the lead officer has conducted a sweep of the room, he or she will lead the way during the entry process and the second officer will follow, using the same techniques just described for the immediate clear. However, when conducting a delayed entry, the officers might decide not to enter the room at all. If the lead officer detects or engages a threat while conducting the sweep, both officers might decide to hold position or pull back. The officers can then "call out" the adversary or wait for a better time and place to make entry.

DELAYED ENTRY: CENTER-FED OPEN DOOR

LEAD OFFICER STEP 1 - Approach the Door

The lead officer approaches the open door from the outside of the room, positioned close to the wall, several yards from the doorway. The lead officer should avoid touching or bumping into the wall because doing so will make noise and might also increase the chances of getting shot, since bullets tend to travel along walls.

APPROX 10 DEGREES

DELAYED ENTRY: CENTER-FED OPEN DOOR

LEAD OFFICER STEP 2 - Conduct Sweep Movement

Next, the lead officer will sweep out in a wide arc, keeping his/her weapon focused on the doorway and moving all the way across to a position close to the wall on the opposite side of the door. The purpose of the sweep is to visually clear the room as quickly as possible to identify any threats inside and possibly draw those threats out of the room. When executing the sweep, the officer should move in an arc as fast as possible while keeping the weapon relatively steady and taking care not to trip. It is sometimes necessary to sacrifice some weapon accuracy in order to minimize exposure and vulnerability through speed. Moving quickly along the arc makes it difficult for an adversary to engage effectively and will leave an officer exposed for only a fraction of a second. After completing the initial sweep, the lead officer can conduct additional sweeps if needed to check the room more carefully.

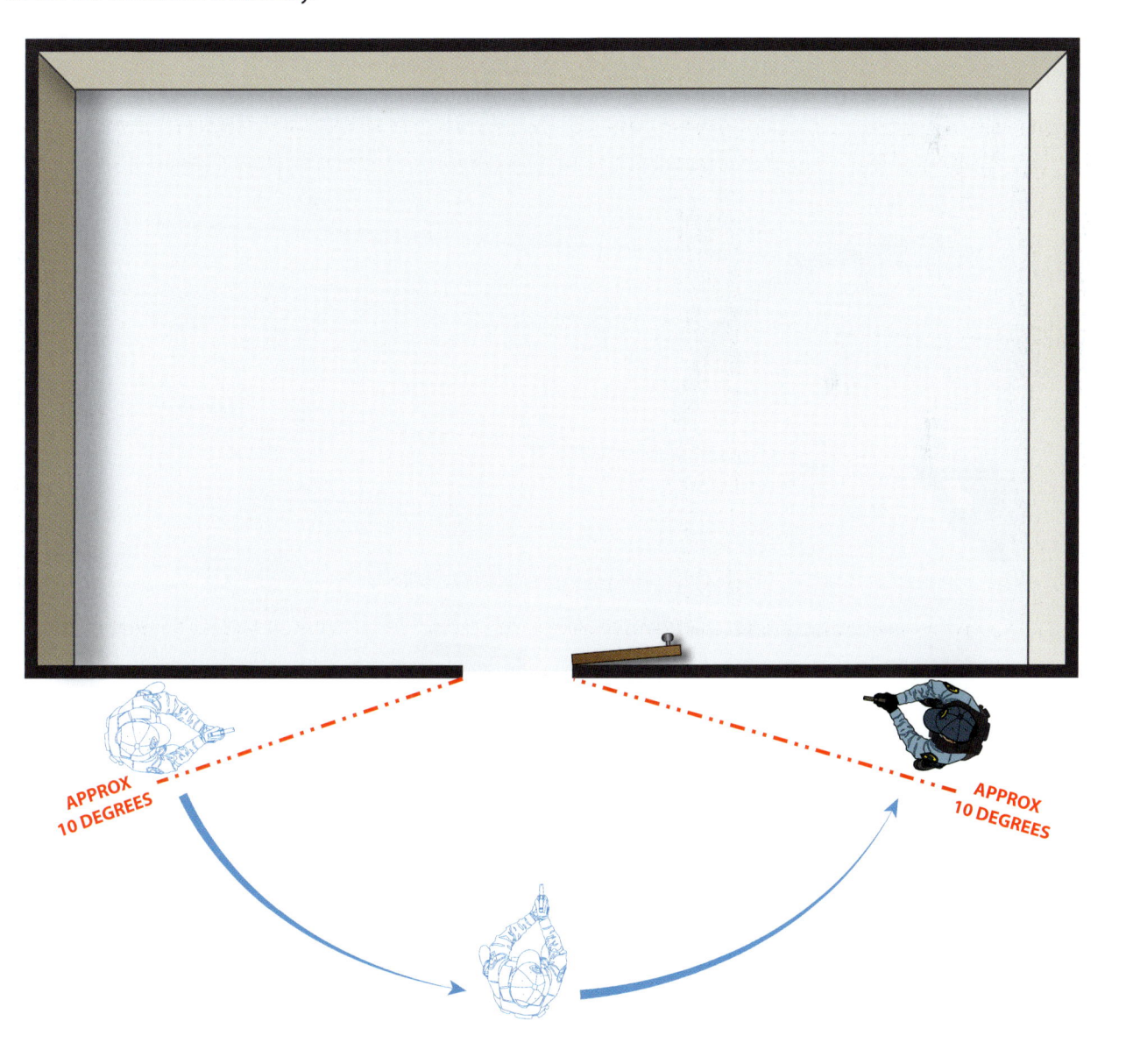

APPROX 10 DEGREES

APPROX 10 DEGREES

DELAYED ENTRY: CENTER-FED OPEN DOOR

LEAD OFFICER STEP 3 - Reverse Sweep and Entry

Once completing the initial sweep, if the team decides to enter the room, the lead officer will sweep along the arc in the opposite direction until he/she facing directly towards the door. The lead officer will then move towards the door remaining alert for deep threats in the center of the room. Once approaching the threshold, the lead officer will scan outward all the way to the corner and then scan back while moving to the domination point, just as in the immediate entry technique.

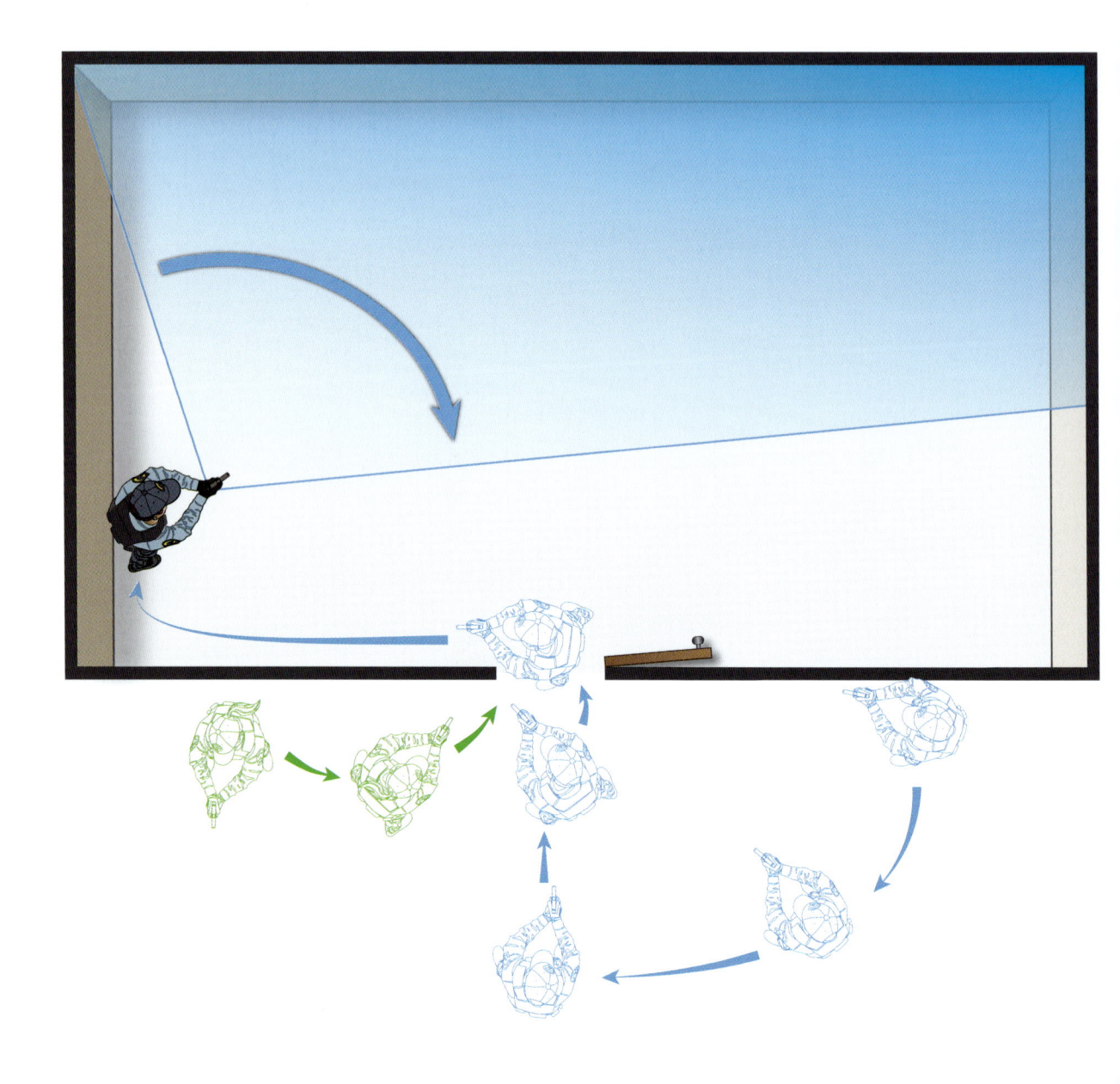

DELAYED ENTRY: CENTER-FED OPEN DOOR

SECOND OFFICER STEP 1 - Scan Outward, Control Door

The second officer will initially keep some distance from the door and allow the lead officer time and space to conduct the initial sweep. If the officers decide to enter the room, the second officer will wait until the lead officer completes the reverse sweep and is moving head-on towards the door. At this point, the second officer will also begin to approach the door, timing his/her entry to cover the back of the lead officer. Upon reaching the door, the second officer will turn in the opposite direction of the lead officer. The second officer will have to choose a good approach angle and use good timing in order to enter the room as close as possible behind the lead officer. As the second officer approaches the threshold, he/she will scan outward all the way to the corner and then scan back while moving to the domination point, just as in the immediate entry technique. If the door opens inward, the second officer will control the door while conducting the scan.

DELAYED ENTRY: CENTER-FED OPEN DOOR

SECOND OFFICER STEP 2 - Check Behind the Door

Once both officers have completed their scans, the second officer will still be controlling the door. If the second officer detects an adversary or any kind of resistance behind the door, the second officer may have to step back and clear behind the door immediately. Otherwise, the second officer will finish scanning the room first, then turn around and check behind the door. It is critical that the second officer step back when checking behind the door to ensure that an adversary is not close enough to jump out and grab the officer's weapon.

DELAYED ENTRY: CENTER-FED CLOSED DOOR

LEAD OFFICER STEP 1 - Open the Door

The technique for a center-fed closed door is almost the same as the technique for clearing the open door with a few minor adjustments. The first difference is that because the door is closed, the lead officer must first open the door before conducting the sweep. To open the door, the lead officer will position close to the wall and away from the door with weapon at the ready and oriented towards the door just in case the door opens and an adversary walks out. The lead officer will quickly move towards the door, grasp the doorknob with the non-firing hand and swing the door open. The lead officer will then back away just in case an adversary fires towards the door.

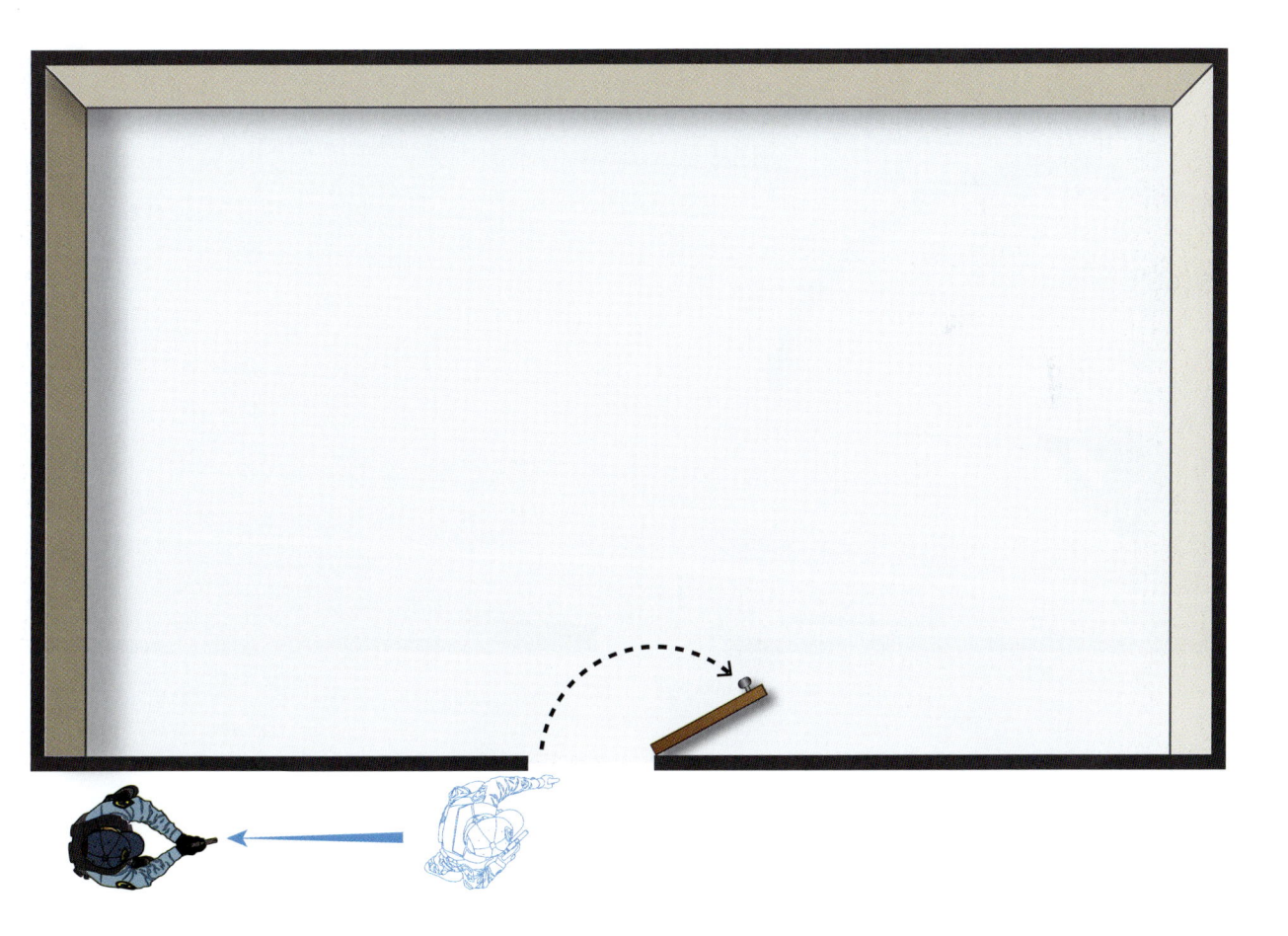

DELAYED ENTRY: CENTER-FED CLOSED DOOR

LEAD OFFICER STEP 2 - Sweep and Enter the Room

Once the door is open, the clearing technique is the same as for a closed door. The lead officer will conduct a sweep across the door, then sweep back in the opposite direction and enter the room. The lead officer will scan outward to the corner and then scan inward while moving to the domination point just as in the immediate entry technique.

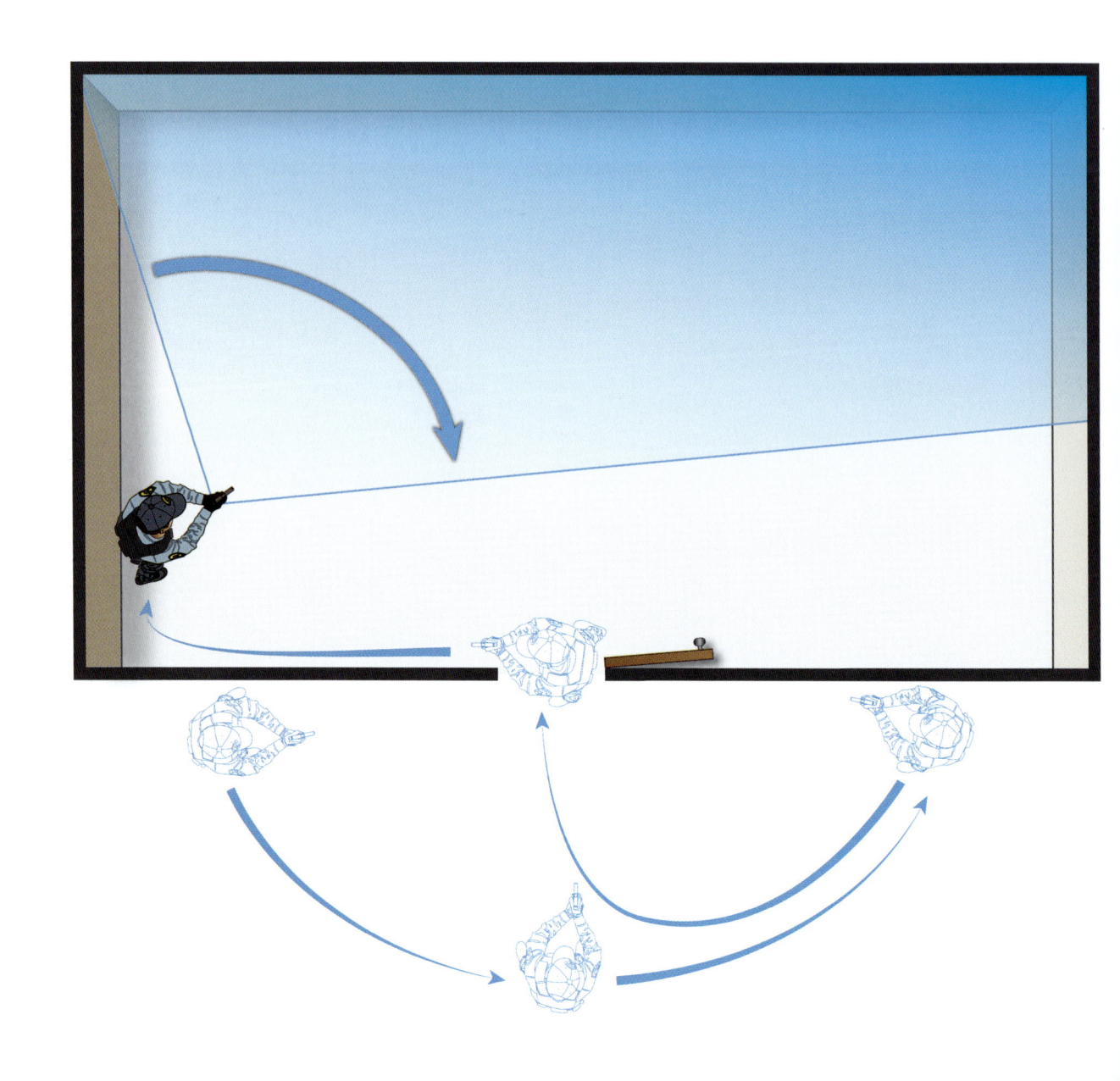

DELAYED ENTRY: CENTER-FED CLOSED DOOR

SECOND OFFICER

The second officer will initially keep some distance from the door and allow the lead officer time and space to conduct the initial sweep. If the officers decide to enter the room, the second officer will wait until the lead officer completes the reverse sweep and is moving head-on towards the door. At this point, the second officer will also begin to approach the door, timing his/her entry to cover the back of the lead officer. Upon reaching the door, the second officer will turn in the opposite direction of the lead officer scanning outward all the way to the corner and then scan back while moving to the domination point, just as in the immediate entry technique. If the door opens inward, the second officer will control the door while conducting the scan, then check behind the door once the scan is complete.

DELAYED ENTRY: CORNER-FED OPEN DOOR

LEAD OFFICER STEP 1 - Conduct Half Sweep

Clearing a corner-fed open door is similar to clearing a center-fed open door. When conducting a delayed entry, the term "corner-fed" or "center-fed" refers to the room where the officers start, as well as the room they are clearing. In some cases, when clearing a corner-fed door the lead officer will only be able to approach from one side and conduct only a "half sweep." The lead officer will position close to the wall while staying several yards away from the door. The lead officer will then sweep out in a quick but smooth arc, maintaining distance from the doorway while clearing the interior of the room.

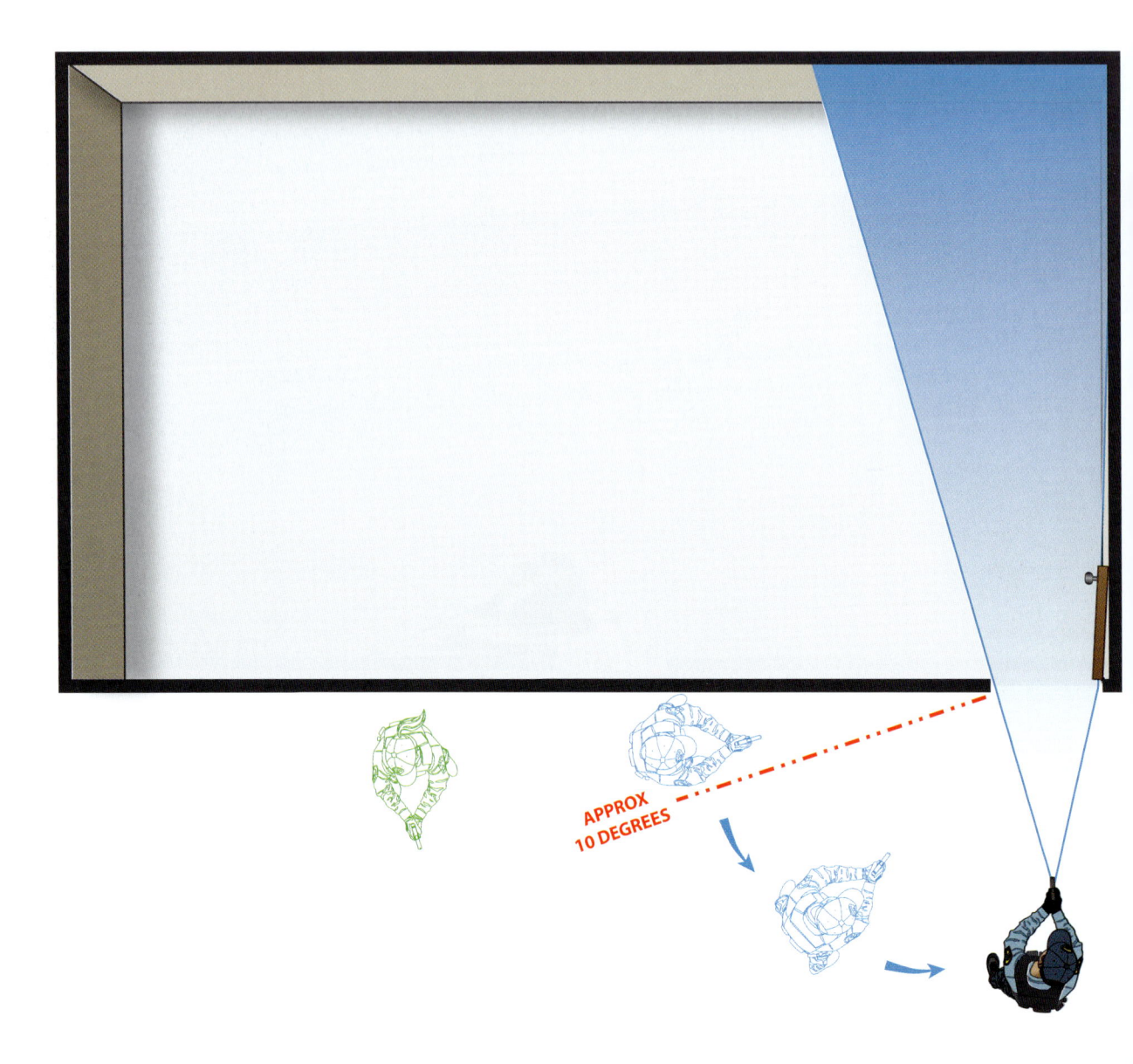

APPROX 10 DEGREES

DELAYED ENTRY: CORNER-FED OPEN DOOR

LEAD OFFICER STEP 2 - Approach the Door and Enter

Once completing the initial half sweep, if the officers decide to enter the room, the lead officer will move towards the door remaining alert for deep threats in the room. Once reaching the threshold, the lead officer will scan outward to the corner and then scan inward while moving to the domination point just as in the immediate entry technique.

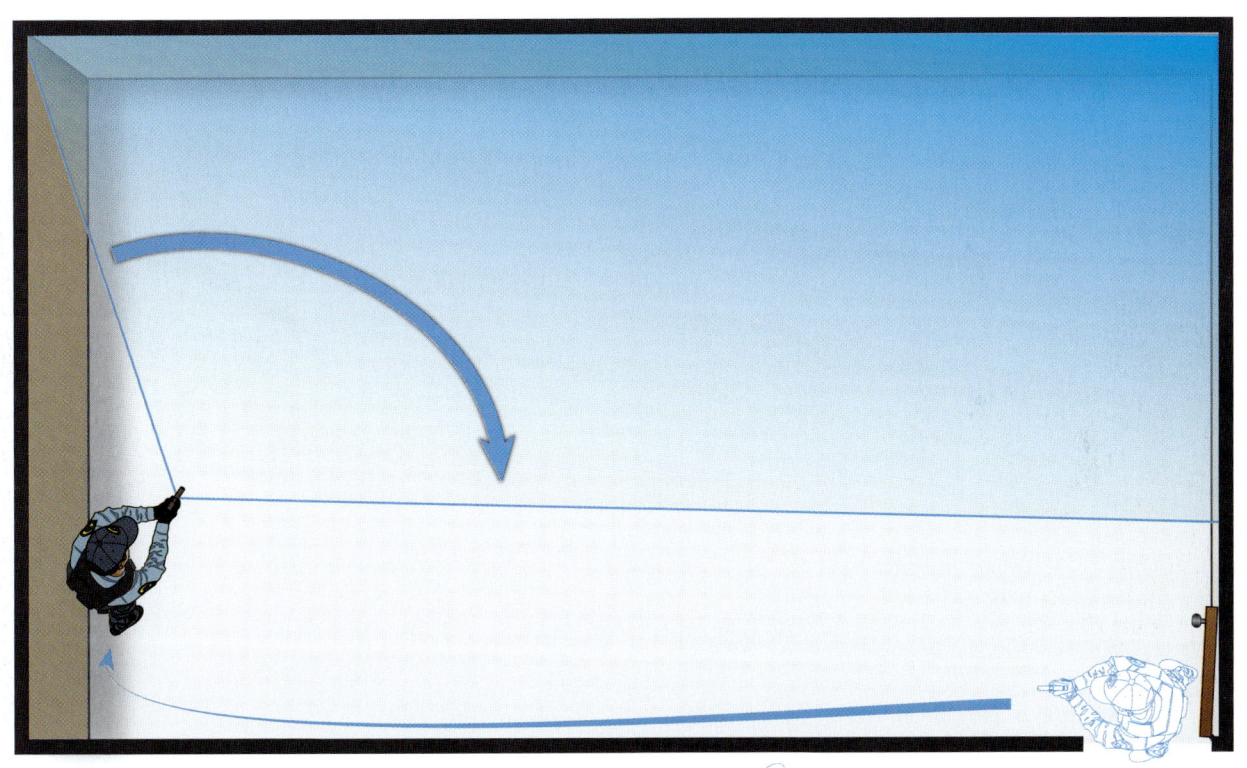

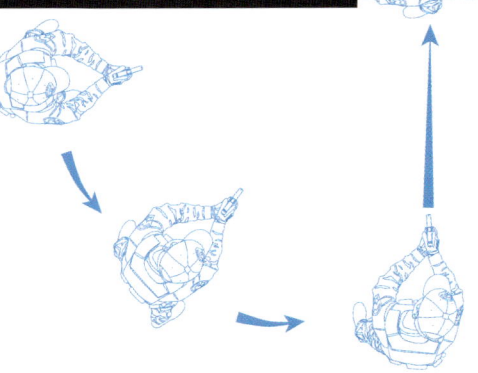

DELAYED ENTRY: CORNER-FED OPEN DOOR

SECOND OFFICER

The second officer will initially keep some distance from the door and allow the lead officer time and space to conduct the initial sweep. If the officers decide to enter the room, the second officer will wait until the lead officer completes the reverse sweep and is moving head-on towards the door. At this point, the second officer will also approach the door and enter right behind the lead officer. Once the second officer enters the room and turns in the opposite direction of the lead officer, he/she will scan from the center of the far wall to the deep corner and engage any threats until they are neutralized. The second officer will then scan inward and move to the domination point just as in the immediate entry technique. If the door opens inward, the second officer will control the door while conducting the scan, then check behind the door once the scan is complete.

DELAYED ENTRY: CORNER-FED CLOSED DOOR

LEAD OFFICER

The technique for a corner-fed closed door is almost the same as the technique for clearing the open door but because the door is closed, the lead officer must first open the door before conducting the sweep. To open the door, the lead officer will position close to the wall and away from the door with weapon at the ready and oriented towards the door just in case the door opens and an adversary walks out. The lead officer will move towards the door quickly, swing the door open and then back away. Once the door is open, the clearing technique is the same as for a closed door. The lead officer will conduct a sweep across the door, then sweep back in the opposite direction and enter the room. The lead officer will scan outward to the corner, then scan back inward while moving to the domination point.

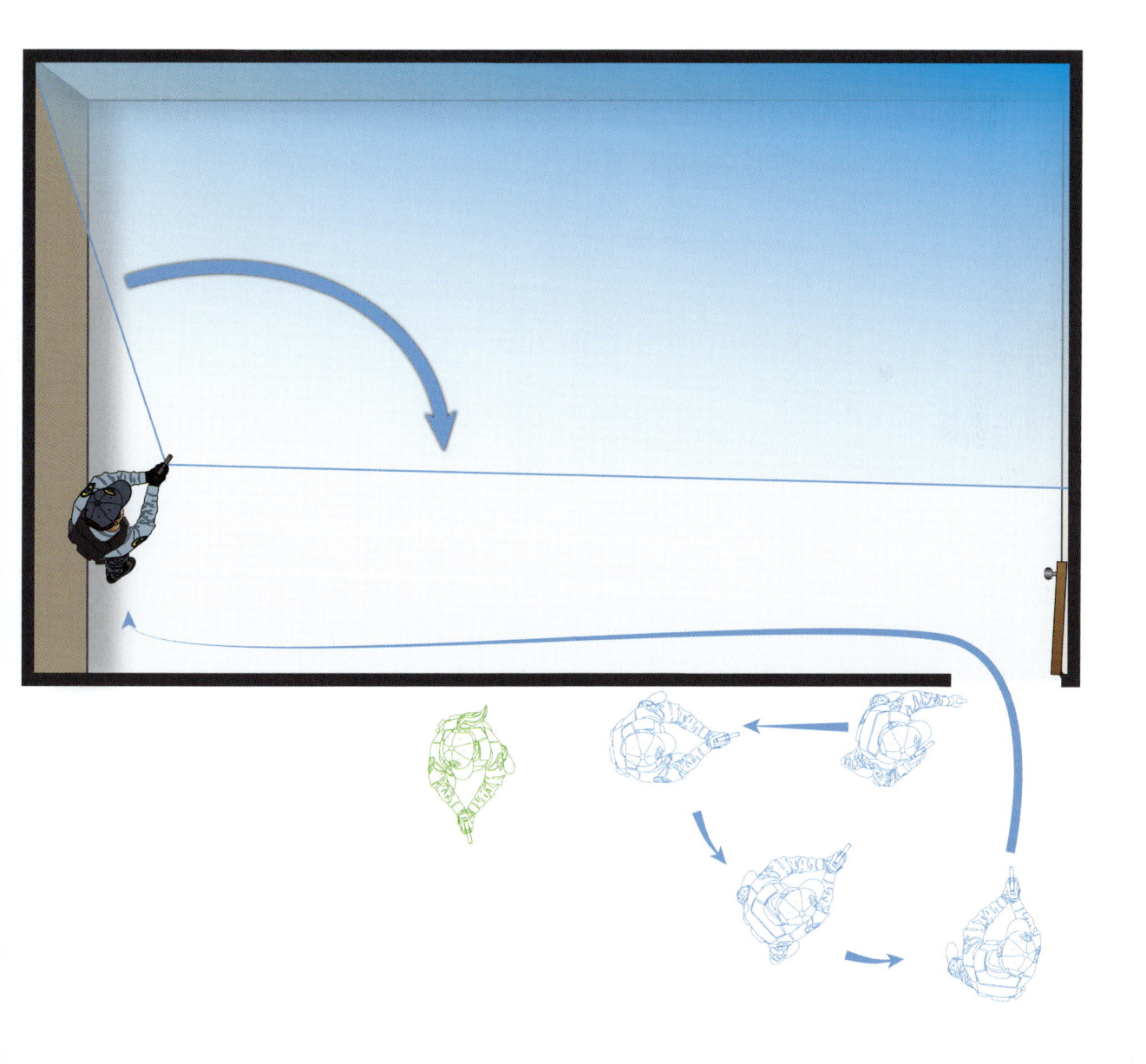

DELAYED ENTRY: CORNER-FED CLOSED DOOR

SECOND OFFICER

The second officer will initially keep some distance from the door and allow the lead officer time and space to conduct the initial sweep. If the officers decide to enter the room, the second officer will wait until the lead officer completes the reverse sweep and is moving head-on towards the door. At this point, the second officer will also approach the door and enter right behind the lead officer. Once the second officer enters the room and turns in the opposite direction of the lead officer, he/she will scan from the center of the far wall to the deep corner and engage any threats until they are neutralized. The second officer will then scan inward and move to the domination point just as in the immediate entry technique. If the door opens inward, the second officer will control the door while conducting the scan, then check behind the door once the scan is complete.

TWO-PERSON OPERATIONS
Multiple Room Immediate Entry

The techniques for moving from one room to the next depend on the positioning of the doors in the room and whether the doors are open or closed. When officers enter a room and encounter an open door, one officer will generally have a better angle of observation into that room. That officer will hold coverage on the open door while the other officer moves towards the door to lead the way into the room. If the officers encounter a closed door, there will be no need to hold long coverage on the door. Instead, one officer will move to the opposite side of the door to act as the breacher.

One of the most challenging configurations is multiple open doors in one room. This is particularly dangerous when there are only two officers to cover multiple doors and danger areas. In this type of situation, it is particularly difficult to apply any predetermined or fixed formula. Instead, officers must use their common sense and judgment to deal with the situation in the safest way possible.

As discussed in the team operations section, a two-person team can employ the "back clear" technique when moving back through a room that was already cleared. Officers may use the back clear if they enter a room with no doors and they must move back to clear another area of the building. Officers might also use the back clear technique to conduct a second, more deliberate clearance of a building to ensure there are no adversaries hiding in concealed locations. For more information on the back clear, see the team operations section.

Officers working in a two-person team can also use the "clear and hold" and "clear on the move" techniques described in the team operations section. However, the clear on the move technique is generally preferable since two officers do not have the manpower to hold multiple danger areas simultaneously. It usually makes more sense for the officers to clear on the move and use speed to their advantage. For more discussion of clearing on the move, see the team operations section.

IMMEDIATE ENTRY: OPEN DOORS

STEP 1 - Dominate First Room, Maintain Long Coverage

The officers will enter and dominate the first room using one of the methods already described. Once the officers are at their domination points, one officer will have a better angle of observation through the open door than the other officer. This officer must both provide long coverage and still be looking over his/her shoulder to provide rear security. The officer covering long may choose to move closer to the door, step farther from the door or adjust position to the left or right to get the best observation angle into the room while still being able to cover the rear. Situational awareness and position shifting is even more important for two-person operations since there are more angles to cover.

IMMEDIATE ENTRY: OPEN DOORS

STEP 2 - Lead Officer Approach the Door

Once long coverage is established, the other officer will approach the door and prepare to enter the next room. Once again, there are no formulas or set rules for how to position the two team members when converging on the door. In general, officers should avoid crossing in front of the open door as much as possible. Therefore, the officer whose domination point is on the right side of the door should generally stay on the right and vice versa. In some cases officers will have no choice but to cross in front of an open door. In these cases, officers should move quickly in an arc movement while maintaining coverage on the door.

IMMEDIATE ENTRY: OPEN DOORS

STEP 3 - Enter and Clear

Once the lead officer is ready, he/she will enter the next room. The second officer must remain alert to be sure to follow right behind the lead officer. The two officers will enter the next room using the same techniques already described for two-person immediate entry.

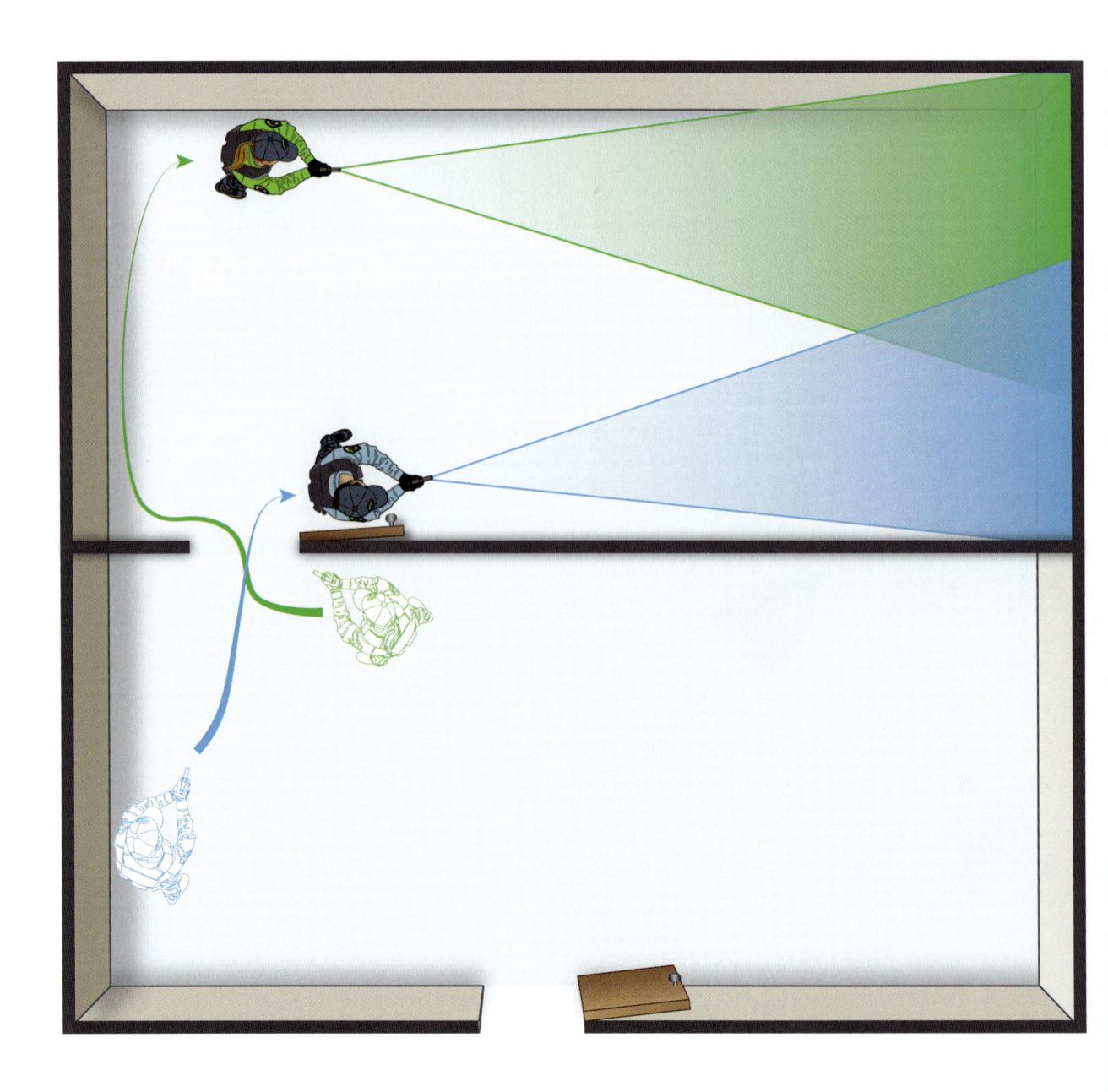

IMMEDIATE ENTRY: CLOSED DOORS

COMPLETE SEQUENCE

Closed doors greatly simplify the process of moving from room to room with two officers. If possible, one officer will open the closed door while the other officer will lead the way into the next room. Officers will enter using the same techniques already described in the two-person immediate entry section. In some cases, if there is no space on the other side of the door, the lead officer will have to open the door. Since there are only two officers, both officers must remain alert and maintain rear security on the move.

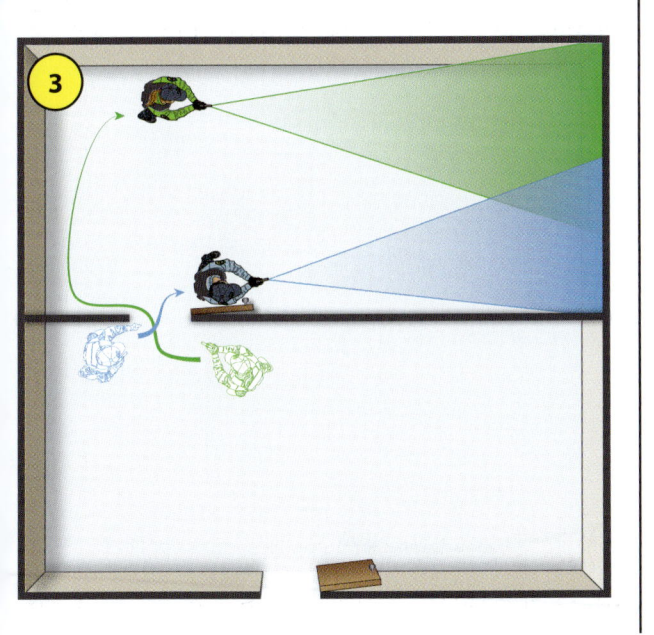

IMMEDIATE ENTRY: MULTIPLE DOORS

COMPLETE SEQUENCE

If there are multiple doors in a room, particularly multiple open doors, that will greatly increase the complexity of the situation for a two-person team. There is no fixed formula for dealing with multiple open doors. However, the general rule is if two officers are facing multiple threats, those officers will want to stay closer together rather than spread apart. If there is only one open door in a room, spreading out can give officers better angles of observation into the room. However, if there are multiple open doors, officers are better able to cover each other's backs if they stay closer together. Therefore, as soon as officers find themselves in a room with multiple open doors, the lead officer will determine which door to enter first and the second officer will move to cover the lead officer's back. Still, officers should maintain some separation to reduce the chances that one shot or burst will hit both of them.

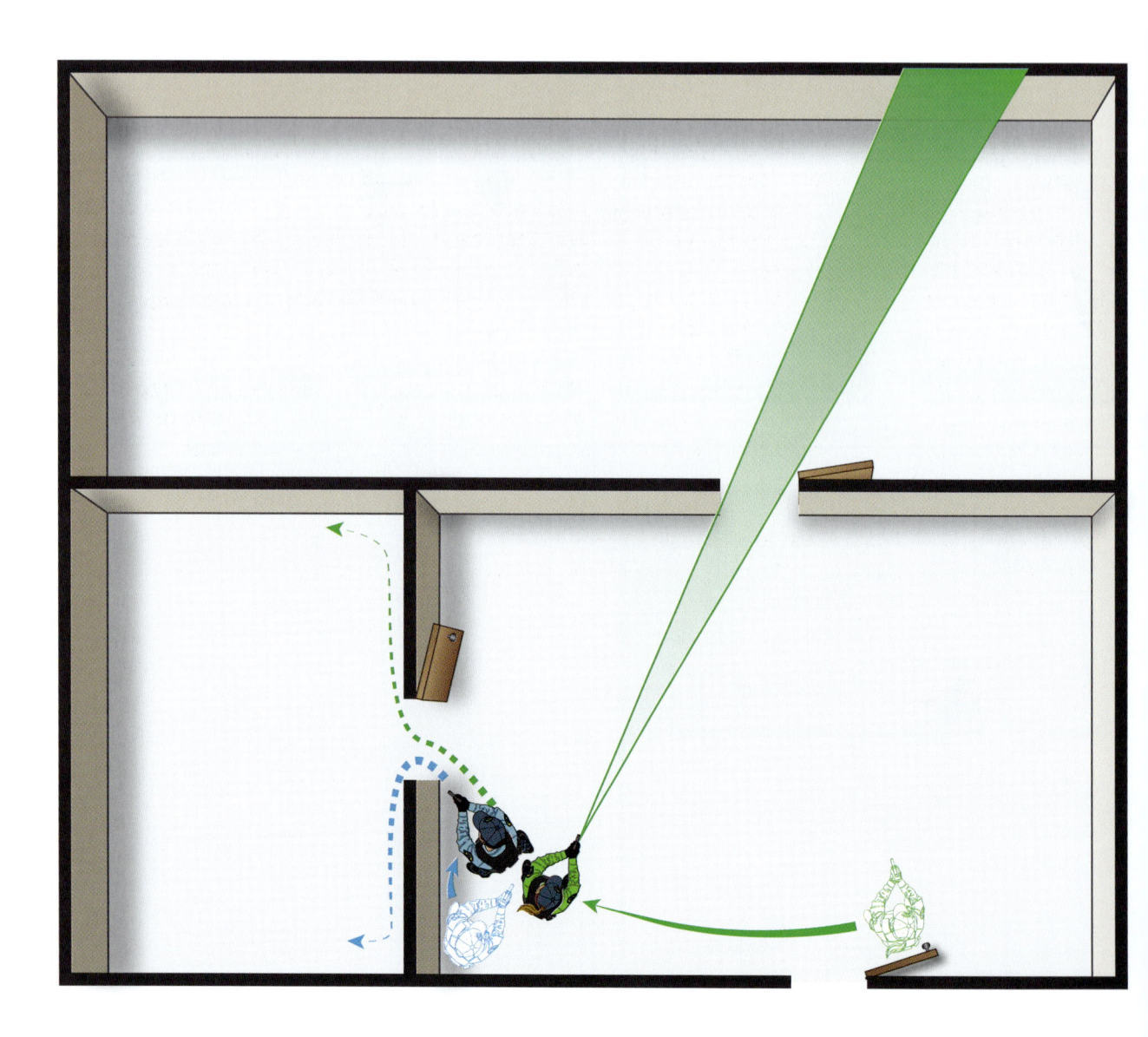

TWO-PERSON OPERATIONS
Multiple Room Delayed Entry

If two officers must move from room to room and there is no imminent danger to innocent civilians, they may choose to use delayed entry instead of immediate entry to minimize risk. The delayed entry technique is particularly useful in situations where the team aims to locate and "call out" a subject without committing too far into a house or building.

Conducting a delayed entry as a two-person element is very similar to executing a delayed entry as a team. For an open door, the officer conducting the sweep will move to a position close to the wall, offering observation as far into the next room's corner as possible. The officer will then sweep around in the same, smooth arc movement described in the single-room delayed entry section. The officer will conduct additional sweeps as needed to check the next room for threats. In other situations, because of the room configuration or the positioning of furniture, the officer might only be able to conduct a partial sweep of the next room.

The procedures for a closed door are the same, except the officer will need to first approach the door, open the door, back away and then conduct the sweep. Once the lead officer opens the door, both officers should remain alert in case an adversary emerges from the door.

Whether the door is open or closed, while the first officer conducts the sweep, the other officer should move away from the door to minimize exposure while providing rear security. The second officer must remain alert and be prepared to converge on the door to follow the lead officer into the room if the lead officer decides to make entry.

DELAYED ENTRY: OPEN DOORS

STEP 1 - Dominate Room, Back Away from the Door

The officers will enter and dominate the first room using one of the methods already described. Once the officers are at their domination points, one officer will have a better angle of observation through the open door than the other officer. However, instead of maintaining long coverage, the officer may give up the angle and choose a more protected position, further from the entry door. Alternatively, the officer with the best observation angle can be the officer to conduct the sweep while the other officer moves away from the door. There are no fixed formulas.

DELAYED ENTRY: OPEN DOORS

STEP 2 - Lead Officer Conduct Sweep

The second officer stays back providing rear security to give the lead officer room to conduct a sweep of the next room. The lead officer may conduct a single sweep or multiple sweeps. If the lead officer decides to enter the next room, he/she will begin moving directly towards the open door.

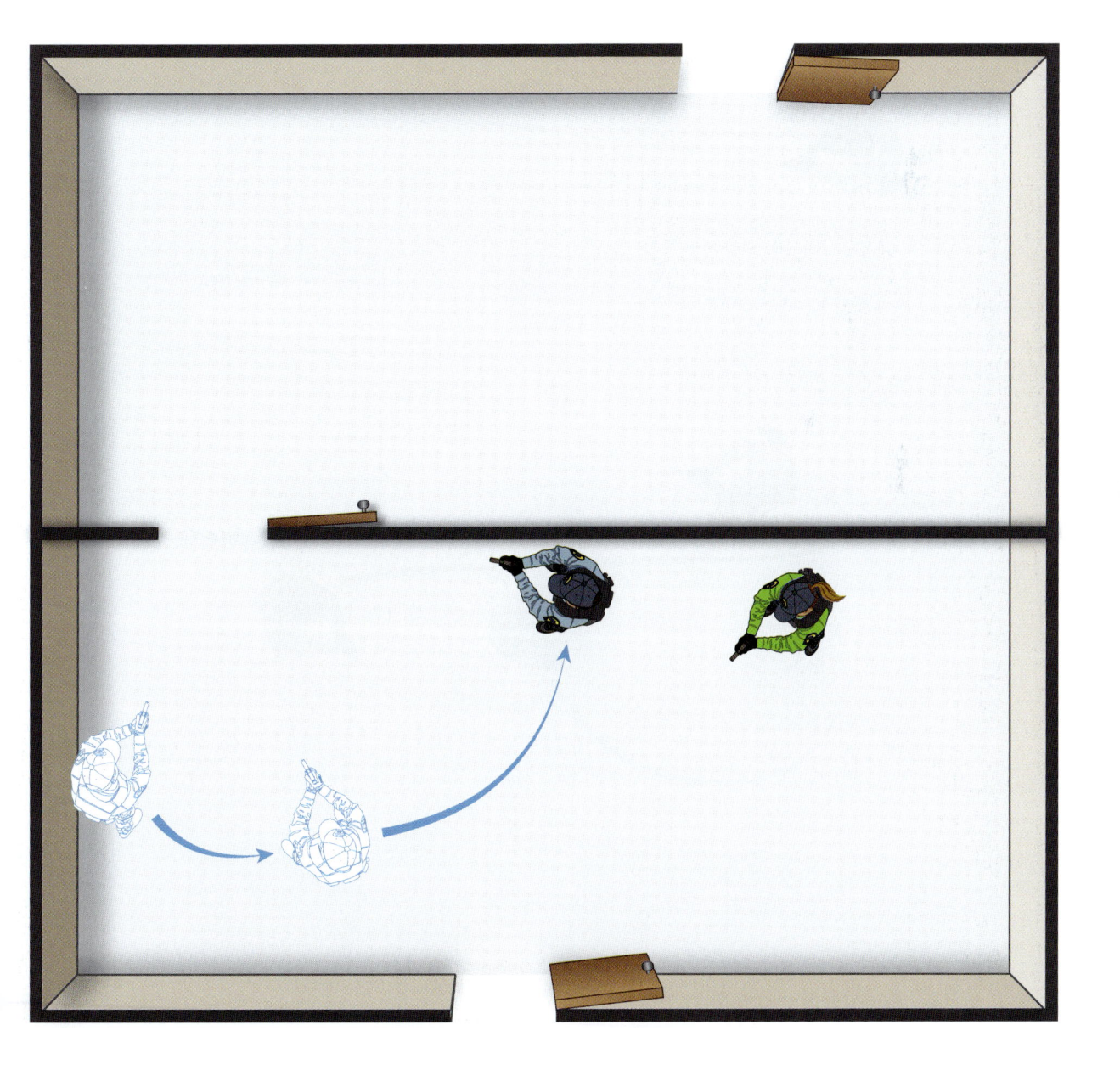

DELAYED ENTRY: OPEN DOORS

STEP 3 - Enter and Clear

Once the sweep is complete and the lead officer is moving towards the door, the second officer will give up rear security to follow the first officer into the next room. The two officers will clear the room using the techniques already described. If the door opens inward, one officer will control the door.

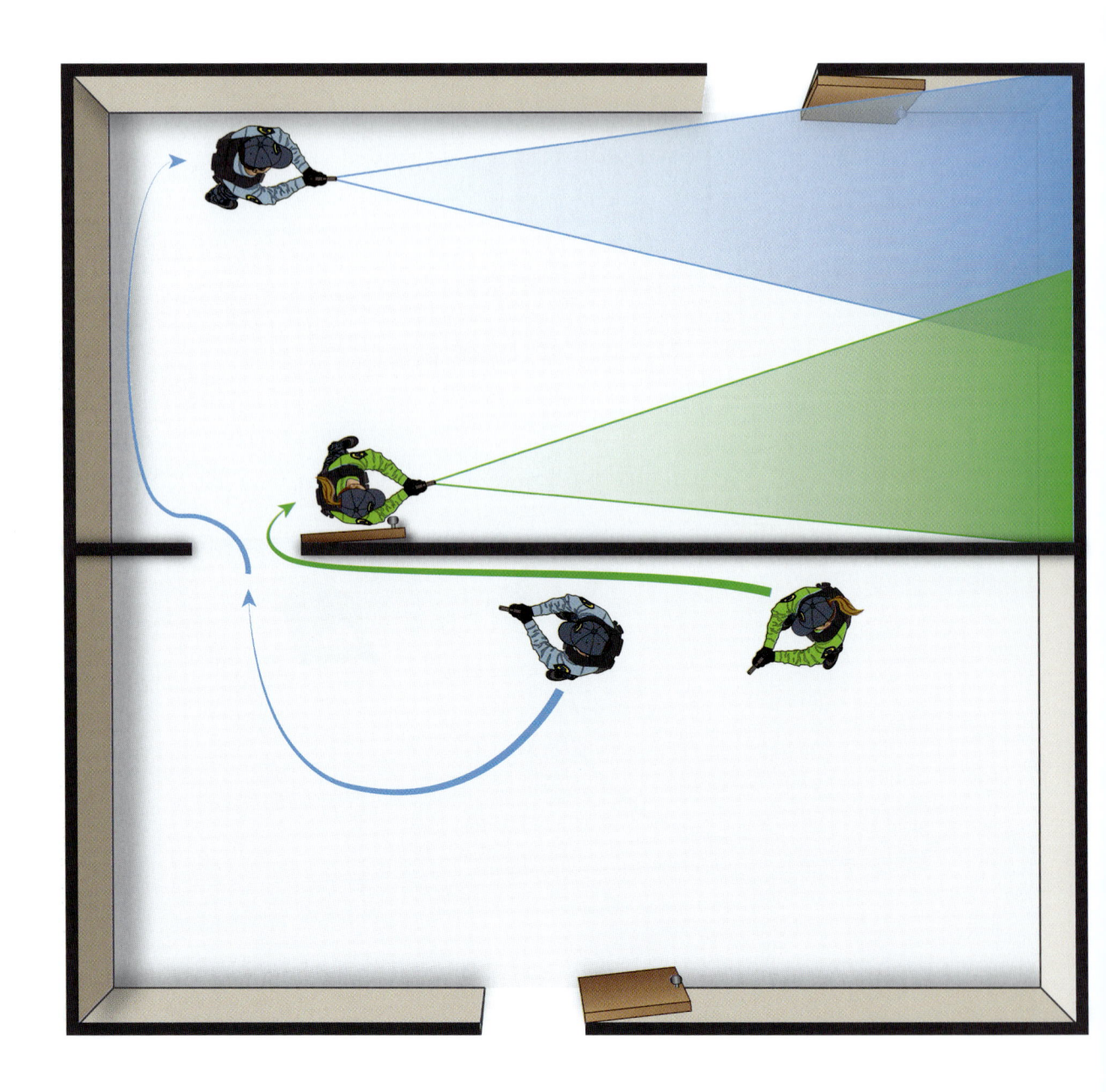

DELAYED ENTRY: OPEN DOORS

STEP 4 - Reposition as Necessary

Once the room is cleared and the second officer has checked behind the door, both officers can reposition as necessary to prepare to conduct a sweep of the next room.

DELAYED ENTRY: CLOSED DOORS

COMPLETE SEQUENCE

Clearing rooms with delayed entry when the door is closed is the exact same process as with open doors except the lead officer will need to quickly approach each door and open it before conducting the scan. In some situations, the other officer might open the door but in general, it is best for the lead officer to both open the door and conduct the scan while the other officer stays back at a safe distance providing rear security.

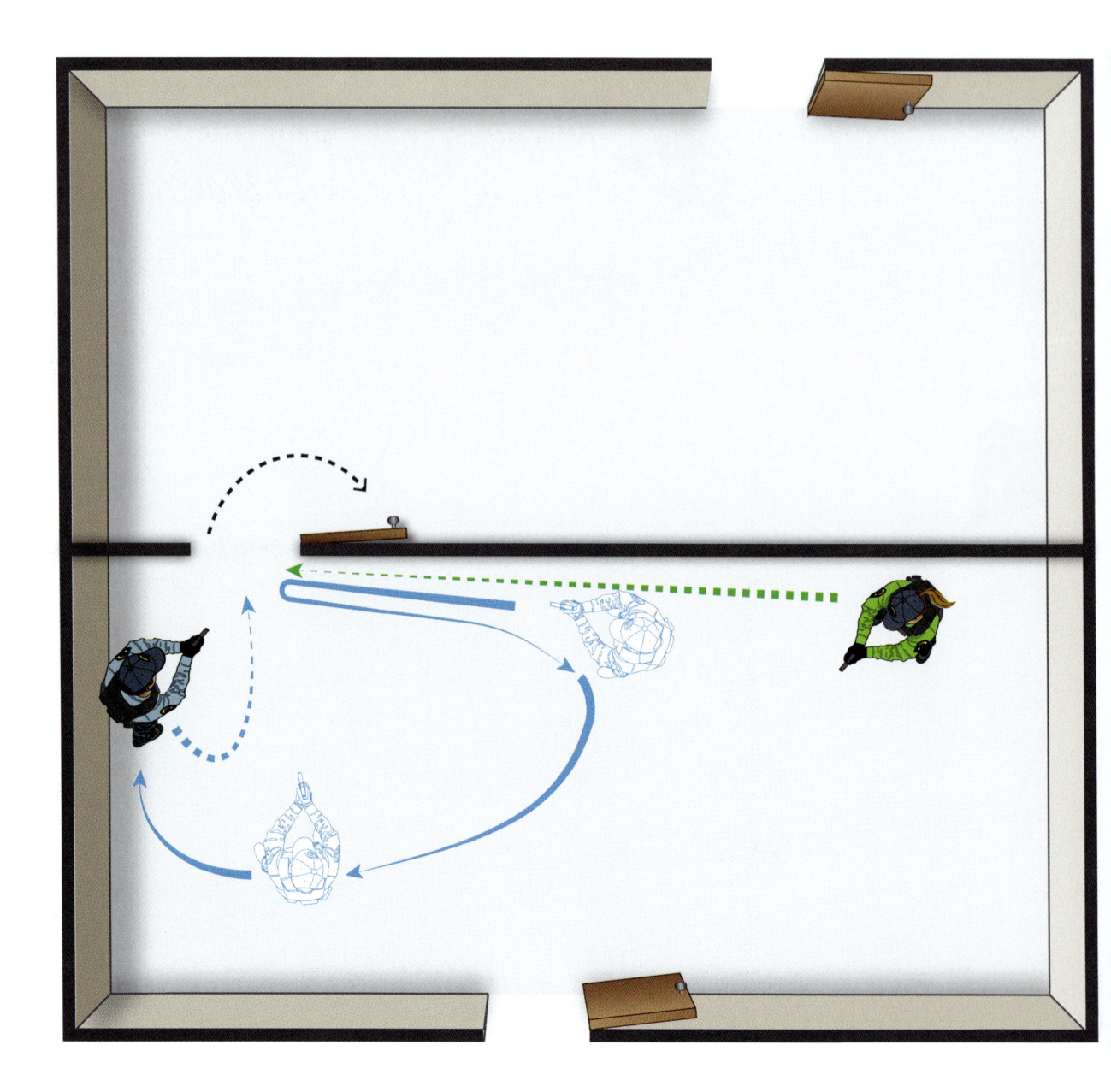

DELAYED ENTRY: MULTIPLE DOORS

COMPLETE SEQUENCE

The process for using delayed entry on rooms with multiple doors is no different than the process for single doors. However, in general, it might not be ideal to use delayed entry from within rooms with multiple open doors. This is because an officer might be exposing his/her back to multiple danger areas while conducting the sweep. Also, conducting a sweep will mean the team is spending longer in the room. Since rooms with multiple open doors are danger areas, it might be best to use immediate clearing techniques to get out of the room, then take a slower approach once the tactical equation is simplified.

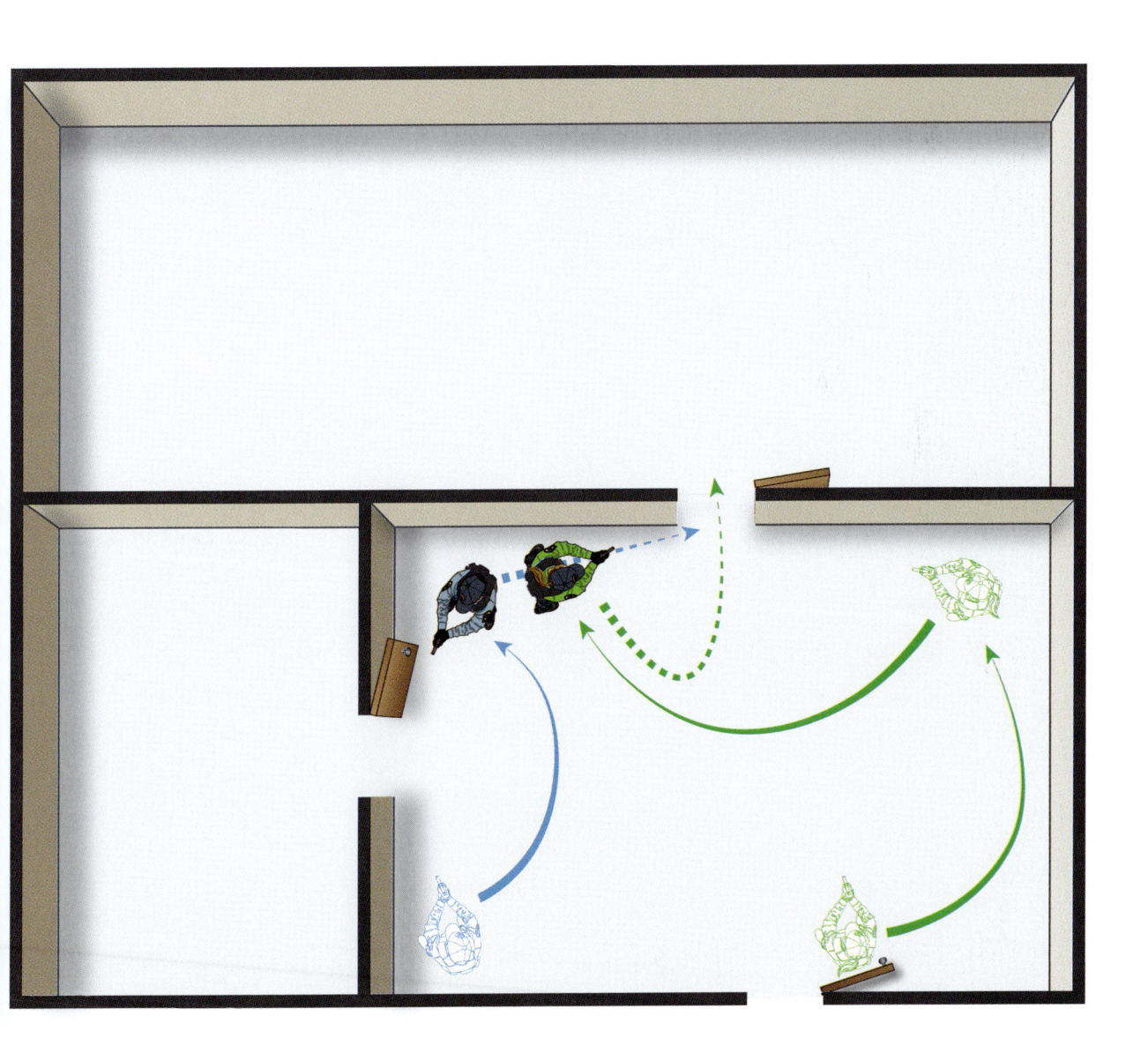

TWO-PERSON OPERATIONS
Hallways Immediate Entry

Hallways are considered danger areas because they generally have many doors running along their length. An adversary could emerge from any one of these doors without warning. More importantly, an adversary could simply extend his/her weapon around the corner and spray indiscriminately. Because of the shape of the hallway, there is a greater chance that this type of indiscriminate fire will cause casualties.

Therefore, officers should move through the hallway quickly, maintaining dispersion. The objective should be to get out of the hallway and into a room that offers better protection. The two officers should maintain "cross coverage" while moving and use the "clear and hold" or "clear on the move" techniques as needed when passing open doors.

When moving from a hallway into a room, or moving from a room into the hallway, the team officers must remain alert for potential threats coming from either direction. If the door is closed, one officer can move across the door to act as a breacher. However, if officers do not want to expose their backs to the hallway, the lead officer can conduct a self-breach and then lead the way into the room.

Probably the most dangerous hallway configurations officers will encounter are hallway intersections. Intersections are danger areas for all of the same reasons as a single hallway. However, when officers pass though an intersection, officers will be exposed from multiple directions instead of just two, increasing the level of risk and presenting more angles for officers to cover. Therefore, officers should try to move through intersections as quickly as possible to get away from the intersection to a safer location.

There are many different intersection configurations but the most common are the L-shape intersection, T-shape intersection and the X-shape intersection.

HALLWAY MOVEMENT

Cross Coverage

When two officers move down a hallway, they will position themselves directly across from each other on each side of the hallway. They will provide cross coverage which means that the officer on the right will cover to the left and the officer on the left will cover to the right. This is because officers have a better angle of observation through doors and openings across the hall than they do on the same side of the hall. In a two-person element, at least one officer should periodically look over his/her shoulder to check the rear. In extremely narrow hallways there might not even be enough room for cross coverage. In these cases, officers should just stagger their formation and cover the front and rear as they move.

HALLWAY MOVEMENT

Moving Past Open Doors - Clear and Hold

As the officers approach an open door they will maintain cross coverage until they reach the door. On the approach, the officer across the hall will have the best angle of vision through the open door. However, this officer will have to momentarily give up cross coverage as the team reaches the door. The officer on the same side as the door will quickly turn and stop momentarily to provide coverage so the team can pass by safely. The covering officer can adjust as needed to achieve the best angle and minimize exposure.

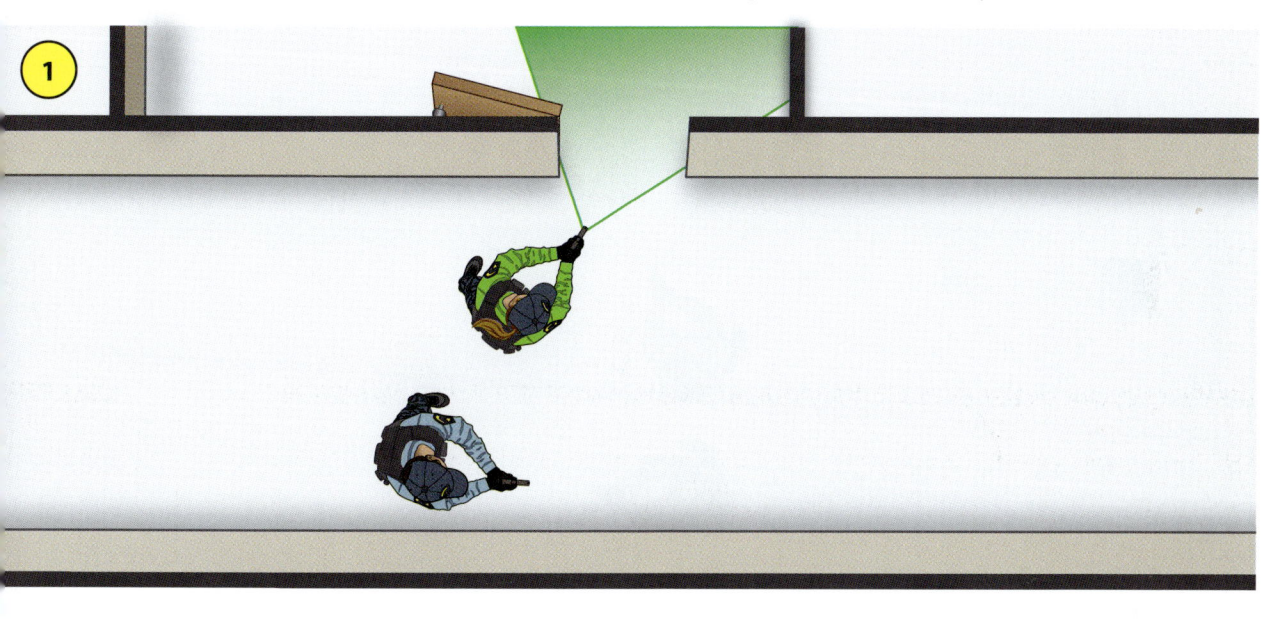

1

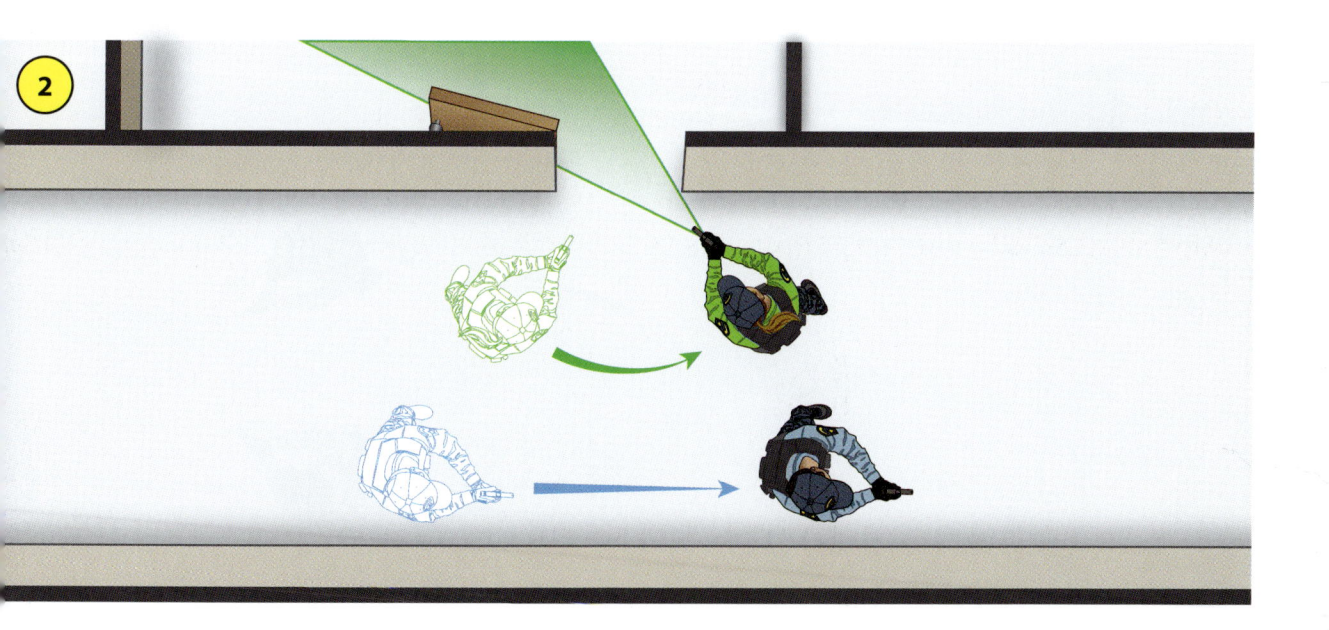

2

HALLWAY MOVEMENT

Moving Past Open Doors - Clear on the Move

The clear on the move technique is less secure but it is faster and easier to execute. Officers will still maintain cross coverage as they move down the hall. However, as an officer reaches an open door, he/she will momentarily pivot to clear the doorway without stopping, continuing movement down the hallway.

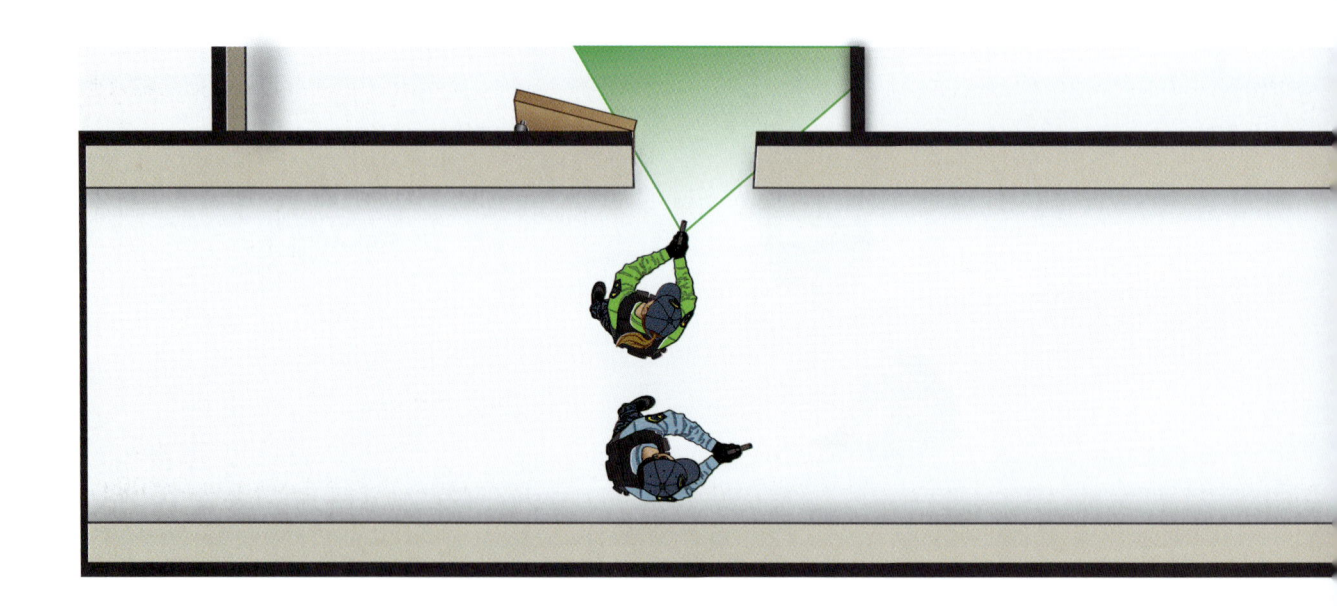

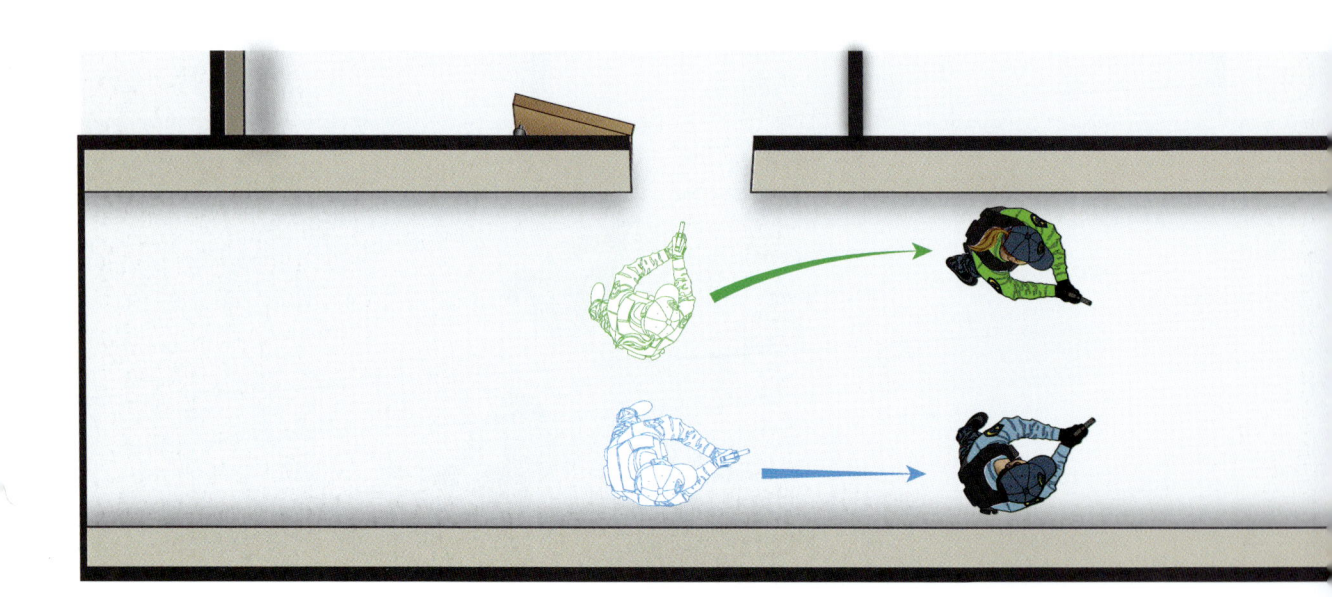

ENTERING AN OPEN DOOR FROM THE HALLWAY

STEP 1 - Approach the Door

As the two officers move down the hallway maintaining cross coverage, one of the officers will identify the open door. They must decide whether or not to enter the room or bypass it. If they decide to enter the room, they will maintain cross coverage until they reach the door.

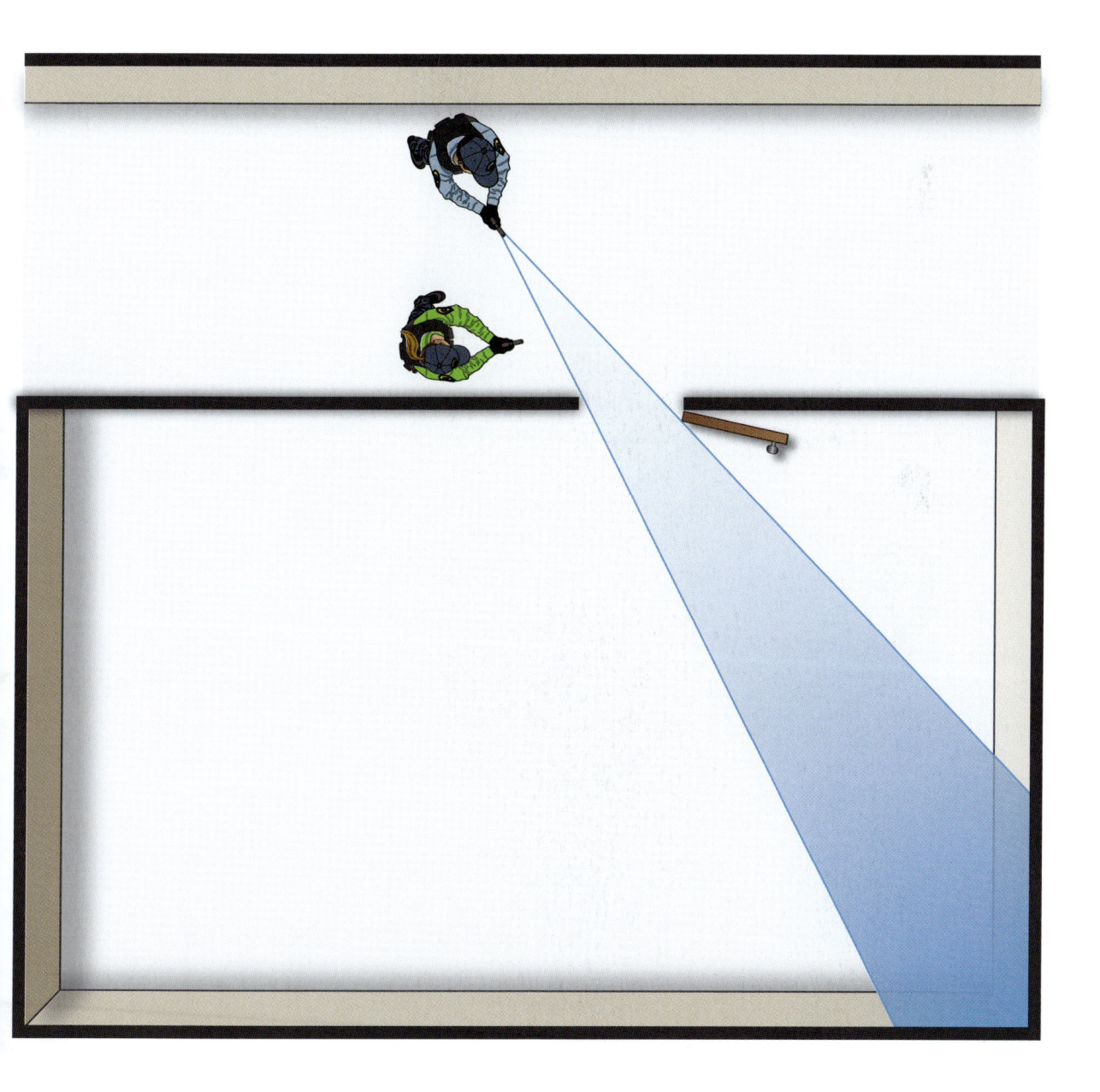

ENTERING AN OPEN DOOR FROM THE HALLWAY

STEP 2 - Stack, Enter and Clear

The officer opposite the side of the open door will move into position to provide long coverage while the other officer prepares to enter the room. If necessary, the entering officer will take a momentary pause before entering to allow the covering officer time to prepare to follow close behind into the room. The lead officer will then enter the room followed by the covering officer, using the techniques already described.

Two-Person Operations: Hallways Immediate Entry   231

ENTERING A CLOSED DOOR FROM THE HALLWAY

STEP 1 - Approach the Door

The two officers will move down the hallway maintaining cross coverage. When the officers identify the closed door, they will decide whether or not to enter the room or bypass it.

ENTERING A CLOSED DOOR FROM THE HALLWAY

STEP 2 - Open the Door

Either one officer can open the door for the other, or the lead officer can open the door with the other officer stacked behind. Either way, since there are only two officers and a hallway is a danger area, the officer should open the door as quickly as possible since his/her back will be exposed to the hallway while opening the door. If officers do not want to expose their backs, another option is for the lead officer to open the door and then enter (self-breach).

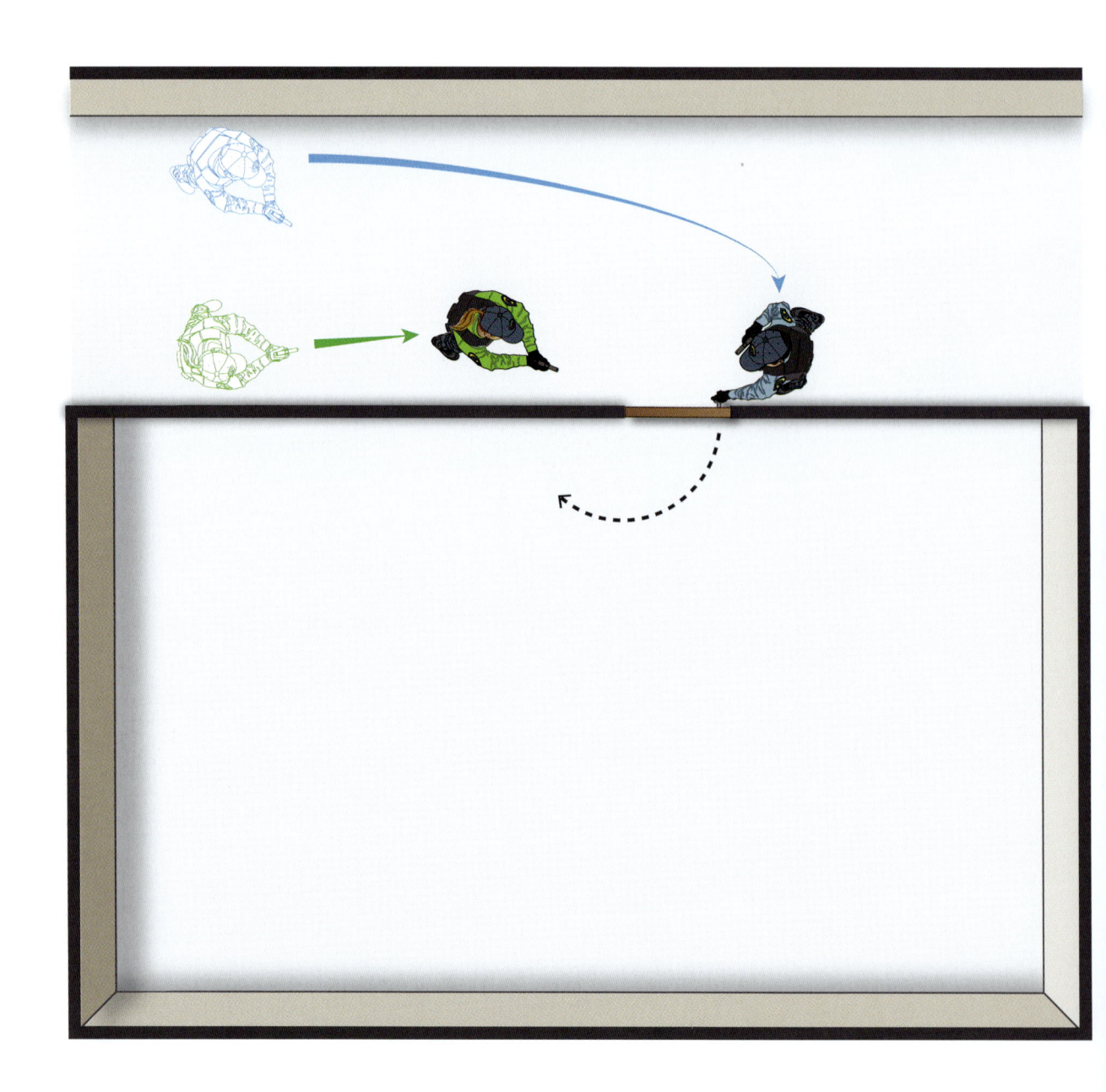

Two-Person Operations: Hallways Immediate Entry   233

ENTERING A CLOSED DOOR FROM THE HALLWAY

STEP 3 - Enter the Room

Once the door is open, the two officers will enter the room using the techniques already described.

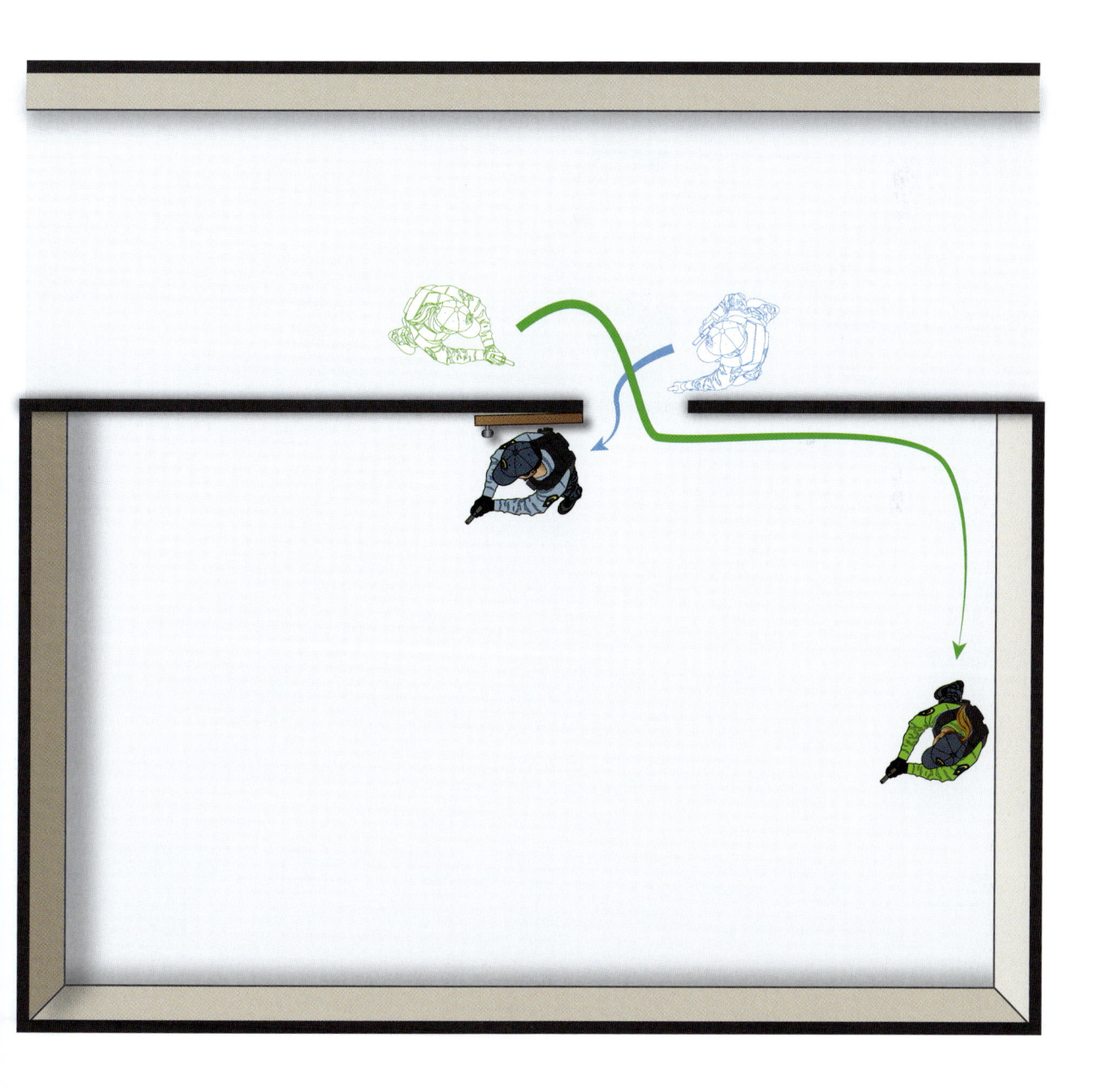

ENTERING OPPOSING OPEN DOORS

STEP 1 - Approach the Door

Opposing open doors (two open doors facing each other) is one of the more difficult configurations officers can face. This is because the officers cannot enter one door without exposing their backs to the other door. The two officers will maintain cross coverage as they approach the opposing doors and decide which door to enter first. If the officers detect sound, movement or light coming from one of the doors, they should generally enter that door first.

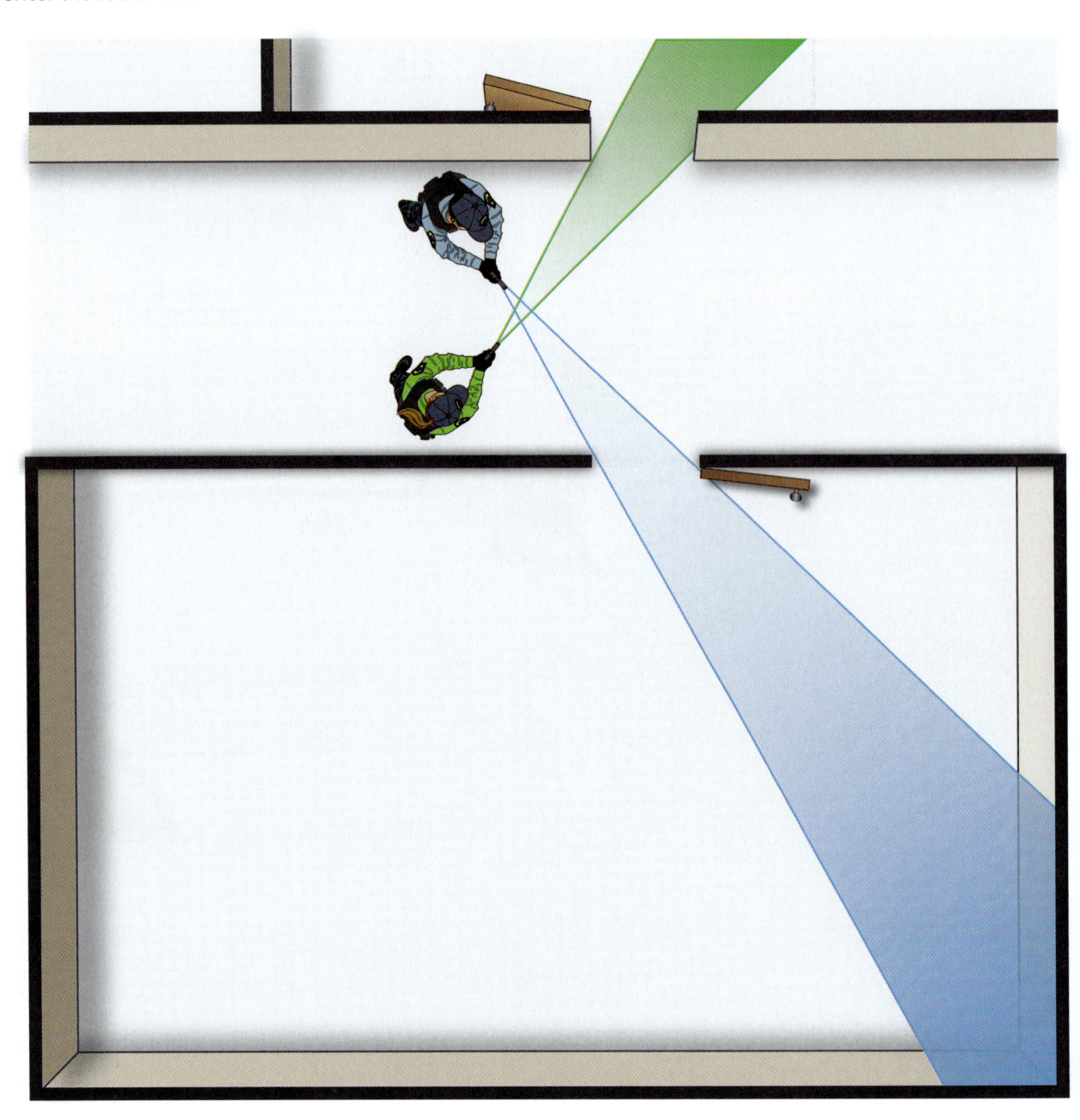

TWO-PERSON OPERATIONS: HALLWAYS IMMEDIATE ENTRY   235

ENTERING OPPOSING OPEN DOORS

STEP 2 - Hold on the Opposing Door and Enter

As the two officers maintaining cross coverage reach the open doors, the officer on the entry side will pause momentarily before entering the room and the other officer will stack right behind the lead officer while covering the opposing door. The second officer will give a squeeze to the first officer and then give up coverage of the opposing door and both officers will enter the room.

MOVING FROM A ROOM INTO THE HALLWAY

STEP 1 - Stack on the Door

When two officers clear a room and then want to move back into the hallway, they will first stack on the door. They will then decide which direction they want to move.

MOVING FROM A ROOM INTO THE HALLWAY

STEP 2 - Clear Left and Right

Once the officers determine which direction they want to move, one officer will move up to the door and quickly clear left and right down the hall, while still taking advantage of the cover and concealment provided by the room.

MOVING FROM A ROOM INTO THE HALLWAY

STEP 3 - Resume Movement in the Direction of Travel
Once the hallway is clear, the lead officer will move back into the hall and the second officer will follow behind.

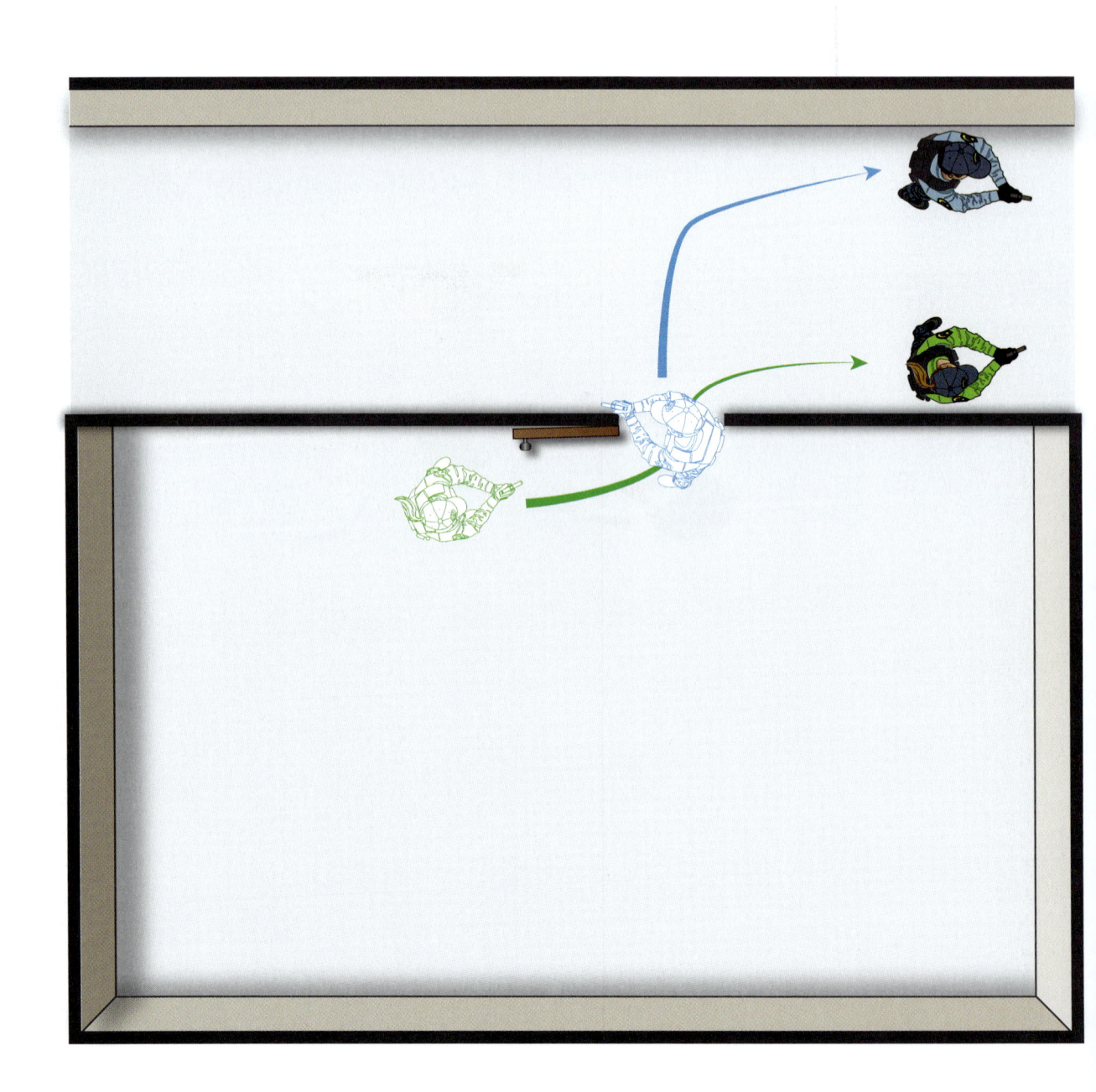

TWO-PERSON OPERATIONS: HALLWAYS IMMEDIATE ENTRY 239

MOVING ACROSS A HALLWAY INTO ANOTHER ROOM

Complete Sequence

When two officers clear a room but then want to move back across the hallway into another room, they will first stack on the door. Because there are only two officers, they will have to "clear on the move" as they cross the hallway. One officer will clear on the move facing right and the other officer will clear on the move facing left. They will then enter the room using the techniques already explained.

L-SHAPE INTERSECTION: HIGH-LOW TECHNIQUE

STEP 1 - Lead Officer Kneels

The high-low technique is used to clear a hallway when speed is not critical and the lead officer expects danger around the corner. Essentially, the high-low can be useful if officers want to maximize the cover and concealment provided by the corner and don't want to overly expose themselves in the hallway. The lead officer will kneel on one knee while maintaining front security. The inside knee nearest to the wall should go down because it offers the best and most natural pivot point. The lead officer should orient his/her weapon at about a 45-degree angle off the corner and be sure not to let the weapon protrude beyond the corner where adversaries might see it. When moving close to the corner, officers should also make sure their shadows do not extend into the hall.

L-SHAPE INTERSECTION: HIGH-LOW TECHNIQUE

STEP 2 - Second Officer Provides Support

The second officer will assume a position at a slight angle away from the lead officer and provide additional cover on the corner. Both officers will be covering the corner but the second officer will be remaining situationally aware and checking the rear as necessary.

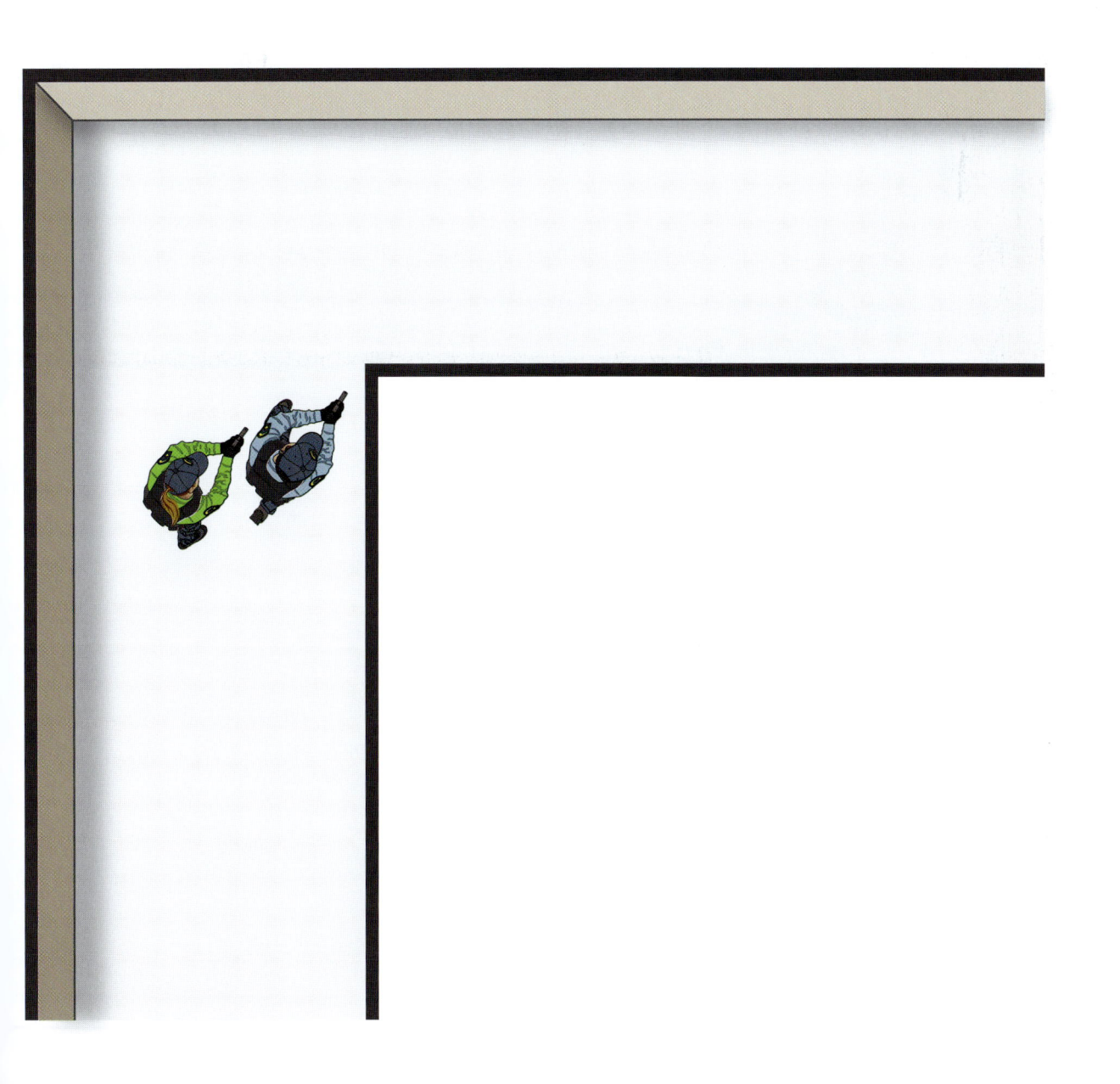

L-SHAPE INTERSECTION: HIGH-LOW TECHNIQUE

STEP 3 - Corner Clear

Once in position, the second officer will give the ready signal (shoulder or arm squeeze) to the lead officer to initiate the corner clearing process. The lead officer will pause briefly to allow the second officer to reset and bring his/her hand back to the weapon. When ready, both officers will shift position outward around the corner and clear the hallway while still taking advantage of the cover/concealment provided by the corner and exposing themselves as little as possible. The second officer also has the option of moving across the hall to get a better angle of observation down the hall and to create more separation with the first officer. However, moving across the hall makes the second officer more exposed to hostile fire.

L-SHAPE INTERSECTION: HIGH-LOW TECHNIQUE

STEP 4 - Pick-up and Move

After clearing the corner, the two officers will continue movement down the hallway, maintaining cross coverage. To initiate movement, the second officer will reach down with the non-firing hand and "pick-up" the lead officer. The lead officer must remain in place and remain kneeling until the other officer picks him/her up. This is important because of the increased risk that can come if a kneeling officer unexpectedly stands up into the line of fire of the other officer.

L-SHAPE INTERSECTION: NEAR-FAR TECHNIQUE

STEP 1 - Lead Officer Prepares to Clear

This technique is similar to the high-low technique but it is faster and easier to execute. For the near-far, the lead officer will not assume a kneeling position, but will instead clear from the standing position. As the two officers reach the corner, the lead officer will cover the corner and provide front security. The lead officer should orient his/her weapon at about a 45-degree angle off the corner and be sure not to let the weapon extend beyond the corner where adversaries might see it. When moving close to the corner, officers should also make sure their shadows do not extend into the hall.

L-SHAPE INTERSECTION: NEAR-FAR TECHNIQUE

STEP 2 - Second Officer Provides Support

The second officer will assume a position at a slight angle away from the lead team officer and provide additional cover on the corner.

L-SHAPE INTERSECTION: NEAR-FAR TECHNIQUE

STEP 3 - Corner Clear

Once in position, the second officer will give the ready signal (shoulder or arm squeeze) to the lead officer to initiate the corner clearing process. The lead officer will pause briefly to allow the second officer to reset and bring his/her hand back to the weapon. When ready, both officers will swing around the corner and clear the hallway. The lead officer will stay close to the corner, taking advantage of cover/concealment. The second officer will push across to the opposite side of the hallway, maintaining good spacing from the lead officer.

L-SHAPE INTERSECTION: NEAR-FAR TECHNIQUE

STEP 4 - Continue Movement

After clearing the corner, the officers will continue movement down the hallway, maintaining cross coverage.

T-SHAPE INTERSECTION

STEP 1 - Approach the Intersection

As the officers approach the intersection they will maintain cross coverage on the corners. Before reaching the intersection they will decide which direction to move. When moving close to the corner, officers should also make sure their shadows do not extend into the hall.

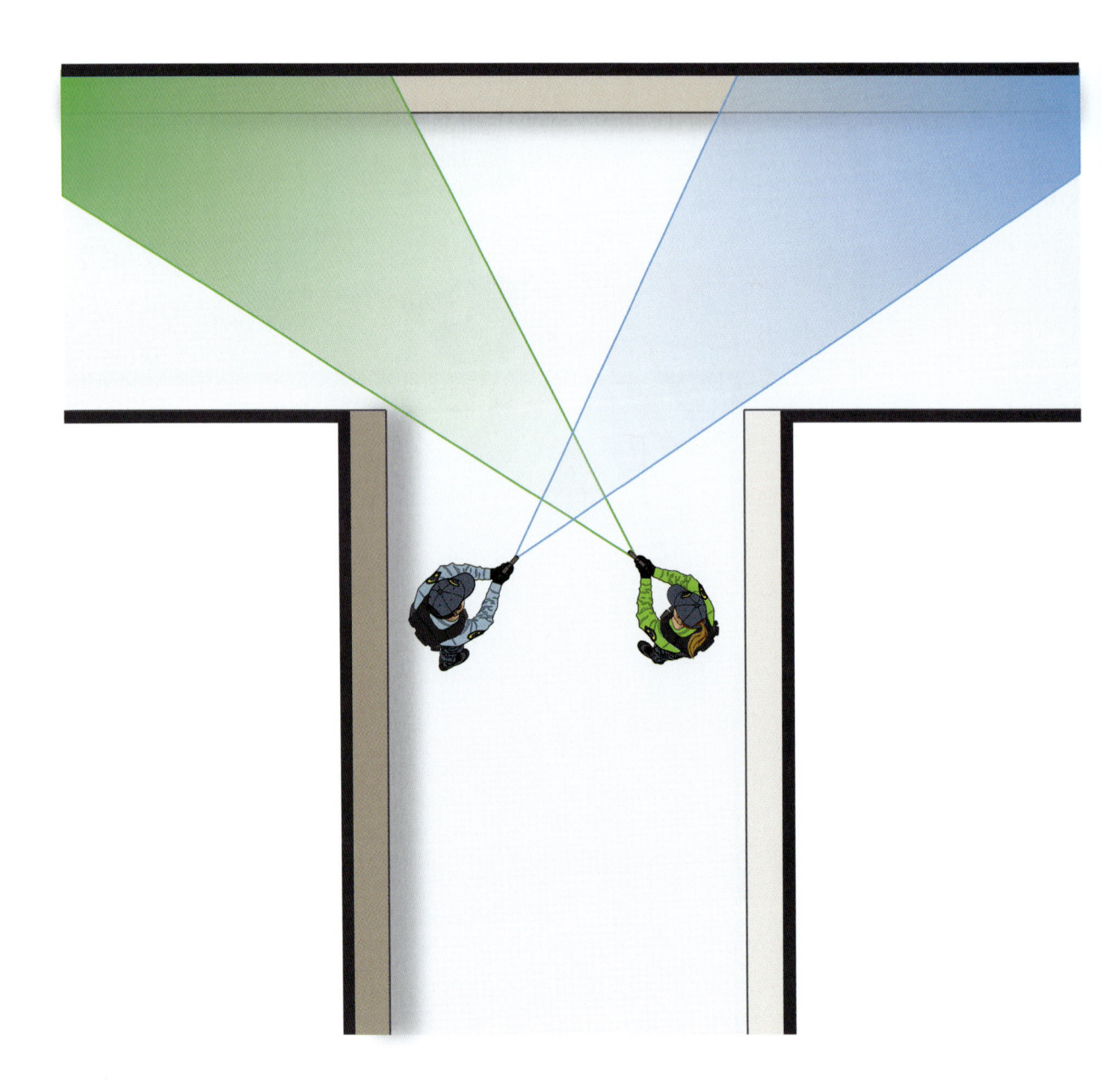

T-SHAPE INTERSECTION

STEP 2 - Clear the Intersection

Once the officers reach their corners they will give up their cross coverage, switch to same-side coverage and clear their corners simultaneously.

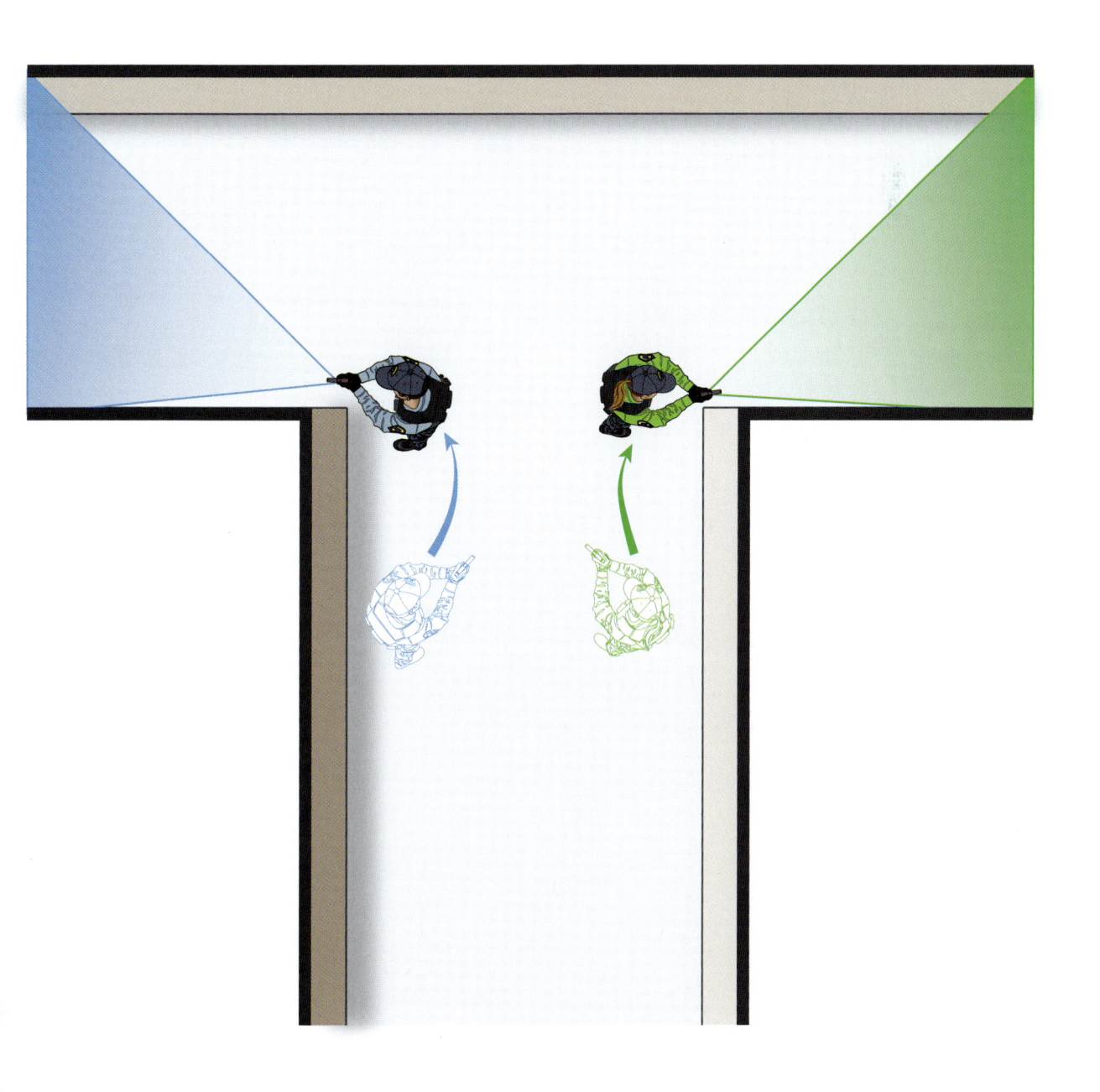

T-SHAPE INTERSECTION

STEP 3 - Move Down the Hall

Once the intersection is clear, the officers will move down the hallway in the desired direction of movement maintaining cross coverage.

Two-Person Operations: Hallways Immediate Entry

X-SHAPE INTERSECTION

STEP 1 - Approach the Intersection

Clearing an X-shape intersection is similar to clearing a T-shape intersection except there is an additional possible direction of travel and additional angles to cover. The officers will approach the intersection maintaining cross coverage but also remaining aware of threats to the front.

X-SHAPE INTERSECTION

STEP 2 - Clear the Intersection

Once the officers reach their corners they will give up their cross coverage, switch to same-side coverage and clear their corners simultaneously.

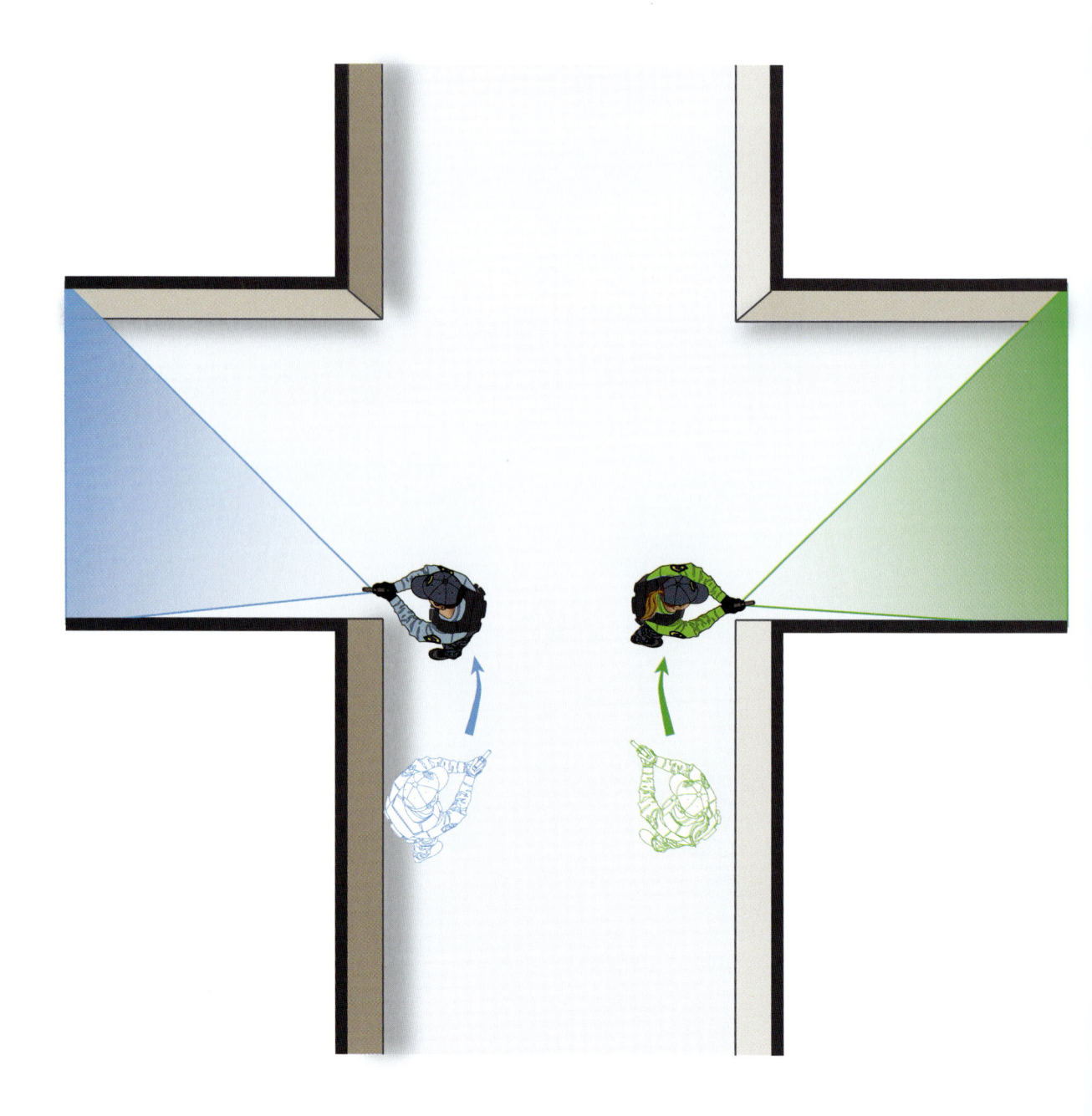

X-SHAPE INTERSECTION

STEP 3 - Move Down the Hall

Once the intersection is clear, the officers will either make a turn and move down the hallway or continue moving straight ahead. It is critical to move quickly away from the intersection to minimize the time that the officers are exposed from four directions.

INTERSECTIONS WITH UNEVEN CORNERS

COMPLETE SEQUENCE

In some situations, two officers may encounter a T-intersection or X-intersection with uneven corners. The clearing process for uneven corners is very similar to the process for even corners. The main difference is that with uneven corners, one officer should clear the near corner slightly before the other officer clears the far corner. If the officers cleared the corners simultaneously, the officer clearing the far corner would be exposing his/her back to the opposing hallway.

CLEARING INTERSECTIONS ON THE MOVE

COMPLETE SEQUENCE

So far, all of the intersection clearing techniques have employed the clear and hold method. However, in an emergency clearing situation where time is critical, two officers can use the "clear on the move" method. Conducting the clear on the move is simple. Officers maintain their general formation and cross coverage and individually clear danger areas as the they pass. For example, to cross an X-shape intersection, the two officers would remain side-by-side but each officer would clear down the hallway on his/her side as the they passed through the intersection.

TWO-PERSON OPERATIONS
Hallways Delayed Entry

If officers are approaching a hallway intersection and detect a potential threat around the corner, they might want to slow down and employ a delayed clearing technique. An example of this is if the officers hear shots fired from around a corner. In that situation, the officers will probably not want to rush towards the intersection and move around the corner, unless there are innocent lives at stake.

If the two-person team decides to employ a delayed hallway clearing technique, one of the officers will move forward towards the intersection while the other officer stays back at a safe distance. The clearing officer will move forward cautiously and may choose to use some of the single-person clearing techniques described later in this book. It is critical that the clearing officer makes as little noise as possible and avoids letting shadows extend into the intersection.

The following diagram only shows how to clear an L-shape intersection. However, the single clearing officer can use the same principle to clear a T-shape or X-shape intersection. For more detailed instructions on single-person clearing, see the single-person operations section of the book.

Once the intersection is clear, the other officer can move forward to continue down the hallway in the desired direction of movement. In other cases, if the clearing officer encounters hostile fire, he/she may choose to fall back. At this point, the two officers can decide whether to attempt to clear the intersection or to fall back to a room or a safer location.

One of the most critical factors to consider is that the clearing officer should not advance so far that the other officer will not be able to provide casualty evacuation. Both officers should remain in visual contact and position themselves to be mutually supporting.

DELAYED ENTRY: L OR T-SHAPE INTERSECTIONS

COMPLETE SEQUENCE

Clearing an L-shape intersection using the delayed technique is very similar to the immediate technique. However, the main difference with delayed intersection clearing is that one officer stays back from the intersection to minimize exposure while the other officer moves up to clear the intersection. The officer can clear the corner from either the standing or kneeling position. Another important difference is that with delayed clearing, once the lead officer clears around the corner, both officers might decide to fall back down the hallway or establish security in a nearby room. Clearing a T-intersection is almost the same process, except the officer will need to conduct a quick-clear to both the left and right.

TWO-PERSON OPERATIONS
Stairwells

Stairwells are even more dangerous than hallways for several reasons. First of all, in commercial or industrial buildings, stairwells typically consist of sturdy metal and concrete construction with steel beams, which means bullets are more likely to ricochet off the solid walls. Adversaries can also toss grenades down the stairs without exposing themselves.

Because officers cannot spread out and create dispersion in the stairwell, they are particularly vulnerable to these sorts of indiscriminate attacks. Officers are even more vulnerable because it is difficult to move quickly up or down stairs without tripping, particularly in the dark.

Therefore, officers should move up or down stairwells as quickly as possible in order to get out of the stairwell to a safer location. While it is critical to move fast, officers must not move so fast that they trip or fall down the stairs. This can be a very real danger, particularly in high-stress situations or when under fire. It is also critical that officers not walk backwards up or down stairs since this makes the chances of tripping even more likely.

The following techniques are the same whether officers are moving up or down the stairwell and are very similar to the procedures for clearing a stairwell with a full team. The officers will first occupy the stairwell's landing or entryway just as they would an ordinary room. At this point the officers will begin to move up or down the stairs, staying as close to the outer railing as possible. This allows the officers to have the best angles of observation around bends in the stairs.

Each time the lead officer reaches a landing, he/she will quickly turn and cover the shaft of the stairwell in the direction of movement. The other officer will then move quickly past to cover the shaft from the next landing. The officers will continue to bound forward in this way from landing to landing. If an officer encounters a landing with a door, he/she will need to stand at an angle to cover both the shaft and the door if possible.

Officers may also encounter "open stairwells," particularly in residential structures. When clearing an open stairwell the two officers will need to move up the stairs to clear the upper floor. When conducting this movement, it is critical that officers not walk backwards up the stairs since doing so can make it very easy to trip. Instead, officers should walk forward up the stairs, pausing or turning as necessary to check various angles of the upper floor.

COMMERCIAL STAIRWELL

STEP 1 - Enter and Clear

Before the two officers can move up or down the stairs, they must enter and clear the stairwell landing just as they would clear a room. The two officers will enter and clear in opposite directions, scanning the landing and checking behind the door.

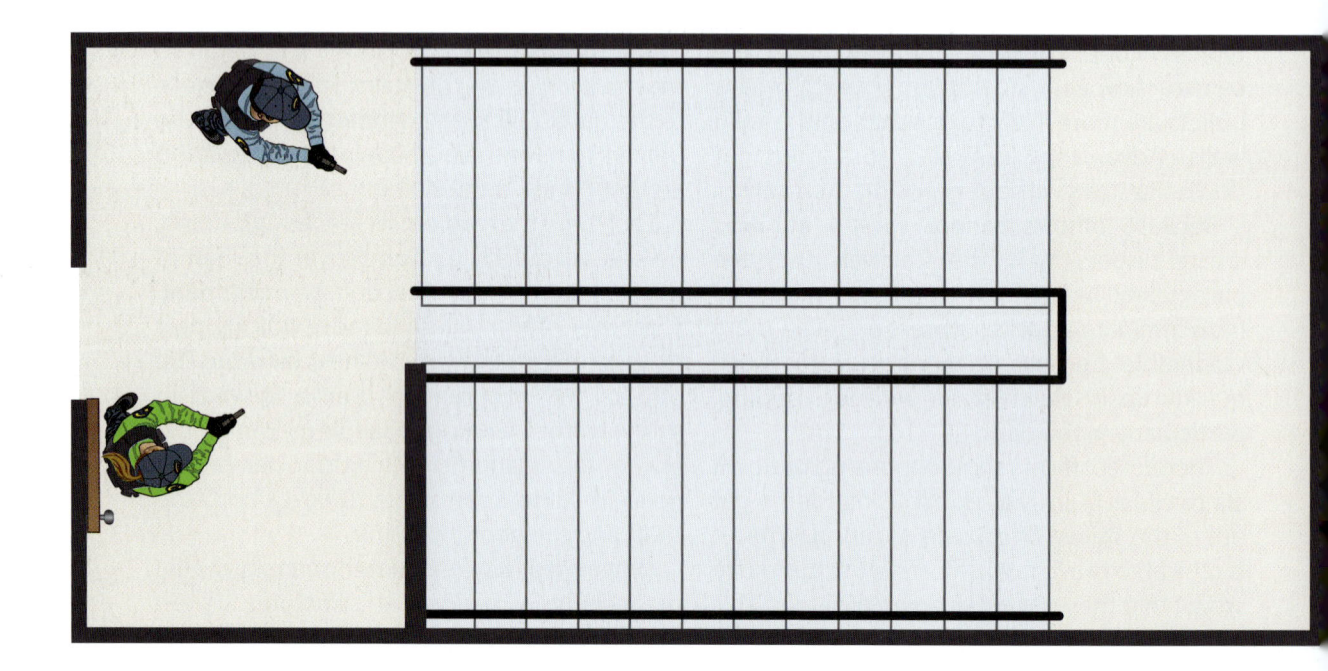

Two-Person Operations: Stairwells   261

COMMERCIAL STAIRWELL

STEP 2 - Move Up/Down the Stairs to the First Landing

Once the initial space is dominated, the officer closest to the stairs will move up or down the stairwell to the first landing, keeping as close as possible to the wall, away from the center banister. This will offer the best angle to see around the bend in the stairs. The lead officer should turn towards the bend in the stairwell as he/she moves, being careful not to trip. This way the officer will be ready to engage any adversaries waiting around the bend in the stairs as soon as they emerge. The lead officer will move all the way to the first landing and then cover the stairwell shaft in the direction of movement.

COMMERCIAL STAIRWELL

STEP 3 - Leapfrog to the Next Landing

When the lead officer reaches the first landing his/her weapon should already be oriented pointing up/down the shaft of the stairwell. At this point the other officer will move around the first officer and head to the next landing to repeat the process. As the moving officer passes behind the covering officer and continues up/ down the stairs, the lead officer will shift coverage to cover the rear. Once the moving officer reaches the next landing and establishes security on the shaft, the other officer will pick up and move, repeating the leapfrog process.

COMMERCIAL STAIRWELL

STEP 4 - Cover the Door

If there is a door on the landing, either open or closed, the covering officer will have to position him or herself in order to cover both the next landing and the door.

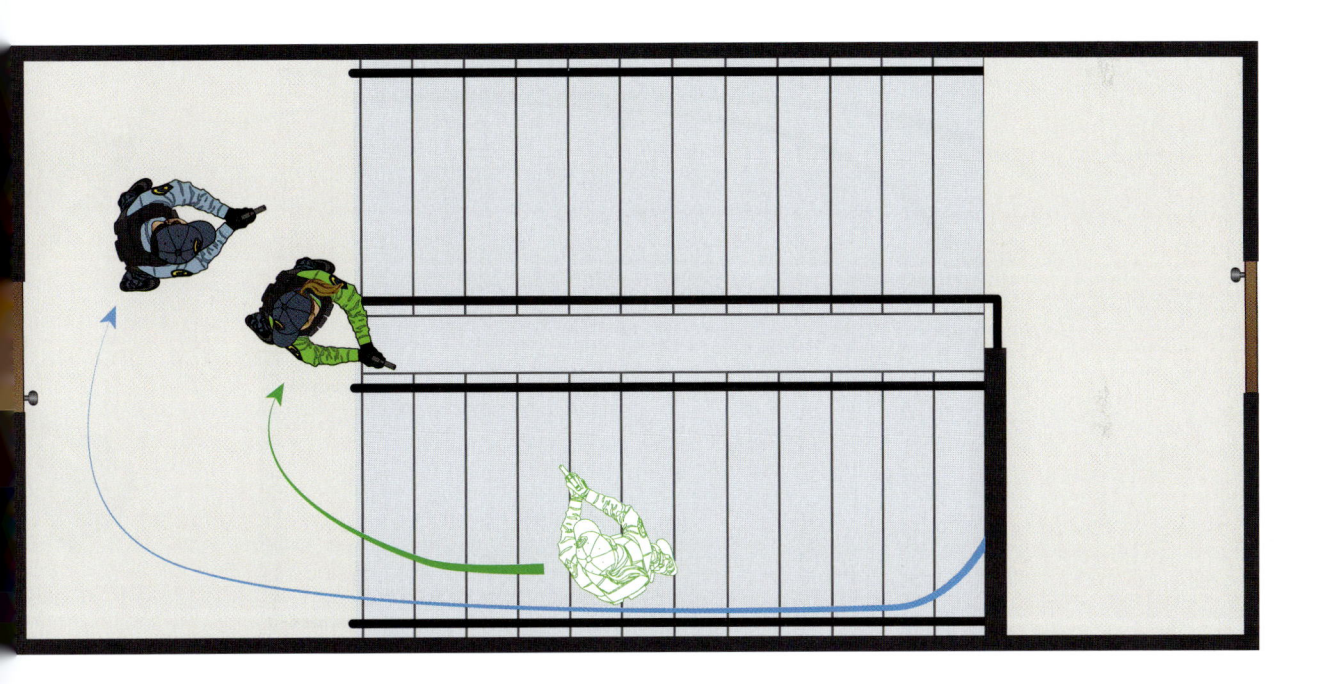

COMMERCIAL STAIRWELL

STEP 5 - Exit the Stairwell

Once the officers reach the desired floor, they will stack on the door and exit the stairwell just as they would exit a normal room

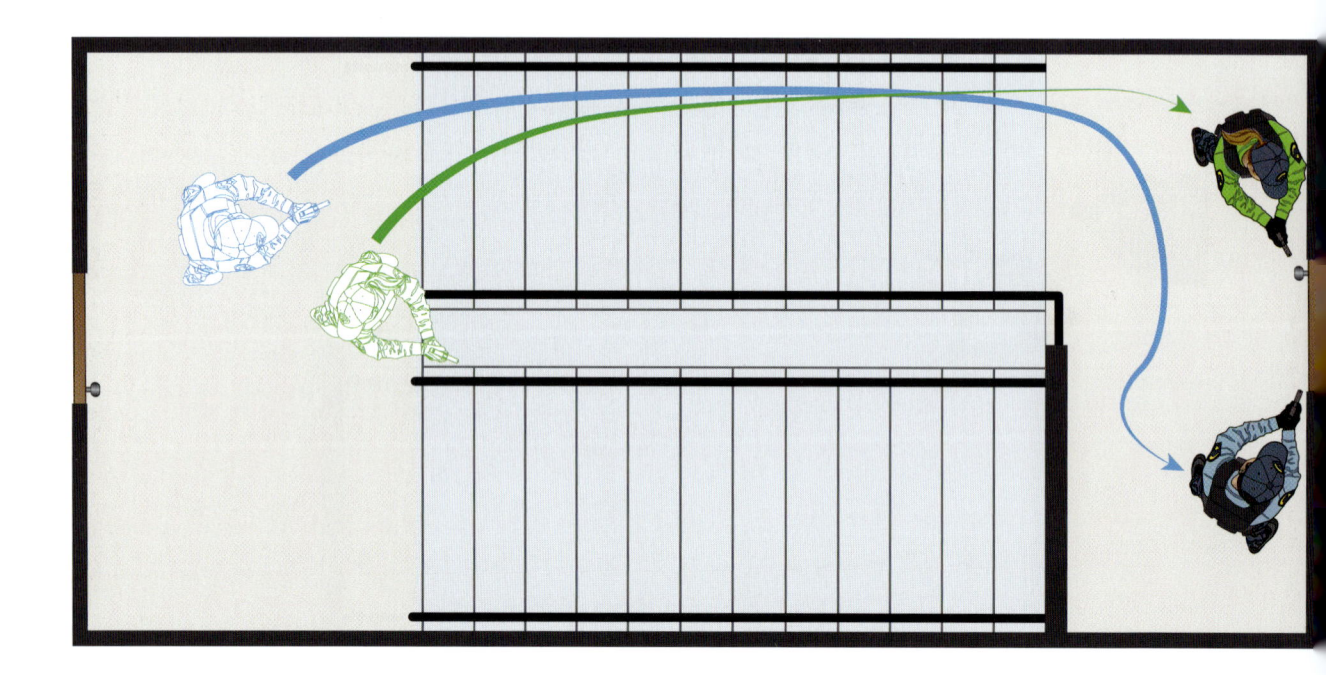

OPEN STAIRWELL

STEP 1 - Check the Upper Floor

Open stairwells that open directly into a room or hallway are common in residential architecture. Open stairwells are particularly dangerous because adversaries have a perfect vantage point from the upper floor to shoot officers as they move up the stairs. Therefore, officers should move quickly to a vantage point where they can ensure the upper floor is secure before moving too far up the stairs. Once reaching the stairwell, the lead officer will cover forward up the stairs. The second officer will turn 180-degrees (or as far as necessary) and look up to check the upper floor.

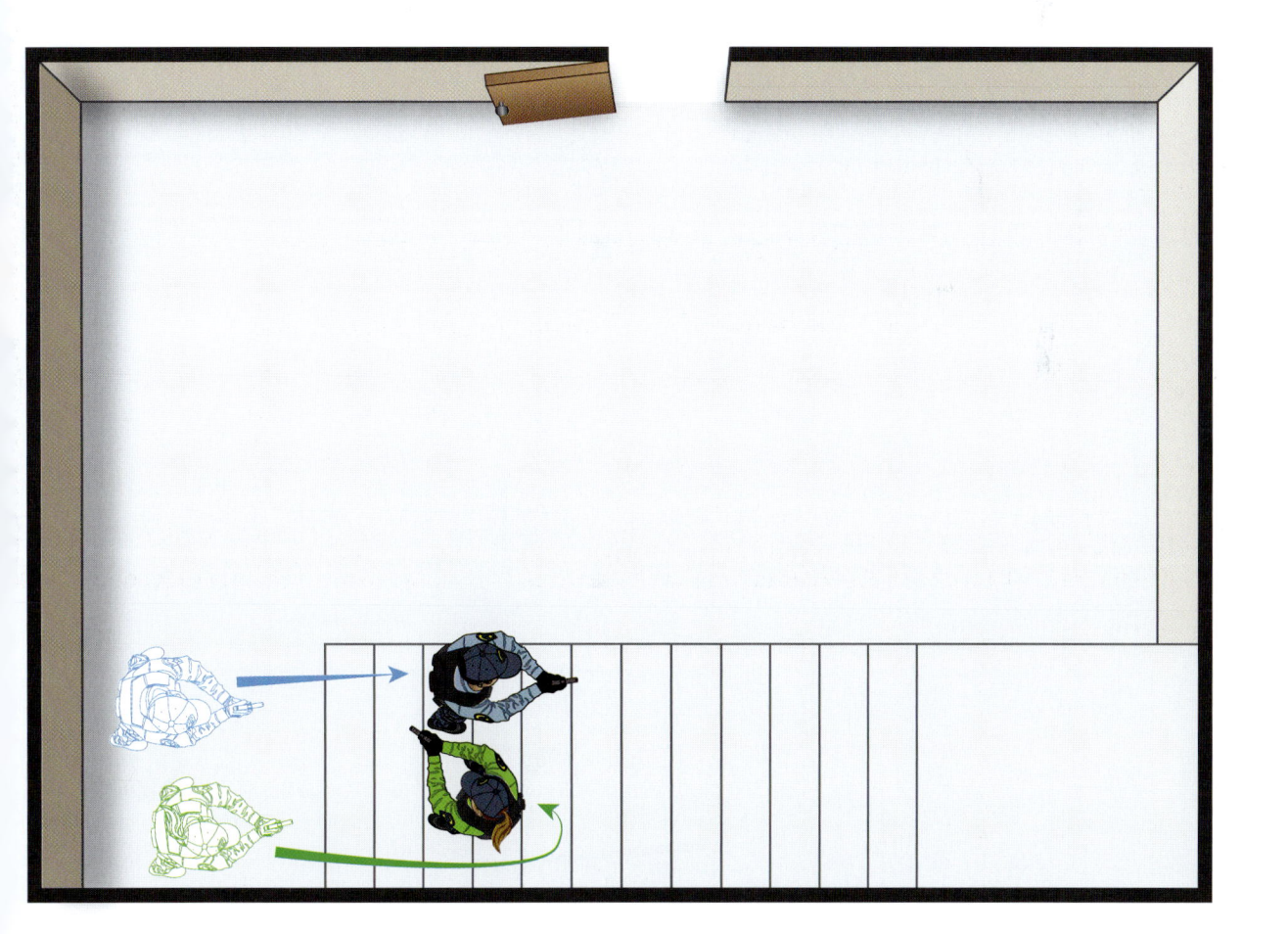

OPEN STAIRWELL

STEP 2 - Move Up the Stairs

If the upper floor appears secure, both officers can move farther up the stairs. It is important that the second officer not walk backwards since doing so can be hazardous. Instead the second officer should walk forwards, moving as quickly as possible, but pause if necessary to turn 180-degrees and recheck the upper floor landing. It is necessary to recheck to ensure an adversary is not crouching or lying in wait. The second officer can pause when needed to ensure the area is clear. At a certain point, when the second officer has moved up far enough to ensure there are no adversaries hiding on the upper floor, both officers can move past the stairwell.

TWO-PERSON OPERATIONS
Complex Configurations and Obstacles

When officers clear houses and buildings in a real-life scenario, they will encounter many different combinations of furniture, obstacles and complex room configurations. This next section provides some basic principles for dealing with these types of tactical problems.

Furniture is the most common obstacle officers will encounter in a room. Furniture deep in the room can provide covered positions for enemies to hide. Officers must be able to move deeper into the room to check behind furniture.

The procedures for moving around furniture placed along the walls of a room is the same as for a full team (see the team operations section for more details). Furniture is often positioned along walls, which naturally interferes with officers' movement towards their domination points. Officers must be prepared to quickly move around obstacles to prevent the team from losing momentum.

Confined areas with multiple openings (such as foyers, entryways or vestibules) are also very common in modern architecture and present a difficult tactical problem for a two-person team. Rather than try to dominate these danger areas, the officers should quickly move past them into a room that offers better protection.

Another common configuration found in commercial structures, are larger rooms filled with cubicles. Cubicles are particularly dangerous since they must each be cleared individually and offer many hiding places for adversaries. When two officers must clear multiple cubicles, it is usually best to split up and clear cubicles simultaneously on both sides of an aisle.

LARGE OBSTACLE DEEP IN THE ROOM

STEP 1 - Dominate the Room

In some cases, two officers will dominate a room but there will still be large obstacles or pieces of furniture deep in the room where an adversary might be hiding. In these cases, the officers will first dominate the room as they usually would, watching carefully in case adversaries pop out from behind furniture deep in the room.

LARGE OBSTACLE DEEP IN THE ROOM

STEP 2 - Officer Calls "Going Deep"

At this point, one officer will identify the obstacle and prepare to move to clear behind it. The officer will call out "going deep" to notify the other officer that he/she will be moving deep into the room. If the two officers have experience working together, they can also use hand-and-arm signals instead of verbal commands to maintain the element of surprise. The officer will begin to move in an arc to clear behind the obstacle or furniture.

LARGE OBSTACLE DEEP IN THE ROOM

STEP 3 - Second Officer Follows in Support

Once the lead officer starts moving, the second officer should move with the lead officer to provide support needed. It is always better to clear an obstacle or danger area with two officers. In some cases the officers will establish a "tactical L" to clear the obstacle from two angles. In other cases, like a large cabinet or closet, one officer might have to open the door while the other officer covers the opening. Once the danger area is clear, the clearing officer will call out "clear" to notify the other officer that it is safe to proceed. If the two officers have experience working together, they can also use non-verbal signals to identify the area as clear.

Two-Person Operations: Complex Configurations and Obstacles   271

CONFINED AREAS WITH MULTIPLE OPENINGS

STEP 1 - Officers Enter and Commit to One Opening

Confined areas with multiple openings are very common in architectural designs. These types of configurations can be found in the entryway or foyer of many residential homes. When the officers enter, they will find themselves in a very vulnerable position with multiple openings and danger areas all around. Therefore, the they will not want to "dominate" this area since it will not really be dominating anything. Instead, the leader will make a quick decision to commit to one of the openings and call out "go right… go right" or "go left… go left."

CONFINED AREAS WITH MULTIPLE OPENINGS

STEP 2 - Hold and Enter

One officer will hold and provide security in the opposite direction while the other officer passes though into the opening. The holding officer will become the last officer into the room. Alternatively, both officers can use the clear on the move technique.

CONFINED AREAS WITH MULTIPLE OPENINGS

STEP 3 - Prepare For Next Movement

Once the officers have dominated a real room and are out of the confined area, they will be in a safer position to look and listen for threats and plan the next move, which could call for moving quickly back across the confined area or moving into other rooms.

CUBICLE CONFIGURATIONS

STEP 1 - Officers Dominate the Entire Room

If the officers enter a room filled with cubicles, the first step is to enter and dominate the room just like a normal room. Once the room is dominated, the officers will prepare to adjust formation to clear each cubicle individually.

Two-Person Operations: Complex Configurations and Obstacles   275

CUBICLE CONFIGURATIONS

STEP 2 - Move to the Center of the Aisle

For clearing very small areas like a cubicle when there are only two officers, the officers can move down the aisle together and clear in opposite directions. This means each officer will clear a cubicle by himself/herself. While this is dangerous, it is the generally the best option when there are just two officers. To prepare for this process, the two officers will move away from their domination points and come together near the center of the room.

CUBICLE CONFIGURATIONS

STEP 3 - Clear Cubicles Simultaneously

The two officers will move down the aisle maintaining cross coverage. As the officers reach the cubicles, they will peel off to clear the two opposing cubicles simultaneously. Once both cubicles are clear, the officers will exit and move to clear the next set of cubicles.

SECTION 3

ONE-PERSON OPERATIONS

ONE-PERSON OPERATIONS
Single-Room Clearing Without Entry

While it is never preferable for an officer to clear a building or house alone, there are some situations when an officer will have no other choice. This is particularly the case with patrol officers or security personnel who may find themselves responding alone to a terrorist attack, home invasion or armed robbery. While it is always safer to wait for backup, if there is an imminent danger to innocent civilians, an officer may choose to respond immediately to attempt to save innocent lives.

When operating alone, officers might often choose to avoid entering a room unless it is absolutely necessary to do so. This will help the officer minimize exposure and maximize personal safety. The officer will clear the room (as much as possible) from the outside and avoid getting drawn into a fight with adversaries who might possess superior numbers and weapons. By remaining outside of a room the officer also makes it easier to pull back away from danger and "call out" the adversary from a covered and concealed location if necessary.

To execute the clear without entry technique, the single officer will conduct a sweep of the target room, just as in the other delayed entry techniques. Once the sweep is complete, the officer may choose to conduct additional sweeps if necessary. Once the officer has cleared as much of the room as possible using the sweep technique, the officer will still need to clear the "deadspace" (or uncleared areas) in the corners of the room. To do this the officer will move forward and quickly clear both corners from the doorway.

Once this process is complete, the officer should not remain standing in the doorway but instead should quickly move away from the door to the next room. In some other cases, the officer might decide to enter the room after all. If the officer decides to enter the room, he/she will use one of the other entry techniques described later in this section.

CLEAR WITHOUT ENTRY: CENTER-FED OPEN DOOR

STEP 1 - Approach the Door

The officer will approach the open door from the outside of the room, and position close to the wall, several yards from the doorway. The officer will stay close to the wall but avoiding touching or bumping into it. Touching the wall will make noise and might also increase an officer's chances of getting shot, since bullets tend to travel along walls.

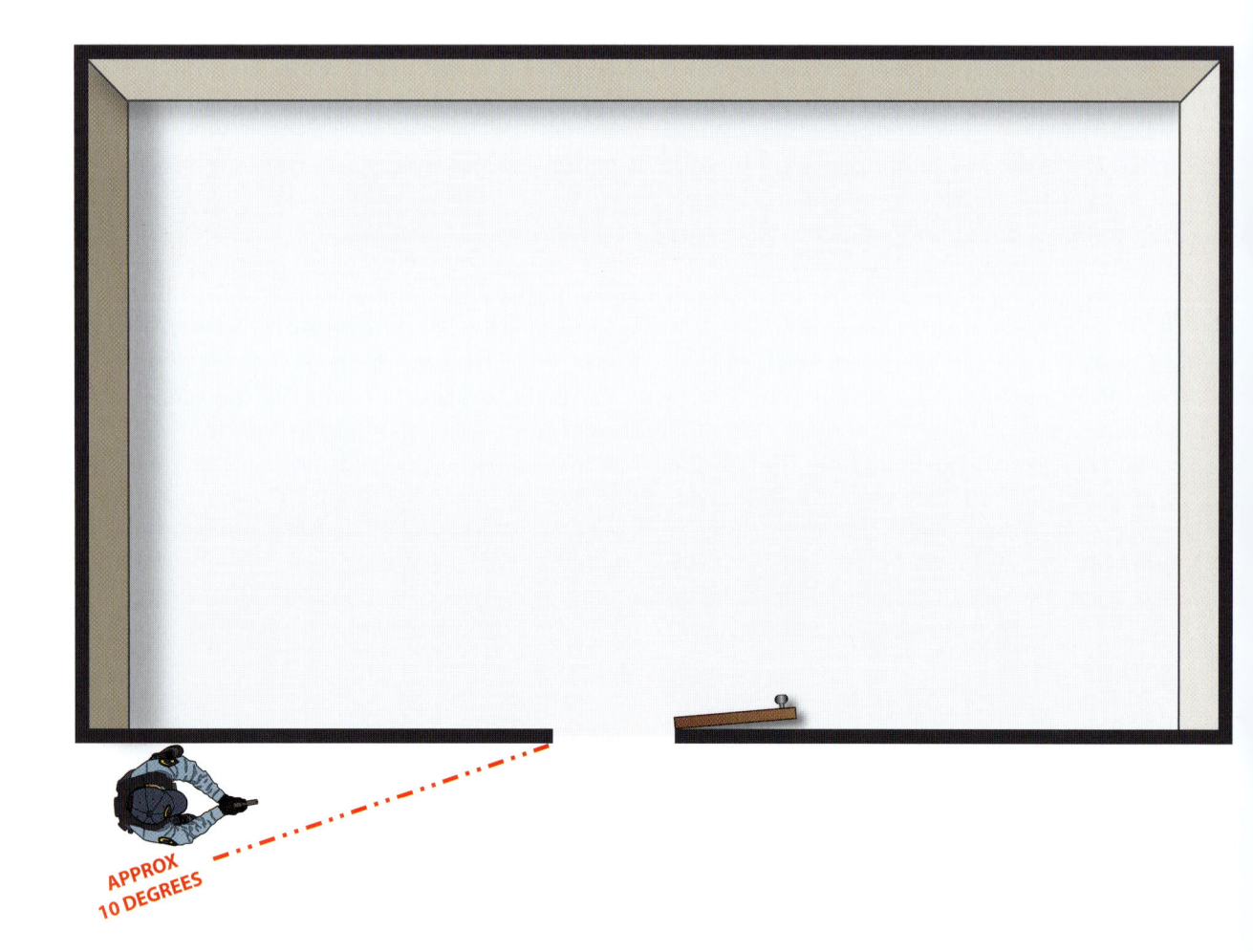

APPROX 10 DEGREES

ONE-PERSON OPERATIONS: SINGLE-ROOM CLEARING WITHOUT ENTRY   281

CLEAR WITHOUT ENTRY: CENTER-FED OPEN DOOR

STEP 2 - Avoid Indiscriminate fire

Staying away from the doorway is also important. Many adversaries, especially terrorists with automatic weapons, will not fire single, aimed shots but will rather spray bullets indiscriminately in the direction of any noise or potential threat. This spray of bullets will generally form an arc several yards wide. If an officer is detected close to a door, he/she might get hit with a barrage of bullets coming through the doorway and the walls surrounding the doorway. Remember, that most interior walls are not bulletproof and the chances of getting shot through a wall are very high. Staying several yards back from the door minimizes the chances of getting hit by indiscriminate fire.

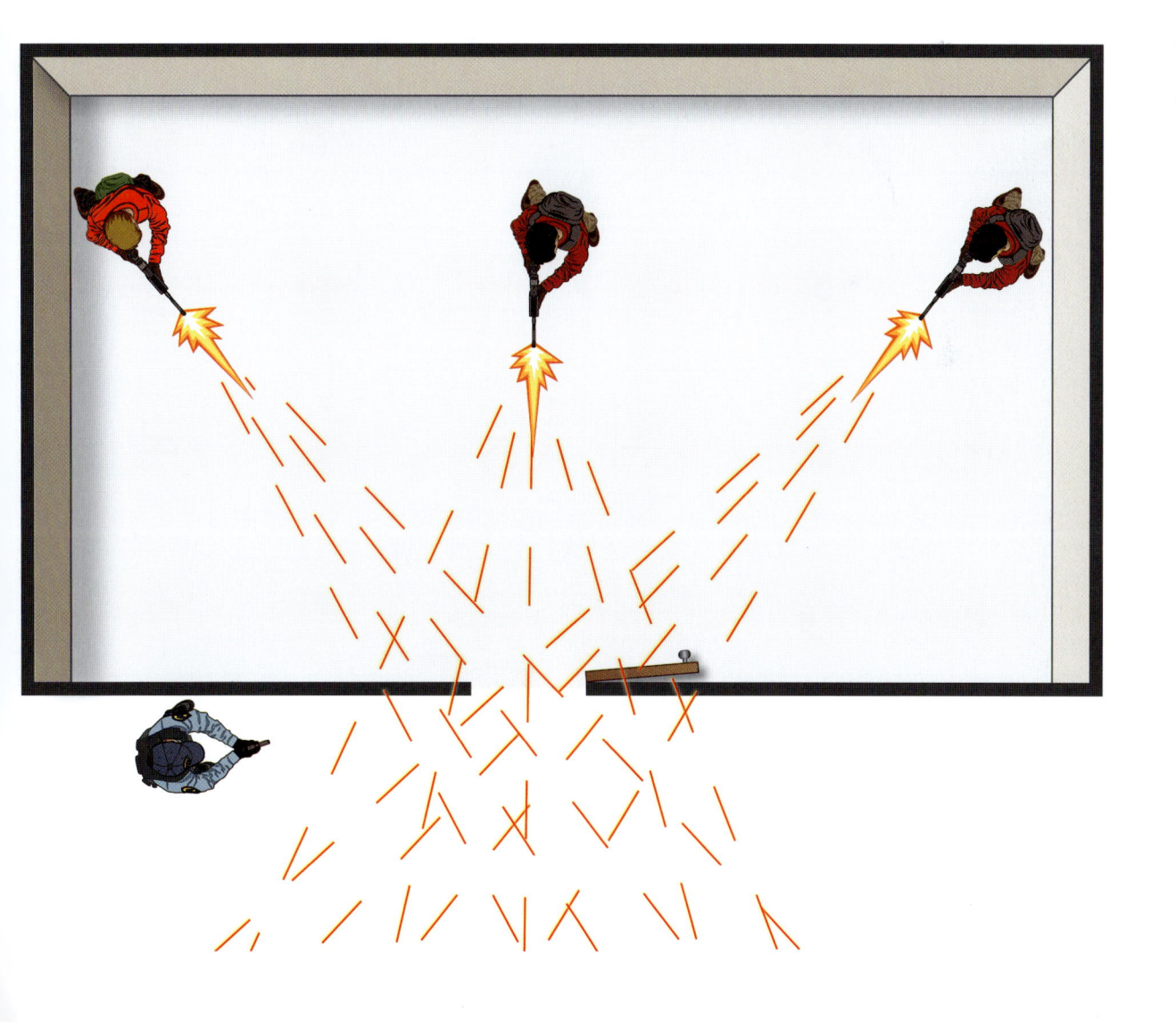

CLEAR WITHOUT ENTRY: CENTER-FED OPEN DOOR

STEP 3 - Watch For Shadow

Staying back from the door also minimizes the chances of detection, especially in terms of shadows created by interior lights. Most buildings have multiple light sources in each room or hallway. This means that when an officer comes close to an open door, someone standing inside the room can most likely see a shadow moving across the floor behind the opening. It is best to keep some distance from the door while remaining aware of shadows while moving. It is also critical to move quietly if possible and keeping away from the door makes it harder for adversaries to hear you.

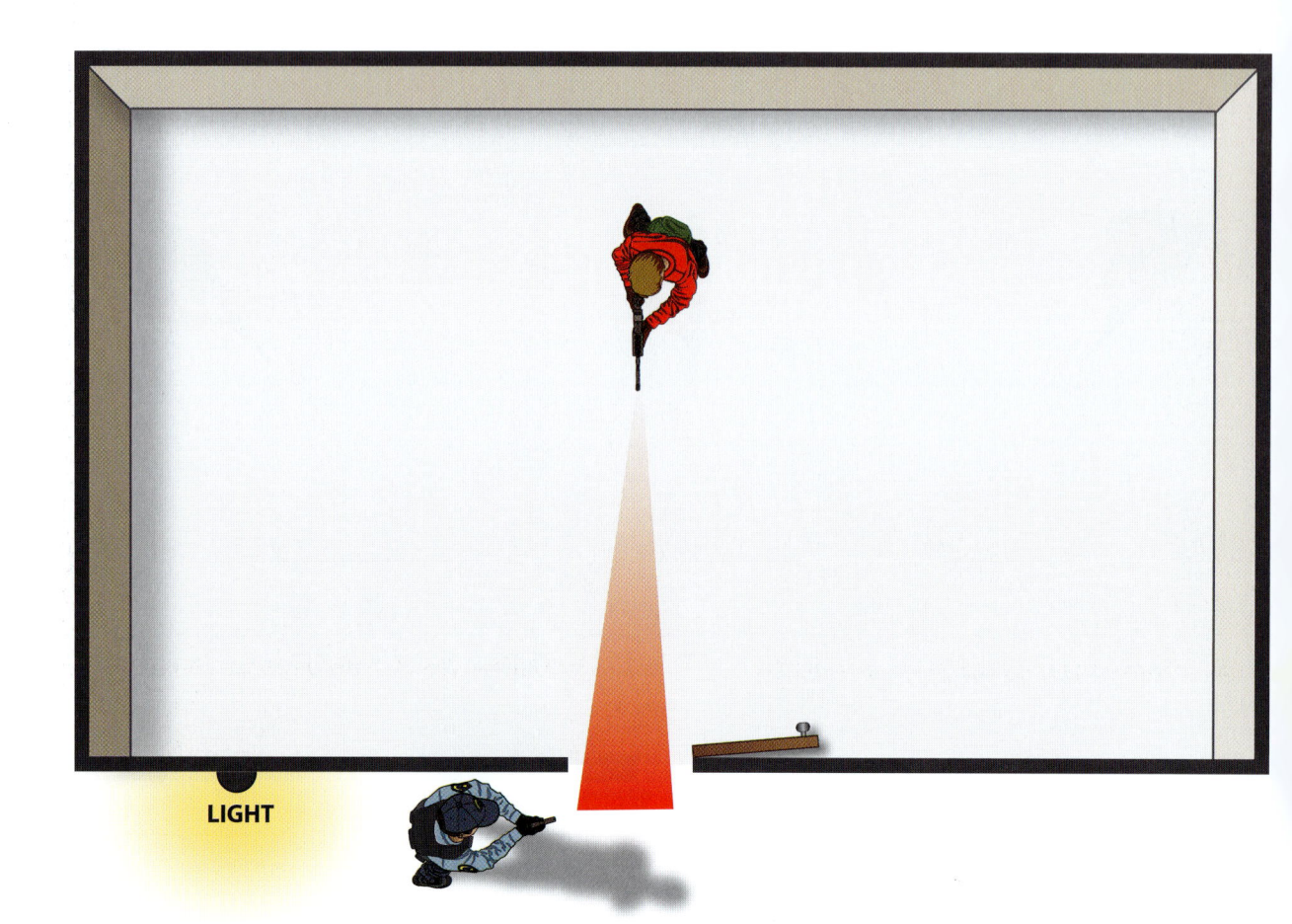

LIGHT

ONE-PERSON OPERATIONS: SINGLE-ROOM CLEARING WITHOUT ENTRY   283

CLEAR WITHOUT ENTRY: CENTER-FED OPEN DOOR

STEP 4 - Conduct "Sweep" Movement

The officer will then sweep out in a wide arc, keeping his/her weapon focused on the doorway. The officer will keep some distance from the door and move all the way across until positioned close to the wall on the opposite side of the door. The purpose of the sweep is to visually clear the room as quickly as possible to identify any threats inside and possibly draw those threats out of the room. When executing the sweep, the officer should move in an arc as fast as possible while keeping the weapon relatively steady and taking care not to trip. This means giving up some weapon accuracy in order to minimize exposure to hostile fire. Moving quickly will make it quite difficult for an adversary to shoot accurately, since the officer will be exposed for only a fraction of a second. Remember that bullets travel very fast and the officer will be an easy target if he/she stops moving. With practice officers can learn to engage targets accurately as they sweep across the door.

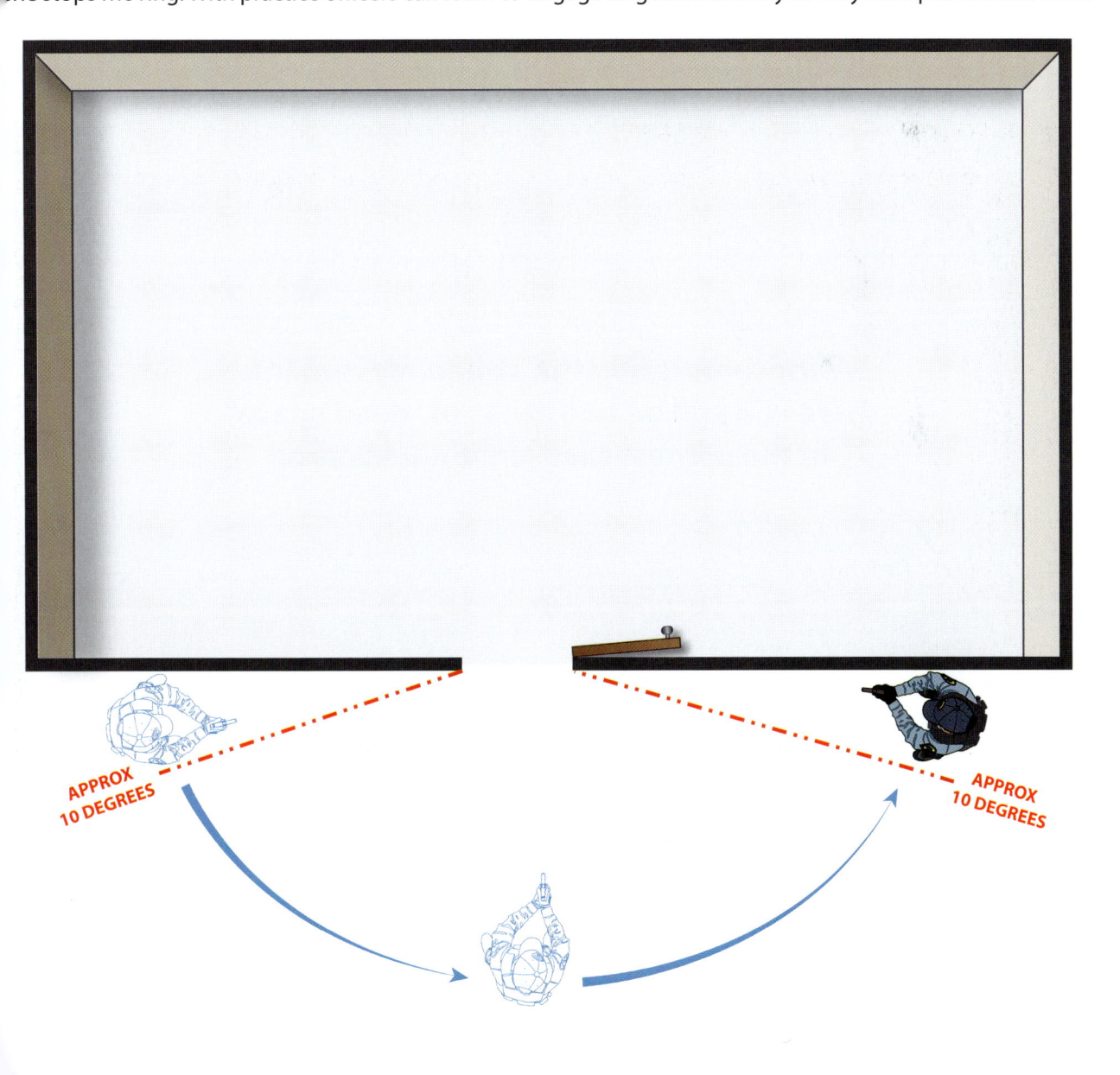

APPROX 10 DEGREES

APPROX 10 DEGREES

CLEAR WITHOUT ENTRY: CENTER-FED OPEN DOOR

STEP 5 - Recognize "Dead Space"

Once the officer reaches the opposite side of the door, he/she will keep some distance from the door since the adversary might fire indiscriminately in the direction of the doorway. The weapon should be at the ready focused on the door. One of the main advantages of the sweep technique is that it can draw adversaries out of the room, directly into the officer's sights as he/she waits covering the door. So, once the sweep is complete, the officer can wait momentarily to draw adversaries out or listen to hear movement coming from inside the room. However, the officer should not wait too long since remaining in place for extended periods can make easier it is for adversaries to maneuver offensively. The task of clearing the room is not yet complete because even if the sweep revealed no threats, there will still be two slices of "dead space" that are not yet clear in each corner of the target room.

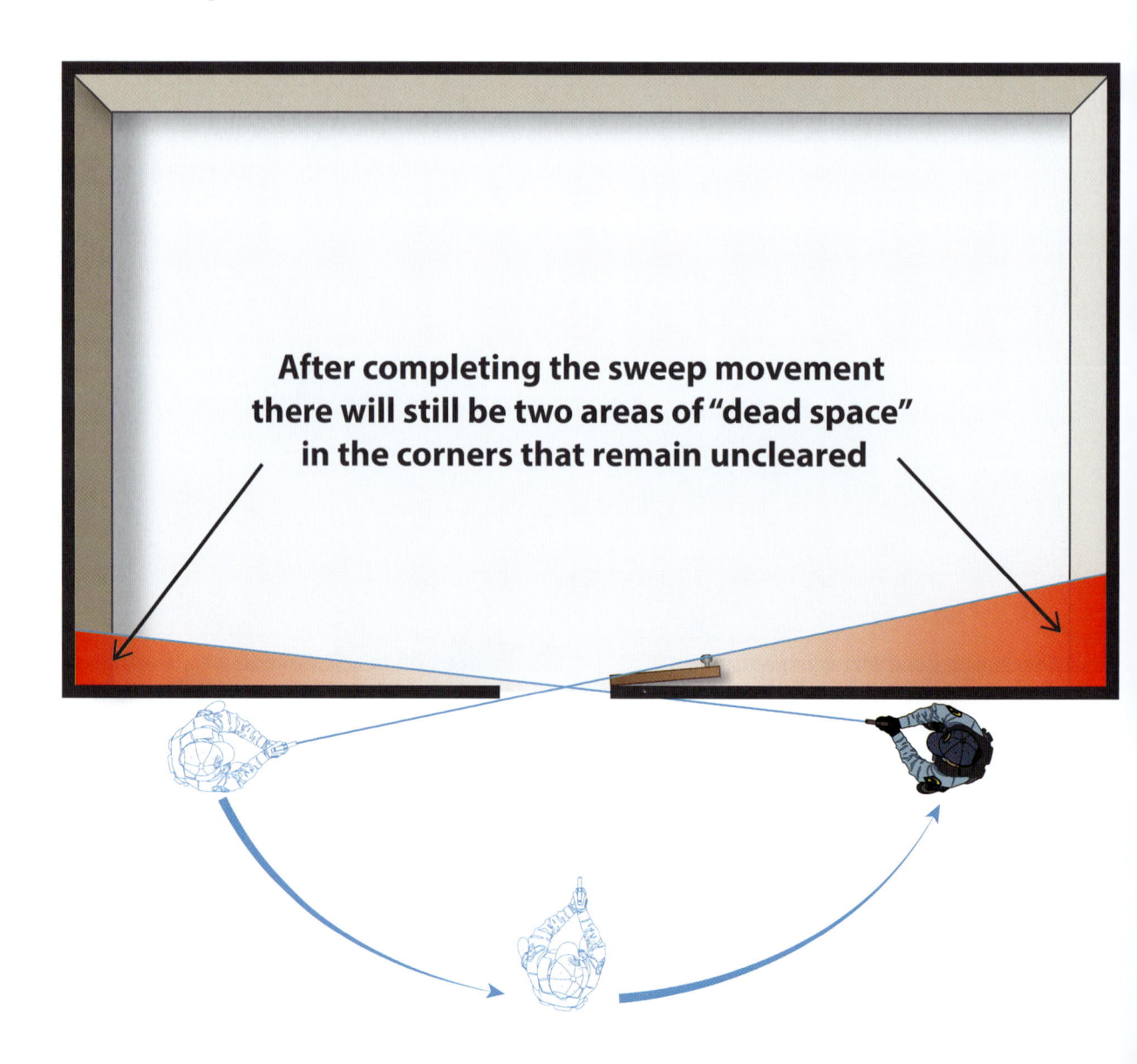

After completing the sweep movement there will still be two areas of "dead space" in the corners that remain uncleared

ONE-PERSON OPERATIONS: SINGLE-ROOM CLEARING WITHOUT ENTRY

CLEAR WITHOUT ENTRY: CENTER-FED OPEN DOOR

STEP 6 - Clear the Corner Away from the Door

To clear the two remaining corners, the officer will sweep along the arc in the opposite direction until he/she is facing directly towards the door. The officer will then move towards the door and lean into the room to clear one of the two corners once reaching the threshold. It is critical to expose as little of the body as possible. Generally, if the door opens inward, it is best to clear first in the direction opposite the swing of the door. However, if the officer hear noise or see light or movement coming from either direction, he/she might want to clear in that direction first, regardless of which way the door opens.

CLEAR WITHOUT ENTRY: CENTER-FED OPEN DOOR

STEP 7 - Clear the Corner Towards the Door

Once the officer has cleared one corner, he/she will rapidly turn 180-degrees and clear the opposite corner. The officer will then immediately back away from the doorway just in case an adversary is hiding in the room behind furniture. This technique is useful for clearing a room from the outside without committing to entering the room.

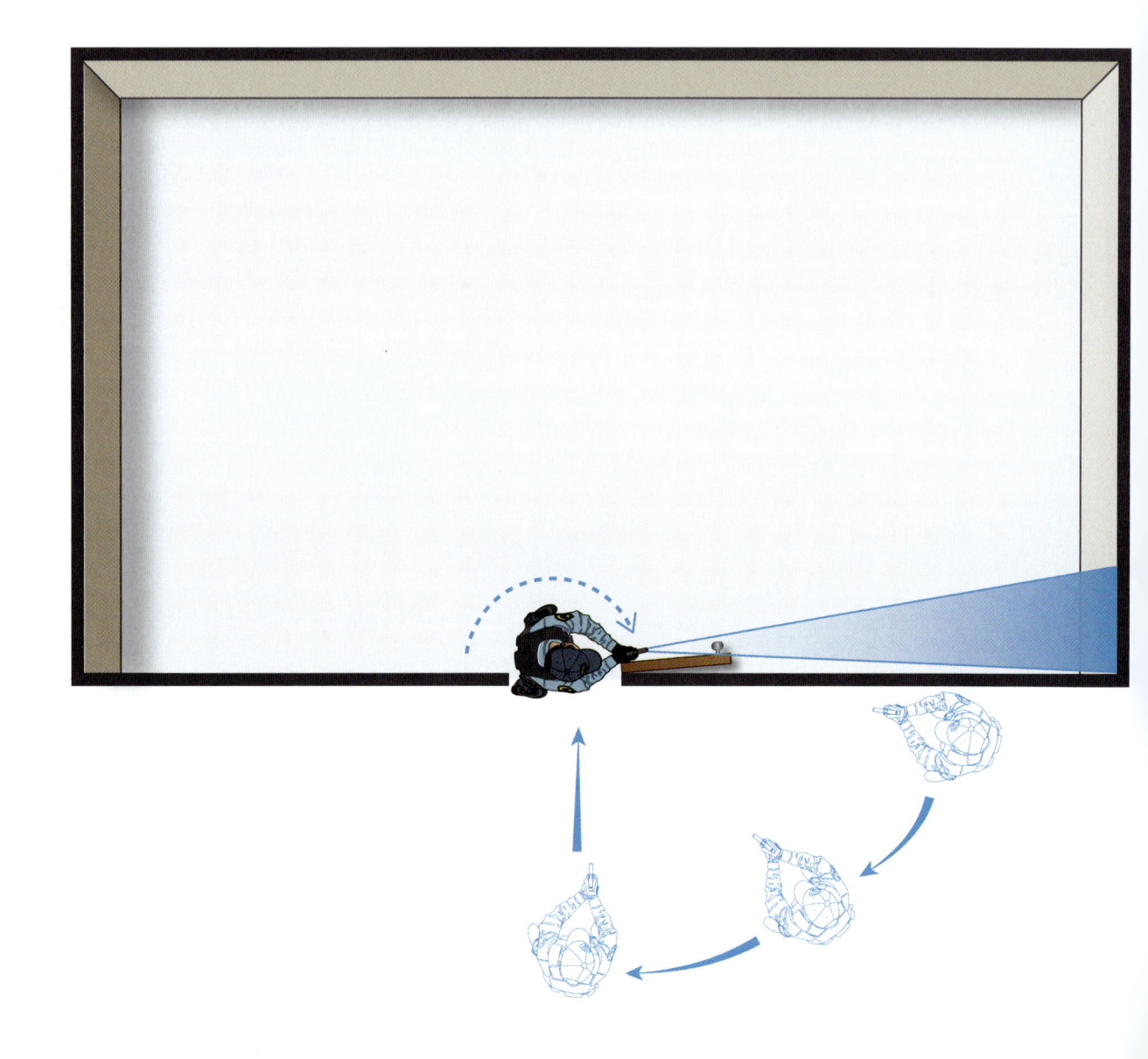

ONE-PERSON OPERATIONS: SINGLE-ROOM CLEARING WITHOUT ENTRY

CLEAR WITHOUT ENTRY: CENTER-FED CLOSED DOOR

STEP 1 - Open the Door

The technique for clearing a center-fed closed door is almost the same as the technique for clearing the open door with a few minor adjustments. The first difference is that because the door is closed, the officer must first open the door before conducting the sweep. To open the door, the officer will position close to the wall and away from the door, just as in the last technique. The officer should keep the weapon at the ready and oriented towards the door just in case the door opens and an adversary walks out. The officer will then move quickly towards the door, grasp the doorknob with the non-firing hand and swing the door open.

CLEAR WITHOUT ENTRY: CENTER-FED CLOSED DOOR

STEP 2 - Back Away

Once the door is open, the officer will back away from the door immediately. The officer should use arm strength to push or pull the door as hard as possible to ensure it swings open while the officer backs away. As the door opens, the first objective is to draw the adversary out or provoke a response that makes it easier to detect the adversary while still keeping distance from the door.

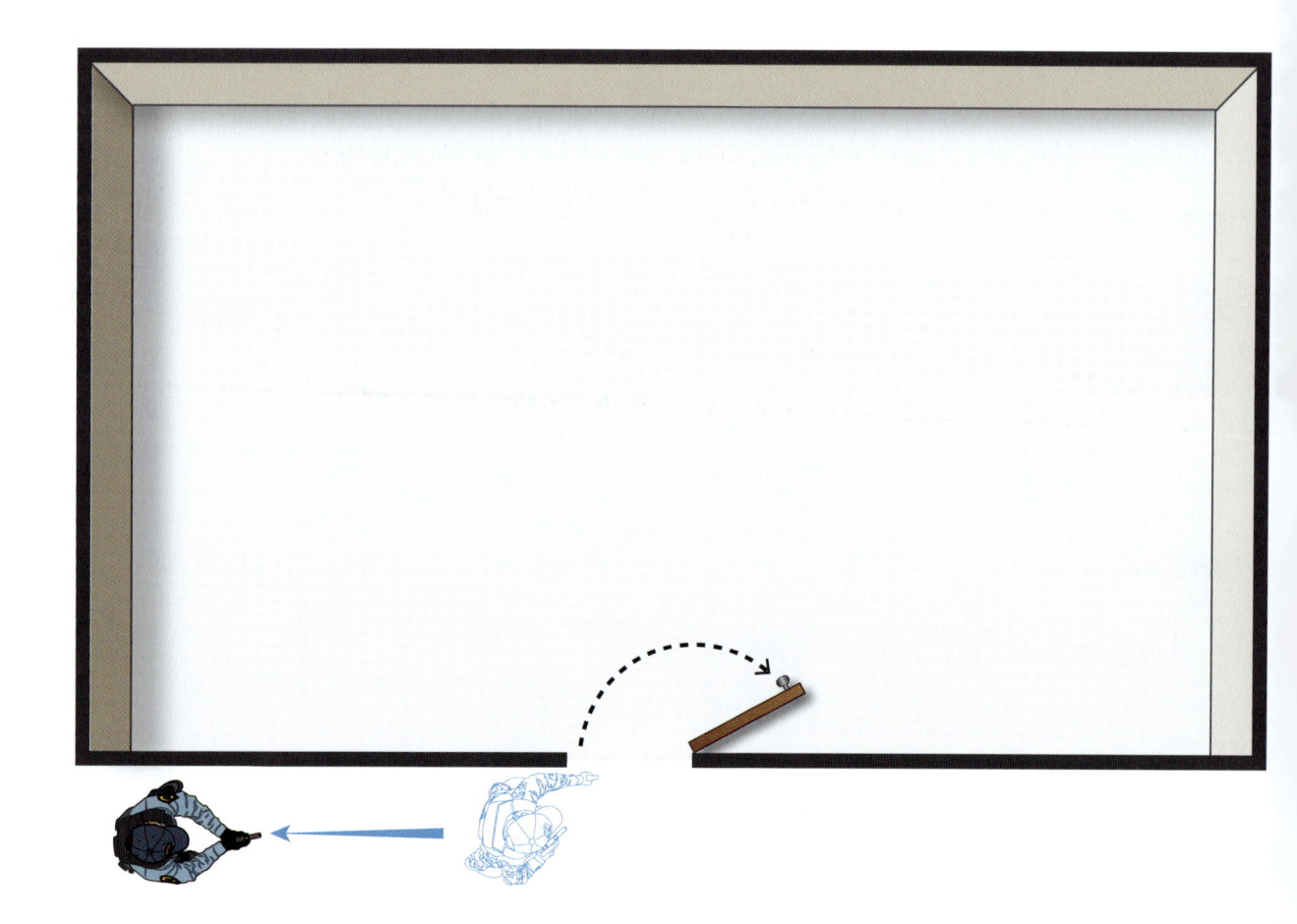

CLEAR WITHOUT ENTRY: CENTER-FED CLOSED DOOR

STEP 3 - Take Advantage of the Door

Which way the door opens and which side the hinges are on is not critical. However, if the door opens inward it is ideal to open the door from the doorknob side if possible. This is because if the door swings inward, the opening door will momentarily conceal the officer as he/she backs away. If the door opens outward, it is ideal to open the door from the hinges side (opposite the doorknob) for the same reason. The opening door will provide at least some degree of concealment and protection, even though it is probably not bulletproof. When opening the door towards the body, it is critical that the officer steps out of the way and lets the door swing open freely so it does not block the officer's vision or weapon.

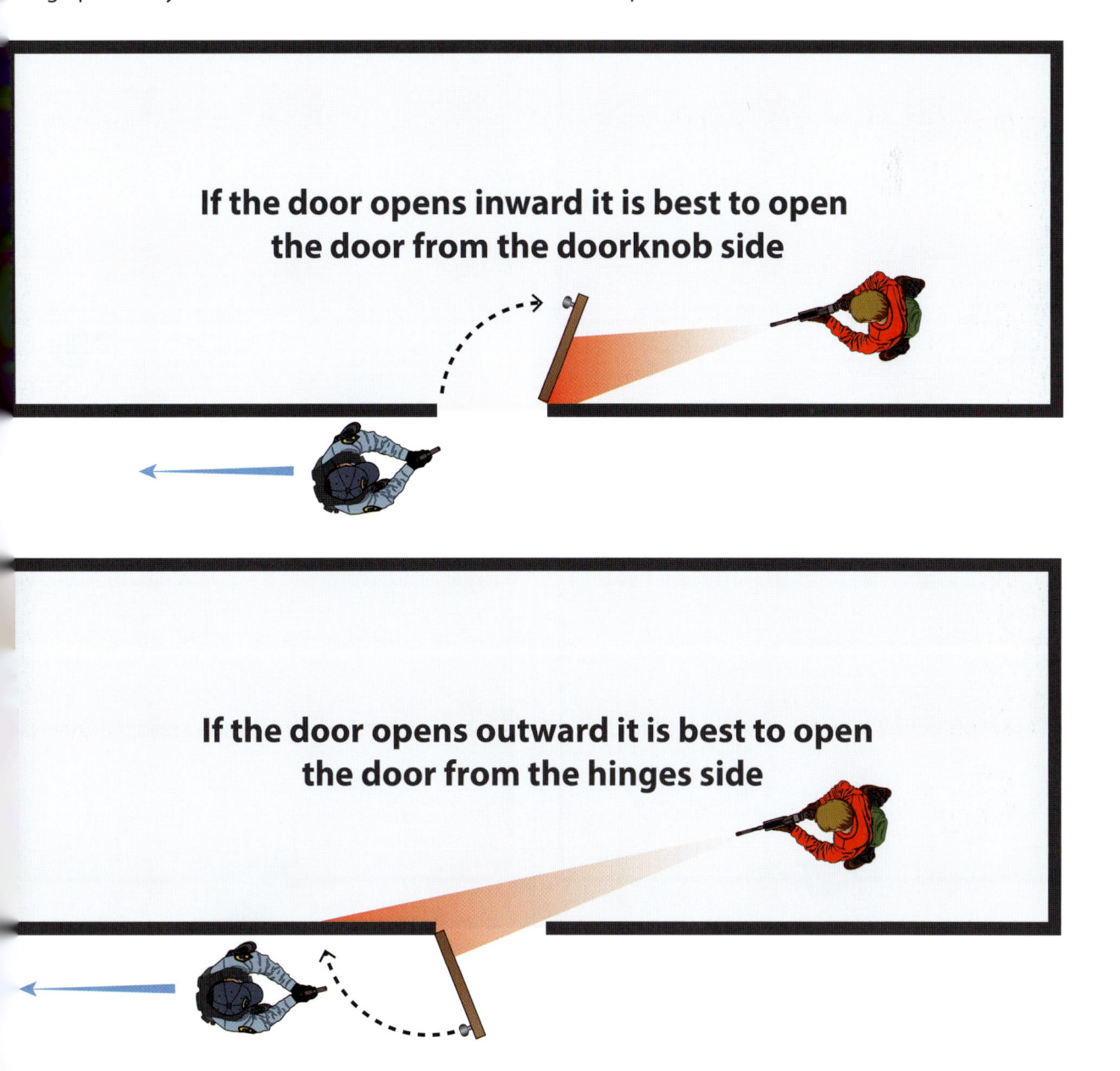

If the door opens inward it is best to open the door from the doorknob side

If the door opens outward it is best to open the door from the hinges side

CLEAR WITHOUT ENTRY: CENTER-FED CLOSED DOOR

STEPS 4 to 7 - Sweep and Clear the Corners

Once the door is open, the officer will be in position to clear the room in exactly the same way described for the center-fed open door. Therefore, in single-person CQB, the main difference between a closed door and an open door is that the officer will have to quickly approach the door, open it, and back away before starting the clearing process.

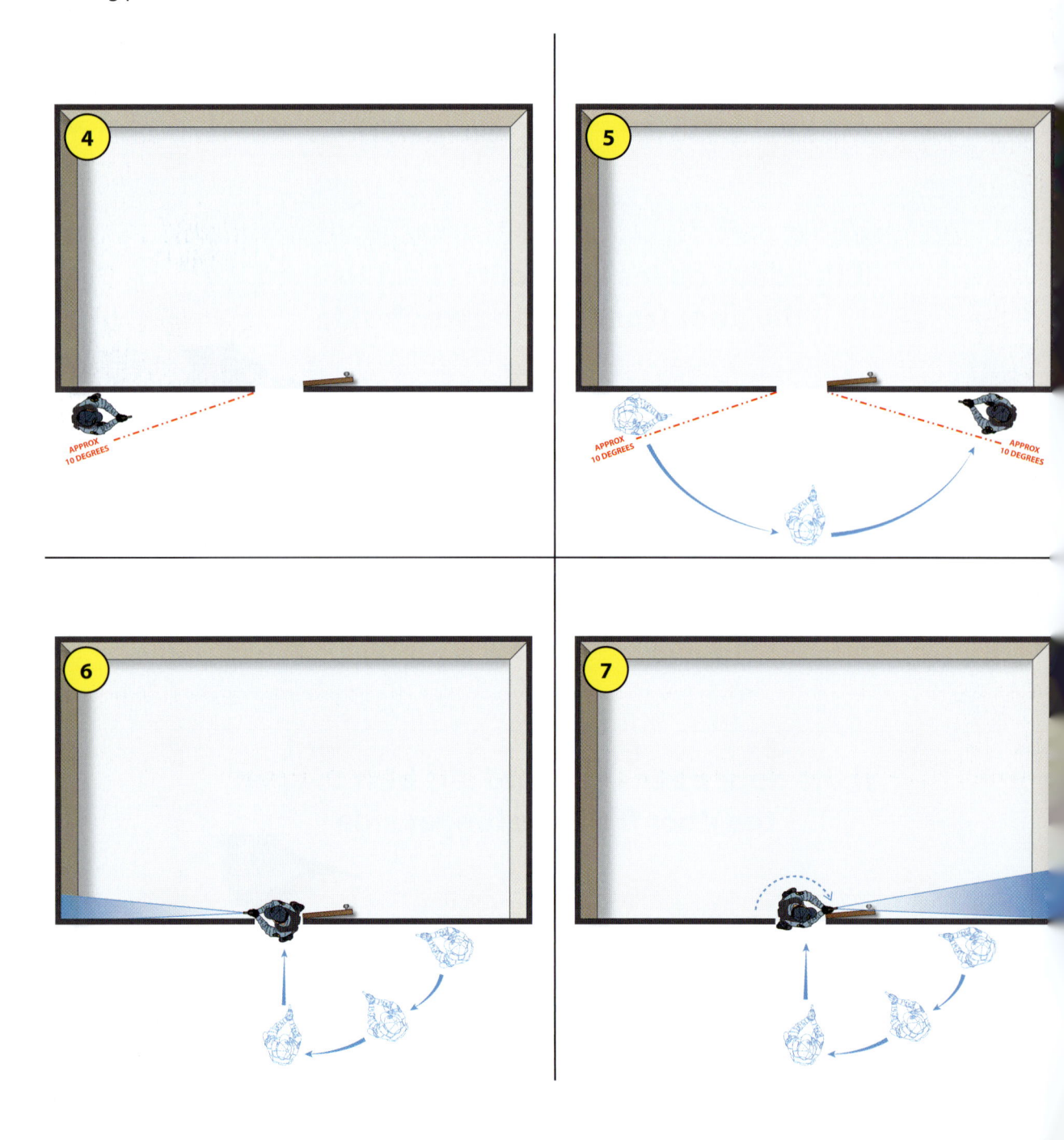

ONE-PERSON OPERATIONS: SINGLE-ROOM CLEARING WITHOUT ENTRY

CLEAR WITHOUT ENTRY: CORNER-FED OPEN DOOR

STEP 1 - Half Sweep

Clearing a corner-fed open door is similar to clearing a center-fed open door. When clearing without entry, the term "corner-fed" or "center-fed" usually refers to the room the officer is in as opposed to the room he/she is clearing. Since the officer is not entering the room, the internal configuration of the target room will have less effect on movement. When clearing a corner-fed door the officer can only approach from one side. He/she will start close to the wall while staying several yards away from the door. As in the previous techniques, the officer will sweep out in a quick but smooth arc, keeping distance from the doorway while clearing the interior of the room.

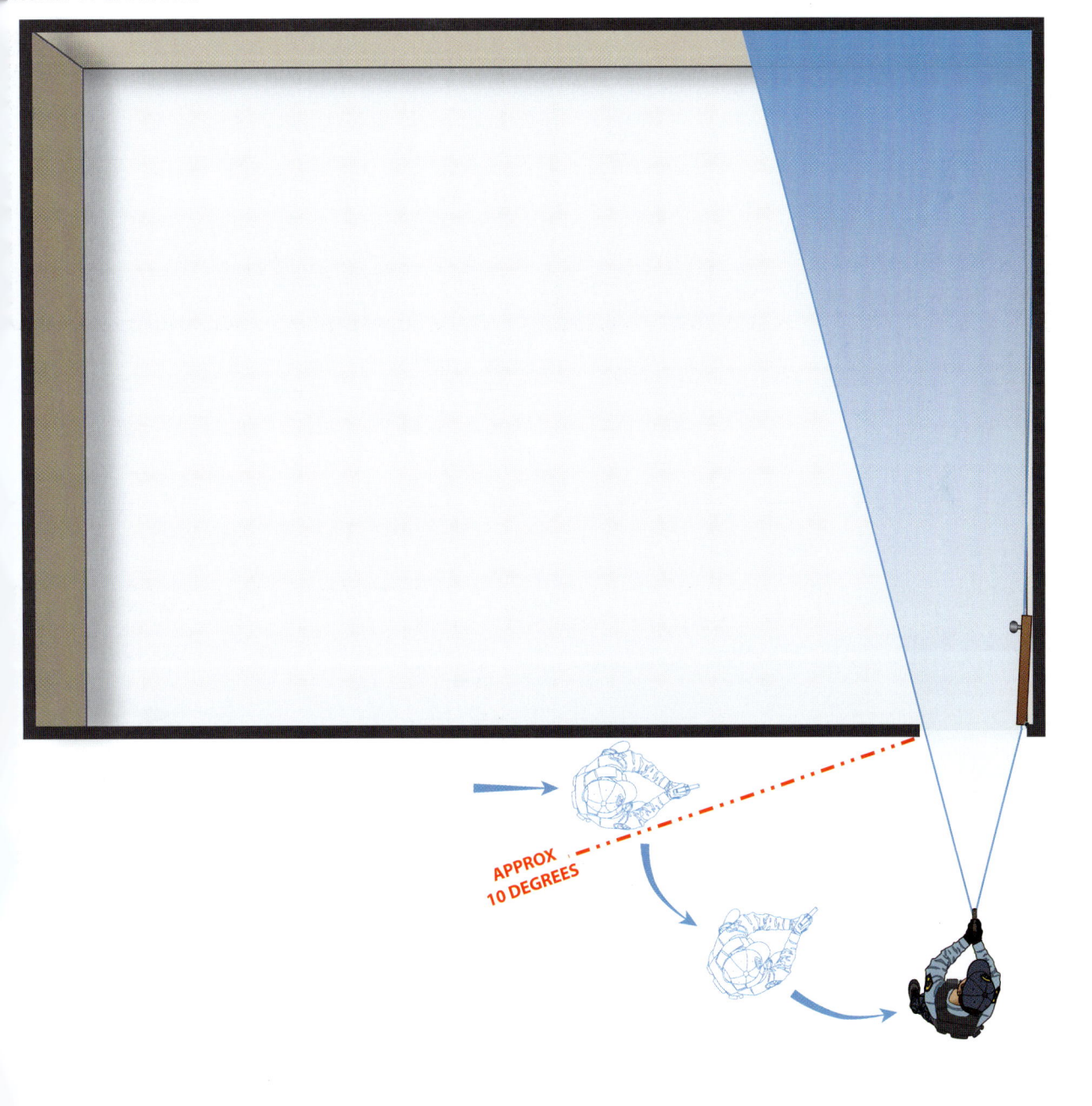

APPROX 10 DEGREES

CLEAR WITHOUT ENTRY: CORNER-FED OPEN DOOR

STEP 2 - Clear the Corner

When clearing a corner-fed door, the officer will only be able to complete half of the sweep. Once the half sweep is complete the officer will be facing the open door and will then only have to clear in one direction. The officer will move towards the door, focusing in the uncleared direction while moving. Upon reaching the threshold, the officer will quickly lean into the room to clear the corner, then back away from the door in case an adversary is hiding somewhere in the room. However, be advised that sometimes corner fed rooms have a small space between the door and the wall where someone could be hiding. In these cases, officers should make sure to clear both corners just as in a center-fed room.

CLEAR WITHOUT ENTRY: CORNER-FED CLOSED DOOR

STEPS 1 to 4 - Open the Door Sweep and Clear

Clearing a corner-fed closed door is very similar to clearing an open door, except the officer will need to quickly approach and swing the door open before starting the clearing process. The method for approaching and opening the door is exactly the same as for a center-fed room. The officer will open the door and back away quickly to avoid getting hit by indiscriminate fire. Once the door is open, the officer will proceed to clear the room in the same manner described for the previous technique.

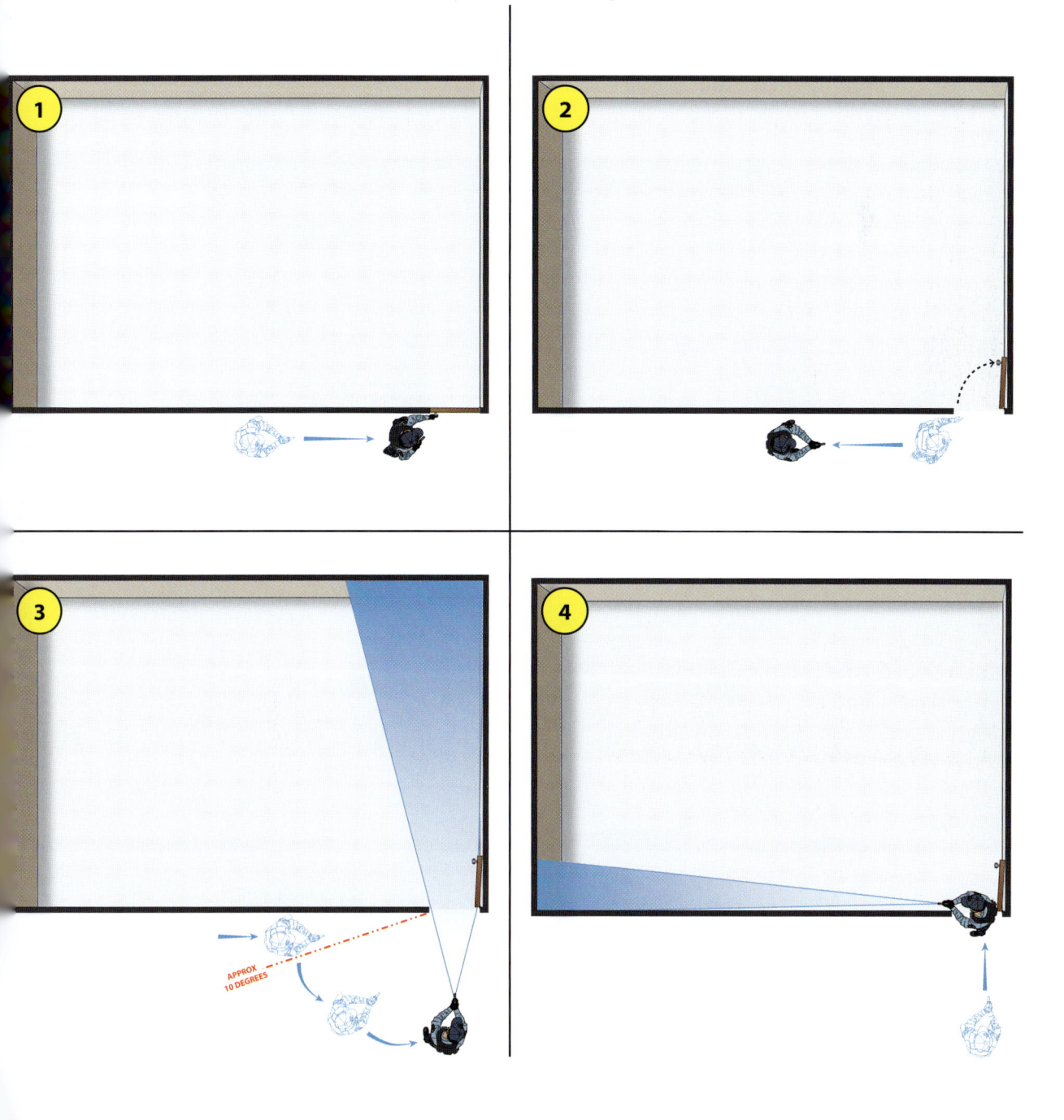

CLEAR WITHOUT ENTRY: QUICK CLEAR

STEP 1 - Clear the Center of the Room

While it is ideal to conduct a full sweep before approaching a doorway, if time is critical or if the room configuration or furniture makes it impossible to conduct the sweep, the officer can clear a room more quickly simply by approaching the door head-on and then clearing each corner in succession. First, the officer will approach the door directly. As the officer approaches, more and more of the room will come into view as the angle of vision widens.

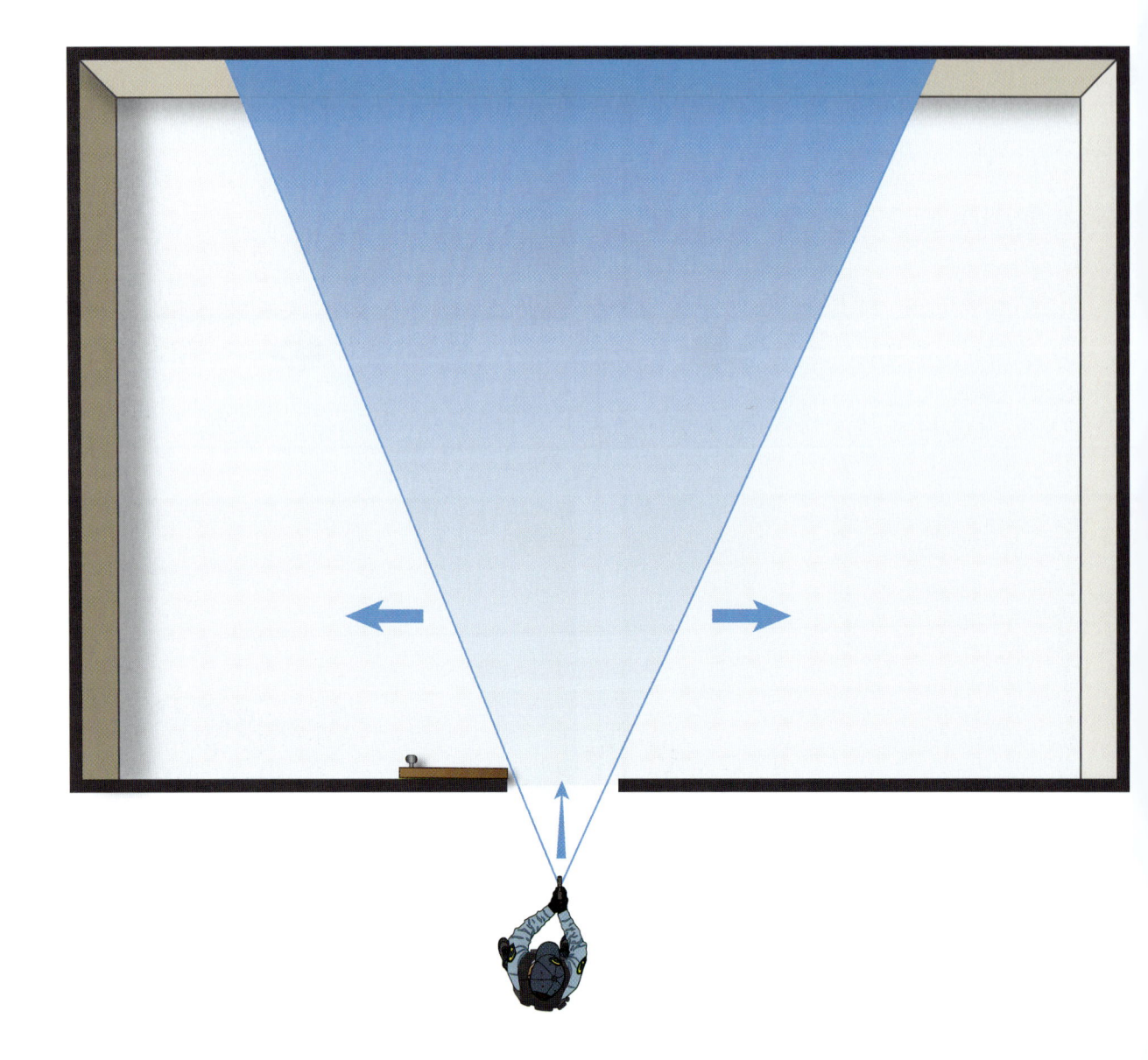

CLEAR WITHOUT ENTRY: QUICK CLEAR

STEP 2 - Clear the First Corner

When the officer reaches the door, he/she will quickly turn to clear one of the two corners. If the officer sees signs of a threat in either corner, he/she will clear that corner first. Otherwise, it is generally a good idea to clear first in the opposite direction that the door opens since the door can sometimes provide a degree of concealment for the exposed back.

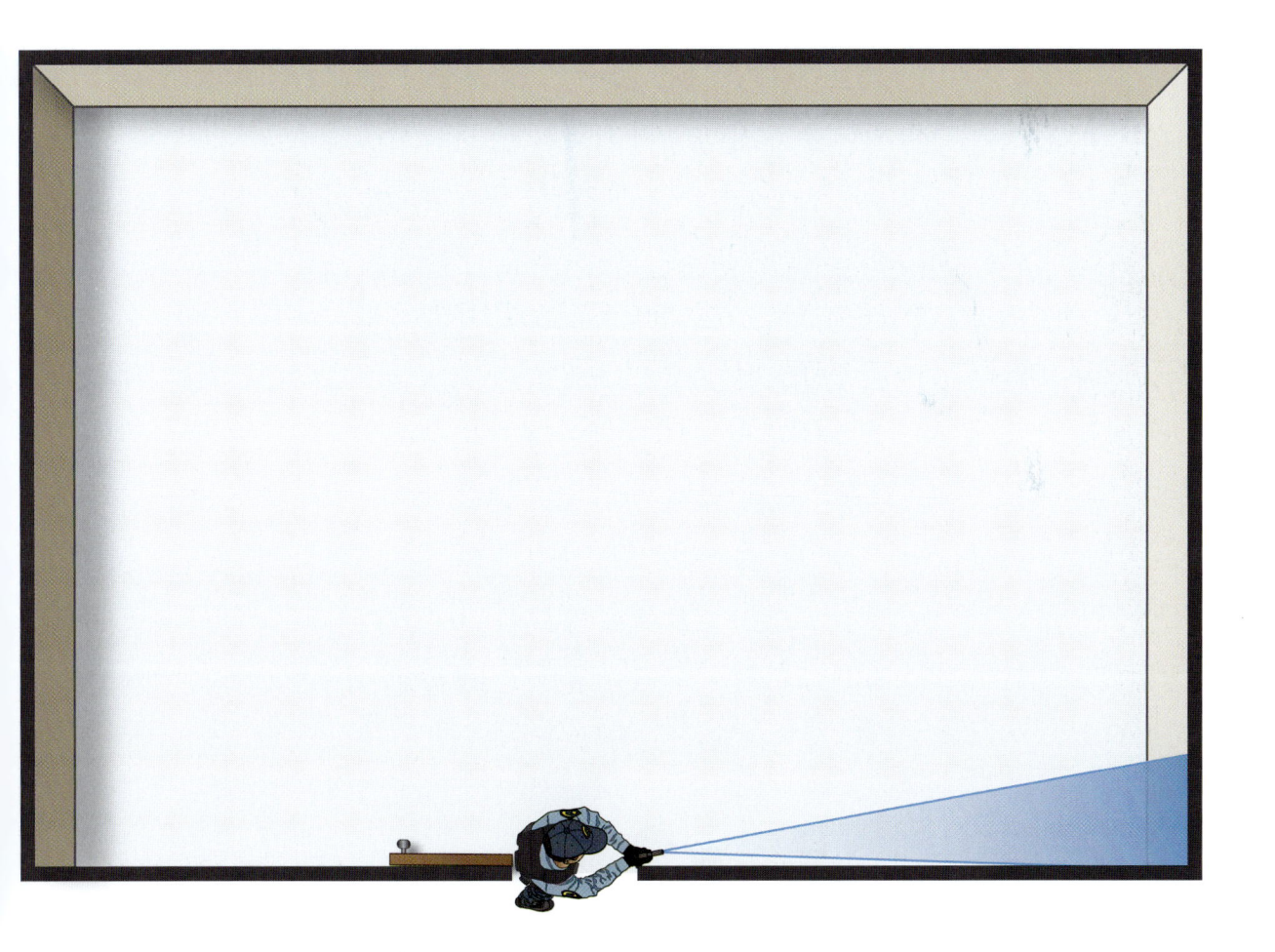

CLEAR WITHOUT ENTRY: QUICK CLEAR

STEP 3 - Clear the Second Corner

After clearing the first corner, the officer will quickly turn and clear the second corner. With practice, it is possible to learn to rapidly clear both corners in a very short time. Once the second corner is clear, the officer can leave the room and move on, or choose to enter the room and conduct a shallow or deep entry. These entry techniques are described in the next chapters.

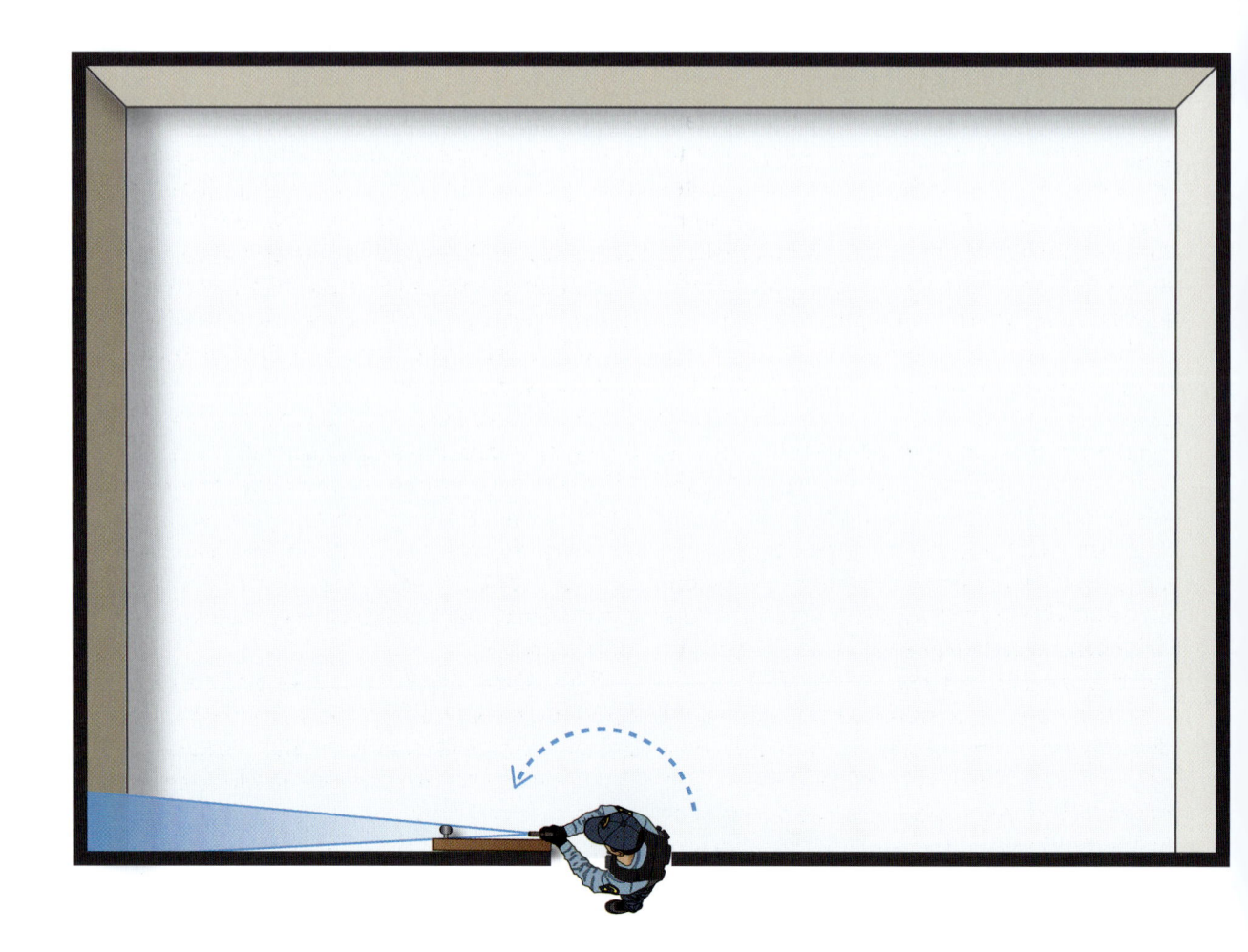

ONE-PERSON OPERATIONS
Single Room Shallow Entry

Another key difference between team operations and single-person operations is that as a single-person, there are many cases when an officer will not want to penetrate too far into a room. The officer may want to get into the room quickly to avoid greater exposure in a hallway, but he/she will want to remain close to the door. This will make it easier for the officer to escape should more adversaries emerge from adjacent rooms.

The shallow entry techniques (sometimes called "limited penetration" techniques) are designed to prevent the officer from becoming over-committed or trapped deep in a target room. In single-person operations, officers will often prefer to remain closer to doors, so they can quickly move through the door to avoid threats coming from either direction. However, officers should still observe the rule of keeping several feet away from the door to avoid getting hit by indiscriminate fire.

If there is a lot of furniture and uncleared dead space in the room, the shallow entry can make an officer vulnerable since he/she has not gone deep enough to see if anyone is hiding behind the furniture. In this situation, the officer might want to penetrate deeper into the room to clear behind the furniture, using the deep entry technique described later on in the manual.

It is also advisable for an officer to go on and complete the deep entry if he/she plans to stay in the room for any length of time. In general, the shallow entry is most useful if the officer wants to quickly enter and clear the room to momentarily get out of an exposed area or hallway. Once ready to keep moving, the officer will exit the room and move along to clear the next room.

The shallow entry techniques begin with the same sweep technique used for the clear without entry. If time is critical, officers can perform any of the shallow entry techniques immediately without first conducting the sweep. However, eliminating the sweep greatly increases the level of risk during the clearing process.

The shallow entry techniques also call for a 180-degree kneeling pivot movement. If an officer has trouble conducting this movement it is possible to execute the shallow entry techniques without kneeling, though kneeling helps reduce the risk of getting shot by an adversary hiding in the corner of the room.

SHALLOW ENTRY: CENTER-FED OPEN DOOR

STEPS 1 to 3 - Sweep and Move Towards the Door

This technique begins with conducting the same steps as directed for the "clear without entry" technique. Therefore, the officer should position near the wall several yards from the door and conduct the sweep all the way across the open door until reaching the opposite side. Then, the officer will conduct a half sweep in the opposite direction until facing the open door. Finally, the officer will move towards the door just as in previous techniques.

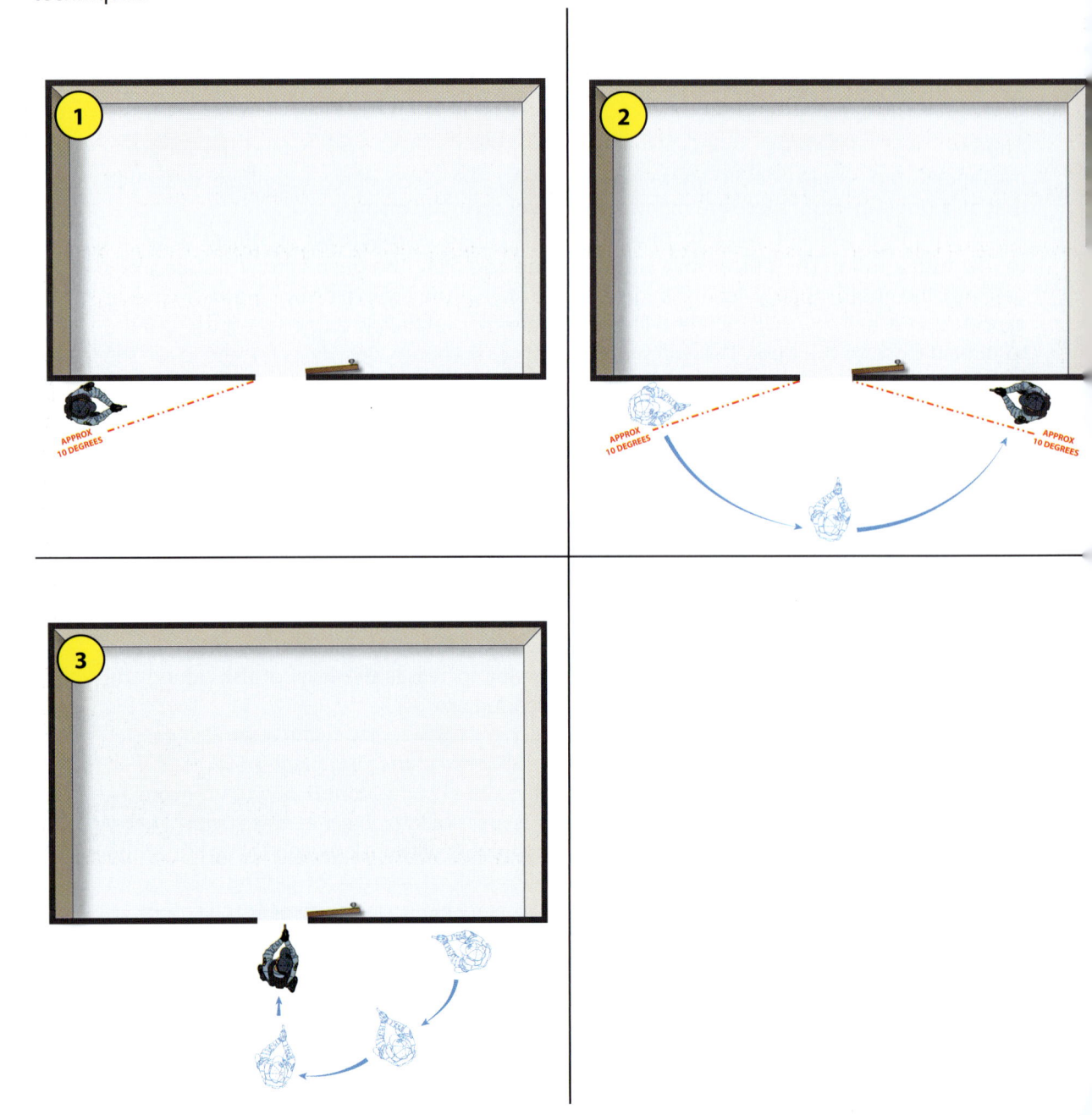

SHALLOW ENTRY: CENTER-FED OPEN DOOR

STEP 4 - Quick-Look Opposite the Direction of Clear

While approaching the doorway, the officer should begin to orient the weapon in the direction he/she is going to clear first. If the door opens inward, it is generally best to clear in the opposite direction of the door, unless noise, movement or light is detected coming from the opposite side. As the officer breaks the plane of the door, he/she should give a quick look over the shoulder in the direction opposite the direction of movement. The officer will then look back in the direction the weapon is pointing and clear that corner. While it might not seem logical to look over the shoulder, away from the direction the weapon is pointing, repeated practice will show that this move actually makes it easier to hit targets in each corner. If officers do not get in the habit of looking over the shoulder when enter the room, it is very easy to get "sucked in" and focus completely on the first corner and be slow to pivot and clear the opposite corner. Looking over the shoulder takes only a fraction of a second and offers a quick snapshot of any adversaries in that corner. This will make it much easier to identify and engage targets after the 180-degree pivot. The movement is similar to quickly looking both ways before crossing the street or checking oncoming traffic before making a turn at an intersection.

Quick glance over the shoulder in the opposite direction of movement

SHALLOW ENTRY: CENTER-FED OPEN DOOR

STEP 5 - Corner Clear

After glancing over the shoulder, the officer will look back in the direction the weapon is pointing and will clear that corner while moving into the room.

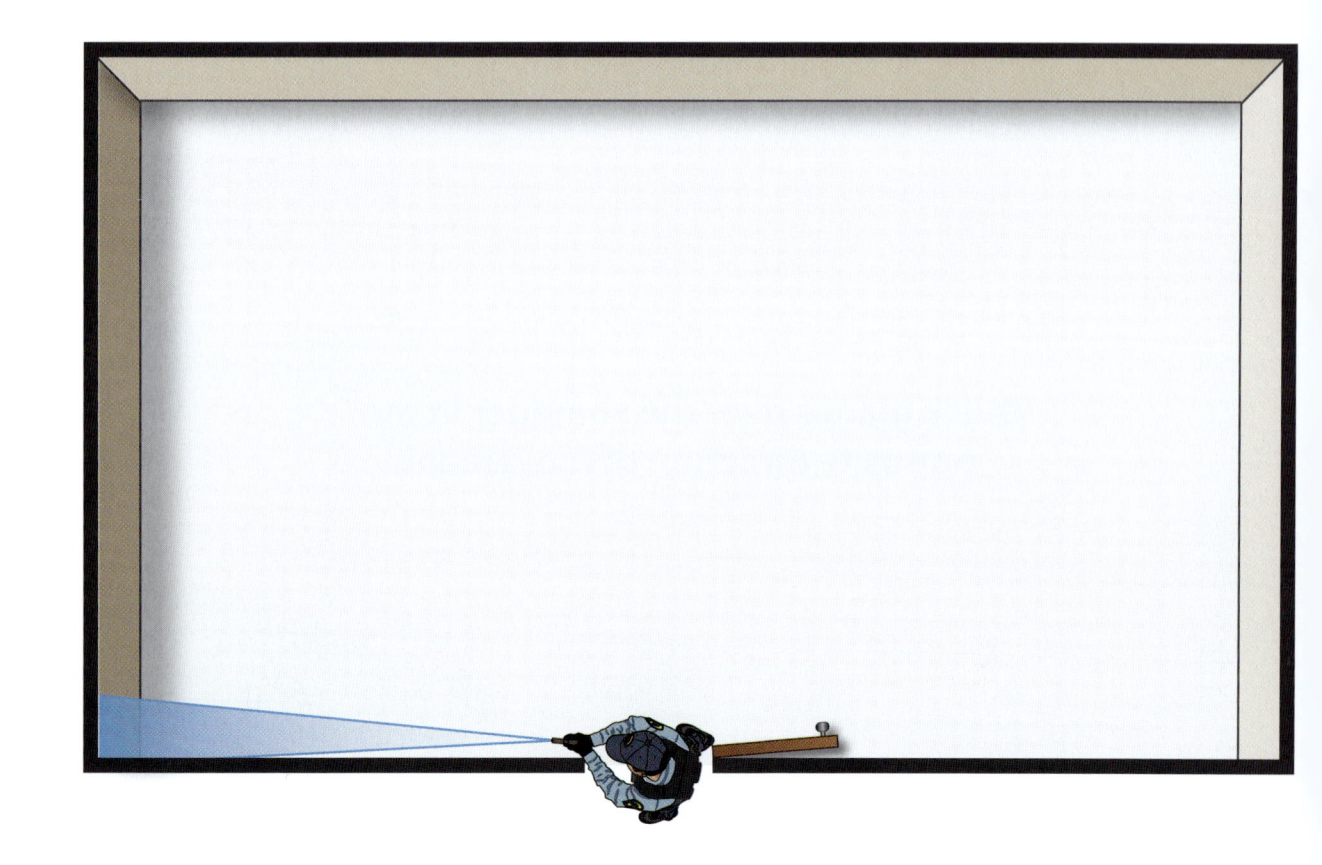

SHALLOW ENTRY: CENTER-FED OPEN DOOR

STEP 6 - Kneeling Pivot

At this point, the officer will pivot 180-degrees, turning towards the direction of the room to clear the opposite corner. If possible, the officer should drop to a knee or squat down while conducting this movement. Dropping to a knee or squatting makes an officer more difficult to hit in the event that there is an adversary in the corner who was about to shoot the officer in the back as he/she entered the room. The officer would see this adversary with the initial glance over his/her shoulder. That initial snapshot will make it easier to engage the adversary after the kneeling pivot. Once both corners are clear, the officer should remain in the room and back away slightly from the door.

SHALLOW ENTRY: CENTER-FED CLOSED DOOR

STEPS 1 to 4 - Complete Sequence

The technique for entering a center-fed closed door is almost the same as the technique for the open do except that the officer will need to open the door, just as in the previous techniques. Keeping distance fro the door, the officer should approach quickly to open it and then step back to create distance. The officer w then conduct the sweep and move in to execute the shallow entry technique as described above.

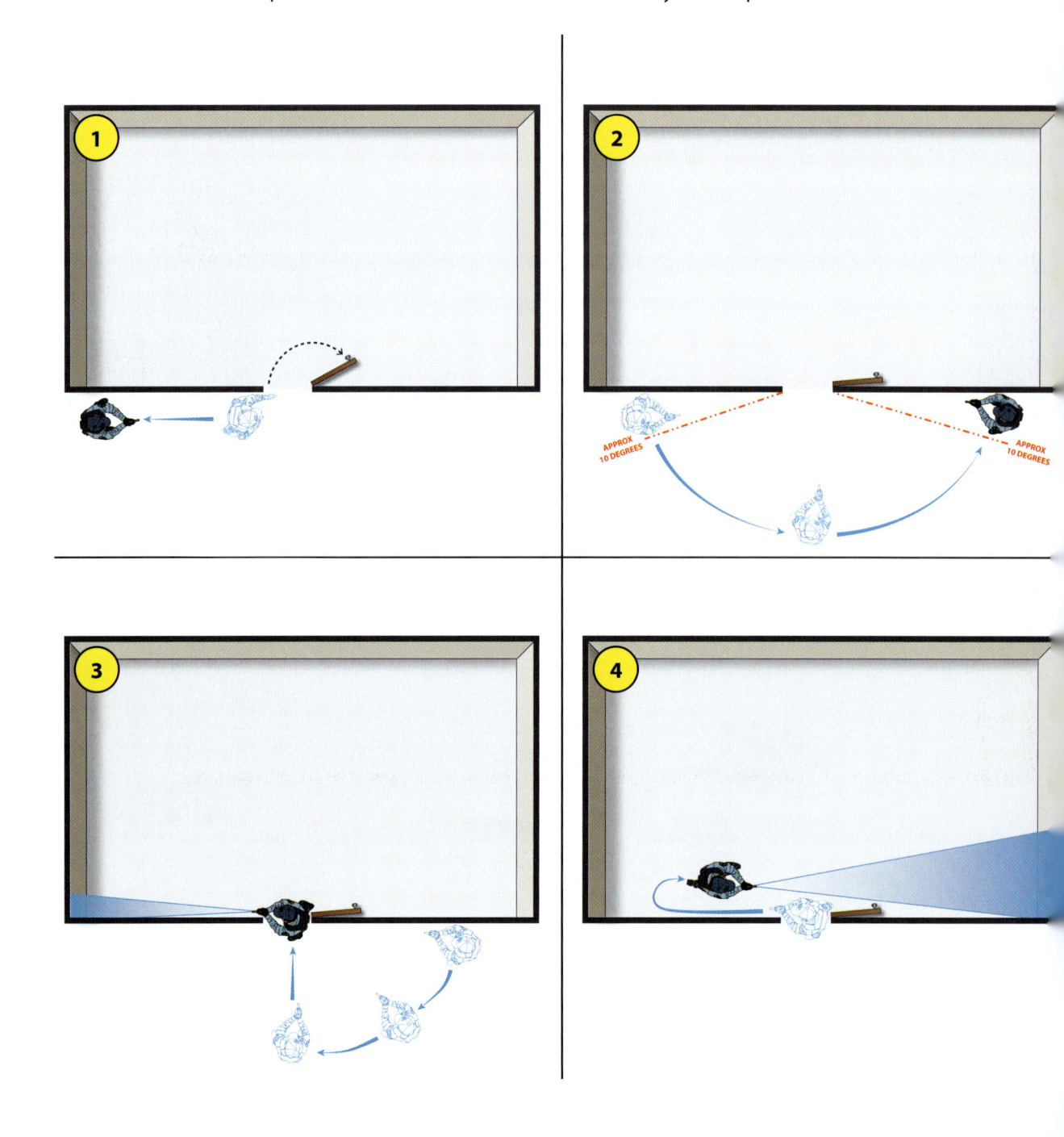

One-Person Operations: Single-Room Shallow Entry | 303

SHALLOW ENTRY: CORNER-FED OPEN DOOR

STEP 1 - Half Sweep

Entering a corner-fed open door is similar to entering a center-fed open door. First, the officer will conduct a half sweep, then approach the door and prepare to make entry, beginning to focus attention towards the remaining uncleared corner.

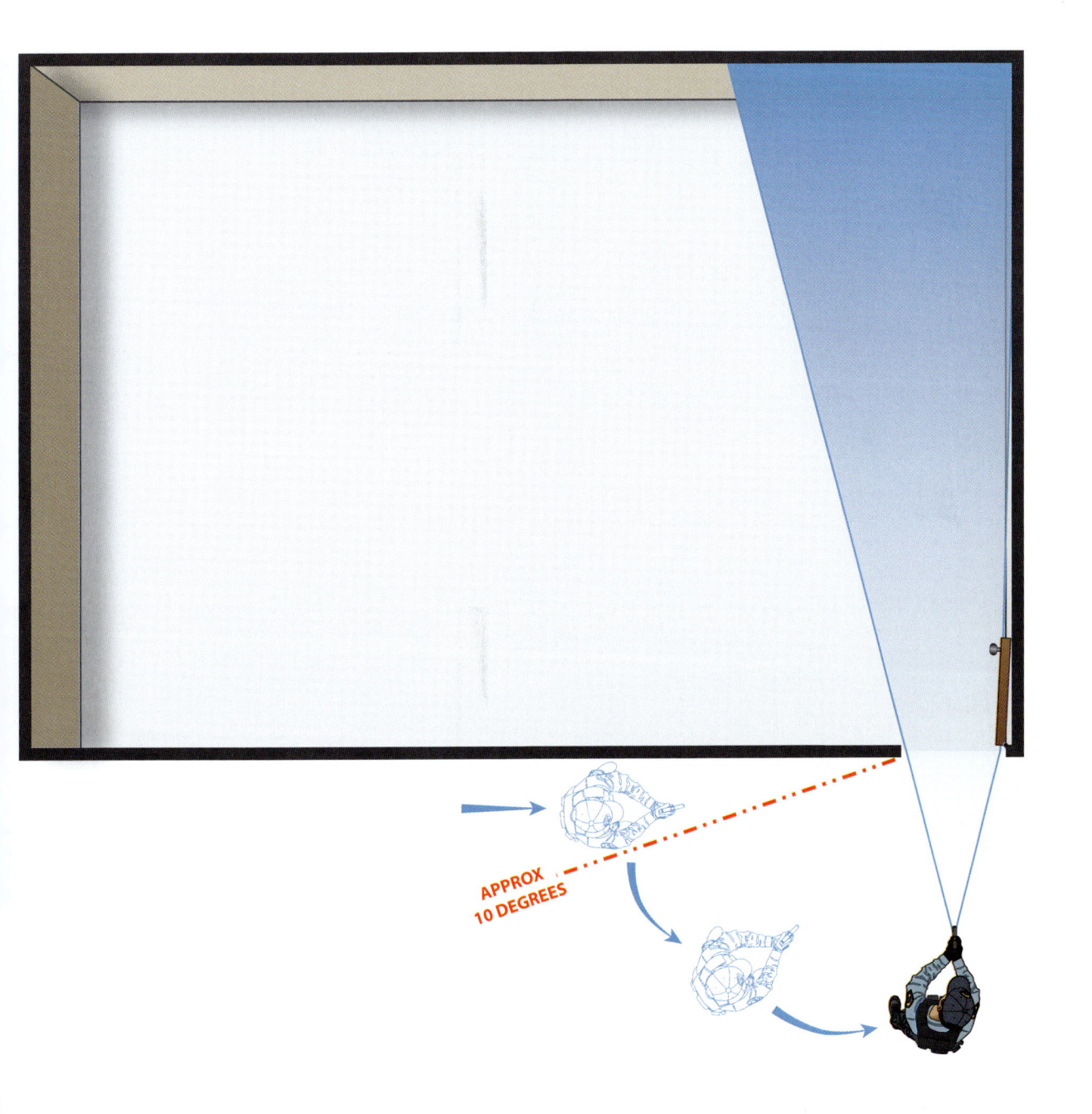

APPROX 10 DEGREES

SHALLOW ENTRY: CORNER-FED OPEN DOOR

STEP 2 - Clear the Corner

As the officer breaks the plane of the door, he/she will clear the corner and move into the room.

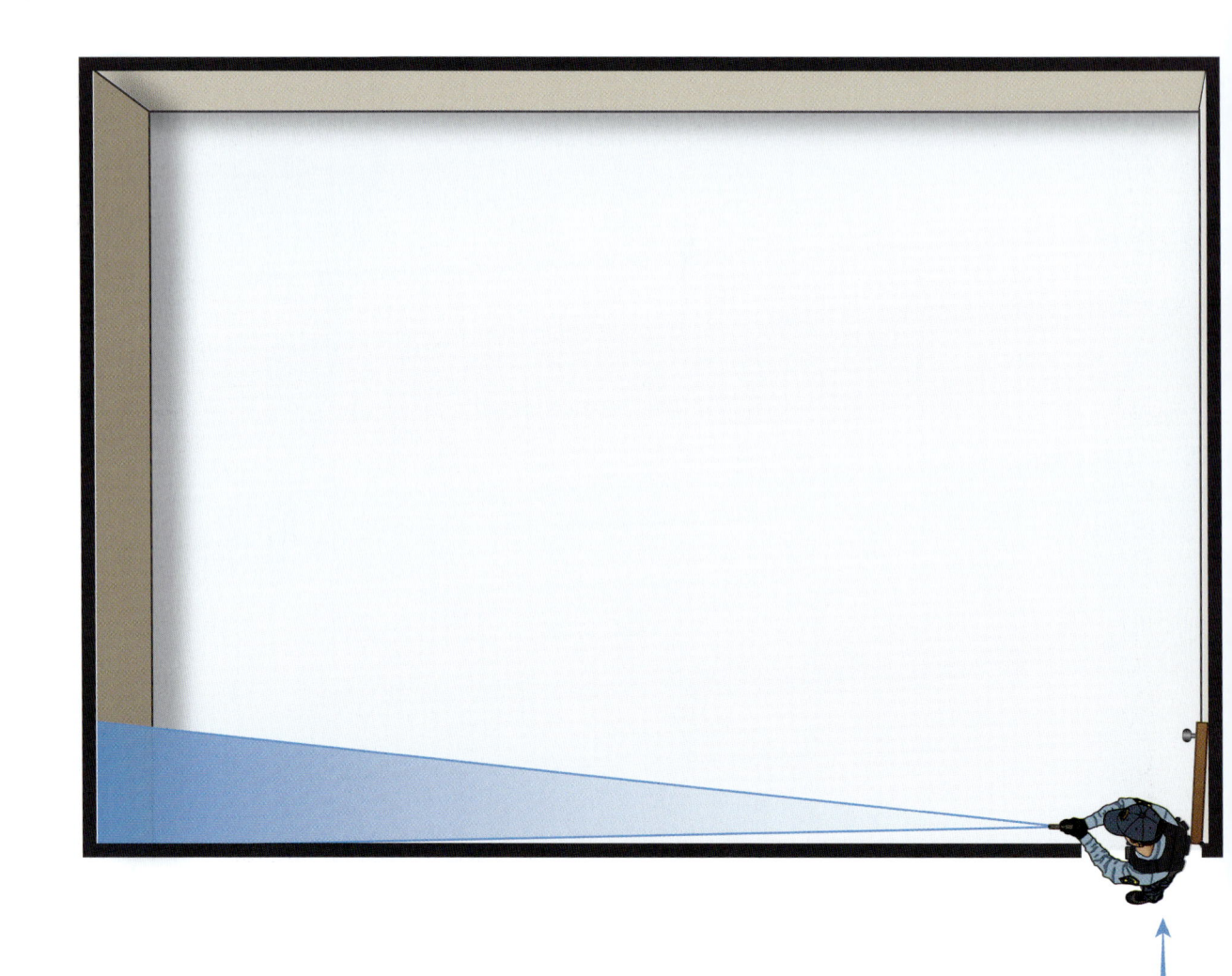

SHALLOW ENTRY: CORNER-FED OPEN DOOR

STEP 3 - Enter the Room

After entering the room, the officer will assume a good defensive position within a few yards of the door and cover in the direction of the most likely threat. In some cases this will mean turning around to provide rear security on the entry door.

SHALLOW ENTRY: CORNER-FED CLOSED DOOR

STEPS 1 to 4 - Complete Sequence

Entering a corner-fed closed door is similar to entering an open door, except the officer will need to quickl* approach and swing the door open before starting the clearing process. The officer will then back away quickl* to avoid getting hit by indiscriminate fire. Once the door is open, the steps for clearing the room are the sam* as those described for the previous technique.

ONE-PERSON OPERATIONS
Single-Room Deep Entry

While shallow entry helps the officer avoid getting overly committed in the room and keep close to a path of escape, there are situations where the officer will want to clear the room completely. This is of particular importance in situations where officers plan to remain in the room for an extended period of time, use the room as a safe area for innocent civilians, or if there is a lot of furniture in the room. Deep entry involves penetrating fully into the room, clearing behind furniture and ensuring no adversaries are hiding behind the door.

When conducting deep entry techniques, an officer will penetrate only as far into the room as he/she needs to. The advantages of staying close to the door still apply. Therefore, unless there is furniture or dead space deep in the room, the officer should conduct the clearing movement relatively close to the door. An officer can also start by conducting a shallow entry and then move on to a deep entry after having had time to assess the layout of the room and the situation.

When executing the deep entry, the officer should try to move as quickly as possible, sacrificing some shooting accuracy in order to reduce vulnerability. If there are multiple threats in the room, the officer will be extremely vulnerable once passing through the door and the best option is to move quickly enough so adversaries find it difficult to shoot accurately. Still, while speed is important, the officer should not move so fast that he/she will trip over objects in the room or completely lose the ability to shoot accurately.

In most rooms, the furniture is located near the walls. Therefore, when conducting the deep entry and moving along the wall, the officer may need to adjust his/her path or scan to deal with various furniture configurations. There are no fixed formulas or solutions, so officers must use their common sense.

DEEP ENTRY: CENTER-FED OPEN DOOR

STEPS 1 to 4 - Sweep and Clear the Corner

The officer should position near the wall, several yards from the door and conduct the sweep all the way across the open door until reaching the opposite side. Then, the officer will conduct a half sweep in the opposite direction until facing the open door. Next, the officer will move towards the door and enter the room just as in the shallow entry, looking quickly over the shoulder in the opposite direction of movement, then turning back forward to clear the corner.

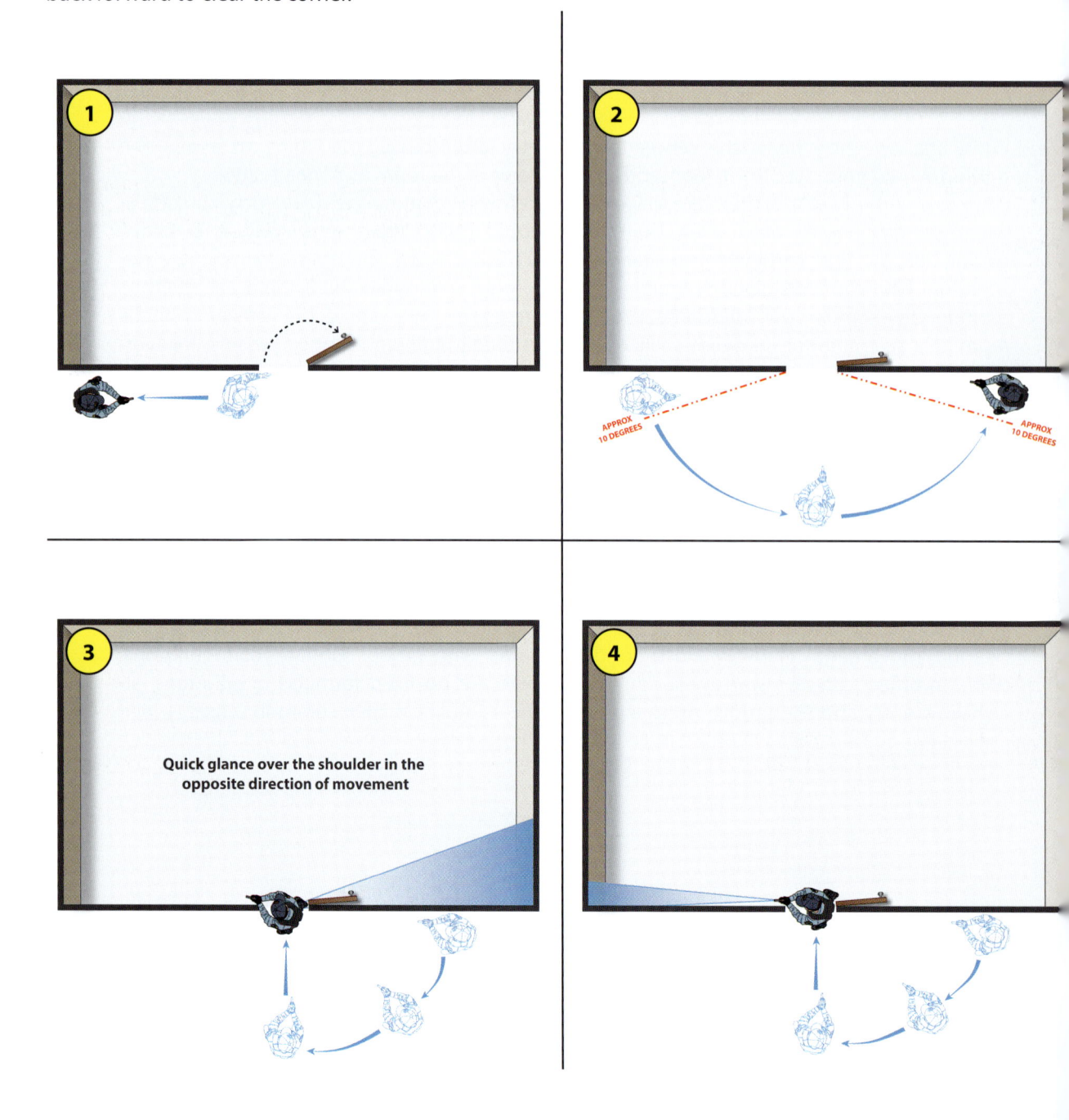

3 — Quick glance over the shoulder in the opposite direction of movement

ONE-PERSON OPERATIONS: SINGLE-ROOM DEEP ENTRY   309

DEEP ENTRY: CENTER-FED OPEN DOOR

STEP 5 - Scan and Clear the Deep Corner

For the deep entry, the quick look over the shoulder is even more important. If the officer looks over his/her shoulder and sees a possible adversary, it is possible to then immediately switch to the shallow entry technique to address the threat, pivoting 180-degrees and dropping to a knee. If the officer does not see an adversary when looking over the shoulder, he/she will continue to move into the room along the wall while scanning towards the deep corner.

DEEP ENTRY: CENTER-FED OPEN DOOR

STEP 6 - Continue Scan

The officer will continue to scan while moving away from the wall, penetrating deeper into the room. Moving in an arc like this will offer the best angles to see behind any objects or furniture in the room where adversaries might be hiding. Depending on the situation, the officer can also move in a much narrower arc to clear the entire room more quickly.

DEEP ENTRY: CENTER-FED OPEN DOOR

STEP 7 - Scan to Clear the Next Deep Corner

The office will continue to scan to the next deep corner while moving further into the room. However, it is best to only move as deep into the room as necessary to clear behind objects and furniture. In general, it is best to use a smaller arc and stay closer to the door in case there is a need to make a quick exit.

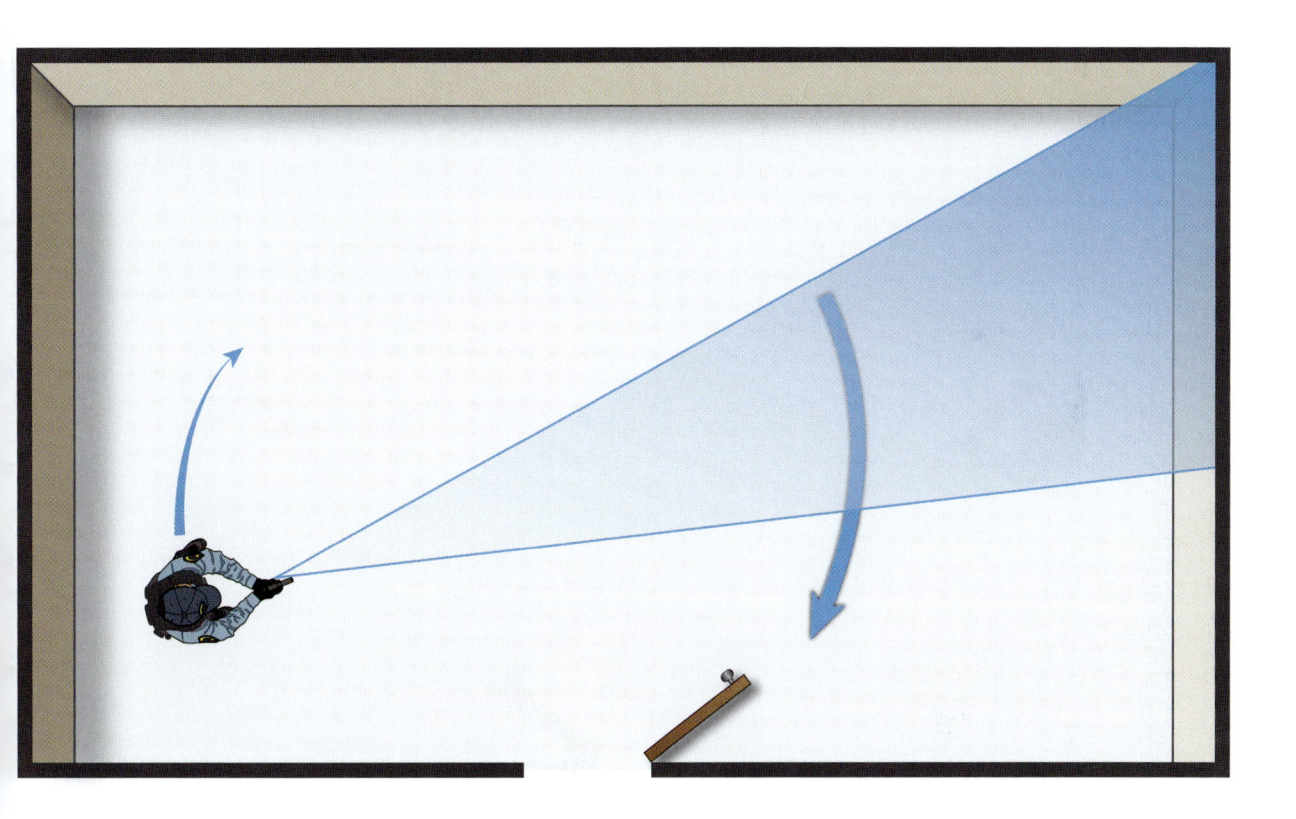

DEEP ENTRY: CENTER-FED OPEN DOOR

STEP 8 - Complete Scan

Continue to scan all the way around to the doorway though which you entered. Be sure to penetrate deep enough to clear behind objects and furniture in the room. At this point the room is clear except for the dead space behind the door.

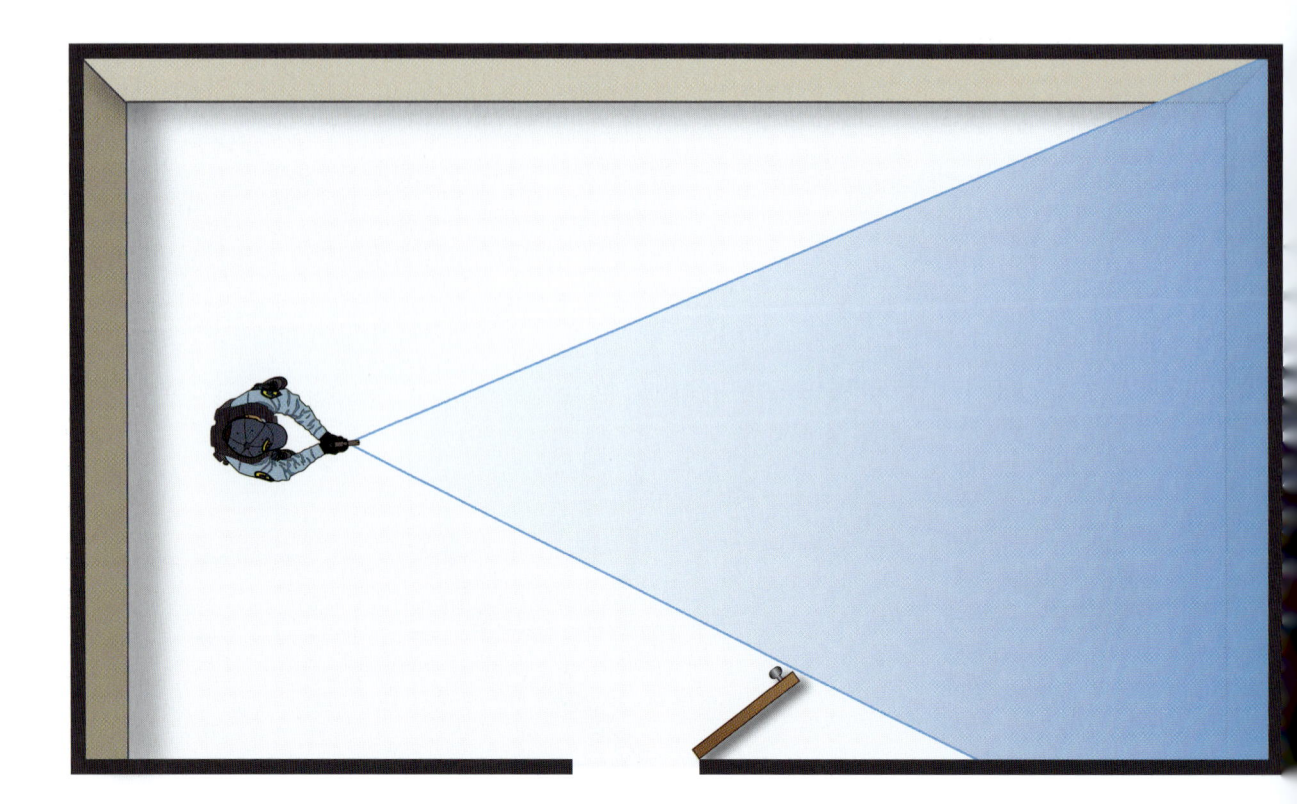

ONE-PERSON OPERATIONS: SINGLE-ROOM DEEP ENTRY

DEEP ENTRY: CENTER-FED OPEN DOOR

STEP 9 - Scan Back to the First Deep Corner

Before moving deeper into the room to check the door, the officer should complete a secondary scan all the way back to the near deep corner. This second scan helps the officer ensure that he/she has checked behind all objects and furniture in the room before exposing his/her back to potential threats by penetrating deeper into the room. Highly experienced officers may eliminate this second scan if time is critical. However, it is always a good idea to take extra precautions given how easy it is to make mistakes in a stressful combat environment.

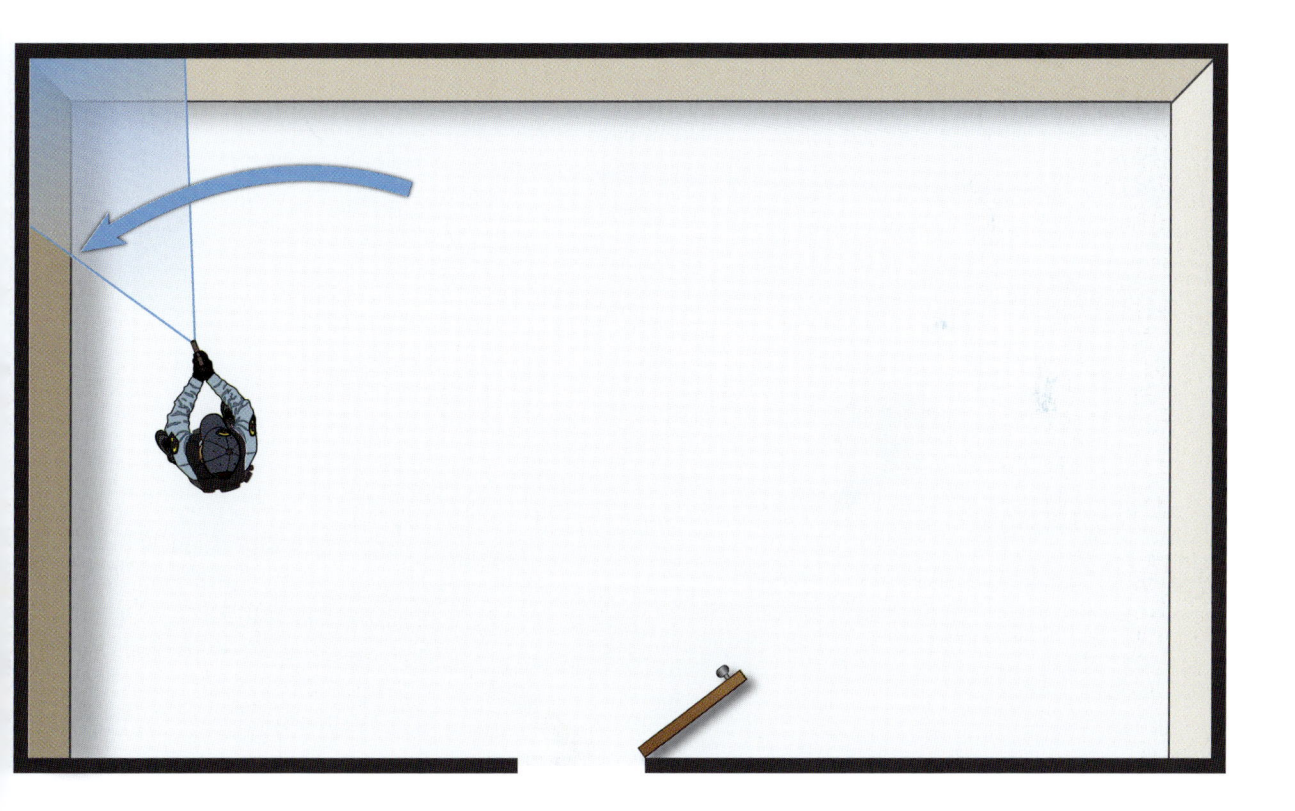

DEEP ENTRY: CENTER-FED OPEN DOOR

STEP 10 - Focus on the Door

Once the officer has completed the second scan, he/she should turn to focus on the door and the uncleared dead space behind it. The officer must be prepared to engage an adversary who jumps out from behind the door. Obviously, this step is only needed if the door opens inward. Also, if the door is completely flush with the wall and there is no way to hide behind it, it is possible to skip this step entirely if time is critical. However, it is possible for smaller adversaries to flatten themselves tightly to the wall behind the door. In other cases, buildings are designed in a way that leaves a small space or indentation behind the door. Finally, in a high stress situation, the officer may think the door is flush against the wall when it actually is not. Because of these factors it is always preferable to check behind the door.

ONE-PERSON OPERATIONS: SINGLE-ROOM DEEP ENTRY 315

DEEP ENTRY: CENTER-FED OPEN DOOR

STEP 11 - Sweep to Clear Behind the Door

The officer will begin to sweep deeper into the room, keeping focused on the door and the space behind it. The angle of the door will determine how wide a sweep is necessary in order to check behind the door. While moving through the room, the officer must move carefully to avoid tripping over furniture or objects lying on the ground.

DEEP ENTRY: CENTER-FED OPEN DOOR

STEP 12 - Clear Behind the Door

The officer will continue to sweep until he/she is able to clear behind the door. If furniture blocks the path to checking behind the door, the officer may have to approach the door and quickly move it away from the wall with the non-firing hand. While doing this, it is critical for the officer to back away quickly to prevent anyone who is hiding behind the door from rushing forward and grabbing the officer's weapon. At this point the room is clear.

One-Person Operations: Single-Room Deep Entry   317

DEEP ENTRY: CENTER-FED CLOSED DOOR

STEPS 1 to 4 - Sweep and Clear the Corner

The technique for entering a center-fed closed door is the same as the technique for the open door except that the officer will need to open the door, just as in the previous techniques. The officer will keep distance from the door, approach quickly to open it and then step back to create distance. The officer will then conduct the sweep and move in to execute the deep entry technique as described above.

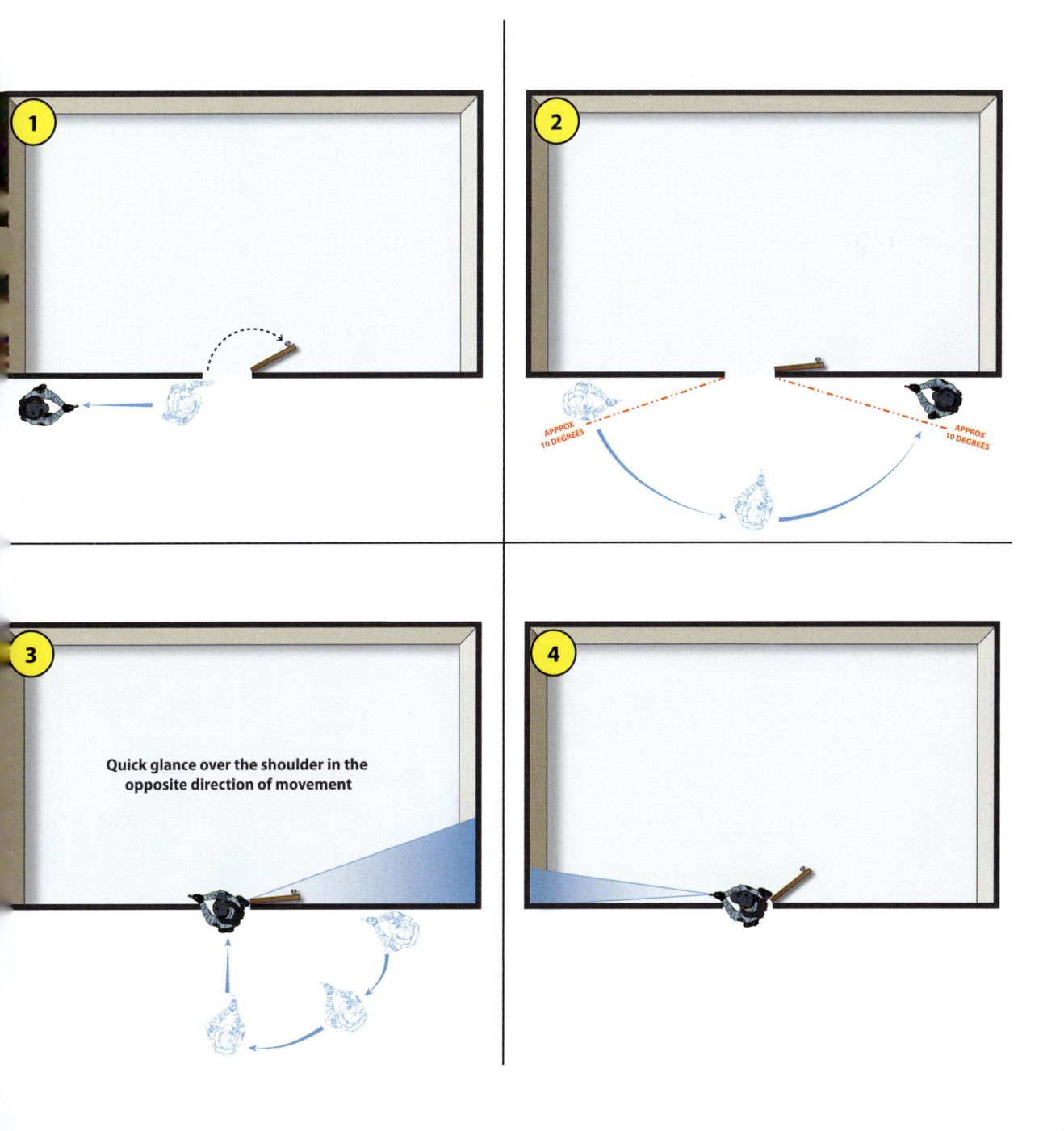

1

2

APPROX 10 DEGREES   APPROX 10 DEGREES

3

Quick glance over the shoulder in the opposite direction of movement

4

DEEP ENTRY: CENTER-FED CLOSED DOOR

STEPS 5 to 8 - Complete the Scan

After looking over the shoulder and clearing the corner, the officer will continue to scan in the direction of the room while moving along the wall. The officer will then turn to penetrate deeper into the room while continuing to scan until the sights of the weapon reach the door through which the officer entered.

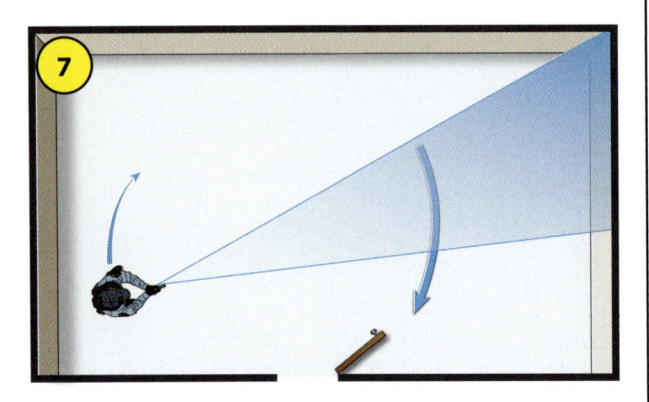

ONE-PERSON OPERATIONS: SINGLE-ROOM DEEP ENTRY 319

DEEP ENTRY: CENTER-FED CLOSED DOOR

STEPS 9 to 12 - Check Behind the Door

After completing the scan, the officer will conduct the second scan back to the near deep corner. Once the second scan is complete, the officer will focus on the door and the uncleared dead space behind it, then sweep around to clear behind the door.

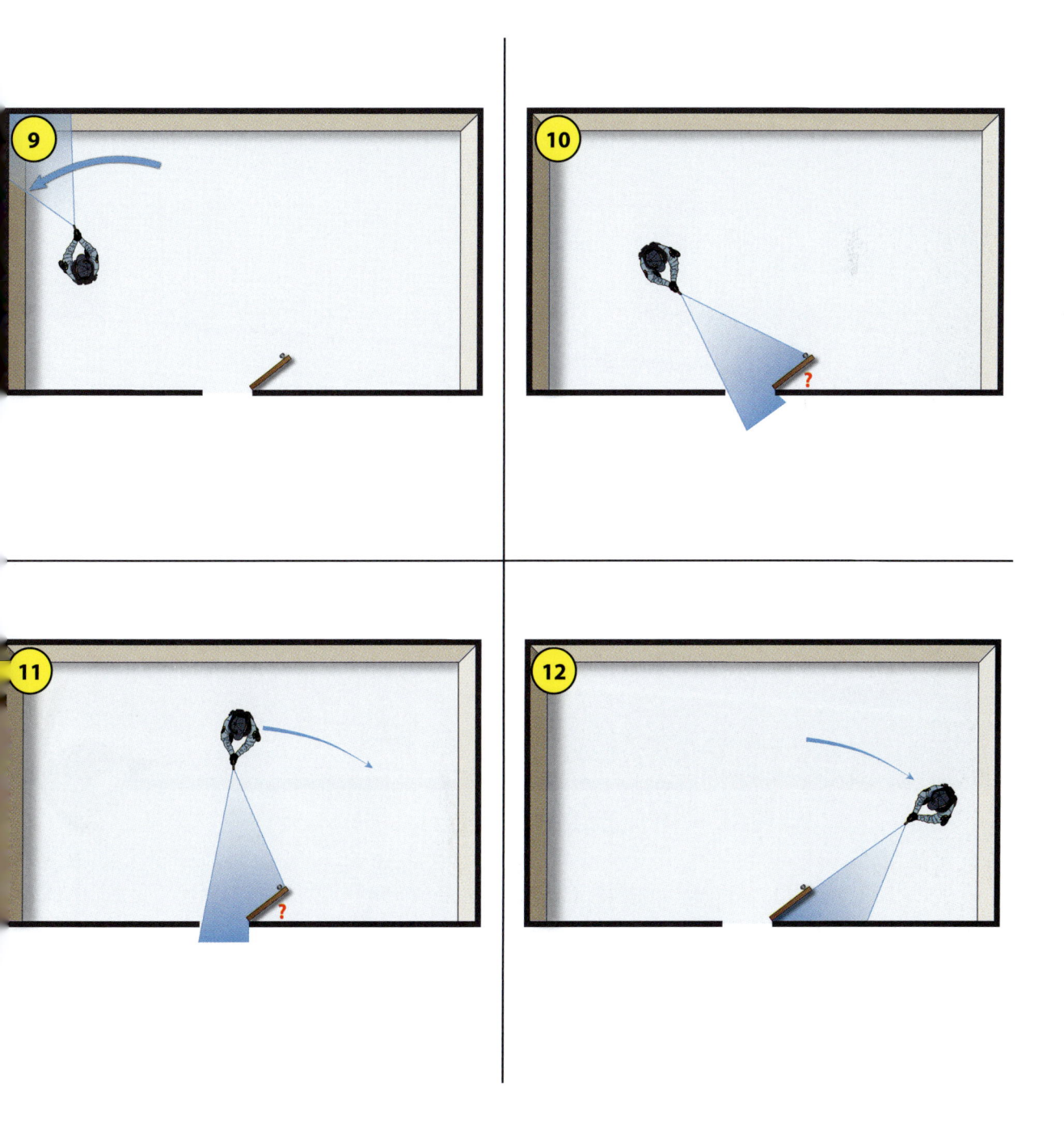

DEEP ENTRY: CORNER-FED OPEN DOOR

STEP 1 - Sweep and Clear the Corner

The officer will conduct a half sweep, then move towards the door and clear the corner. At this point, it is possible to slam the door against the wall to ensure no one is hiding behind it. However, it is preferable not to touch the door and stay focused on possible threats within the room since slamming the door will require attention and energy. Also, if there is someone hiding behind the door, slamming it might provoke an immediate physical confrontation and the adversary will be close enough to grab the officer's weapon. Given these factors it might be better to move away from the door into the room or conduct a shallow entry.

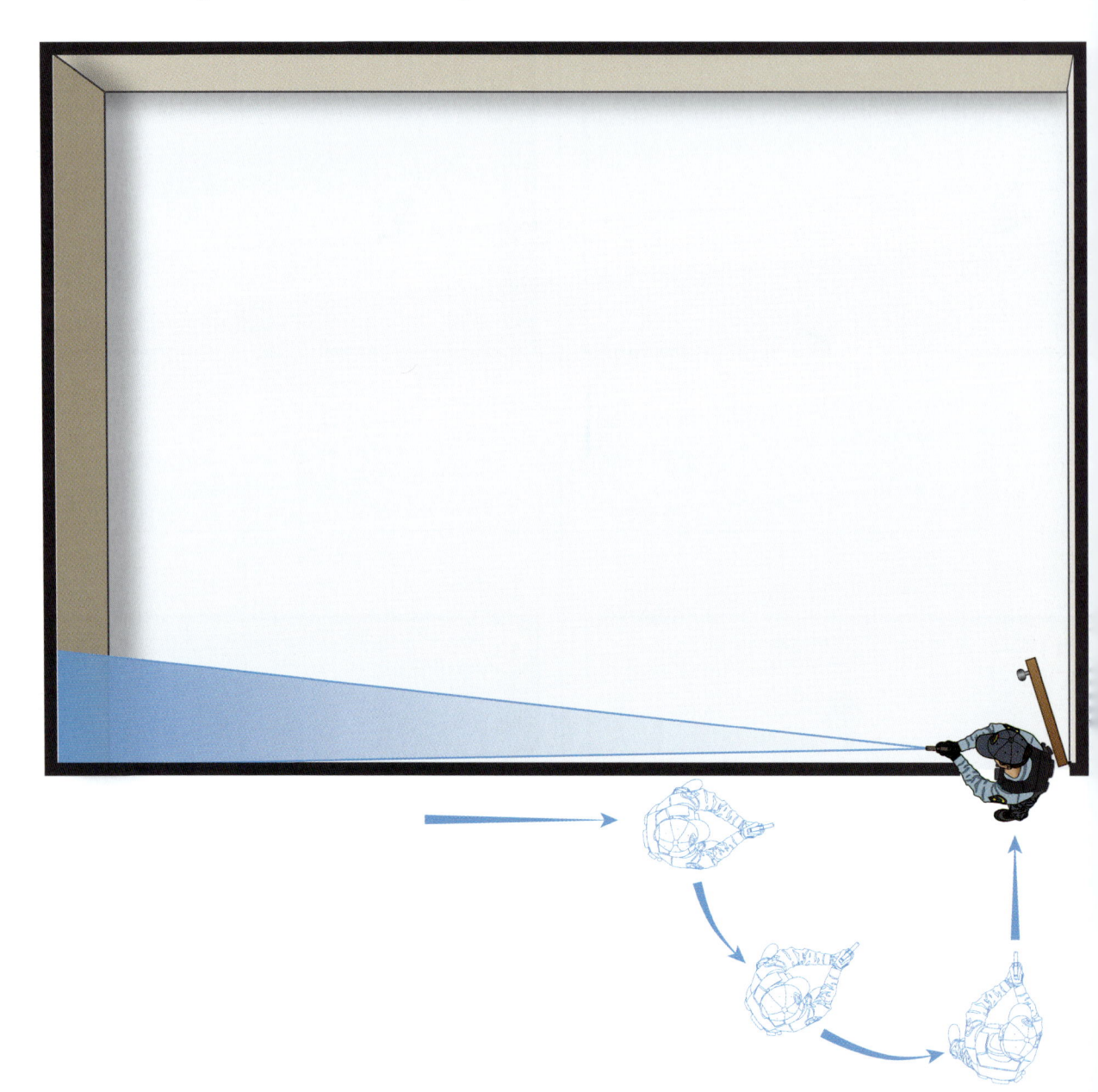

DEEP ENTRY: CORNER-FED OPEN DOOR

STEP 2 - Scan and Clear the Deep Corner

The officer will continue to move into the room along the wall while scanning towards the deep corner.

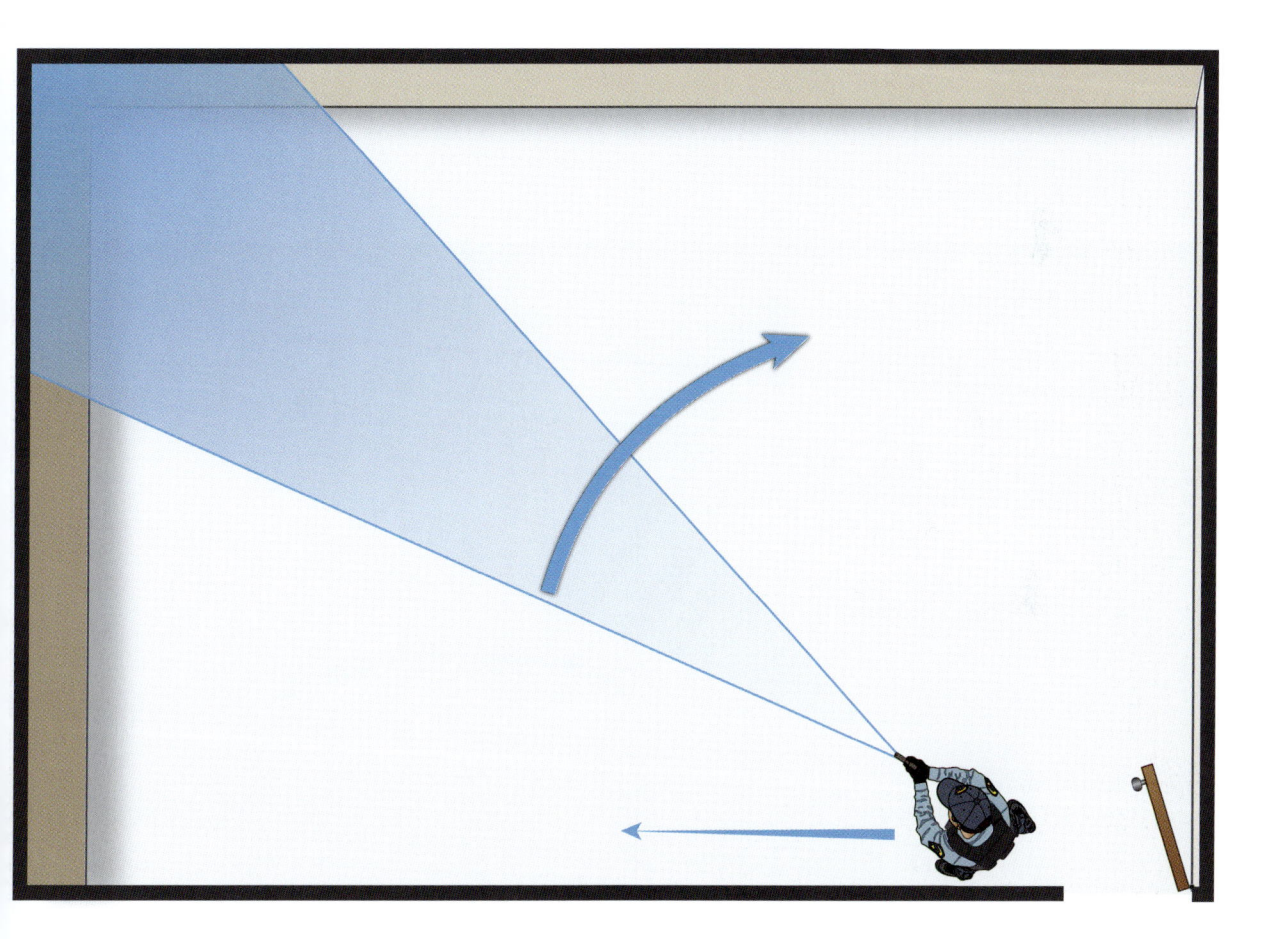

DEEP ENTRY: CORNER-FED OPEN DOOR

STEP 3 - Continue to Scan

The officer will continue to scan while moving along the wall, checking behind any obstacles or furniture in the room.

ONE-PERSON OPERATIONS: SINGLE-ROOM DEEP ENTRY

DEEP ENTRY: CORNER-FED OPEN DOOR

STEP 4 - Clear the Next Deep Corner

The officer will continue the scan to the next deep corner. Depending on the configuration of the room, the officer should also be starting to move away from the wall, deeper into the room. This will provide the correct visual angle to check behind objects and furniture. However, as before, it is best to penetrate only as far into the room as necessary in order to clear these areas of dead space.

DEEP ENTRY: CORNER-FED OPEN DOOR

STEP 5 - Complete the Scan

The officer will complete the scan by clearing all the way around to the entry door. At this point the only remaining uncleared dead space is behind the door. Once again, if the door is completely flush with the wall it might not be necessary to clear behind it.

DEEP ENTRY: CORNER-FED OPEN DOOR

STEP 6 - Move to Clear Behind the Door

The officer will begin sweeping deeper into the room while keeping the weapon oriented towards the door and the uncleared dead space behind it.

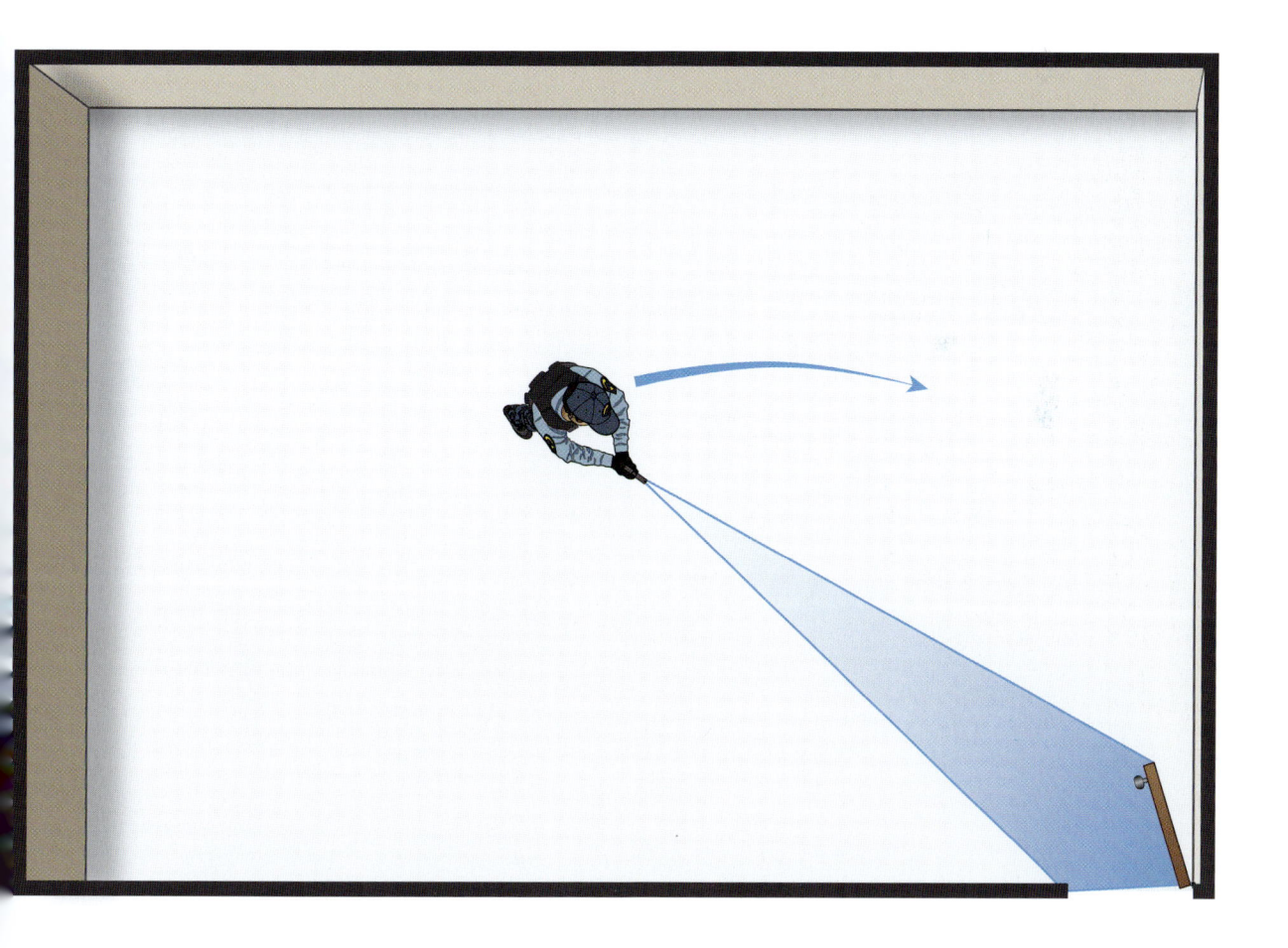

DEEP ENTRY: CORNER-FED OPEN DOOR

STEP 7 - Clear Behind the Door

The officer will continue to sweep until he/she is able to clear behind the door. . If furniture blocks the path t checking behind the door, the officer may have to approach the door and quickly move it away from the wa with the non-firing hand. While doing this, it is critical for the officer to back away quickly to prevent anyon who is hiding behind the door from rushing forward and grabbing the officer's weapon. At this point the roor is clear.

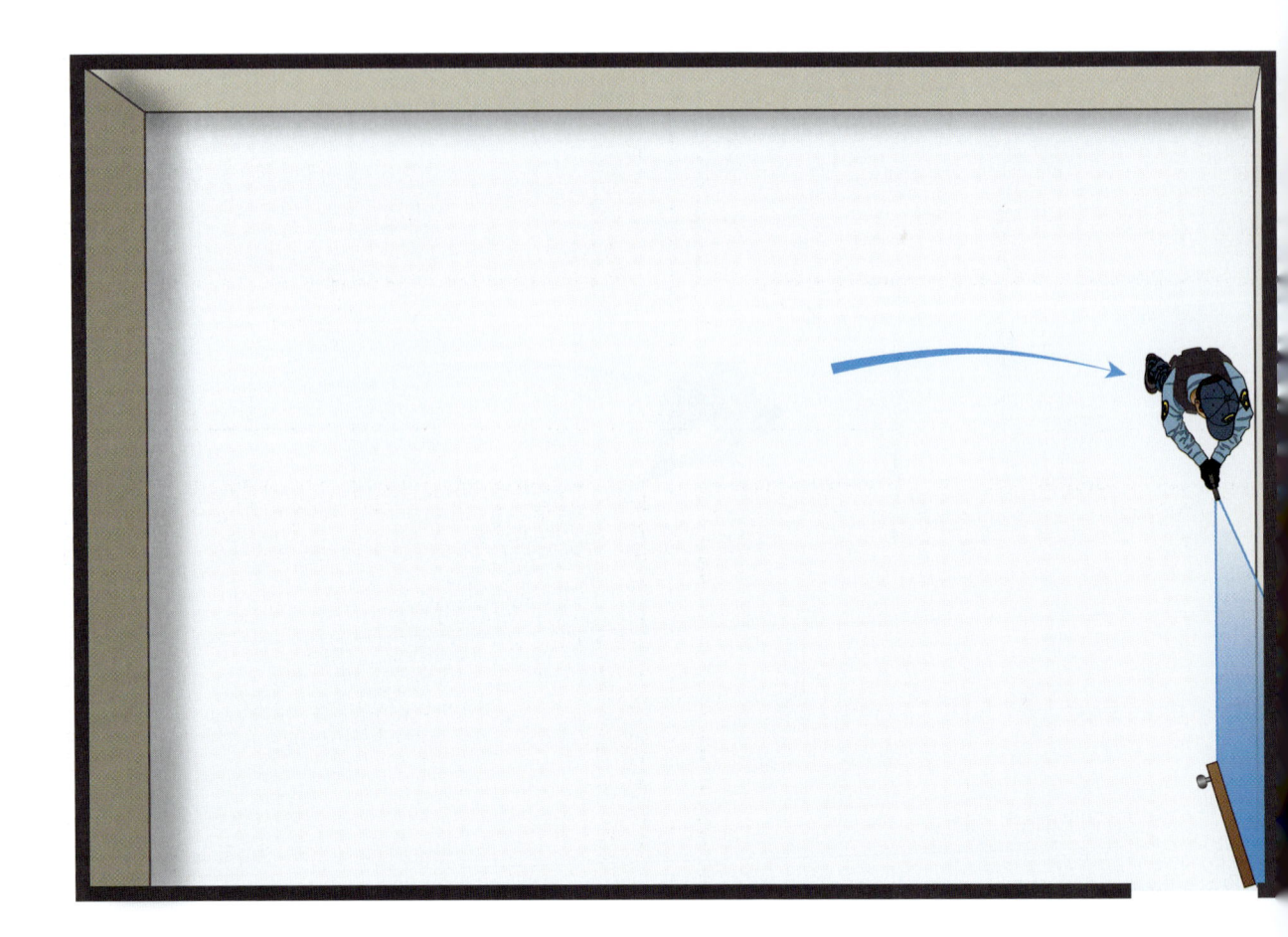

ONE-PERSON OPERATIONS: SINGLE-ROOM DEEP ENTRY

DEEP ENTRY: CORNER-FED CLOSED DOOR

STEPS 1 to 4 - Sweep and Clear the Corner

Entering a corner-fed closed door is similar to entering a corner-fed open door, except that the officer will need to quickly approach and swing the door open before starting the clearing process. The officer will open the door and back away quickly to avoid getting hit by indiscriminate fire. Once the door is open, the officer will conduct the sweep, clear the first corner and begin to scan while moving deeper into the room.

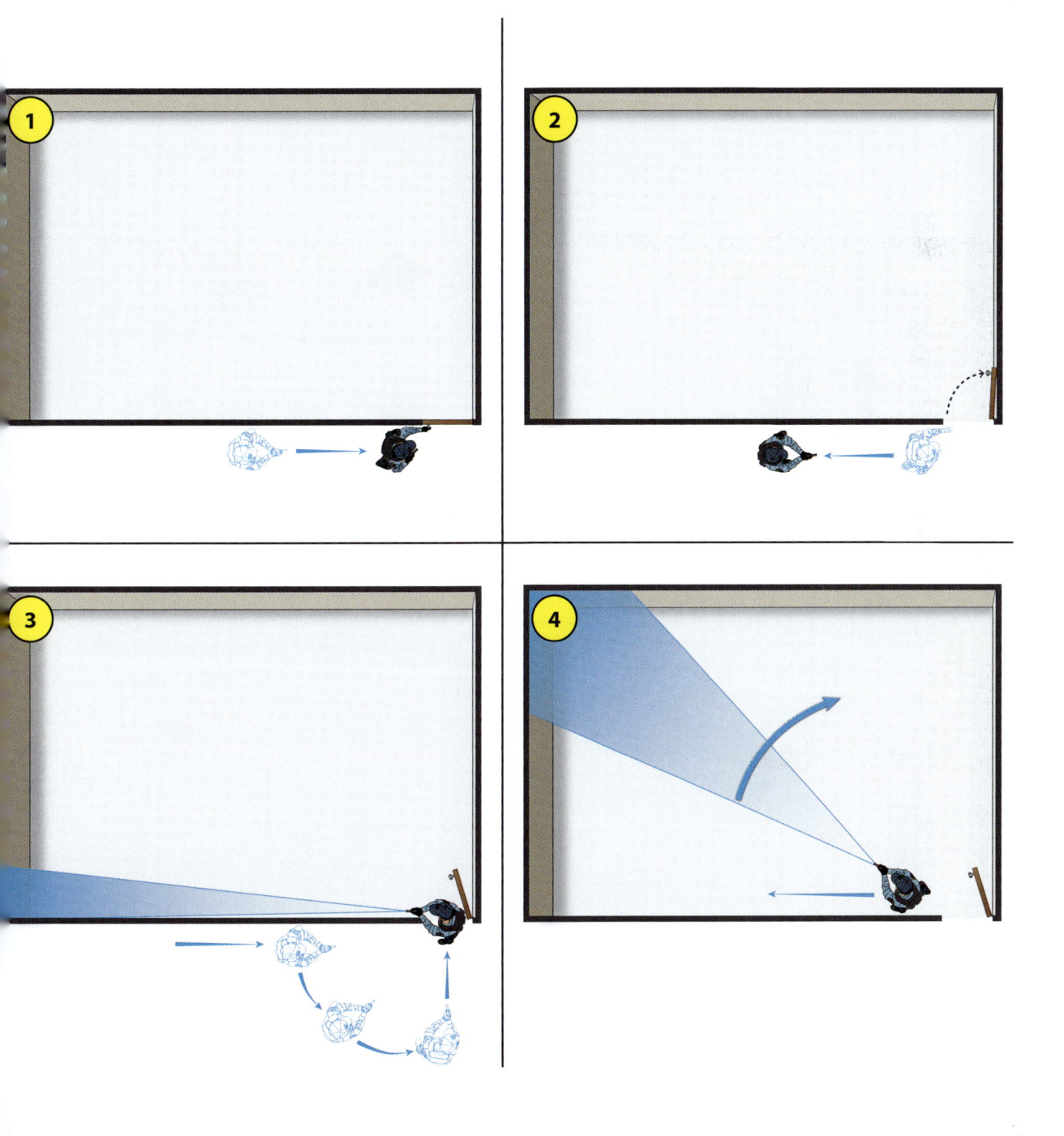

DEEP ENTRY: CORNER-FED CLOSED DOOR

STEPS 5 to 8 - Complete Scan and Check Behind the Door

The officer will continue to move deeper into the room while continuing to scan, clearing behind objects and furniture while moving. Once the scan is complete, the only remaining uncleared area should be the dead space behind the door. The officer will focus attention on the door and sweep around the room to a position to clear behind the door.

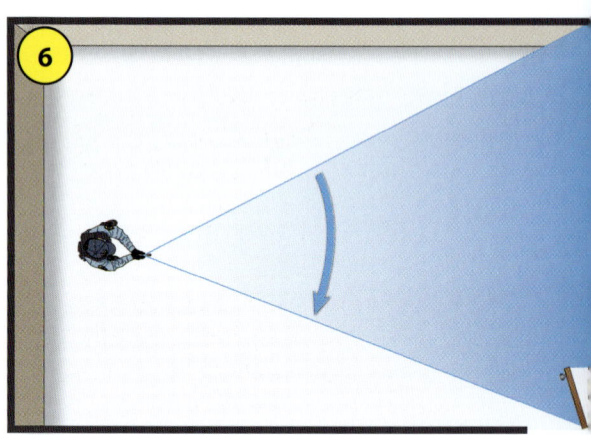

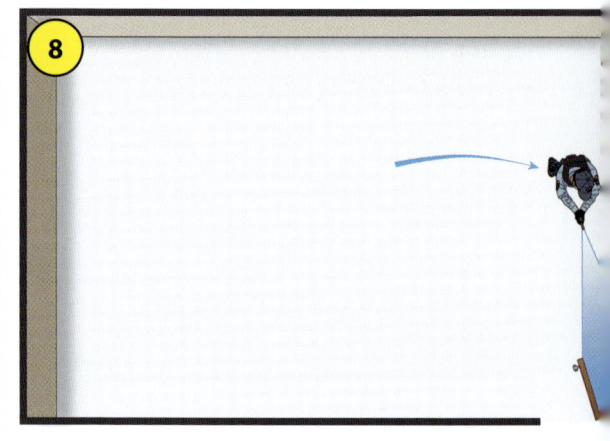

ONE-PERSON OPERATIONS
Multiple Rooms

Moving from room to room is difficult and dangerous when operating alone. Because a lone officer can only look and fire in one direction at a time, there is no perfect technique that eliminates all risk and covers all angles.

If all doors are closed, moving from room to room is not as difficult, since the sound of an opening door will give the officer time to pivot and orient the weapon towards the threat. When doors are closed, the officer can treat each room as a separate problem, opening doors in sequence and using the various clearing techniques described so far to move through the entire house or building.

Open doors present a more difficult problem for the single officer. The officer must quickly analyze the layout of the room as much as possible so that he/she is able to clear one room while moving into position to conduct a sweep of the next room. While moving, the officer should take advantage of cover and concealment in the room as much as possible and be prepared to fall back if necessary.

Multiple open doors in one room present one of the most dangerous challenges for the lone officer. However, with practice, a skilled officer can quickly clear multiple doorways, danger areas and rooms using a combination of the various techniques described so far.

For single-person operations, it is even more difficult to apply fixed rules or formulas to solve tactical problems. Unfortunately, operating as a lone officer is one of the most dangerous scenarios, particularly when facing heavily armed adversaries. However, a well trained officer with good shooting skills can use speed and good tactics to quickly gain the upper hand and resolve a potentially disastrous situation.

OPEN DOOR ON THE FAR WALL

STEP 1 - Conduct Deep Entry

The officer will enter the first room using the deep entry technique. If possible, the officer should choose t[o] enter in the direction of greatest threat. If no threat is detected, the officer should choose the direction tha[t] offers the best cover and concealment or the best observation behind furniture in the room. Depending o[n] the situation, the officer may also choose to execute a shallow entry instead of a deep entry.

OPEN DOOR ON THE FAR WALL

STEP 2 - Prepare to Enter Next Door

As the officer completes the deep entry movement, he/she will be approaching the open door on the far wall and in the ideal position to conduct a sweep on the open door.

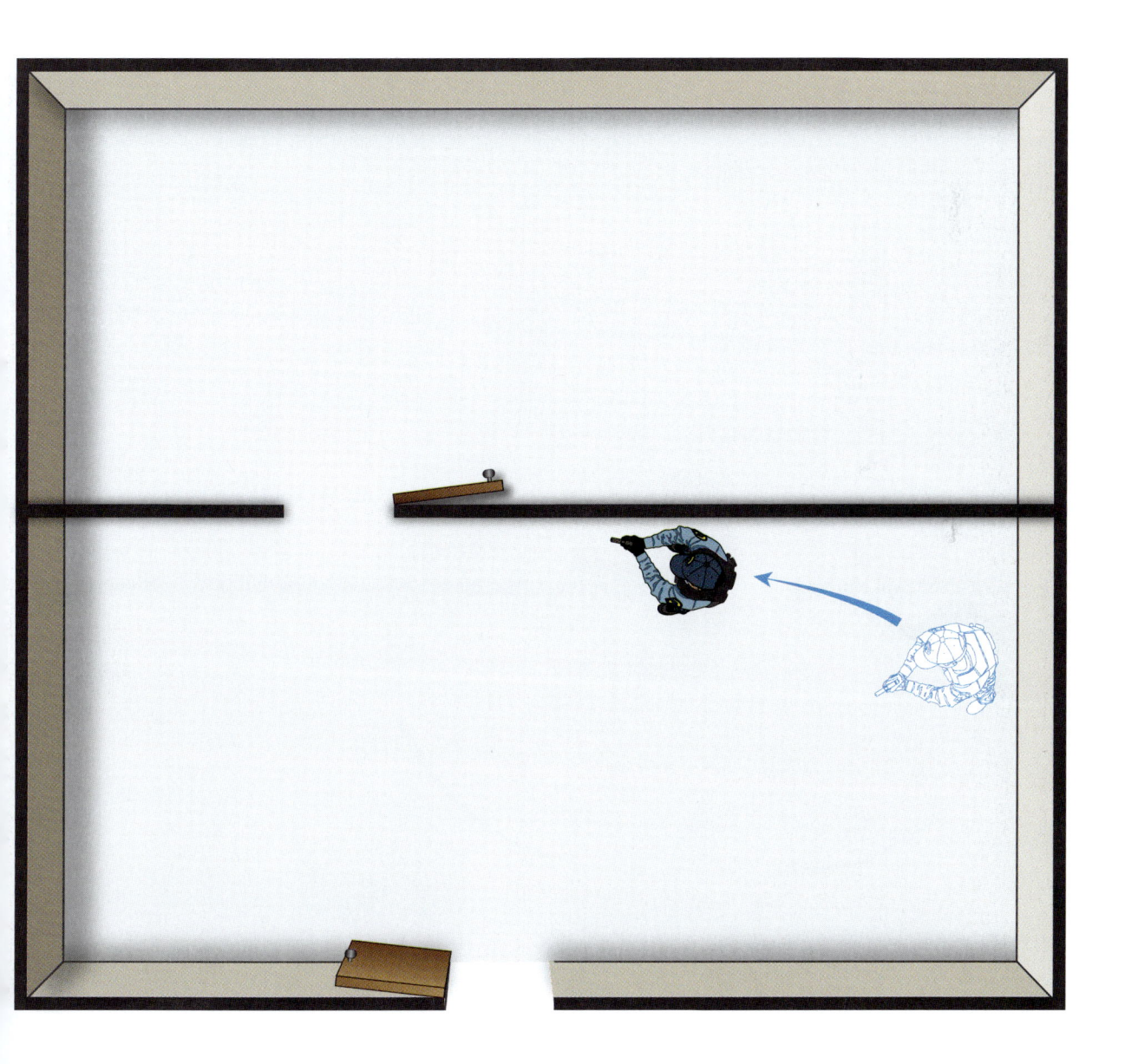

OPEN DOOR ON THE FAR WALL

STEP 3 - Conduct Sweep

The officer will conduct a sweep on the open door while maintaining awareness of his/her surroundings as much as possible. This might mean looking over the shoulder to check the rear periodically, or stopping momentarily to take cover behind solid furniture. There is no fixed formula and maximum situational awareness is critical.

ONE-PERSON OPERATIONS: MULTIPLE ROOMS   333

OPEN DOOR ON THE FAR WALL

STEP 4 - Enter the Next Room

Once the sweep is complete, the officer will conduct a half sweep and then move straight towards the next door to conduct another deep or shallow entry as needed.

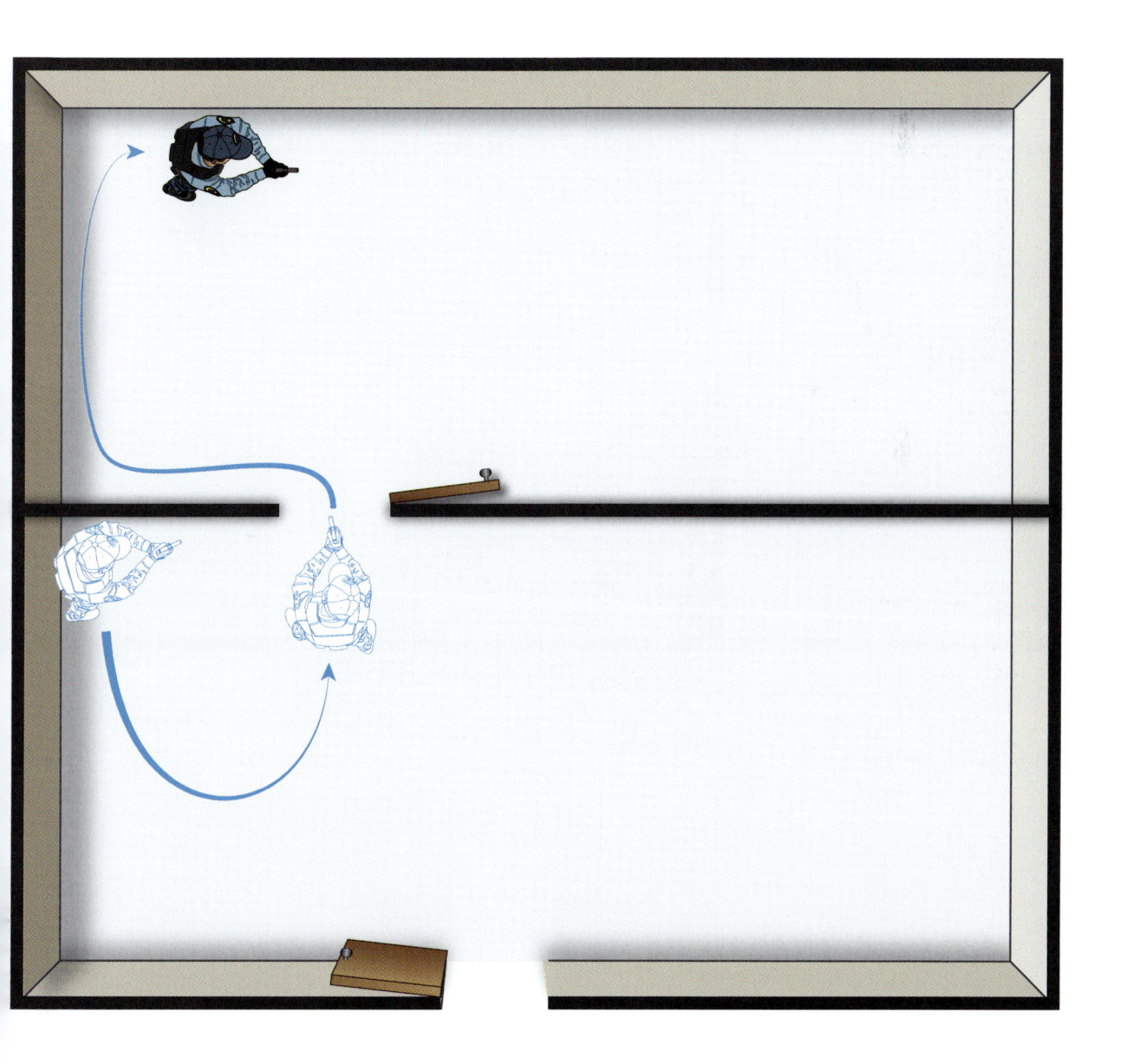

OPEN DOOR ON THE SIDE WALL

STEP 1 - Conduct Deep Entry

The officer will enter the first room using the deep entry technique. The officer should generally choose to enter in the opposite direction of the next open door. This will prevent the officer from having to expose his/her back to the door and will give the officer some observation into the next room while conducting the deep entry. **NOTE: The following steps show only one example of how to handle this configuration. The officer might choose to use other combinations of shallow entry, deep entry and quick-clear etc.**

ONE-PERSON OPERATIONS: MULTIPLE ROOMS — 335

OPEN DOOR ON THE SIDE WALL

STEP 2 - Prepare to Enter Next Door

After conducting the deep entry the officer will continue to move until he/she is in position to conduct a sweep on the next door.

OPEN DOOR ON THE SIDE WALL

STEP 3 - Conduct Sweep

The officer will conduct a sweep or half sweep on the open door while maintaining awareness of his/her surroundings as much as possible. This might mean looking over the shoulder to check the rear periodically, or stopping momentarily to take cover behind solid furniture. There is no fixed formula and maximum situational awareness is critical.

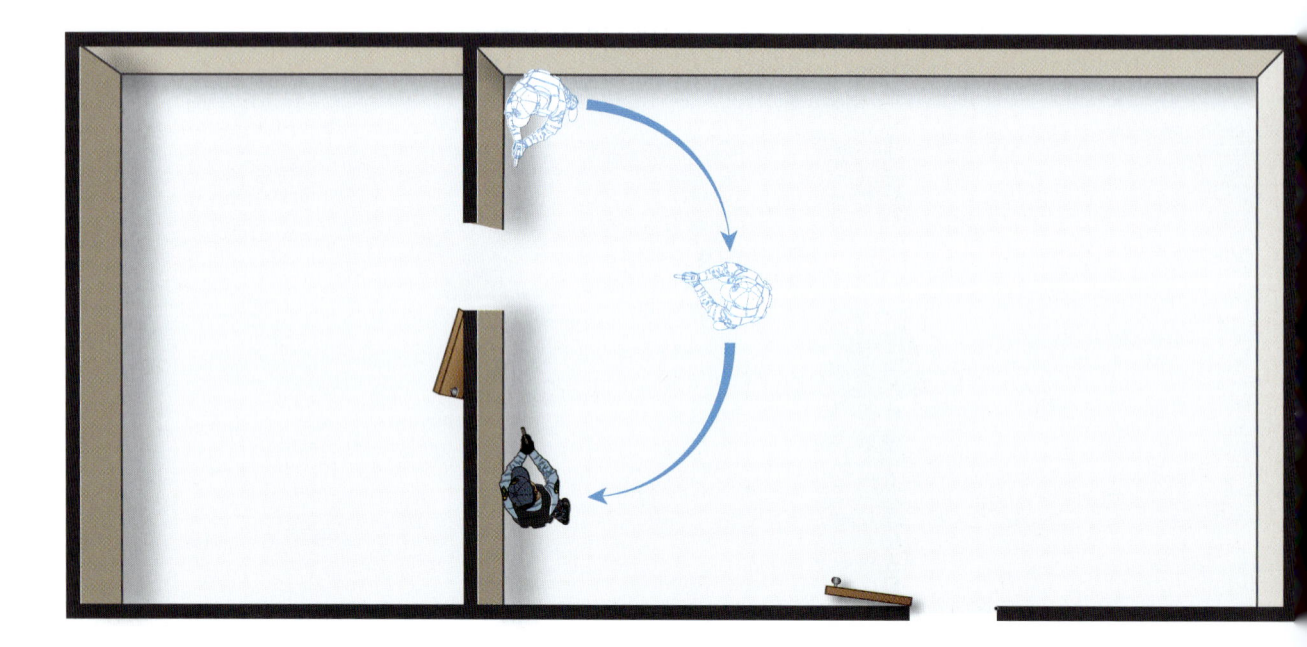

ONE-PERSON OPERATIONS: MULTIPLE ROOMS   337

OPEN DOOR ON THE SIDE WALL

STEP 4 - Enter the Next Room

Once the sweep is complete, the officer will conduct a half sweep and then move straight towards the next door to conduct another deep or shallow entry as needed.

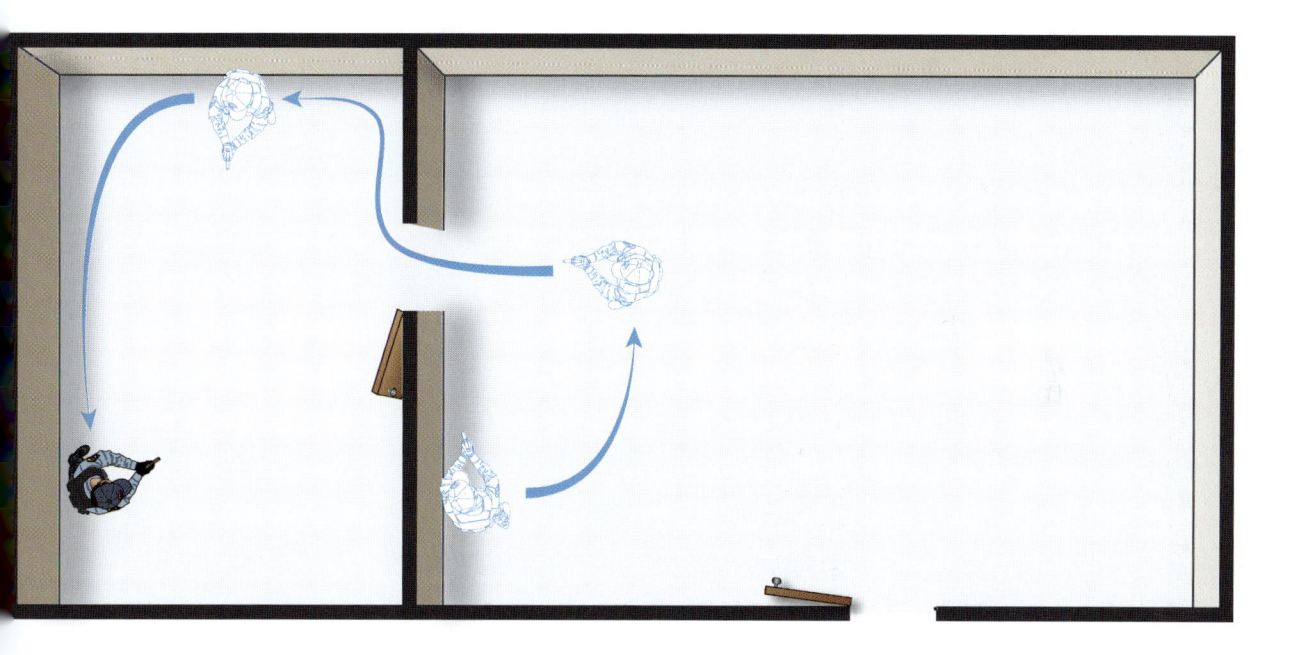

CLOSED DOORS

COMPLETE SEQUENCE

Moving from room to room through closed doors as a single officer is much easier than dealing with open doors. The officer will simply open each door, back away and conduct a sweep before entering the next room.
NOTE: The sweep movement is highlighted with red arrows to make the sequence easier to follow.

MULTIPLE DOORS

COMPLETE SEQUENCE

Encountering multiple doors in a room as a single officer is one of the most challenging problems, particularly if all of the doors are open. If some doors are open and others are closed, the officer should generally clear through the open doors first. There is no fixed formula for dealing with multiple open doors. The officer should move quickly, maintaining situational awareness and taking advantage of cover and concealment when possible. The officer can use any combination of clearing techniques just described. The quick clear can be particularly useful when checking multiple open doors for threats. **NOTE: The illustration below shows one example of how to handle this configuration. The sweep movement is highlighted with red arrows to make the sequence easier to follow.**

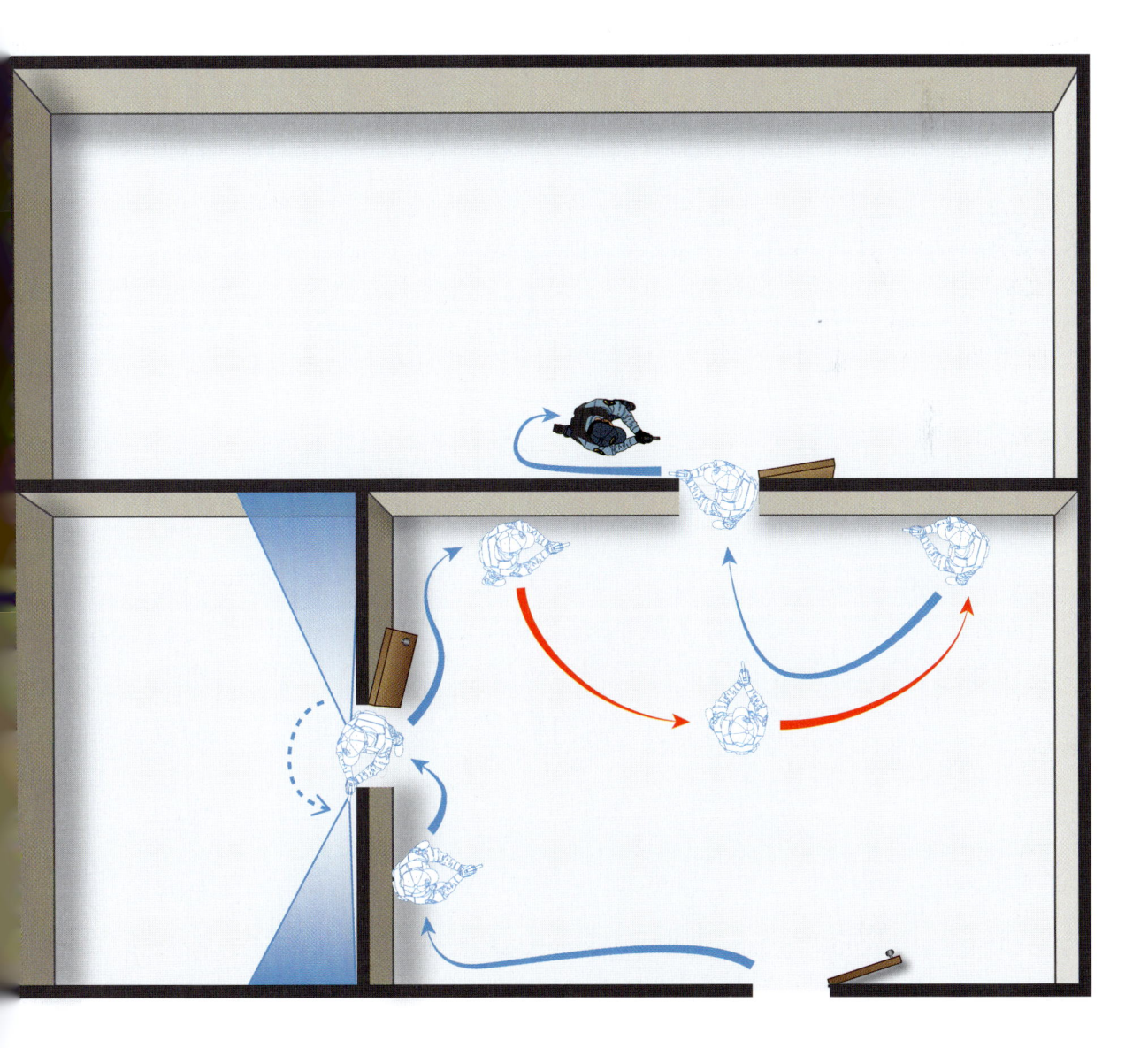

ONE-PERSON OPERATIONS
Hallways

Hallways can be found in the vast majority of residential and commercial buildings. Hallways, by nature, are danger areas. When moving through a hallway, the officer's first objective should be to get out of the hallway as soon as possible. Hallways frequently have multiple doors all along their length, offering many potential openings from which adversaries might emerge. Hallways also frequently have little furniture that can be used for cover and concealment. Finally, the shape of the hallway makes it easy for an enemy at either end to spray a large number of bullets down the hallway that will most likely hit anyone standing exposed. For all these reasons, hallways are danger areas and the officer should try to spend as little time in the hallway as possible.

Most of the following techniques focus on the most deliberate and thorough methods for hallway clearing. However, keep in mind that once officers understand and master these techniques, there may be situations when they will want to simplify or modify the techniques in the interest of speed. This might mean not conducting a full sweep when standing in a hallway but rather moving directly into the room and conducting a shallow or deep entry. In other cases, the officer's best course of action might just be to run down the hallway as quickly as possible to try to find a covered and concealed position before addressing the threat. There are no fixed solutions. The key point is to avoid being exposed in the hallway, improvising as necessary to minimize risk.

A lone officer must provide his/her own rear security. To do this, the officer will simply look over the shoulder frequently and watch out for possible threats coming from any direction. However, it is important to never walk backwards since walking backwards makes it very easy to trip and fall down, especially in the dark. In team operations, the eyes and the weapon are usually pointing in the same direction. For single-person operations it is necessary for officers to keep the "head on a swivel," constantly looking around to identify danger areas and potential threats. Situational awareness is especially critical in one-person operations.

HALLWAY MOVEMENT

Moving Down the Hallway

When moving down a hallway it is best to remain near the middle of the hallway while moving. This will give the officer the best angle to observe doorways or openings on each side of the hallway as early as possible, giving the officer time to react and plan his/her movements. If the officer stays very close to one wall or the other, it will be more difficult to see doors on that side of the hallway and determine if they are open or not. Therefore, it is generally best to stay near the middle of the hallway while moving. Also, bullets traveling down the hallway will often hug the walls, making the space near the walls more dangerous.

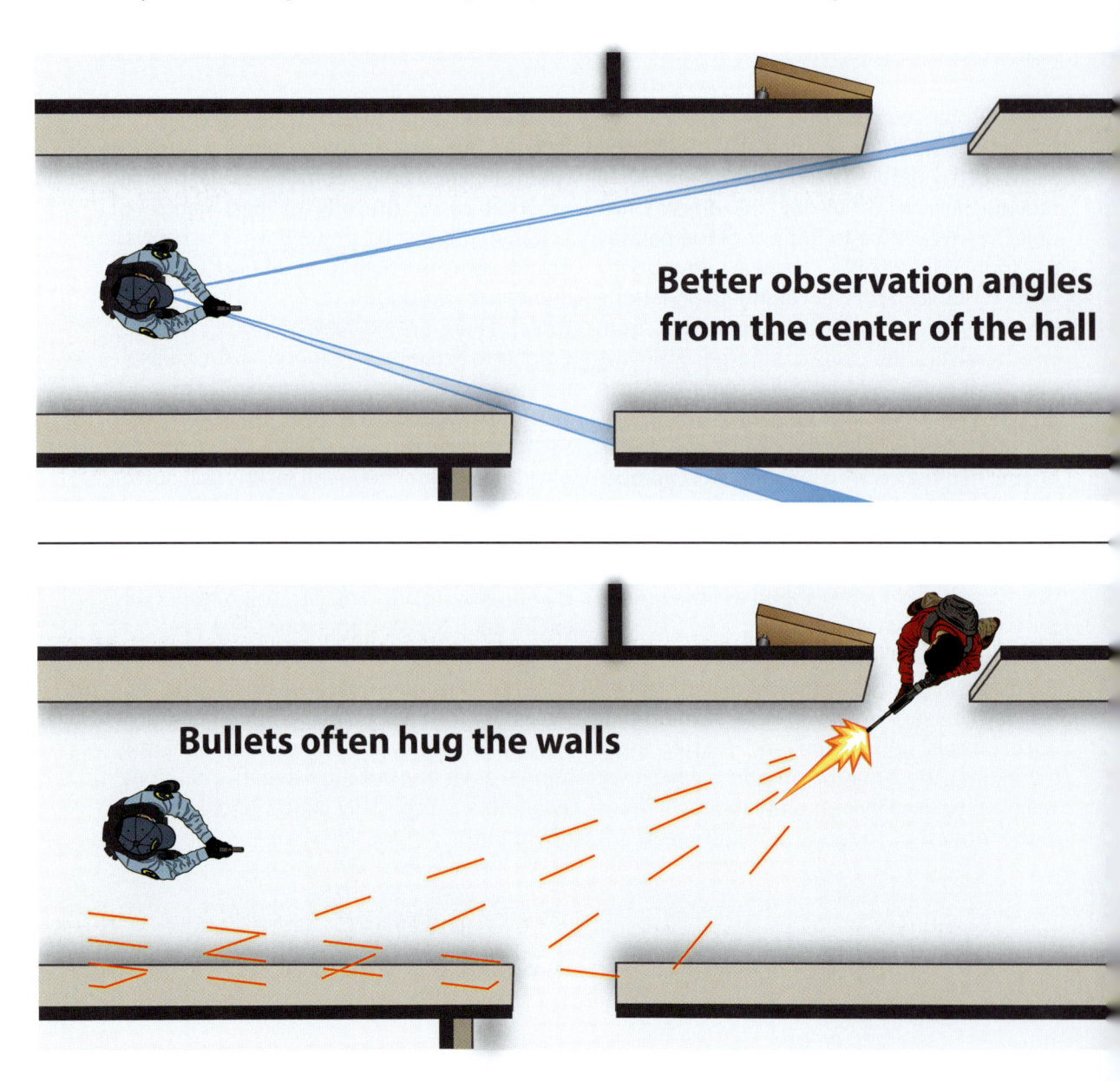

Better observation angles from the center of the hall

Bullets often hug the walls

HALLWAY MOVEMENT

Passing Open Doors

Once the officer identifies an open door down the hall, he/she can begin to move towards the opposite wall. This will give the officer the best field of vision into the room. Essentially, the officer will be widening his/her path to conduct a hasty sweep of the door in passing. By moving in this way, the officer will be "weaving" down the hall, covering each door as it emerges. This technique only applies to alternating open doors. Opposing open doors (doors directly across from one another) require a different technique that will be explained later in this chapter.

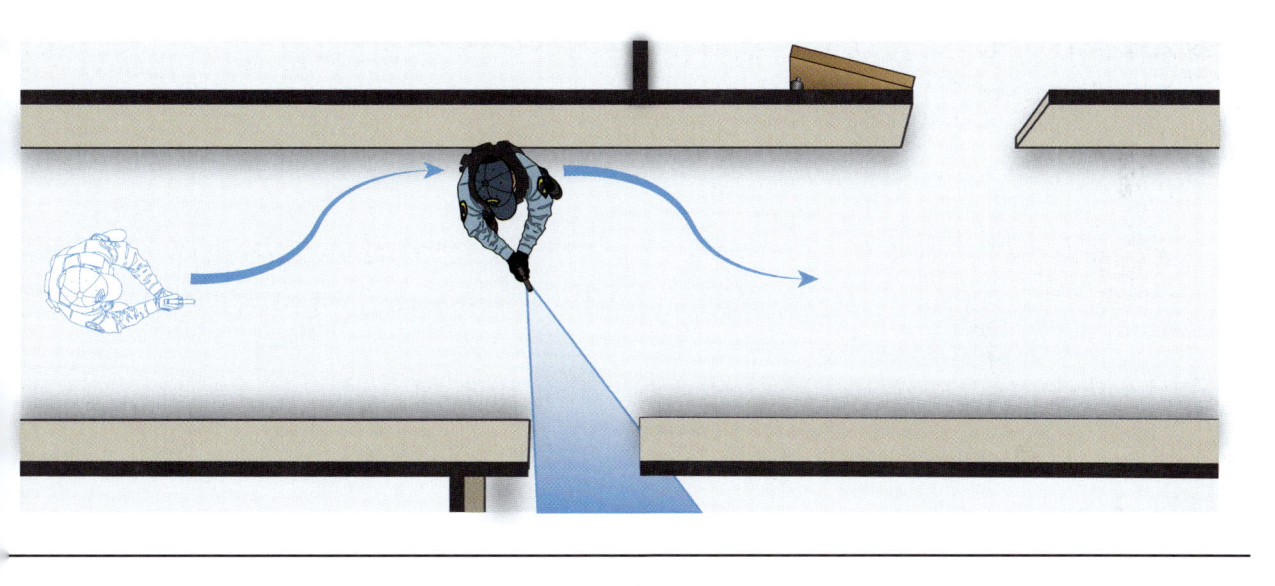

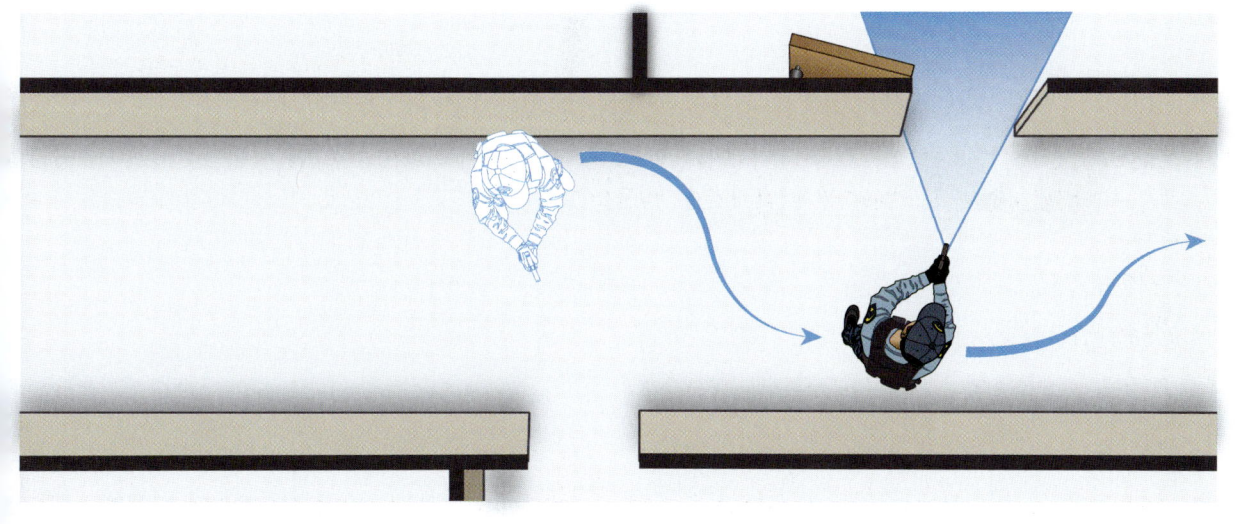

HALLWAY MOVEMENT

Entering a Room From the Hallway

The procedures for entering a room from a hallway are similar to the room clearing procedures described s far. The officer can use any of the techniques already described to clear a room from a hallway including cle without entry, quick clear, shallow entry and deep entry. However, the main difference is that the depth of th sweep will be limited by the width of the hallway.

HALLWAY MOVEMENT

Moving from a Room into the Hallway

When the officer is finished clearing a room and wants to move back out into the hallway, it is best not to just walk through the door assuming the hallway is still clear. The safest approach is to clear the hallway again before walking out. The officer can clear the hallway using any of the clearing techniques already described for clearing rooms. However, probably the easiest and fastest is to just conduct a quick clear by checking right and left from the door. Once the hallway is clear the officer can resume movement down the hallway in the desired direction of travel.

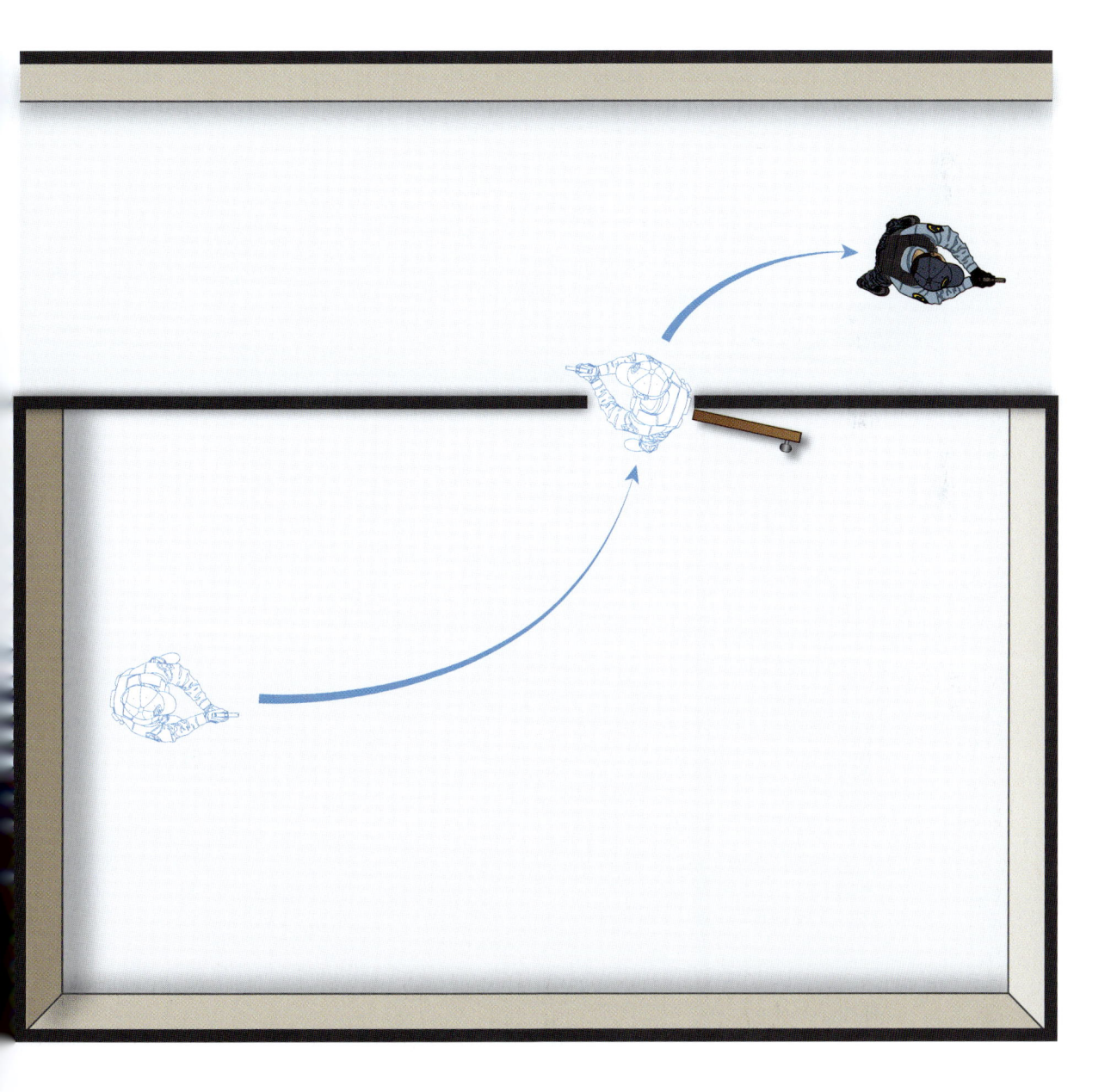

HALLWAYS: L-SHAPE INTERSECTION

COMPLETE SEQUENCE

The L-shape is the simplest of the hallway intersections. To clear an L-shape intersection the officer will positio close to the corner, then quickly step out and direct the weapon around the corner. The key point is to expos as little of the body as possible. It is best not to step or jump fully into the hallway but rather to move ju enough to get the weapon around the corner, using the wall for cover and concealment. While the wall probably not bulletproof, it will at least provide some protection. Once the hallway is clear, the officer ca continue movement in the desired direction.

HALLWAYS: T-SHAPE INTERSECTION

STEP 1 - Conduct Sweep Before the Intersection

The officer will stop short of the T-intersection to avoid exposure and to ensure his/her shadow does not extend into the hall where it might be seen by adversaries around the corner. This stopping point is marked with the dashed red line below. From this position, the officer will conduct a sweep to clear as far as possible to the right and left down each hallway. The officer will not be able to see all the way down either hallway but the sweep will help identify any adversaries hiding behind the corners. In general, it is best not to take too much time conducting the sweep. The officer is still in a danger area and should conduct the sweep as quickly as possible and then move on.

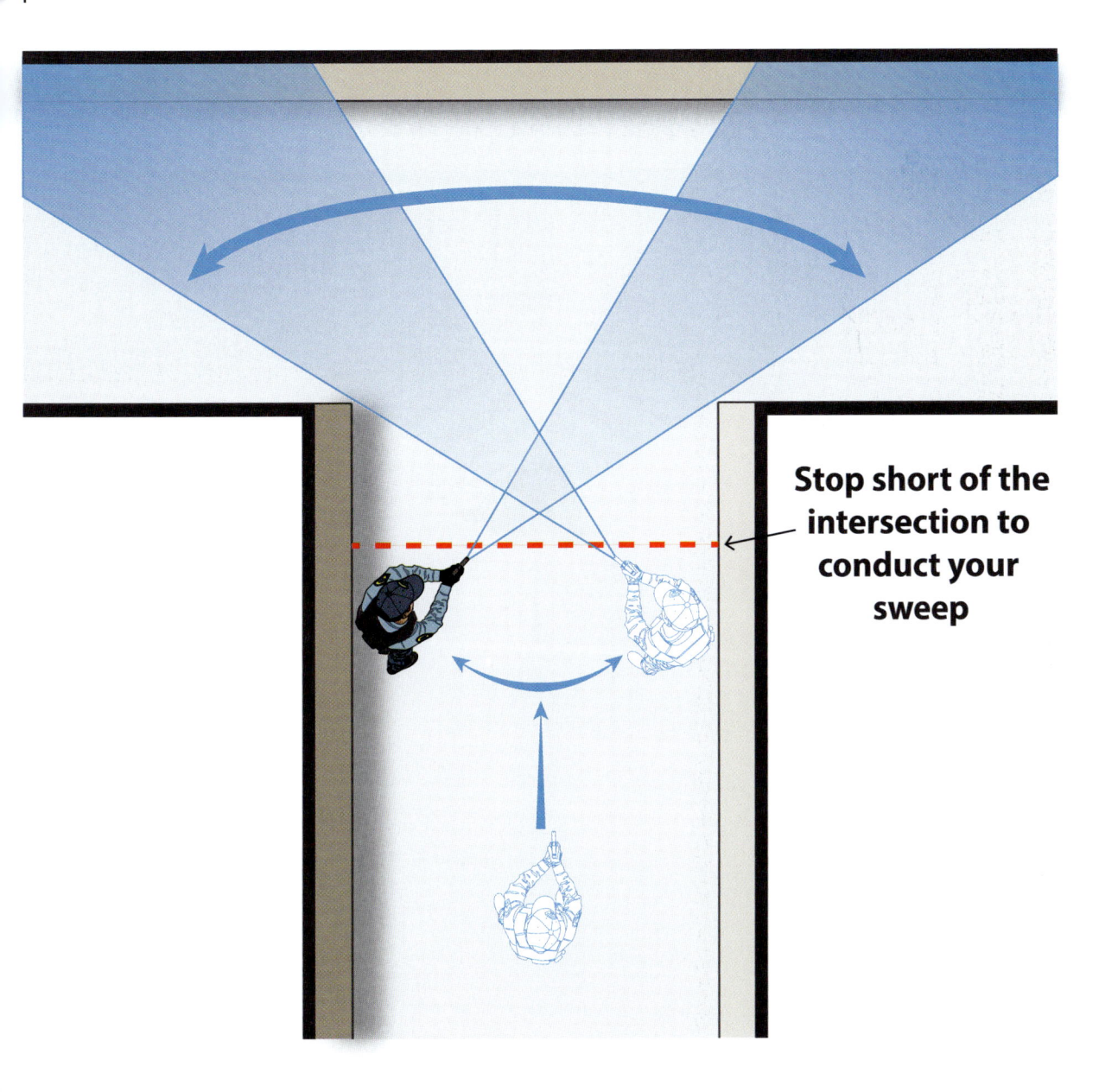

Stop short of the intersection to conduct your sweep

HALLWAYS: T-SHAPE INTERSECTION

STEP 2 - Clear the First Hallway

By conducting the sweep and listening for sounds coming from either direction, the officer must determine which direction to clear first. Ideally, if the officer hears something or sees something coming from either side during the sweep, he/she will clear that side first. If the officer does not hear or see anything it is generally easier to clear the strong side (weapon hand side) first. When ready, the officer will move up quickly to the intersection and bring the weapon around the corner. The officer should expose the body as little as possible while still ensuring he/she can see all the way down the hallway.

HALLWAYS: T-SHAPE INTERSECTION

STEP 3 - Clear the Second Hallway

Once the officer has cleared down one hallway, he/she will quickly turn 180-degrees to clear down the opposite hallway. If the officer has identified adversaries to either the left or right he/she can either decide to remain in place and engage them from the corner, or the officer might decide to quickly fall back to a room or covered position and try to draw the adversaries out.

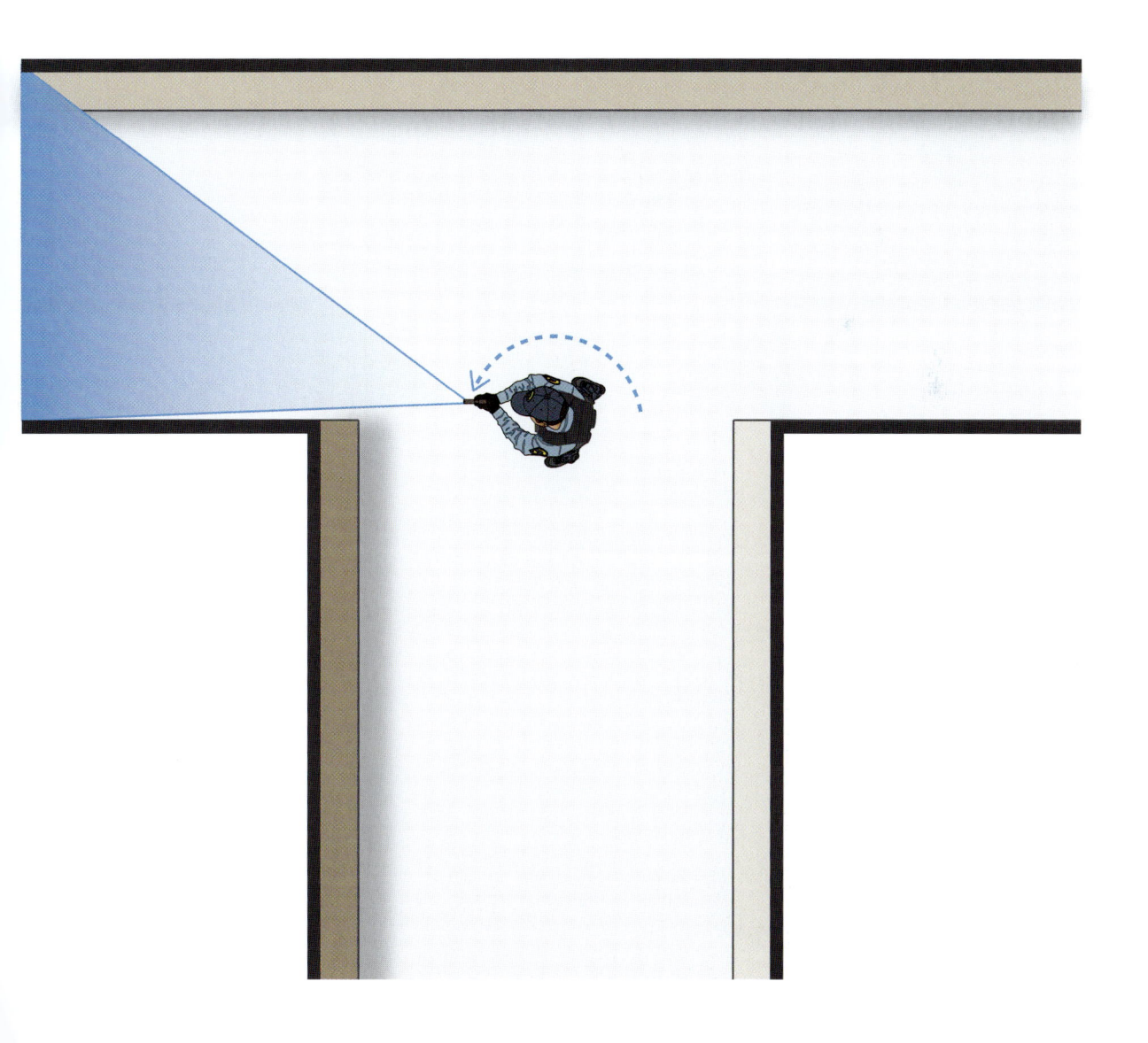

HALLWAYS: T-SHAPE INTERSECTION

STEP 4 - Continue Movement

Once the hallway is clear, the officer can continue moving in the desired direction. Remember that hallways are danger areas so it is critical to continue moving quickly and get out of the hallway as soon as possible. Also officers must remain aware of their surroundings, listen for footsteps and periodically check the rear.

One-Person Operations: Hallways   351

HALLWAYS: X-SHAPE INTERSECTION

STEP 1 - Conduct Sweep Before the Intersection

The officer will stop short of the X-intersection to avoid exposure and to ensure his/her shadow does not extend into the hall where it might be seen by adversaries around the corner. This stopping point is marked with the dashed red line below. From this position, the officer will conduct a sweep to achieve maximum visibility down the hallways to the left, right and front. As with the T-intersection, it is best not to take too much time conducting the sweep. The hallway is a danger area so the officer should conduct the sweep as quickly as possible and then move on.

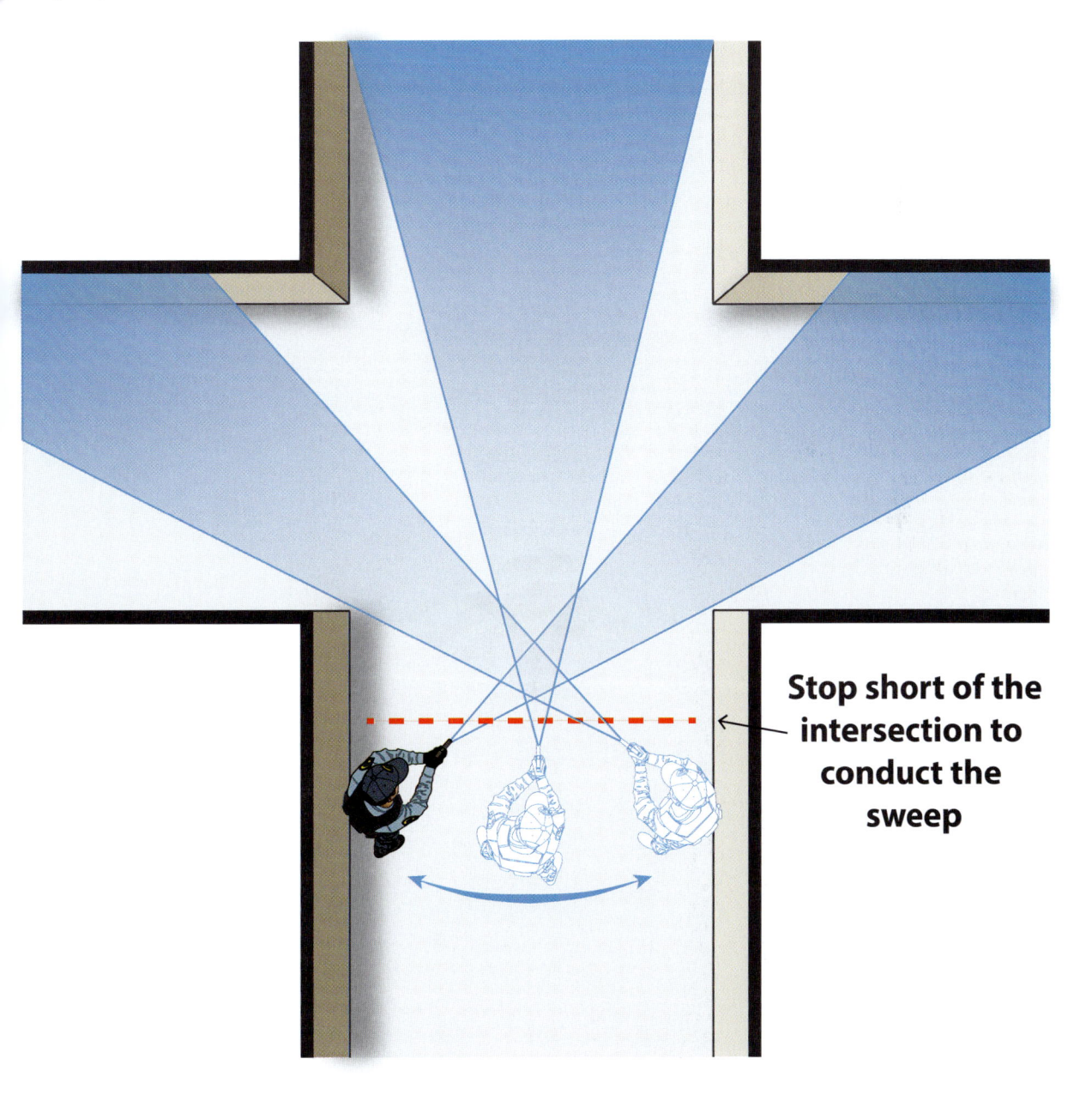

Stop short of the intersection to conduct the sweep

HALLWAYS: X-SHAPE INTERSECTION

STEP 2 - Clear to One Side

By conducting the sweep and listening for sounds coming from either direction, the officer must determine which direction to clear first. Ideally, if the officer hears something or sees something coming from either side during the sweep, he/she will clear that side first. If the officer does not hear or see anything it is generally easier to clear the strong side (weapon hand side) first. When ready, the officer will move up quickly to the intersection and bring the weapon around the corner. The officer should expose the body as little as possible while still ensuring he/she can see all the way down the hallway. In an X-shape intersection, the officer must also remain alert for possible threats to the front.

HALLWAYS: X-SHAPE INTERSECTION

STEP 3 - Clear the Other Side

Once the officer has cleared down one hallway, he/she will quickly turn 180-degrees to clear down the opposite hallway. If the officer has identified adversaries to either the left or right he/she can either decide to remain in place and engage them from the corner, or the officer might decide to quickly fall back to a room or covered position and try to draw the adversaries out.

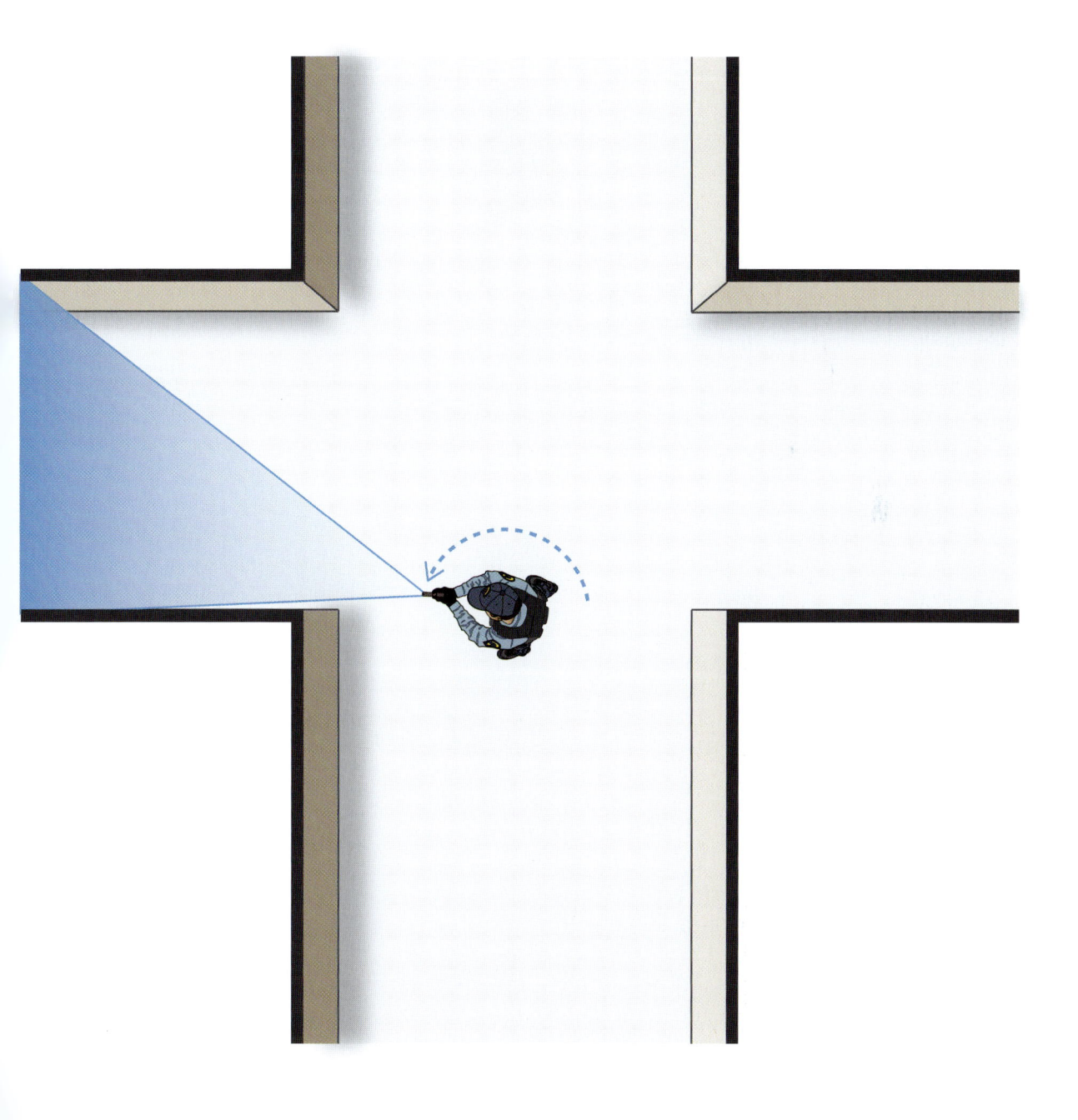

HALLWAYS: X-SHAPE INTERSECTION

STEP 4 - Continue Movement

Once the hallway is clear, the officer can continue moving in the desired direction. Remember that hallway are danger areas so it is critical to continue moving quickly and get out of the hallway as soon as possibl Also, officers must remain aware of their surroundings, listen for footsteps and periodically check the rear. the officer chooses to move forward, he/she should not stop right after passing the intersection but instea keep moving quickly and create distance from the intersection, minimizing exposure.

ONE-PERSON OPERATIONS: HALLWAYS   355

HALLWAYS: OPPOSING OPEN DOORS

STEP 1 - Conduct Sweep

Opposing open doors present one of the most dangerous challenges in single-person CQB because as a single officer it is impossible to cover two directions at once. There is no perfect solution to this problem and the officer will be assuming some risk whatever he/she chooses to do. The safest way to approach the problem is to begin by conducting a sweep at a safe distance from the opposing doors. This distance is represented by the red dashed line in the diagram below. The officer is keeping distance to minimize exposure and to prevent noise or shadow from alerting the adversary. The officer will conduct a sweep in order to clear as much of the two rooms as possible while remaining at a safe distance.

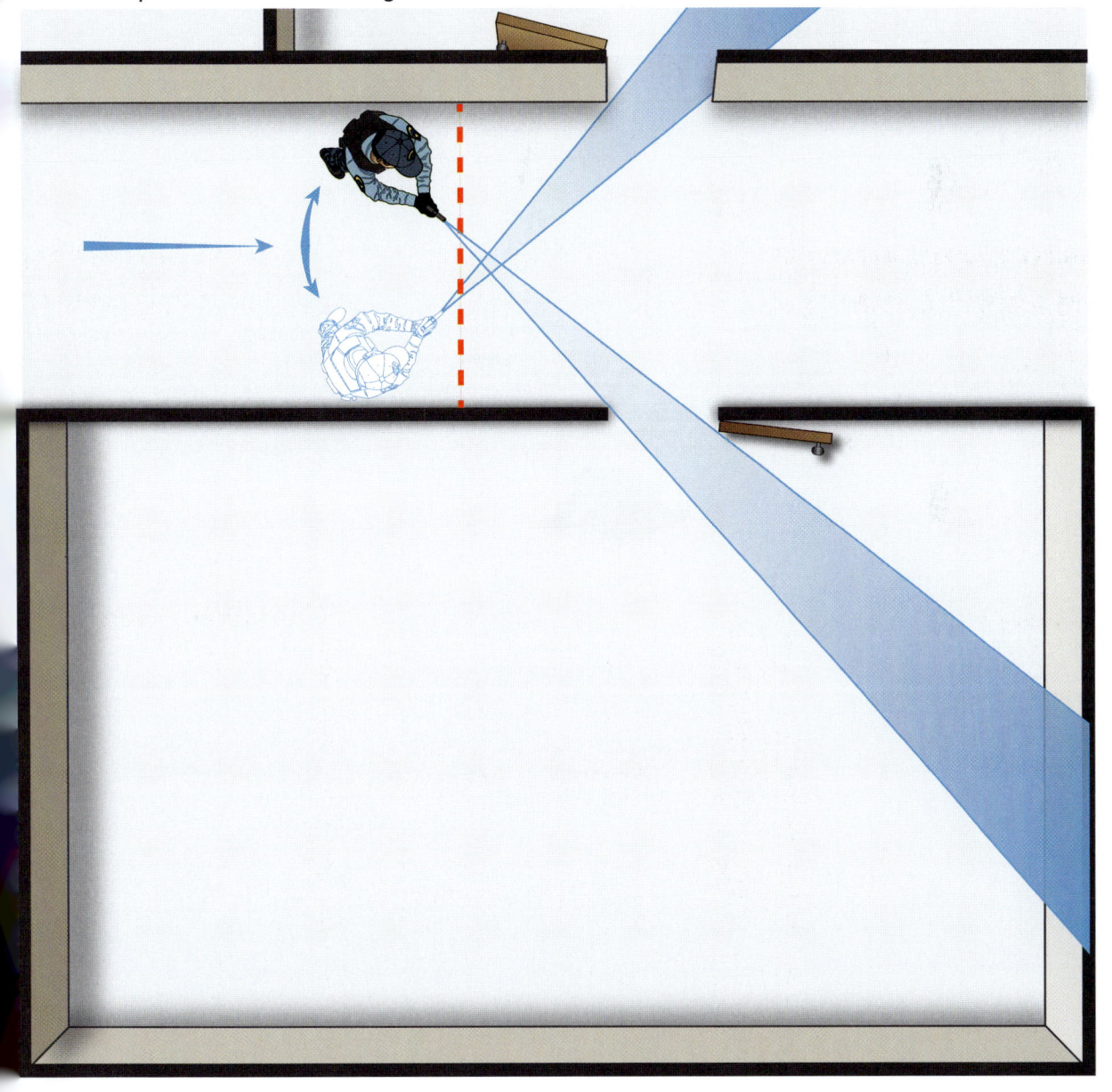

HALLWAYS: OPPOSING OPEN DOORS

STEP 2 - Enter One Room

Conducting the sweep and listening for movement should help the officer prioritize which room to enter firs
Ideally, the officer will want to enter the room with the greatest potential threat first. However, by turning t
enter one room, the officer will be exposing his/her back to the opposing door. The best way to minimize th
risk is to momentarily turn and clear the opposing door, then enter the room quickly using either a shallow
deep entry technique.

ONE-PERSON OPERATIONS: HALLWAYS   357

HALLWAYS: OPPOSING OPEN DOORS

STEP 3 - Quick Clear the Hallway Again

Clearing the first room will simplify the tactical equation. Once the first room is clear, all the officer has to do is re-enter the hallway and move across to clear the second room. Before entering the hallway, it is best to perform a quick clear from the doorway, checking both left and right before moving.

HALLWAYS: OPPOSING OPEN DOORS

STEP 4 - Move Across to Clear the Other Room

After performing the quick clear, the officer will move across the hall and enter through the opposing door t clear the second room using either shallow or deep entry. Once the second room is clear, the officer can safe continue to move down the hallway. It is possible to bypass opposing open doors in an emergency situatio where time is critical.

ONE-PERSON OPERATIONS
Stairwells

Clearing stairwells as an individual is very dangerous and you should avoid stairwells if at all possible. If you must enter a stairwell, the clearing process is actually relatively simple because there is only so much you can do to cover all of the potentially exposed angles in a stairwell. As in the hallway, your best option is to use speed to your advantage and get out of the stairwell as quickly as possible. Stairwells are danger areas so move through quickly and find a better fighting position. In commercial or industrial buildings, stairwells typically consist of sturdy metal and concrete construction with steel beams, making them particularly dangerous since bullets are more likely to ricochet off the solid walls.

Whether you are moving up a stairwell or down a stairwell, the technique remains the same. Orient your weapon in the direction of travel (up or down) and keep as close as possible to the wall, away from the center banister. This will give you the best angle to see around the bend in the stairs. Turn your body towards the bend in the stairwell as you move, being careful to watch your step and not trip. This way you will be ready to engage any adversaries waiting around the bend in the stairs as soon as they emerge.

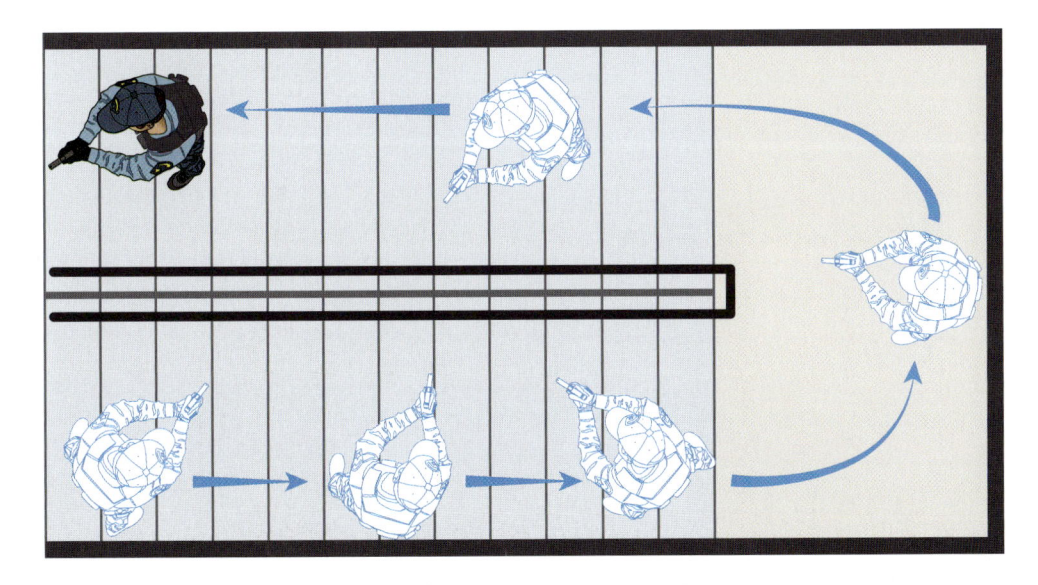

ONE-PERSON OPERATIONS
Complex Configurations

When an officer clears a house or building in a real-life scenario, he/she will encounter many different combinations of furniture, obstacles and complex room configurations. In many cases, the techniques for dealing with these situations is the same as for team operations. However, in other cases the procedures are different. Complex configurations are particularly dangerous for single officers since they have no backup and cannot cover more than one direction at a time.

The procedure for dealing with furniture as a single officer is relatively simple. Because there are no other officers present to perform a coordinated movement, the single officer will simply move quickly to pass by obstacles in the room or check behind furniture for adversaries.

Confined areas with multiple openings (such as foyers, entryways or vestibules) are also very common in modern architecture and present a difficult tactical problem for the single officer. Rather than try to dominate these danger areas, the officer should quickly move past them into a room that offers better protection.

Another common configuration, found in commercial structures, are larger rooms filled with cubicles. Cubicles are particularly dangerous since they must each be cleared individually and offer many hiding places for adversaries. When a single officer must clear a room full of cubicles, quick movement is critical since the officer will be exposed from many angles while moving. The officer can choose to move diagonally or laterally from cubicle to cubicle, looking for threats. Generally, the officer should clear the closest cubicle first and move down the row, crossing over as needed.

CONFINED AREAS WITH MULTIPLE OPENINGS

STEP 1 - Officer Commits to One Opening

Confined areas with multiple openings are very common in architectural designs. When the officer enter he/she will be in a very vulnerable position with multiple openings and danger areas all around. Therefor the officer will want to move out of this danger area as quickly as possible. He/she will make a fast decisic to commit to one of the doors and move towards it quickly while clearing on the move. It can be usef for the officer to give a quick glance over his/her shoulder, opposite the direction of movement, to increa situational awareness.

ONE-PERSON OPERATIONS: COMPLEX CONFIGURATIONS 363

CONFINED AREAS WITH MULTIPLE OPENINGS

STEP 2 - Enter and Clear

Once the officer passes through the door, he/she will conduct either a shallow or deep entry technique to clear the room. Once again, the officer quickly entered the room because he/she was vulnerable in the entryway or hallway.

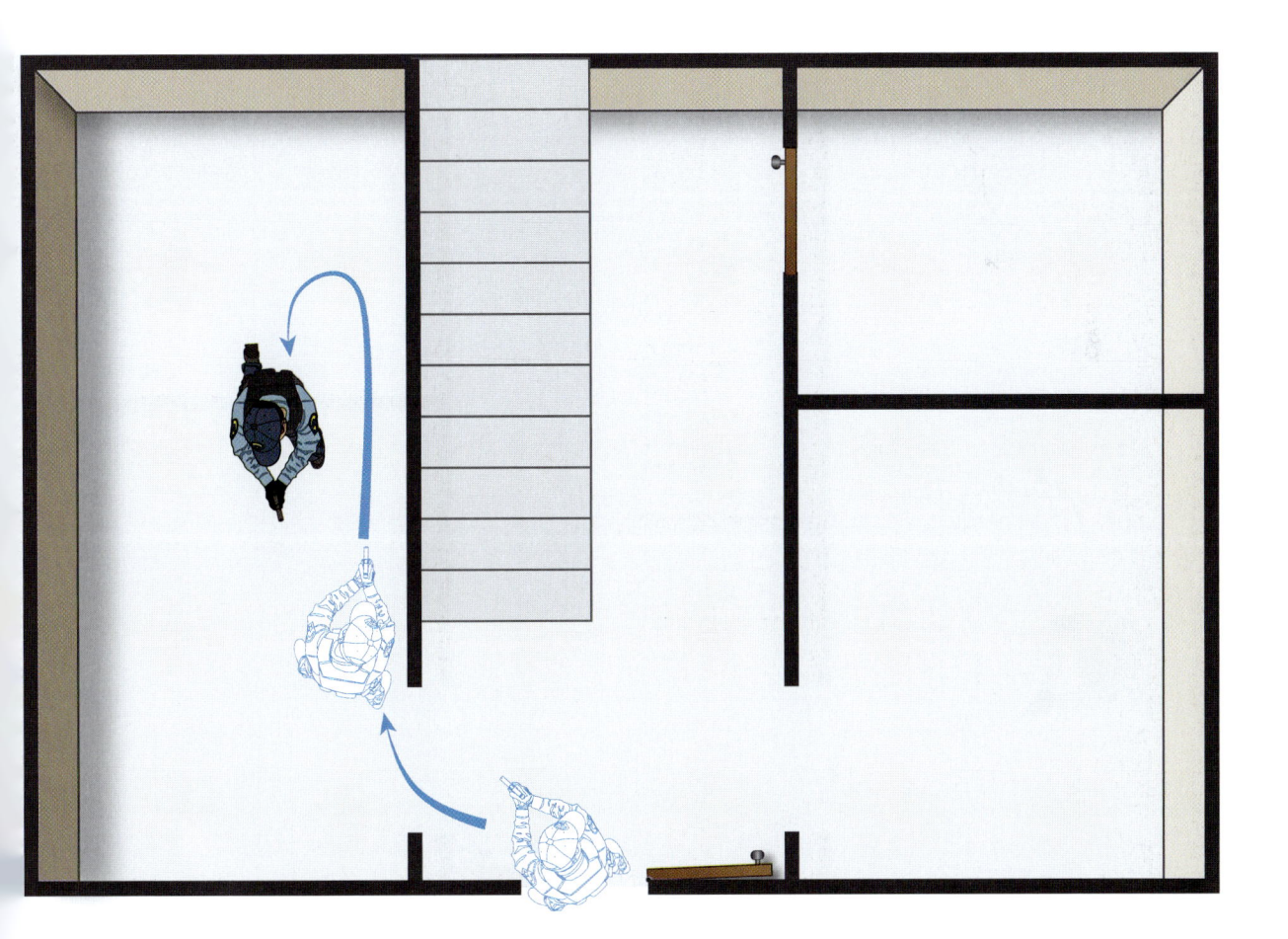

CONFINED AREAS WITH MULTIPLE OPENINGS

STEP 3 - Prepare For Next Movement

From inside the room, the officer will be in a safer position to look and listen for threats and plan the next move, which could call for moving quickly back across the confined area or moving into other rooms. It might also call for conducting partial or full sweeps of the door the officer just entered through.

ONE-PERSON OPERATIONS: COMPLEX CONFIGURATIONS   365

CUBICLE CONFIGURATIONS

STEP 1 - Clear Without Entry or Shallow Entry

To enter the room containing the cubicles, the officer can use any of the entry techniques already explained. However, the best option would most likely be the shallow entry or clear without entry techniques, since this will minimize the officer's exposure. Once the clear or entry is complete, the officer can prepare to move towards the cubicles.

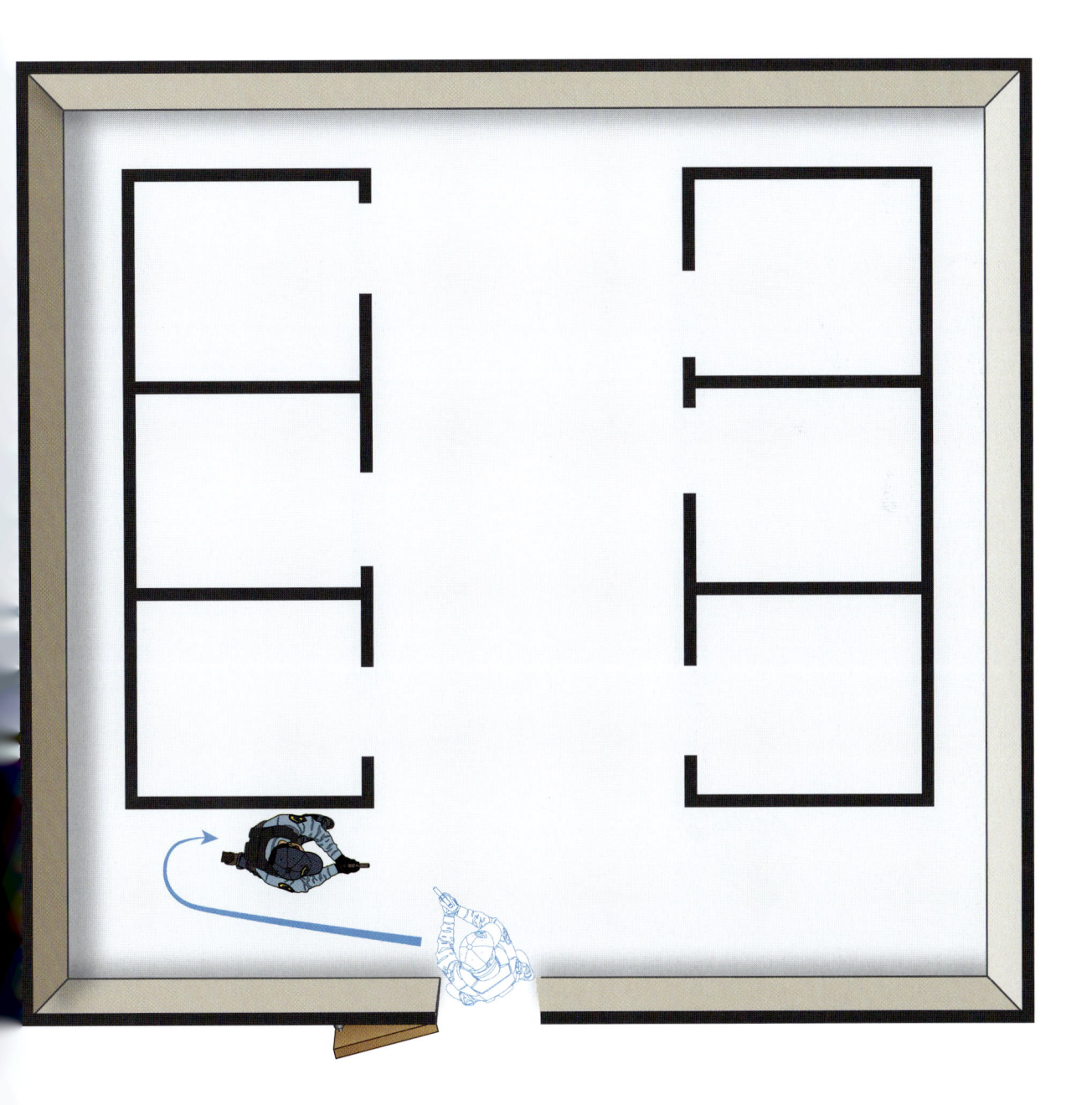

CUBICLE CONFIGURATIONS

STEP 2 - Choose Which Cubicle to Enter

If the openings to the cubicles are uneven, the officer will aim to clear the closest opening first. This will he[lp] the officer avoid exposing his/her back to the opposite cubicle. If the openings are even, the officer mu[st] choose which cubicle to enter first. If there are any signs of threat (noise, light or movement) coming from on[e] of the cubicles, the officer should attempt to clear that cubicle first.

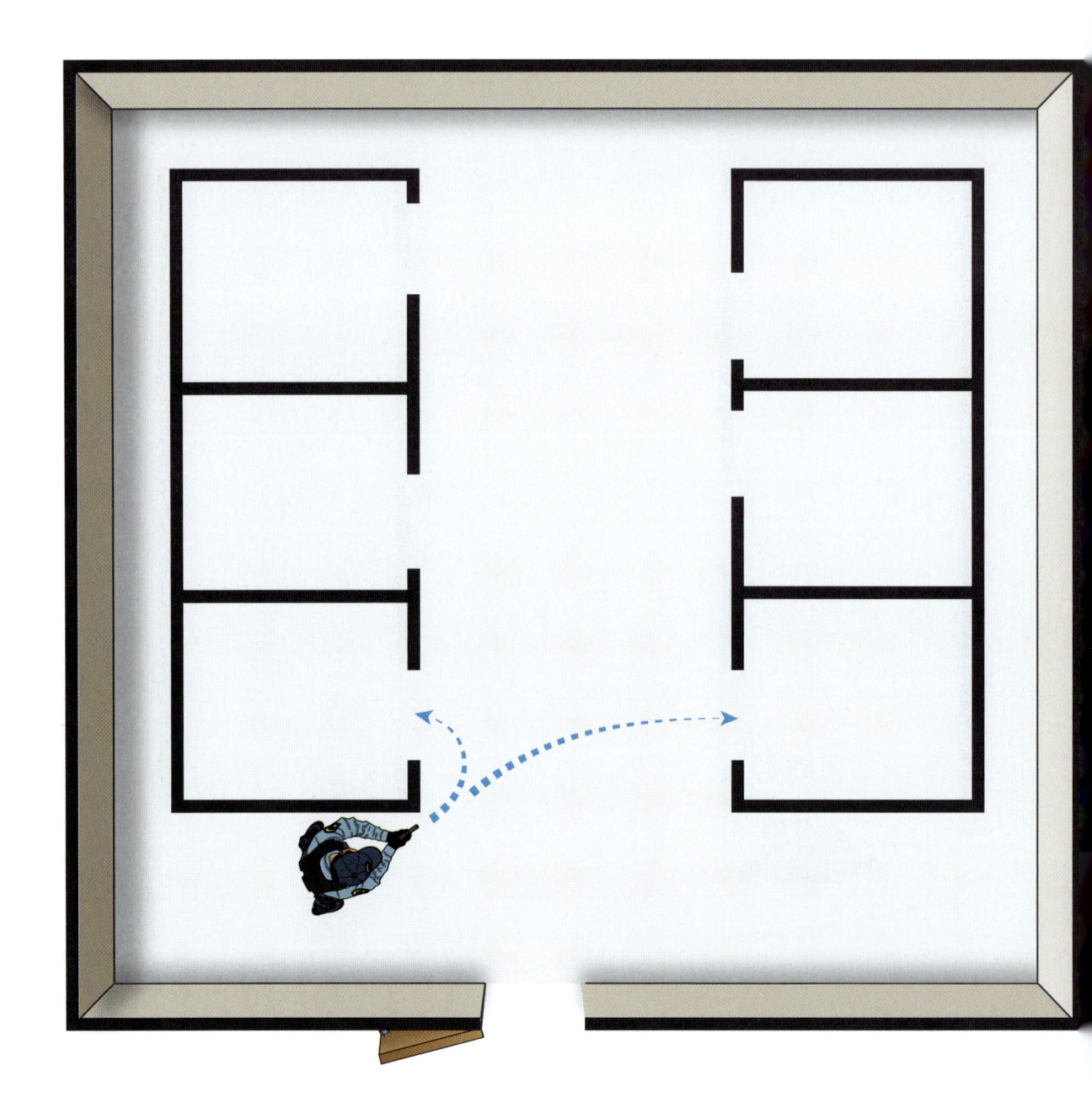

ONE-PERSON OPERATIONS: COMPLEX CONFIGURATIONS   367

CUBICLE CONFIGURATIONS

STEP 3 - Enter and Clear the First Cubicle

Once the officer chooses which cubicle to enter, he/she will enter and clear using a movement similar to the deep entry technique but with tighter arc. The officer will clear one corner, then scan across the cubicle to clear the opposite corner while moving into the cubicle. The officer will end up facing back out of the cubicle towards the next cubicle.

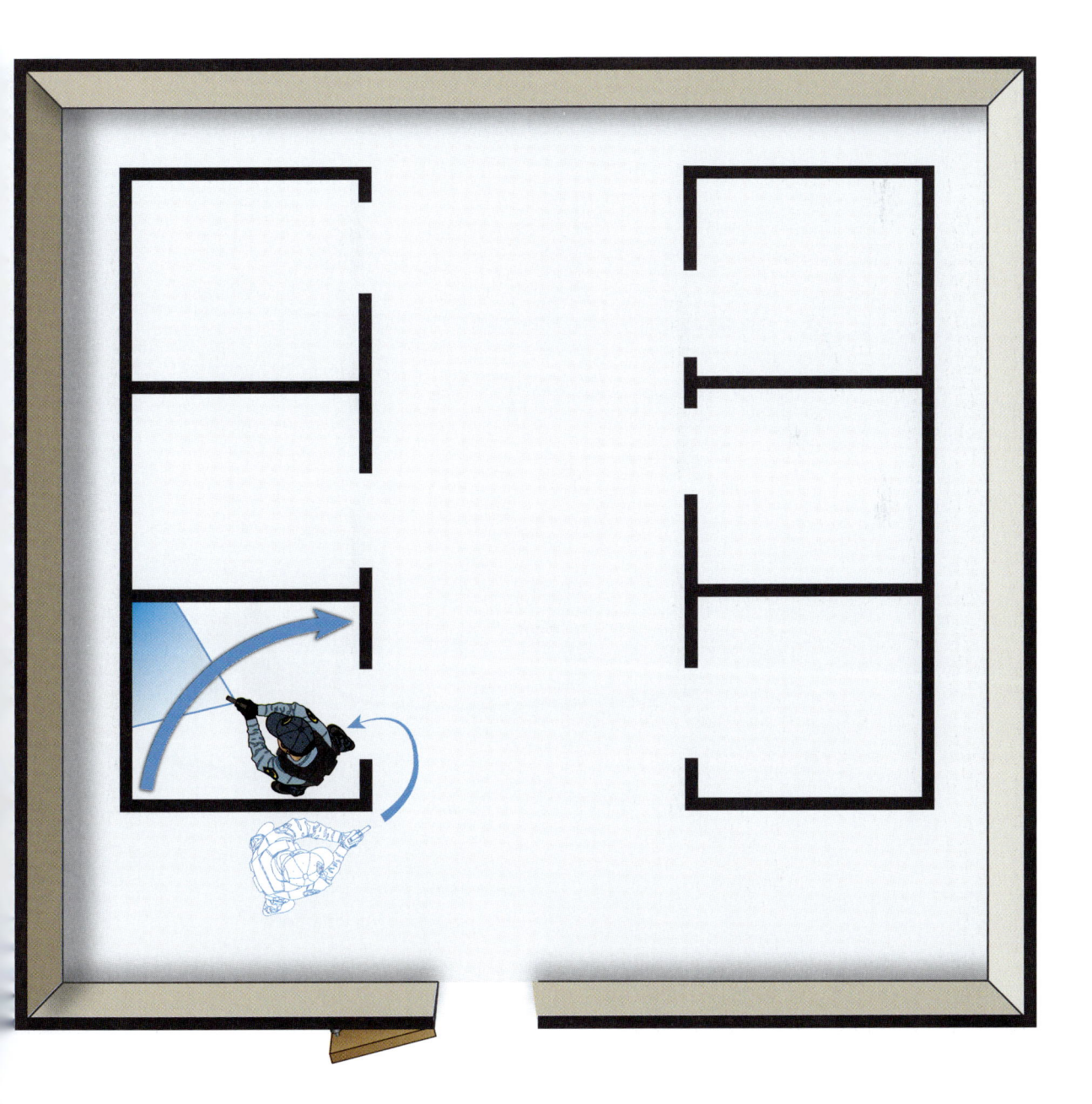

CUBICLE CONFIGURATIONS

STEP 4 - Cross to Clear the Opposite Cubicle

Once the first cubicle is clear, the officer will quickly move across to clear the opposing cubicle using the same technique.

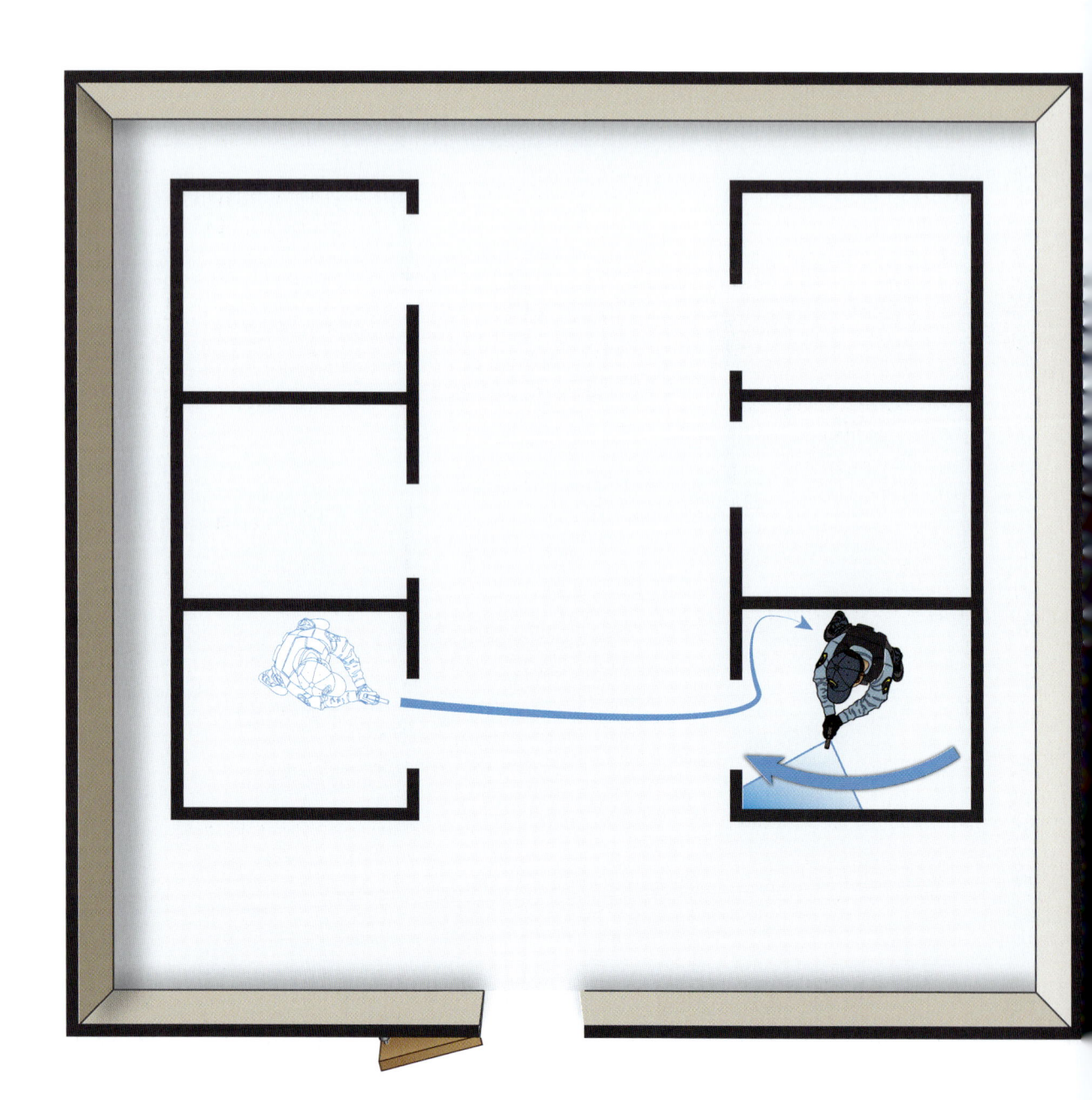

CUBICLE CONFIGURATIONS

STEP 5 - Advance to Next Cubicle (Diagonal Movement)

Once the first two opposing cubicles are clear, the officer will have to choose whether to move to the next cubicle on the same side (lateral movement) or cross over to the next cubicle on the opposite side (diagonal movement). Once again, the officer should generally choose to enter whichever door is closer. For the diagonal movement, the officer will cross over to the cubicle on the far side while quickly glancing over the shoulder to check the cubicle on the near side. Once the officer reaches the cubicle, he/she will enter and clear using the same technique already explained.

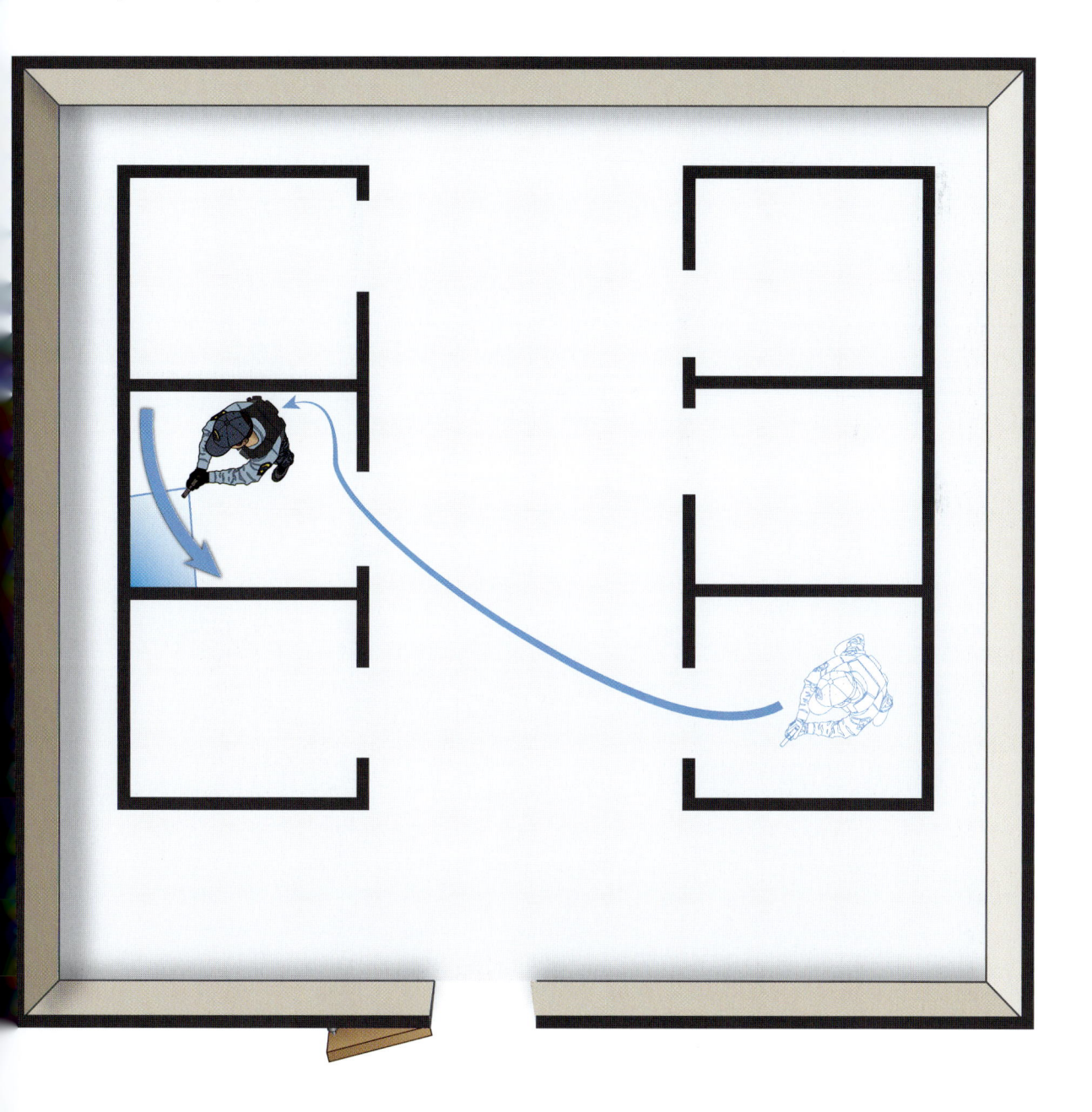

CUBICLE CONFIGURATIONS

STEPS 6 - Cross to Clear the Opposite Cubicle

After conducting the diagonal move, the officer will quickly move back across to clear the opposing cubicle

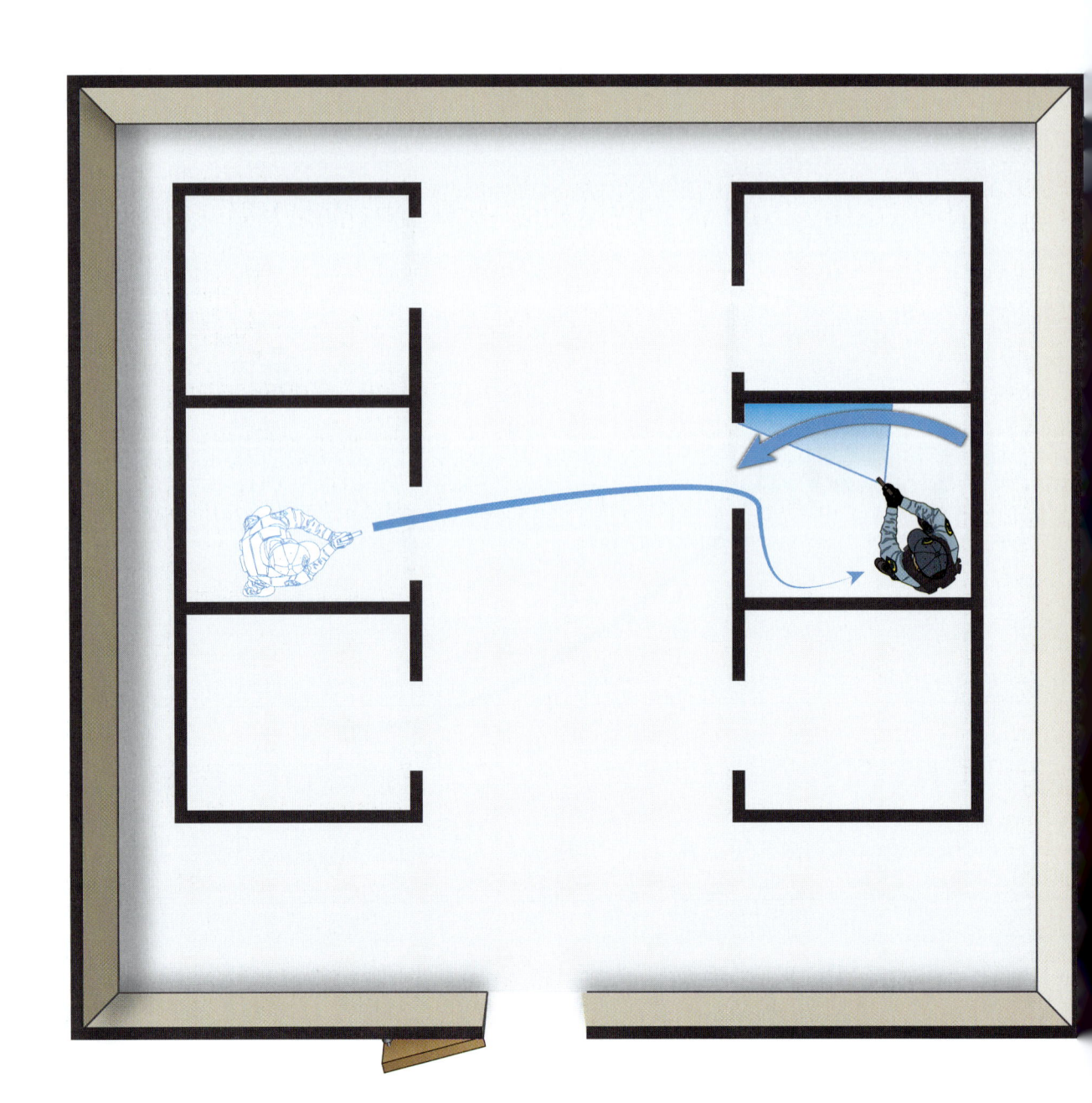

CUBICLE CONFIGURATIONS

STEP 7 - Advance to Next Cubicle (Lateral Movement)

In some cases, the officer will decide to clear the next cubicle on the same side (lateral movement). For this movement, the officer will momentarily glance to check the cubicle on the opposite side, then turn to enter and clear the cubicle on the same side using the technique already explained.

SECTION 4

MULTIPLE-TEAM OPERATIONS

FEAR NOT

MULTIPLE TEAM OPERATIONS
Entry and Movement

Larger tactical teams might need to employ multiple elements simultaneously. A single team with more than six officers can become difficult to control. Three to six officers is a good size for a single team. Conducting an entry with seven or more officers generally calls for splitting into multiple teams.

Operating with multiple teams offers several advantages. Increased manpower and firepower raises the odds of success and survival. Having more officers on site also makes it easier to evacuate casualties and innocent civilians in an emergency. However, operating with multiple teams also presents several challenges.

Whenever two elements are moving in a building independently, there is a much greater risk of friendly fire. In a high-stress situation, there is a significant chance that two teams will accidentally shoot at each other. For this reason, multiple team tactics is considered a more advanced skill and should ideally be executed only by experienced units that have had time to practice frequently.

Even if the two teams do not engage each other directly, there is still a risk of accidental friendly fire. If two teams are clearing adjacent rooms, there is a chance that stray bullets will pass through the wall, causing friendly fire casualties. Experienced teams can use a combination of pinpoint shooting accuracy and awareness of the building layout to prevent these types of accidents. Given these risks, teams that have not had the opportunity to practice multiple team operations should stick together and operate as a single element if possible.

More experienced units that have practiced conducting multiple team operations will generally use three different movement techniques: leapfrog, trail in direct support and simultaneous clear. Multiple teams can also be useful in clearing hallways, since one team can clear the rooms on one side of the hallway while the other team clears the rooms on the opposite side.

INITIAL ENTRY

STEP 1 - Blue Team Stacks on the Door

Blue team will approach the initial entry point and stack on the door. Green team will stay back from the do[or] providing security from behind covered and concealed positions. This is a better option than having gree[n] team stack right behind blue team. A long line of officers running along the side of the building will make a[n] easy target for adversaries, particularly if the adversaries are armed with automatic weapons.

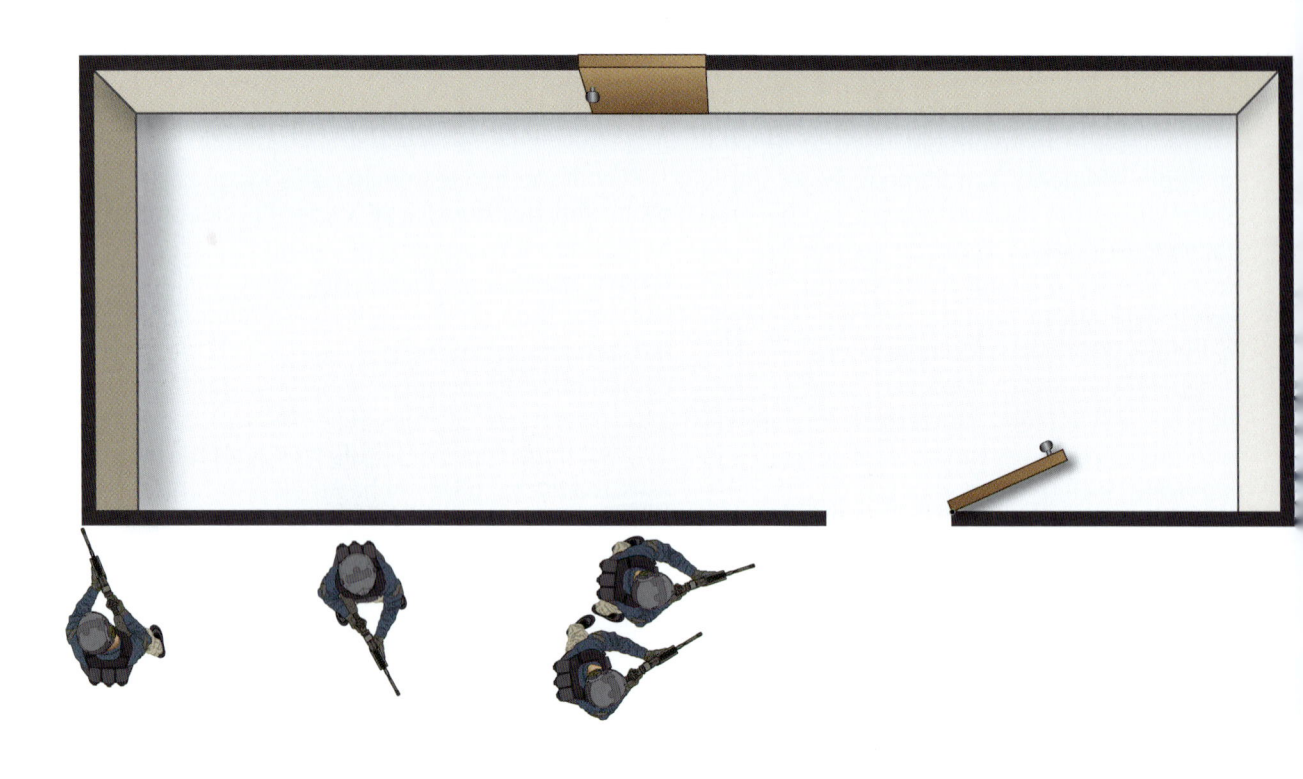

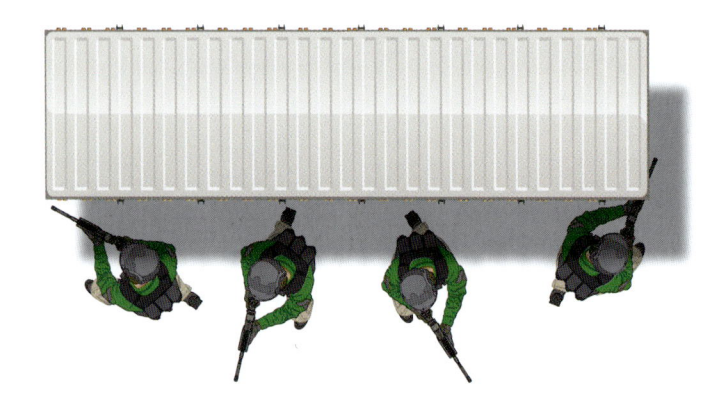

MULTIPLE TEAM OPERATIONS: ENTRY AND MOVEMENT | 377

INITIAL ENTRY

STEP 2 - Blue Team Enters

Blue team will enter the building using any of the techniques described in previous chapters. Once the team has entered the first room, the team leader will turn around and provide rear security. However, since there is a follow-on team, the team leader's objective will be less to provide security and more to provide a coordination point with the next team. This is why it is helpful to have the team leader be the third officer in the stack. If the team leader is first or second into the room, he/she will not be in a good position to turn around and coordinate with the follow-on team.

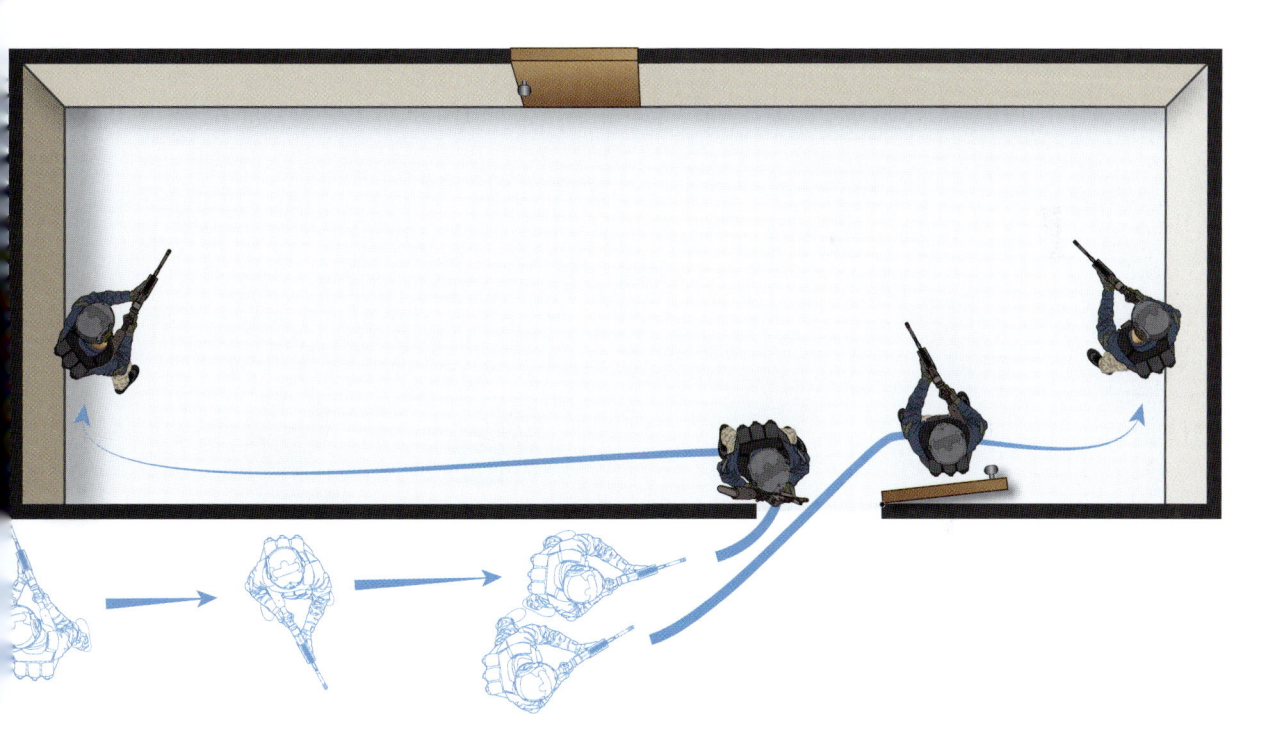

INITIAL ENTRY

STEP 3 - Green Team Stacks in Support

Once blue team enters through the door, green team will give up their covering positions and begin to converge on the door to stack in support of blue team. Stacking in support means that green team is ready to enter the room at a moment's notice to provide any help that the blue team leader might request. The blue team leader will be facing out the door in a good coordination point to be able to communicate with green team.

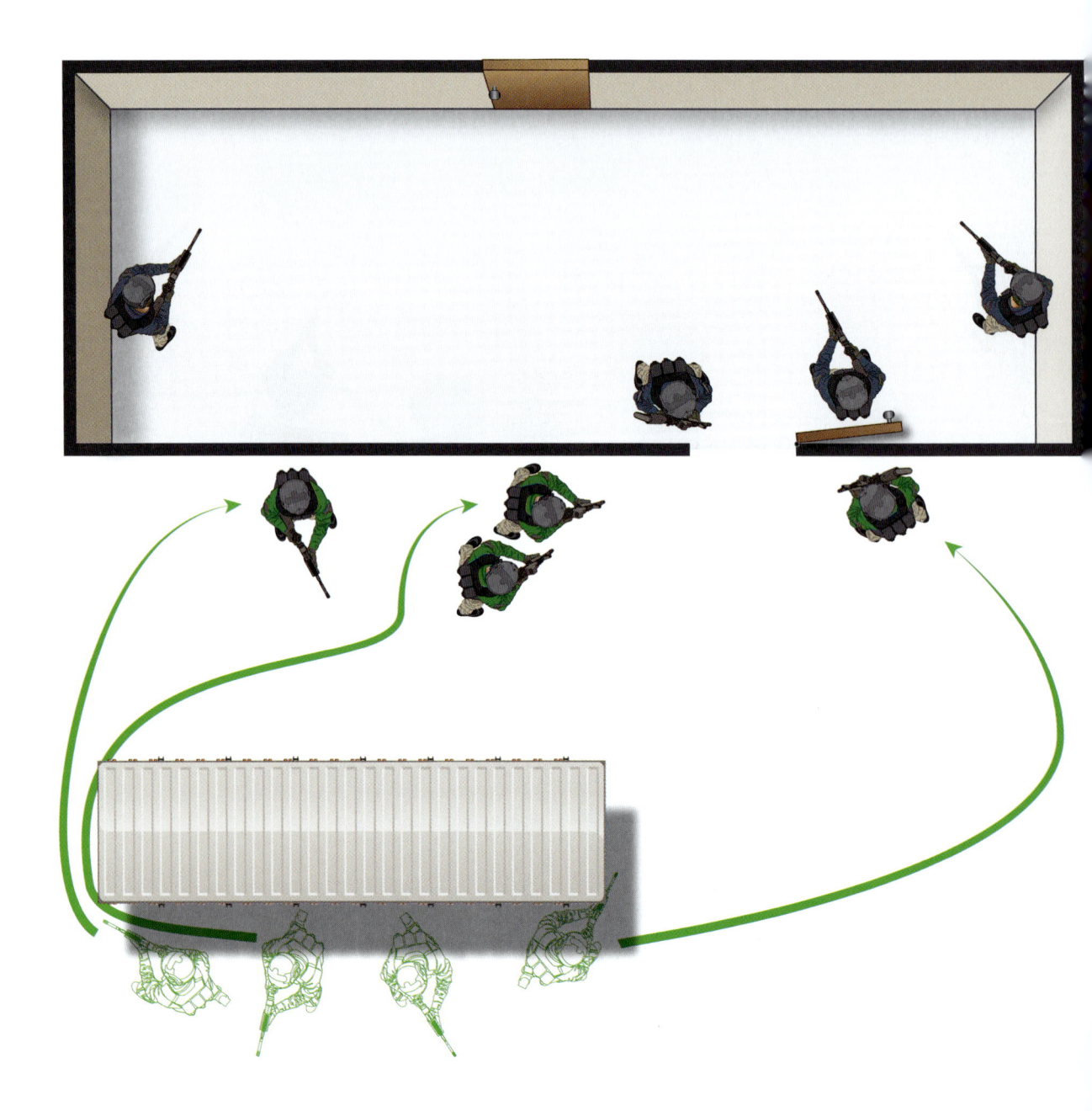

MULTIPLE TEAM OPERATIONS: ENTRY AND MOVEMENT   379

INITIAL ENTRY

STEP 4 - Blue Team Calls Green Team Into the Room

Ideally, green team should not stay stacked outside the door for long. They should only stack momentarily until the blue team leader can determine the next move. Once the blue team leader determines the course of action, he/she will call green team into the room, saying "green team come in." The lead officer in green team will reply with, "green team coming in." Once both teams are in the building there are several different ways to proceed that will be discussed in the following sections.

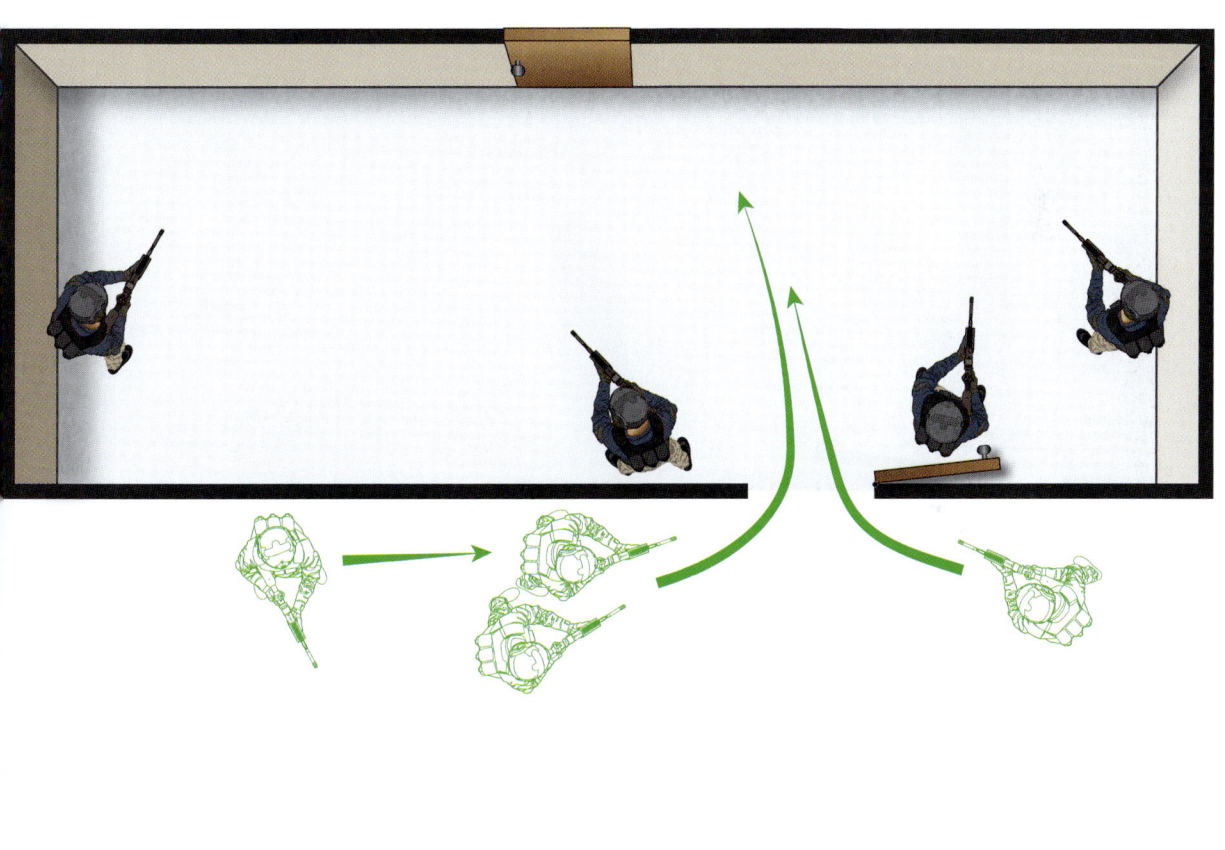

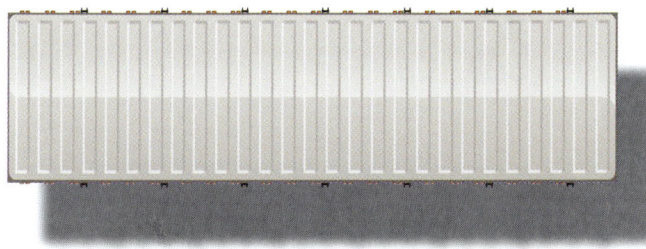

MOVEMENT: LEAPFROG

STEP 1 - Blue Team Enters

Blue team will enter the first room using the technique of their choosing. Once the team has entered the team leader will turn around and provide a coordination point with the next team. This is why it is helpful to have the team leader be the third officer in the stack.

Multiple Team Operations: Entry and Movement   381

MOVEMENT: LEAPFROG

STEP 2 - Blue Team Calls Green Team Into the Room

Once blue team has dominated the room, green team should already be stacked in support outside the door. If the blue team leader identifies a door in the room and decides to use the leapfrog technique, the blue team leader will call green team into the room and tell them to stack on the door, saying "stack… stack… stack" or simply by pointing to the door with the non-firing hand. Green team will move straight to the door and stack, ready to enter the next room.

MOVEMENT: LEAPFROG

STEP 3 - Green Team Enters

Green team will enter the next room using the technique of their choosing. Once the team has entered th green team leader will turn around and provide a coordination point with the blue team. Blue team will b stacked in support, ready to enter.

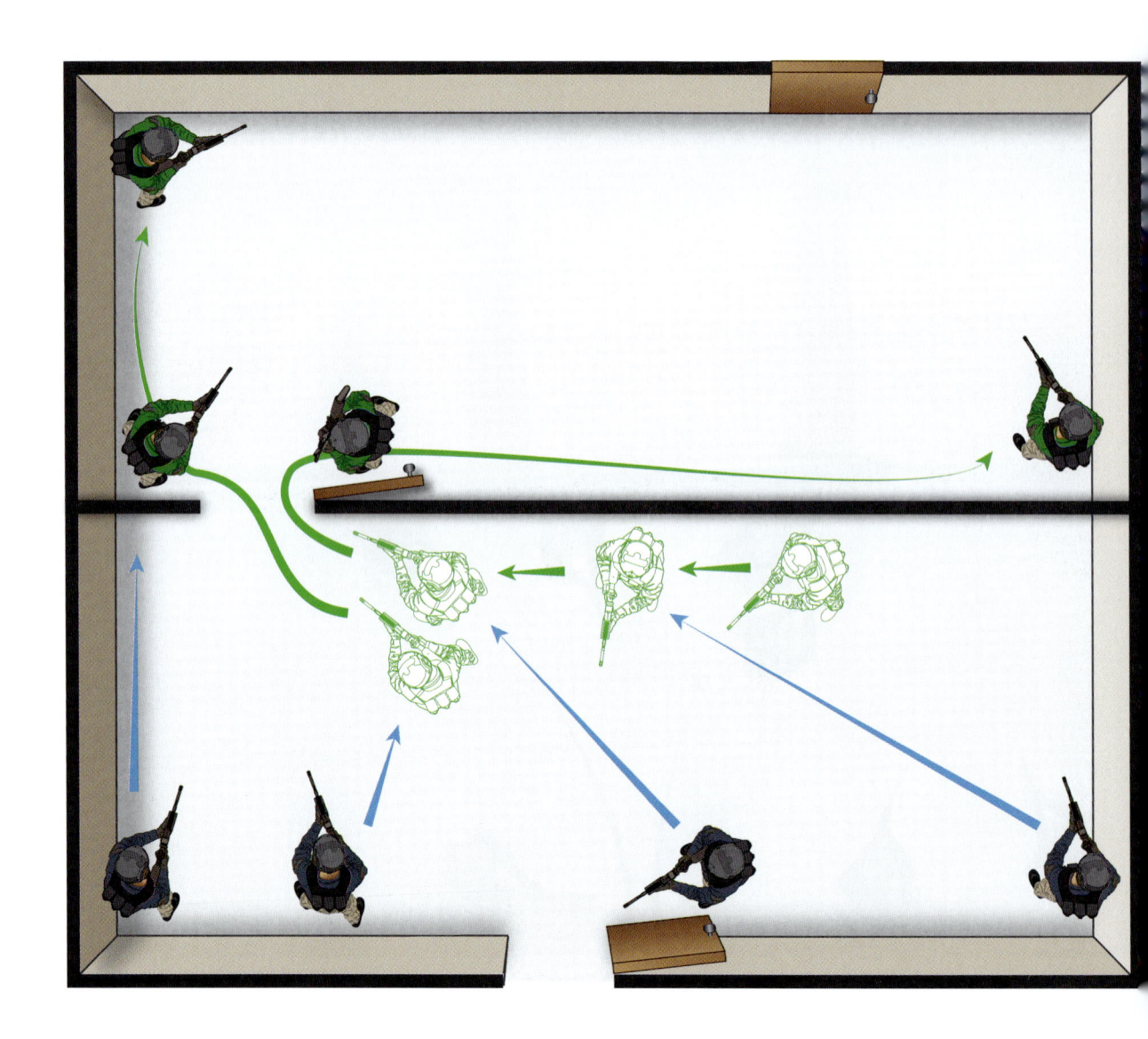

MULTIPLE TEAM OPERATIONS: ENTRY AND MOVEMENT   383

MOVEMENT: LEAPFROG

STEP 4 - Green Team Calls Blue Team Into the Room

Blue team will be stacked in support outside the door. If the green team leader identifies a door in the room and decides to use the leapfrog technique, the green team leader will call blue team into the room and tell them to stack on the door, saying "stack… stack… stack" or simply by pointing. The process will then repeat, with each team leapfrogging ahead of the next from room to room.

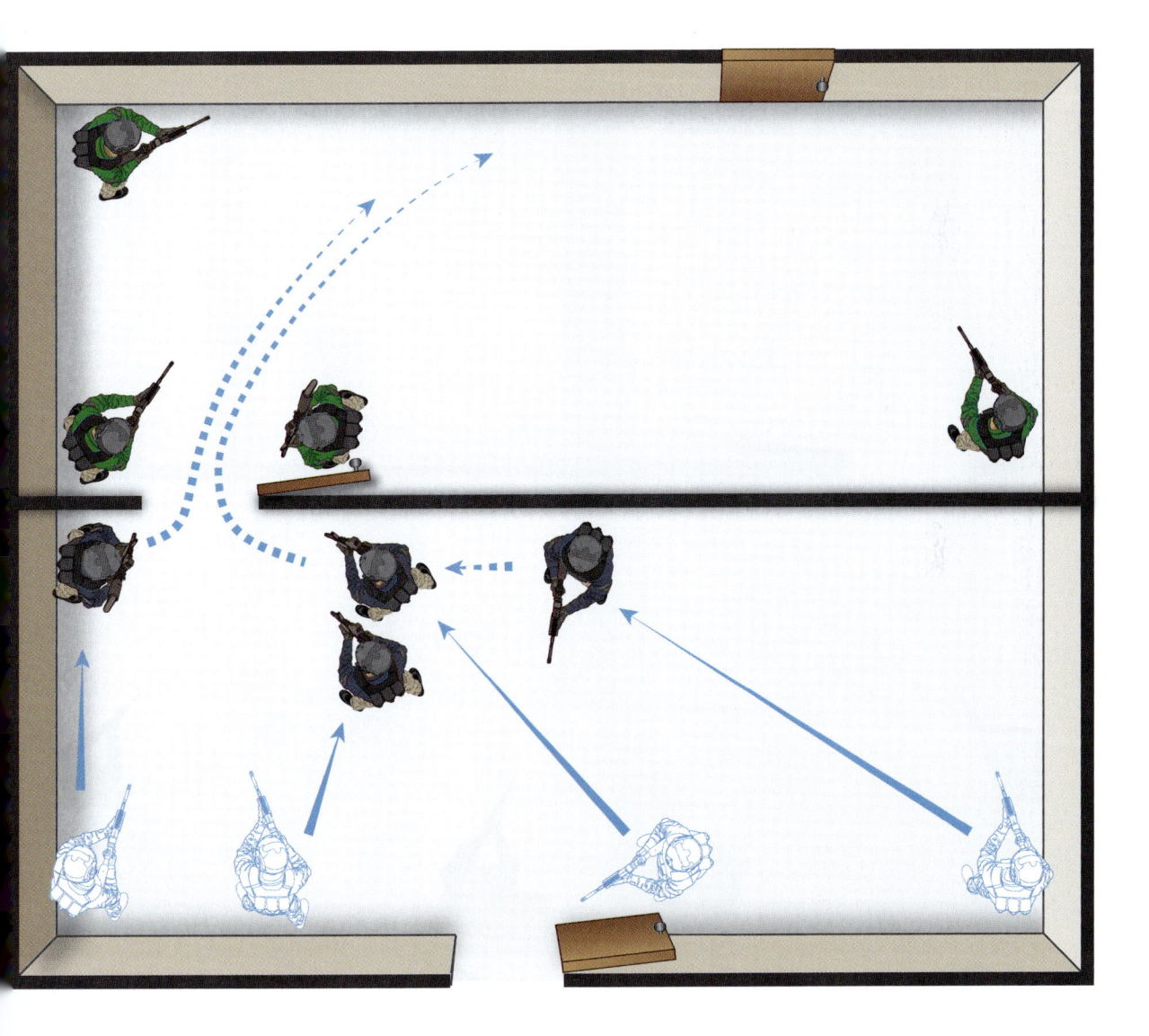

MOVEMENT: TRAIL IN DIRECT SUPPORT

STEP 1 - Blue Team Enters

Blue team will enter the first room using the technique of their choosing. Once the team has entered the team leader will turn around and provide a coordination point with the next team. This is why it is helpful to have the team leader be the third officer in the stack.

Multiple Team Operations: Entry and Movement   385

MOVEMENT: TRAIL IN DIRECT SUPPORT

STEP 2 - Blue Team Stacks on the Next Door

Once blue team has dominated the room, if the blue team leader decides to use the trail technique, blue team will stack on the next door and prepare to lead the way into the next room.

MOVEMENT: TRAIL IN DIRECT SUPPORT

STEP 3 - Blue Team Calls Green Team Into the Room

After blue team stacks on the next door (or simultaneously) the blue team leader will call green team into the room. Green team will enter the room as they normally would, moving to domination points. Or, if blue team is already on the way into the next room, the green team leader might choose not to re-dominate the room but instead will move directly to the door and stack in support of blue team.

MULTIPLE TEAM OPERATIONS: ENTRY AND MOVEMENT 387

MOVEMENT: TRAIL IN DIRECT SUPPORT

STEP 4 - Blue Team Enters the Next Room

As green team comes into the room in a trailing position, blue team will lead the way into the next room, enter and clear. The process will repeat with blue team leading the way into the next room and green team trailing behind. It is possible for blue team and green team to be separated by up to one room, as long as the team leader of blue team (coordination point) and the lead officer of green team are able to see each other and communicate.

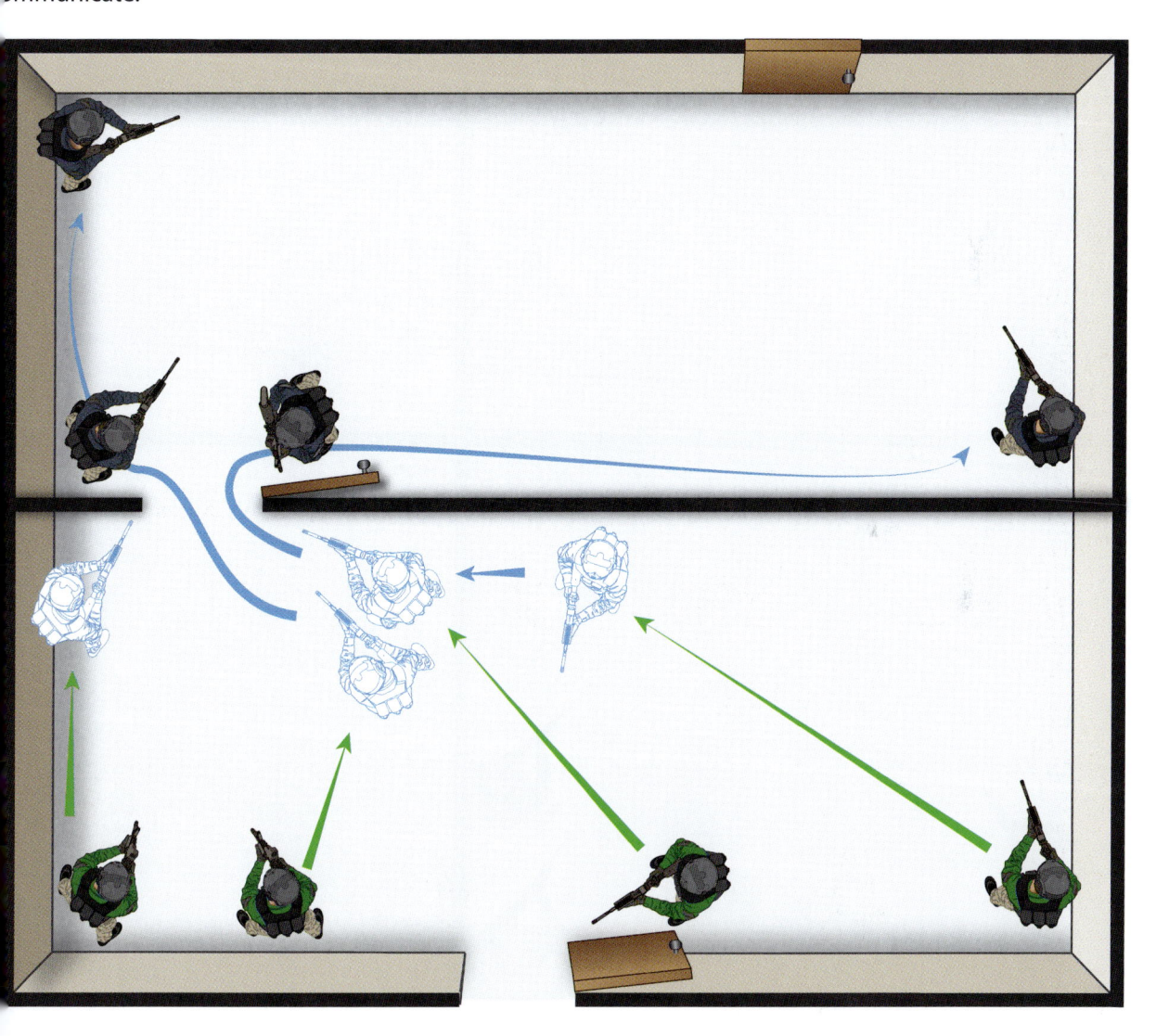

SIMULTANEOUS ENTRY

STEP 1 - Blue Team Enters

Blue team will enter the first room using the technique of their choosing. Once the team has entered the team leader will turn around and provide a coordination point with the next team.

SIMULTANEOUS ENTRY

STEP 2 - Blue Team Calls Green Team Into the Room

Once blue team has dominated the room, green team should already be stacked in support outside the door. If the blue team leader identifies two doors in the room and decides to use the simultaneous clearing technique, the blue team leader will call green team into the room and tell them to stack on one of the two doors. Green team will move straight to the door and stack, ready to enter the next room. Blue team will converge and stack on the other door.

SIMULTANEOUS ENTRY

STEP 3 - Blue and Green Teams Enter Simultaneously

With both teams stacked on different doors, the second officers in each stack will make eye contact and coordinate the ready signals (squeeze) to initiate entry. Both teams will enter their respective rooms simultaneously. Once both teams have entered, the team leaders of each team will post next to the door to provide the coordination point. The two team leaders will be able to see each other and communicate, in order to decide which direction to go next.

MULTIPLE TEAM OPERATIONS: ENTRY AND MOVEMENT

SIMULTANEOUS ENTRY

STEP 4 - Coordination Point and Resume Movement

The two teams should not move any farther apart, since they will lose the ability to communicate using the coordination points. Unless the operation was heavily rehearsed and the floor plan carefully studied, it is preferable for teams never to break visual contact with each other for safety reasons. Therefore, with one room separating the two teams, either blue team can call in green team, green team can call in blue team or one of the teams can back clear to lead the way in the opposite direction.

HALLWAY MOVEMENT

STEP 1 - Team Configuration

When moving down a hallway with two teams, generally one team will focus on the right side of the hallway while the other team focuses on the left side of the hallway. However, this is not a fixed rule and depending on the configuration of rooms, teams may switch sides as needed. Teams will generally alternate, clearing the next door in the hallway. Since the leader of each team will be positioned in a coordination point near the door, the two team leaders will be able to communicate across the hall to coordinate movement.

MULTIPLE TEAM OPERATIONS: ENTRY AND MOVEMENT   393

HALLWAY MOVEMENT

STEP 2 - Blue Team Enters the First Room

Blue team will enter and dominate the first room. The blue team leader, at the coordination point, will look down the hallway and see that the next door is on the opposite side of the hall. The team leader will call green team forward to enter and clear the next room.

HALLWAY MOVEMENT

STEP 3 - Green Team Enters the Next Room

Green team will enter and dominate the next room. The green team leader, at the coordination point, will lo[ok] down the hallway and see that there are opposing open doors down the hall. The team leader will call bl[ue] team forward so both teams can clear the opposing doors simultaneously. Blue team will exit the room a[nd] begin moving down the hall.

MULTIPLE TEAM OPERATIONS: ENTRY AND MOVEMENT   395

HALLWAY MOVEMENT

STEP 4 - Blue and Green Teams Enter Simultaneously

As blue team approaches green team, blue team will converge to one side along the wall to make room for green team to exit the room. As blue team passes green team, green team will exit so both teams are moving side by side. The lead officer of blue team and the lead officer of green team will provide cross coverage as they approach the open doors. Once both teams reach the open doors, they will enter the two rooms simultaneously.

INTERSECTIONS

STEP 1 – Lead Team Clears the Intersection

When operating with multiple teams, there are no changes to the techniques for clearing intersections. The team leader will decide which team will clear the intersection and which team will follow behind. Generally is not a good idea to use two teams to clear an intersection since intersections are danger areas and two team will be very vulnerable if they are bunched in an intersection.

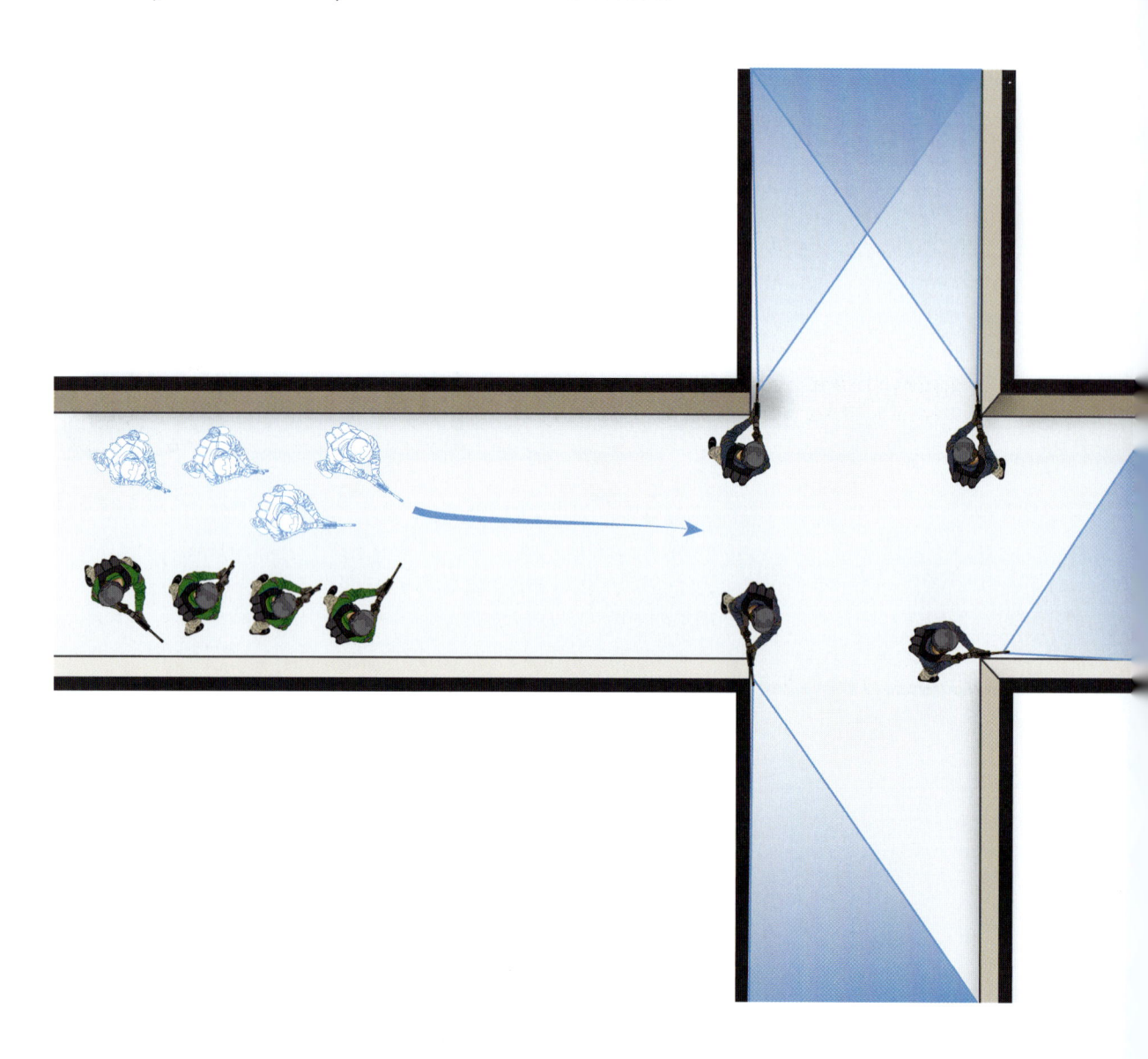

INTERSECTIONS

STEP 2 – Teams Choose Movement Directions

Once the intersection is clear, the two teams may decide to move in the same direction, or they might decide to split up and move in different directions. If teams move in opposite directions down a hallway, both team leaders must remain very alert since there is an increased chance that the teams will accidentally shoot each other if they are not in close contact.

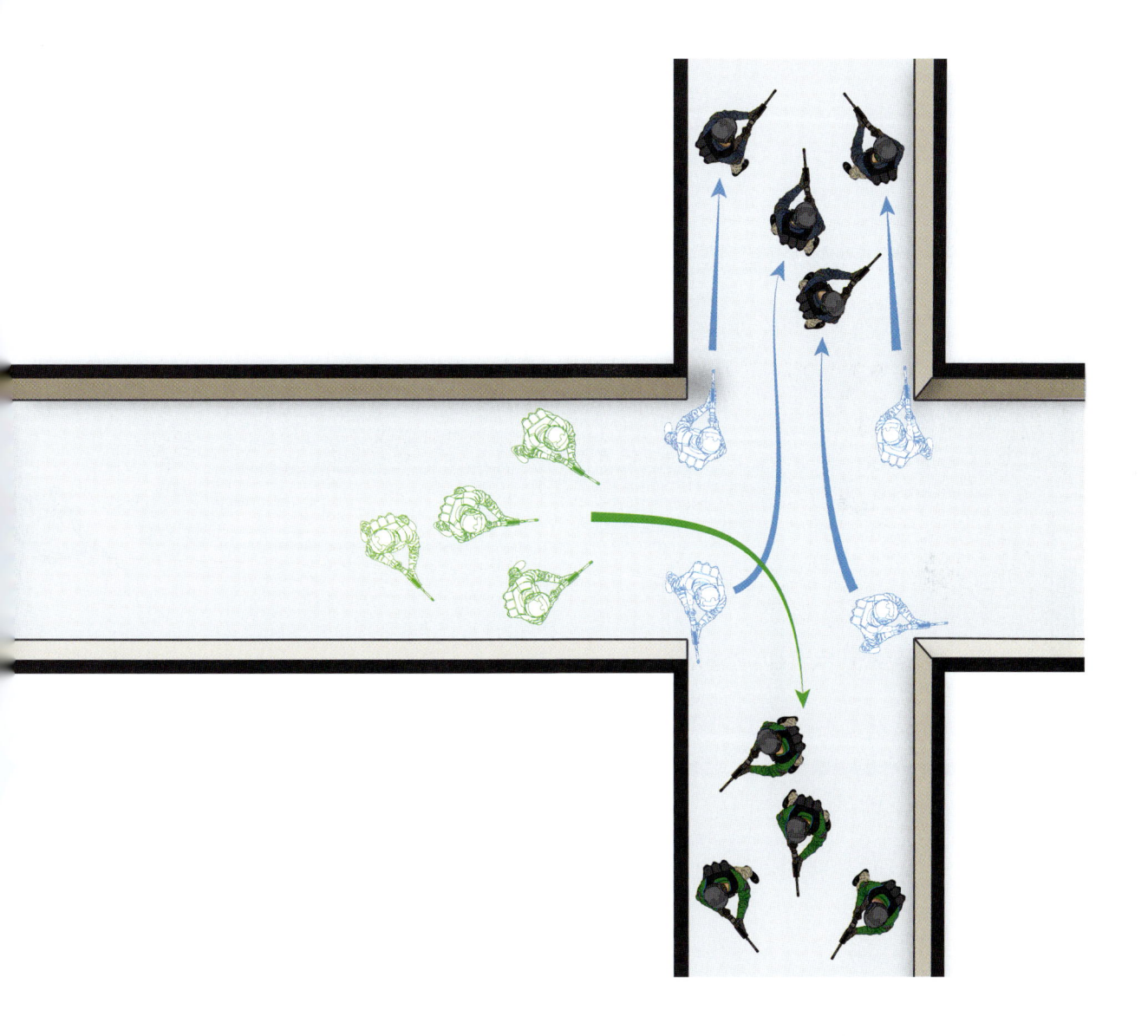

STAIRWELLS

COMPLETE SEQUENCE

When operating with multiple teams, there are no changes to the techniques for clearing stairwells. The team leader will decide which team will lead and which team will follow behind. The two teams can move in the stairwell simultaneously or one team can wait for the other to reach the next landing or floor before entering the stairwell. Either way, the teams will be very vulnerable in the stairwell and should try to move out of the stairwell as quickly as possible.

MULTIPLE TEAM OPERATIONS: ENTRY AND MOVEMENT   399

CONFINED AREAS WITH MULTIPLE OPENINGS

STEP 1 - Blue Team Enters and Commits to One Opening

Confined areas with multiple openings are very common in architectural designs. These types of configurations can be found in the entryway or foyer of many residential homes. When blue team enters, they will find themselves bunched up in a very vulnerable position with multiple openings and danger areas all around them. Therefore, blue team will not want to "dominate" this area since they will not really be dominating anything. Instead, the blue team leader will make a fast decision to commit to one of the openings. The team leader will call out "go right… go right" or "go left… go left." One officer (usually the lead officer) will hold and provide security in the opposite direction while the rest of the team passes though into the opening. The holding officer will become the last officer into the room.

CONFINED AREAS WITH MULTIPLE OPENINGS

STEP 2 - Green Team Fills in Through the Other Opening

Since green team is stacked in support, the lead officer will recognize the situation and see that blue team is committing to the opening on the right. This will automatically alert green team to flow in to the left support. Green team will enter and clear the room on the left in support

CONFINED AREAS WITH MULTIPLE OPENINGS

STEP 3 - Both Teams Coordinate Next Move

With blue team dominating the room on the right and green team dominating the room on the left, the two team leaders will be able to communicate from their respective coordination points to plan the next move. The tactical equation will be much simpler with the two rooms dominated.

SECTION 5

SPECIAL EQUIPMENT

SPECIAL EQUIPMENT

FEAR NOT

SPECIAL EQUIPMENT
Shotgun, Flashbang, Shield and Mirror

Some teams, particularly dedicated tactical units, will have access to special equipment such as breaching shotguns, flashbangs, ballistic shields and tactical mirrors. These tools can prove extremely useful for a tactical team and greatly reduce risk to officers. It is also useful for patrol officers to familiarize themselves with these tools since they may be called upon to use them in an emergency situation.

The breaching shotgun is very useful for bypassing locked doors. Each tactical team will generally have at least one (preferably two) trained breachers equipped with shotguns. All of the instructions in this section for shotgun employment can also apply to other mechanical breaching tools like the ram or Halligan tool.

Flashbangs are distraction devices that are designed to stun adversaries in a room and reduce the risk to the entry team. Flashbangs are particularly useful for reducing the risks associated with immediate entry techniques. If the team needs to move fast into a room, without hesitation, it can be wise to employ a flashbang to give the team an advantage against adversaries in the room.

The ballistic shield can provide protection for a tactical team in a high-risk situation. However, it is critical for a team to understand the protective limitations of every shield they use. In many cases, shields are not rated to protect against high velocity or armor piercing ammunition. More importantly, the shield provides limited protection for standing officers since it does not protect an officer's lower body. Wounds to the lower body, particularly to the pelvic girdle, can be as lethal as wounds to the upper body. Therefore, officers should recognize that while the shield can be a lifesaving tool, it also has limitations.

The tactical mirror, snake/pole cameras and even a common mobile phone can help a tactical team identify threats around a corner. However, it is critical to remember that an officer employing a mirror or camera is particularly vulnerable and may also be shot through the wall. For this reason, it is preferable to employ the mirror in conjunction with the ballistic shield to provide added protection. It is also useful to have another officer close by to cover the officer who is employing the mirror or camera.

SHOTGUN EMPLOYMENT

STEP 1 - Call Breacher Into Position

In order to execute a shotgun breach, the officer with the shotgun must move to the opposite side of the door as the team. The team leader will call out "breacher!" to order the breacher forward into position. The lead officer can also call the breacher forward since the lead officer might be able to see that the door is locked or obstructed. In some other cases, an officer might try to open the door and find that the door is locked. In these cases the opening officer should call "breacher!" and quickly move out of the way to make way for the breacher. In a hallway this works out well since the officer who failed to open the door can quickly turn 180-degrees and push forward to cover the breacher's back.

BREACHER!

SHOTGUN EMPLOYMENT

STEP 2 - Prep and Signal

Once the breacher is in position, he/she will prep the shotgun for action, step in front of the door and then turn to look at the lead officer. When the breacher looks at the lead officer this will be the signal that the breacher is ready. When the lead officer is ready, he/she will nod without breaking focus from the door. It is important that the lead officer stay focused on the door and not get distracted by looking at the breacher when delivering the nod.

SHOTGUN EMPLOYMENT

STEP 3 - Shotgun Breach

Once the breacher sees the nod, he/she will proceed to breach the door using the shotgun. There are sever[al] ways to do this including targeting the locking mechanism or the hinges. Specific breaching techniques a[re] discussed in more detail in Special Tactics' dedicated breaching manuals. After disabling the lock or hinges, th[e] breacher will open the door. The standard way of doing this is a strong, flat-footed kick. This kick can requi[re] some leg strength so it is wise to choose a strong team member to serve as the breacher. Once the door [is] open, the breacher will quickly move out of the way of the opening, secure his/her shotgun and prepare [to] enter the room behind the rest of the team.

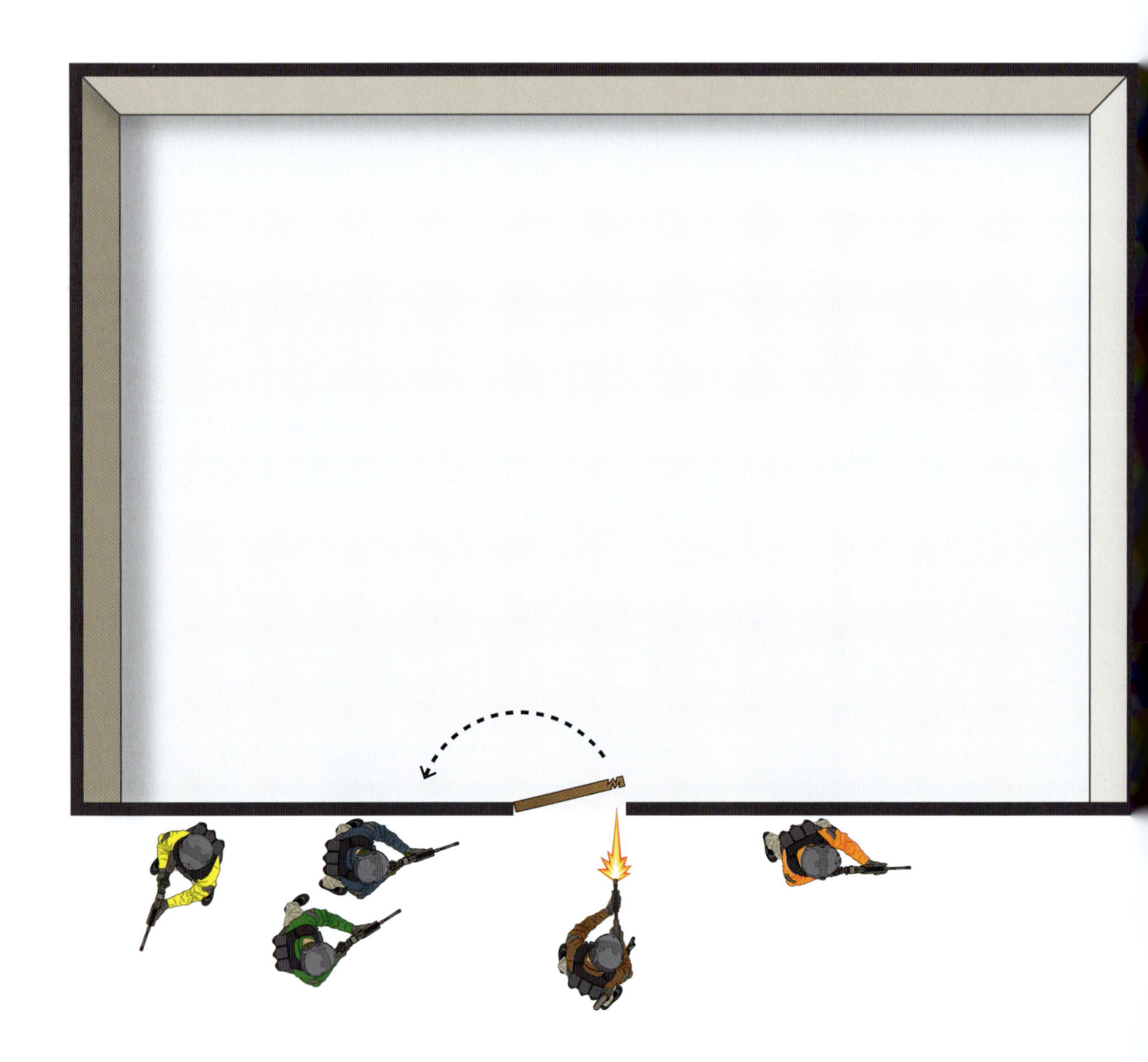

BREACHING AND TOOLS 409

SHOTGUN EMPLOYMENT

STEP 4 - Enter and Clear

With the door open, the team will enter and clear the room using the technique of their choosing. The breacher will become the last officer into the room and be prepared to check behind the door or cover the rear. If the team is using a loose stack, the breacher might become the third officer to enter the room instead of the last officer, depending on how far away the other officers are from the door.

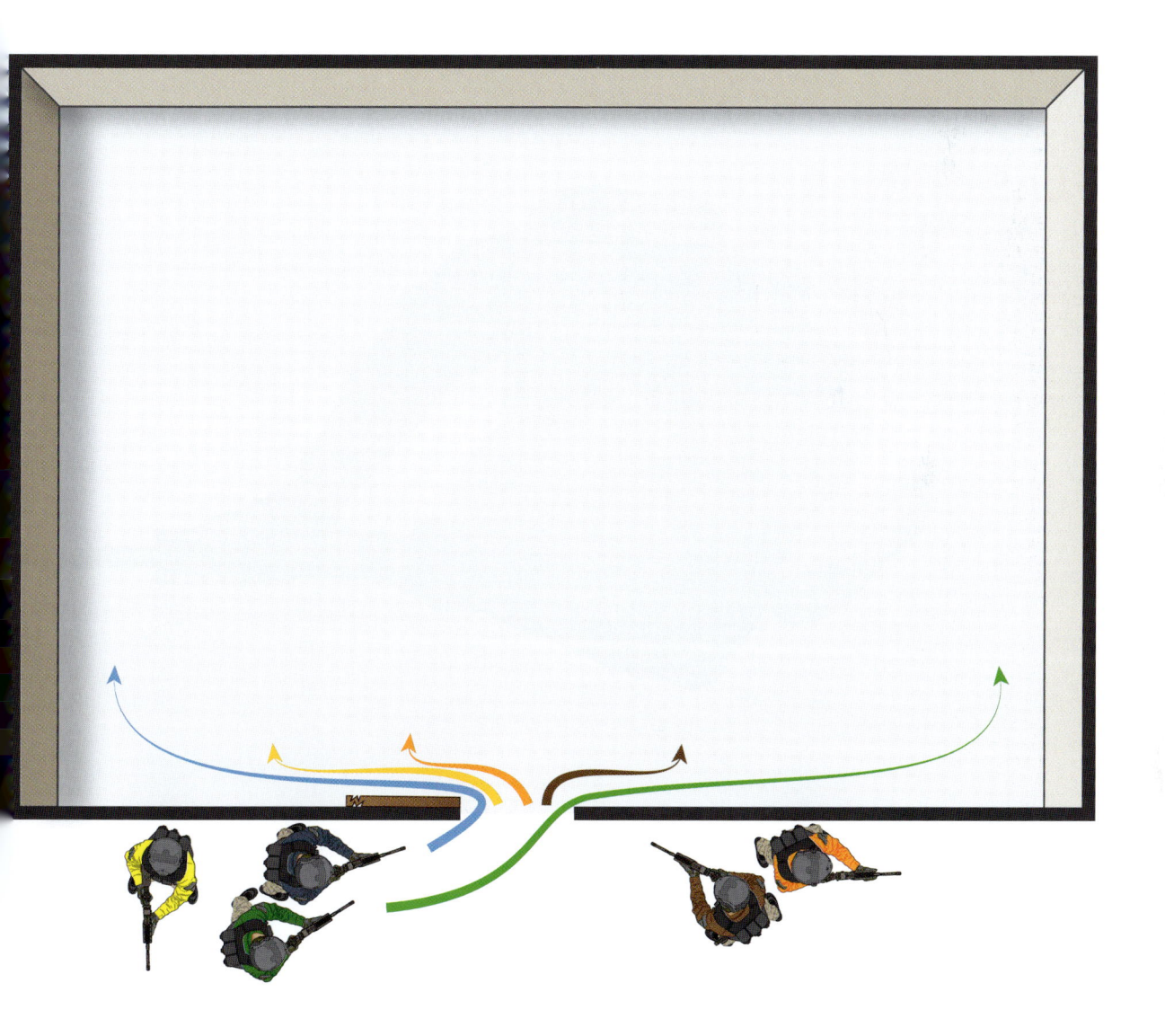

FLASHBANG EMPLOYMENT: OPEN DOOR

STEP 1 - Proper Carry of the Flashbang

The standard way of carrying flashbangs is to store them in pouches on each officer's upper back. This allow an officer standing behind to easily reach up and equip the flashbang. Officers can also carry one or tw flashbangs on the belt or vest for personal use if needed. **SAFETY NOTE: Once you have pulled the pin fro a flashbang, never try to replace it. Instead toss the flashbang in a safe direction. It is also useful practice tossing a dummy flashbang through a door in a safe environment prior to an assault.**

FLASHBANGS

Breaching and Tools | 411

FLASHBANG EMPLOYMENT: OPEN DOOR

STEP 2 - Call for the Flashbang

The team leader will call for the flashbang by calling out "banger!" The lead officer can also call for the flashbang since the lead officer may be in the best position to see or hear signs of a threat in the room. Experienced teams might choose to use hand-and-arm signals instead of verbal commands.

BANGER!

FLASHBANG EMPLOYMENT: OPEN DOOR

STEP 3 - Equip and Prep the Flashbang

Once the call for a flashbang is made, the second officer in the stack will temporarily stow his/her weapon leave both hands free to manipulate the flashbang. The second officer will open one of the flashbang pouch on the back of the lead officer's vest and draw a flashbang. The second officer will then prep the flashbang removing any safeties prior to pulling the pin.

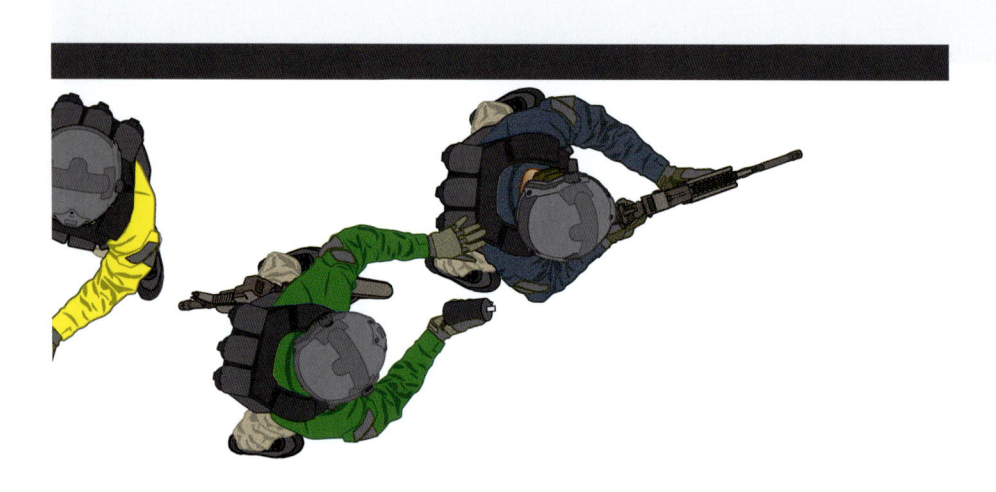

FLASHBANG EMPLOYMENT: OPEN DOOR

STEP 4 - Show the Flashbang

Once the flashbang is prepped, the second officer will extend it out next to the lead officer's head so the lead officer can clearly see the flashbang through his/her peripheral vision. When the lead officer sees the flashbang, he/she will nod to acknowledge the flashbang. This process of showing and acknowledging the flashbang is an extra precaution to verify that the lead officer knows the flashbang is about to be used. It is critical that the lead officer wait until the flashbang goes off before entering the room in order to capitalize on the positive effects of the flashbang. If for any reason the lead officer runs into the room before the flashbang goes off, the rest of the team must follow the lead officer into the room to provide support.

FLASHBANG EMPLOYMENT: OPEN DOOR

STEP 5 - Pull the Pin and Toss the Flashbang

Once the lead officer acknowledges the flashbang, the second officer will bring the flashbang back to his/h chest, pull the pin and then toss the flashbang around the lead officer into the room in a smooth sweepir motion. It is important that the second officer toss the flashbang with a forehand (not backhand) motion a toss it directly through the door, into the center of the room. Trying to toss the flashbang in more complicat ways or bouncing the flashbang off of walls can cause the flashbang to bounce back at the team or e up in a suboptimal location for entry. **NOTE: If the officer tossing the flashbang sees highly flammab materials (gasoline, propane, ammunition etc.) in the room, he/she should discard the flashbang ir safe direction.**

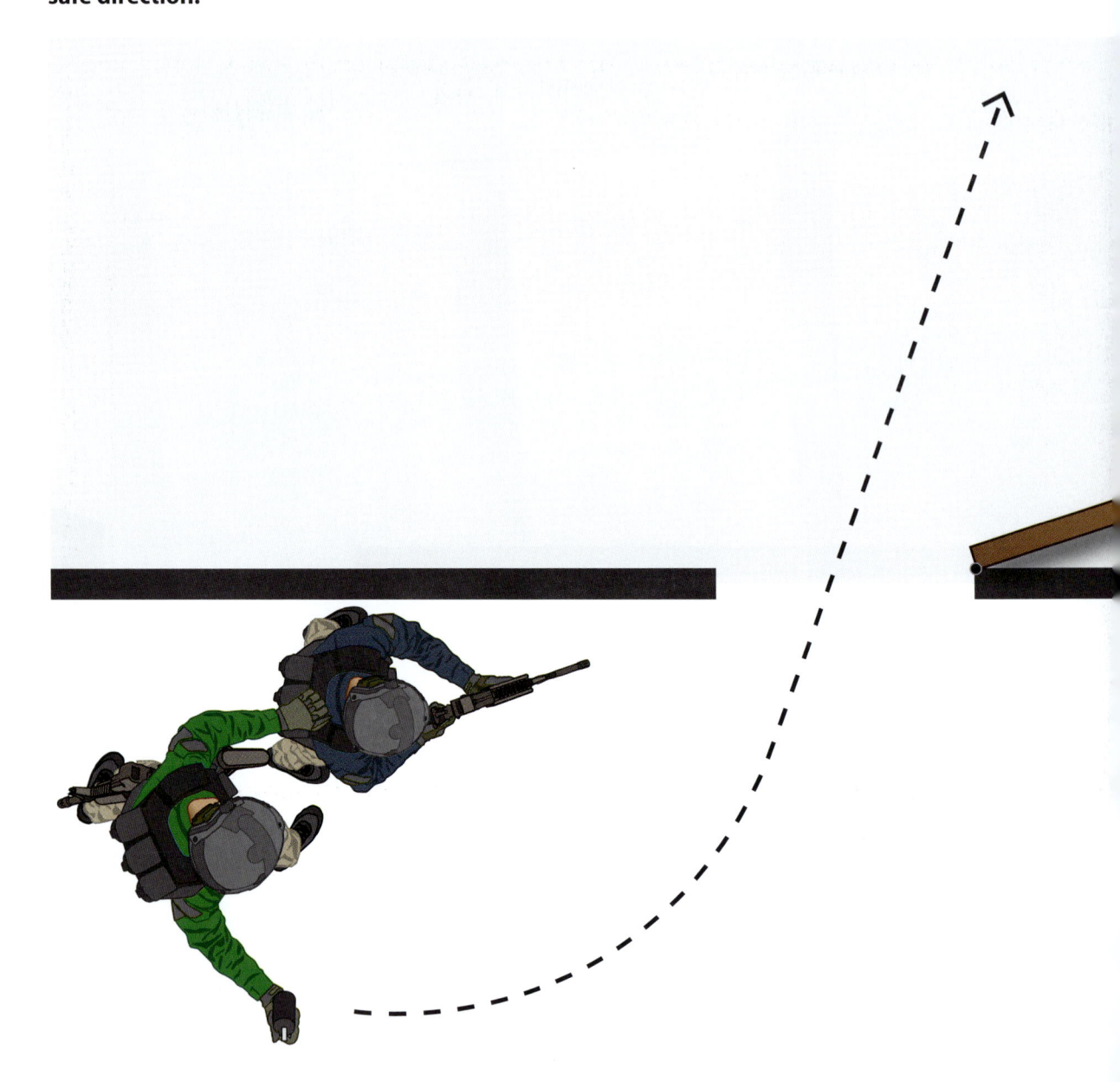

FLASHBANG EMPLOYMENT: OPEN DOOR

STEP 6 - Enter and Clear

Once the flashbang goes off, the team will enter and clear the room using the technique of their choosing. It is important that the officer throwing the flashbang use the few seconds before the flashbang goes off to bring his/her weapon back to the ready position and prepare to enter the room.

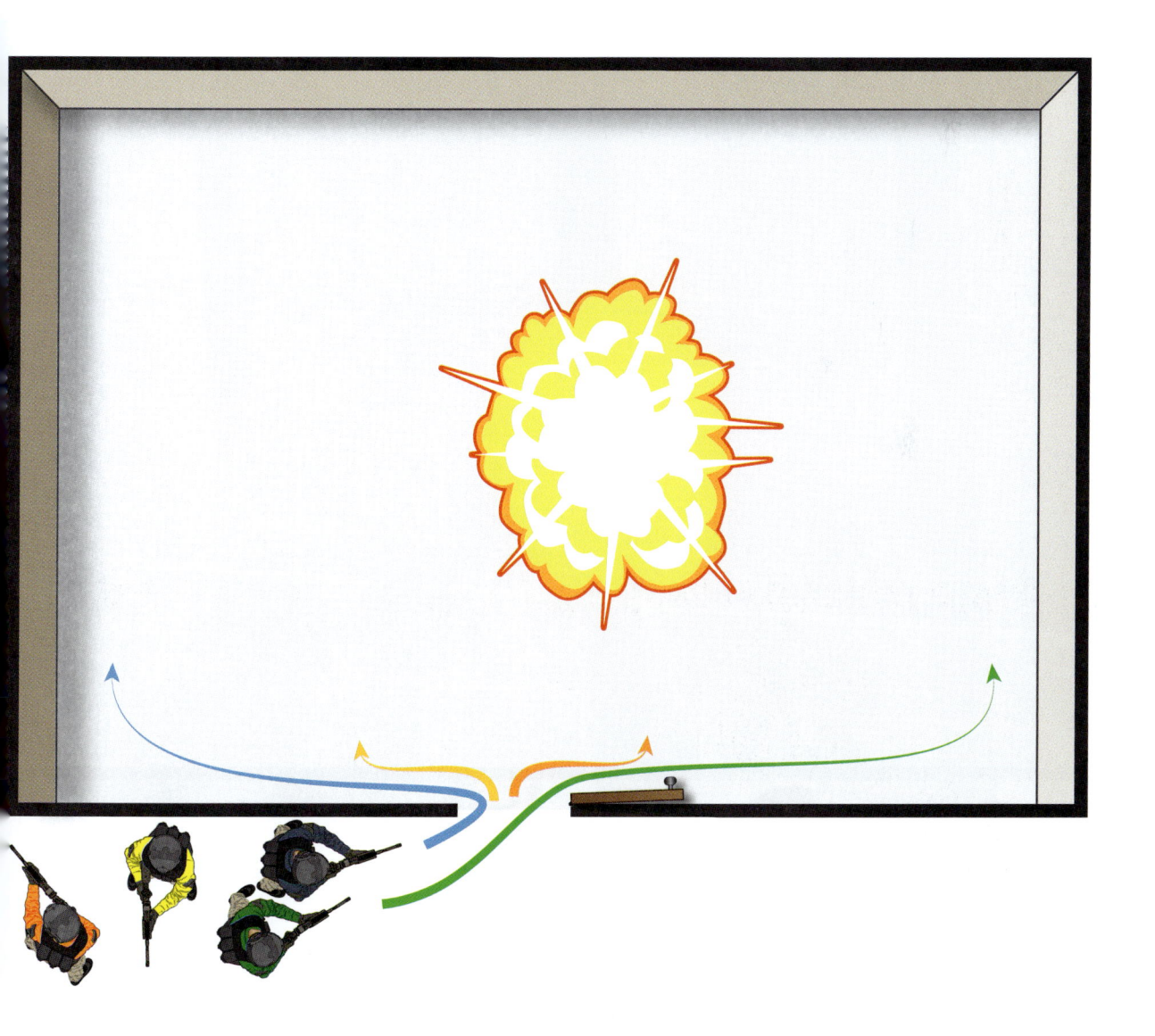

FLASHBANG EMPLOYMENT: CLOSED DOOR

STEP 1 - Call Breacher Into Position

Employing a flashbang on a room with a closed door will require an officer to open or breach the door for the team. The breacher will move to the opposite side of the door and prepare to open or breach the door. If the breacher is using a shotgun, he/she will prep the shotgun as already described and stand by for the nod from the lead officer.

BREACHER!

FLASHBANG EMPLOYMENT: CLOSED DOOR

STEP 2 - Call for the Flashbang

The team leader will call for the flashbang by calling out "banger!" The lead officer can also call for the flashbang since the lead officer may be in the best position to see or hear signs of a threat in the room.

BANGER!

FLASHBANG EMPLOYMENT: CLOSED DOOR

STEP 3 - Equip and Prep the Flashbang

Once the call for a flashbang is made, the second officer in the stack will temporarily stow his/her weapon leave both hands free to manipulate the flashbang. The second officer will open one of the flashbang pouch on the back of the lead officer's vest and draw a flashbang. The second officer will then prep the flashbang removing any safeties prior to pulling the pin.

BREACHING AND TOOLS 419

FLASHBANG EMPLOYMENT: CLOSED DOOR

STEP 4 - Show the Flashbang

Once the flashbang is prepped, the second officer will extend it out next to the lead officer's head so the lead officer can clearly see the flashbang through his/her peripheral vision. When the lead officer sees the flashbang, he/she will nod to acknowledge the flashbang. This nod will also act as the nod to signal the breacher to open or breach the door. The breacher will open the door and step out of the way.

FLASHBANG EMPLOYMENT: CLOSED DOOR

STEP 5 - Pull the Pin and Toss the Flashbang

While the breacher is opening the door, the second officer will bring the flashbang back to his/her chest, p the pin and then toss the flashbang around the lead officer into the room in a smooth sweeping motion aft the door swings open. If for any reason the breacher fails to open the door, the second officer should not ho on to the flashbang but should instead toss it as far as possible away from the team in a safe direction.

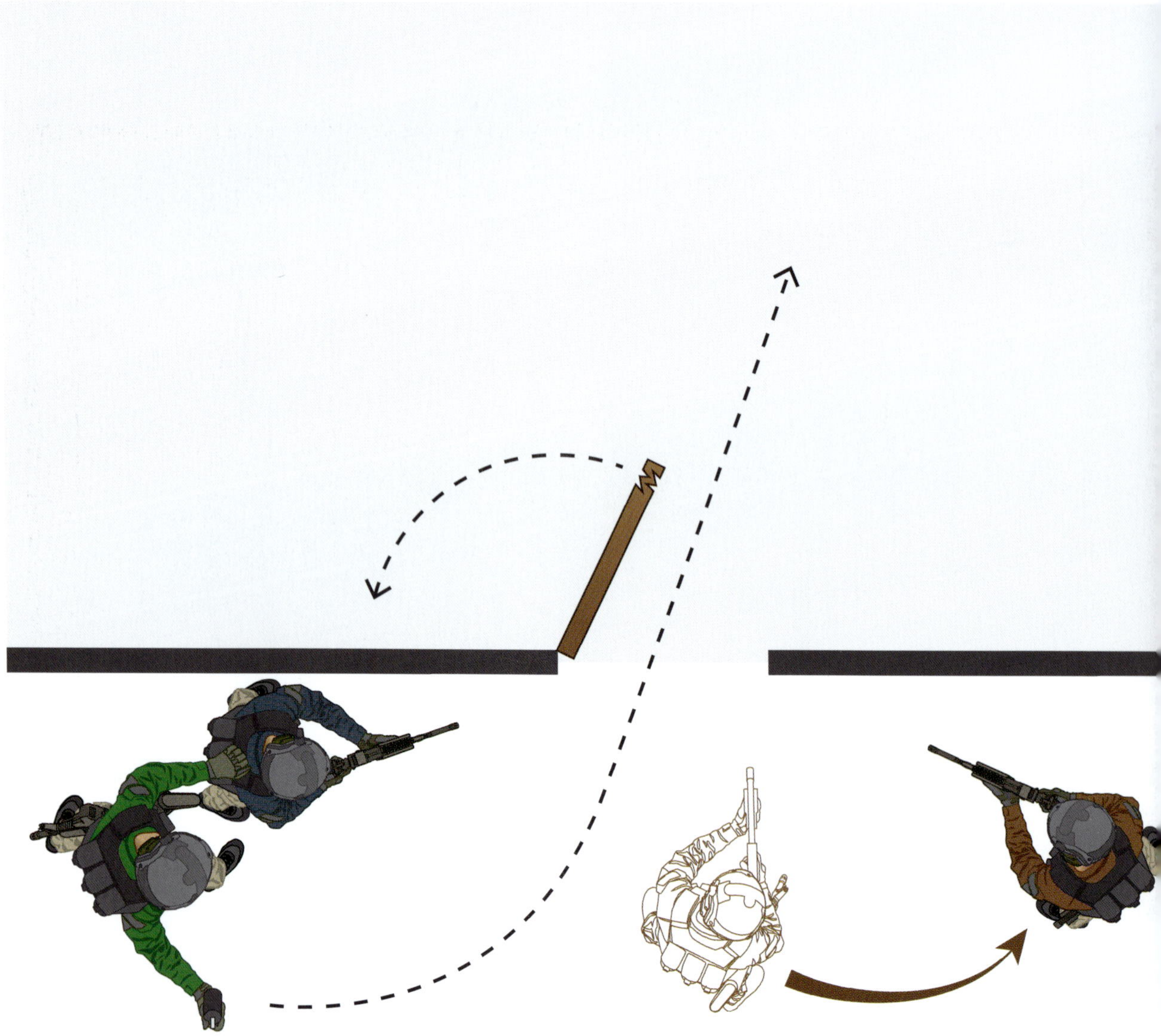

BREACHING AND TOOLS   421

FLASHBANG EMPLOYMENT: CLOSED DOOR

STEP 6 - Enter and Clear

Once the flashbang goes off, the team will enter and clear the room using the technique of their choosing. It is important that the officer throwing the flashbang use the few seconds before the flashbang goes off to bring his/her weapon back to the ready position and prepare to enter the room.

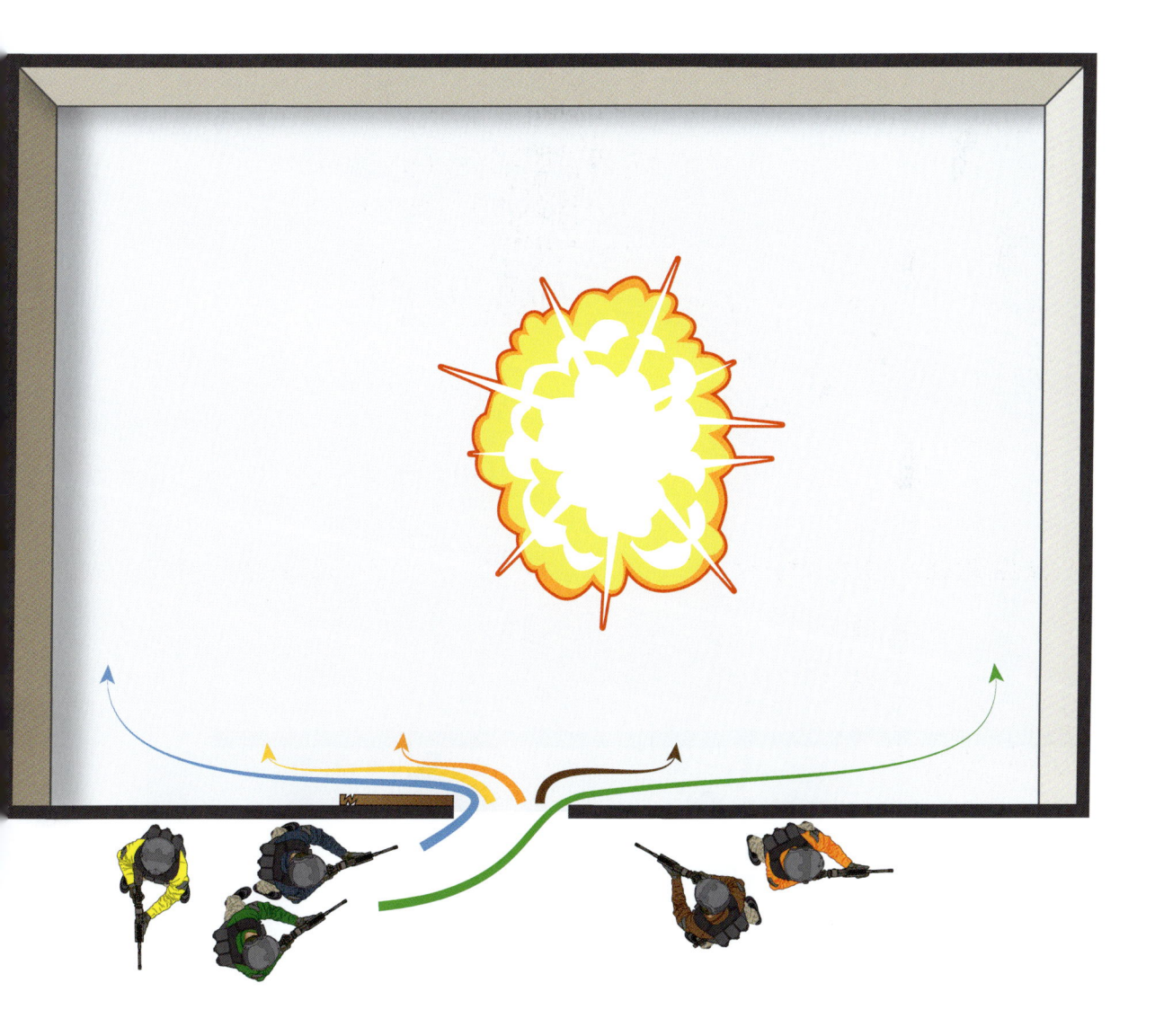

BALLISTIC SHIELD EMPLOYMENT CONSIDERATIONS

Use the Shield to Protect the Lead Officer

In most cases, the ballistic shield will not change the way a team moves through buildings and into room The ballistic shield helps protect the lead officer, who is often the officer who is most at risk. If other office try to hide behind the shield, jamming the formation together, the shield might provide limited protectio but ultimately it will reduce the maneuverability and effectiveness of the team. It is generally best for the lea officer to use the shield for protection while the other officers operate and move as they would if the team d not have the shield.

BALLISTIC SHIELD EMPLOYMENT CONSIDERATIONS

Understand the Protective Limitations of the Shield

It is critical for a team to understand the protective limitations of every shield they use. In many cases, shields are not rated to protect against high velocity or armor piercing ammunition. More importantly, the shield provides limited protection for standing officers. While the shield can protect the head and many of the vital organs, it does not protect an officer's lower body. If an adversary fires a burst of automatic fire at an officer carrying a shield, there is a serious risk that bullets will strike vital areas in the lower body including the pelvic girdle. Wounds to these areas can be as lethal as wounds to the upper body. Therefore, officers should recognize that while the shield can be a lifesaving tool, it also has limitations.

BALLISTIC SHIELD EMPLOYMENT CONSIDERATIONS

The Shield is Best Used from the Crouching Position

While the shield provides some protection for standing officers, it is most useful for slow and deliberate pee around corners from the kneeling position. When employed from the crouching position, the shield c provide effective protection of an officer's entire body from enemy fire, as long as the ballistic rating of t shield is adequate. Therefore, when the team is moving, the ballistic shield provides only limited protecti for the lead officer. However, when the team decides to stop and conduct a deliberate clear around a corn the shield can prove much more effective.

BALLISTIC SHIELD: CORNER CLEARING

STEP 1 - Place the Ballistic Shield Against the Corner

The ballistic shield is most useful for deliberate corner clearing. To employ the ballistic shield, the lead officer should move forward to the corner with another officer positioned behind in a good position to provide support. Once the lead officer reaches the corner, he/she will set the shield down on the floor so it is flush against the wall but not yet protruding around the corner.

BALLISTIC SHIELD: CORNER CLEARING

STEP 2 - Crouch Behind the Shield and Slide Out to Clear

Once the shield is in position the lead officer will crouch behind the shield. It is important for the officer stay behind the shield even if the officer has not peeked around the corner yet. Bullets can go through wa and the shield provides added protection when set against the wall. Once the lead officer is in position, h she will slide the shield slowly outward until the viewport passes the corner. The officer will look through t viewport to ensure the hallway is clear. The lead officer should slide the shield outward, just far enough to able to see down the hall.

BALLISTIC SHIELD: CORNER CLEARING

STEP 3 - Pick Up and Move

Once the hallway is clear, the lead officer will pick up the shield and lead the way down the hall. The rest of the team will follow behind. Once again, while it is good to take advantage of the frontal protection offered by the shield if possible, officers may still decide to spread out and maintain cross-coverage, given the limitations of the shield in the standing position.

TACTICAL MIRROR

STEP 1 - Emplace Ballistic Shield if Possible

The tactical mirror can help officers see around a corner without exposing themselves. However, it is importa[nt] to remember that unless walls are bulletproof, it can be dangerous to extend a tactical mirror around a corn[er] without additional ballistic protection. This is why it is useful to employ the tactical mirror in conjunction wi[th] the ballistic shield. Before employing the mirror, the lead officer should set the ballistic shield on the groun[d] up against the wall and almost flush with the corner. This will reinforce the ballistic protection provided by t[he] wall. **NOTE: Other devices such as snake cameras, pole cameras and even personal mobile phones ca[n] be used in the same way as the tactical mirror.**

TACTICAL MIRROR

STEP 2 - Crouch Behind Ballistic Shield and Equip Mirror

The lead officer should crouch behind the ballistic shield, using it for protection as much as possible. The officer should then draw and extend the tactical mirror with the non-firing hand. To employ the mirror, the lead officer should slide the mirror along the floor to slowly view around the corner at the lowest point, exposing as little of the mirror as possible. The officer should avoid sticking the mirror out farther than necessary, or moving the mirror more than necessary. With practice, an officer can scan the complete area just by angling the mirror slightly in each direction. A second officer should stand behind the lead officer in a good position to provide cover while the lead officer employs the mirror. While using the mirror, the lead officer will extend his/her hand backwards and grasp the second officer's leg or knee.

TACTICAL MIRROR

STEP 3 - Check Around the Corner

While the lead officer employs the mirror, he/she will be holding the second officer's leg. This is so that on the hallway is clear, the lead officer can give a squeeze to signal the second officer to move around the corr and hold the hallway in preparation for the team's movement. The lead officer will then stow the mirror a pick up the shield, preparing to move down the hallway.

TACTICAL MIRROR

STEP 4 - Stow the Mirror and Prepare to Move

Once the lead officer picks up the shield, the team will move around the corner and continue moving down the hallway. Once again, while it is good to take advantage of the frontal protection offered by the shield if possible, officers may still decide to spread out and maintain cross-coverage, given the limitations of the shield in the standing position.

SECTION 6

EXTERIOR MOVEMENT

EXTERIOR MOVEMENT

FEAR NOT

EXTERIOR MOVEMENT
Streets, Alleys and Windows

If officers have to move through an urban environment where threats could emerge from any building or direction, they must be prepared to move tactically in the safest way possible. Urban movement tactics are particularly useful for preparation against terrorist attacks or active shooter scenarios. In these scenarios, the adversaries might not barricade themselves in one building but will rather move freely from building to building, causing as much destruction as possible.

To deal with terrorist or active shooter threats, officers must know how to move outside of buildings as well as inside buildings. The most critical question when moving in the street or between buildings is whether the officers are under fire or not under fire. If officers are not under fire, they can move down the street in a staggered file formation with weapons hanging or at the low ready. If officers take hostile fire, they must employ more deliberate maneuver in order to minimize exposure and address the threat.

When moving under fire, officers must strive to always have one element that is moving and another element providing cover. Officers should avoid trying to move and shoot at the same time while exposed in the street without cover or concealment. Instead of trying to move and shoot at the same time, officers should sprint as quickly as possible to the next covered position and then return fire from a more stable firing platform.

When fighting in the street, officers should always take maximum advantage of cover and concealment. This is the single most important factor that can improve an officer's chances of survival. Officers should take cover behind solid walls or cars. When using cars for cover, officers should position themselves behind the engine block and wheel well for maximum protection. If officers do not take advantage of the protection provided by a car's wheels, bullets can skip under the chassis of a car and hit crouching officers in the legs. Even a curb can provide limited protection against bullets.

MOVING DOWN STREETS

Formation and Positioning

If officers must move down a street in a hostile environment, they should move in a staggered, single-f[ile] formation with 5-10 yards between each officer, remaining close to buildings or other covered positions. Th[is] way if the officers take hostile fire, they can use the buildings as cover. Officers should not move down t[he] center of the street in the open. Also, in many urban environments, there are cars parked along the side [of] the street. If officers move between the cars and the buildings they can take cover to protect themselves fro[m] fire from either side. However, exact positioning will depend on the direction of the threat. Officers will wa[nt] to put cover between them and the potential threat. Ideally, officers should never be more than 5 yards aw[ay] from a covered position.

MOVING DOWN STREETS

Cross Coverage

…officers must move through a very dangerous urban environment and it is uncertain from which direction …threat might emerge, it can be a good idea for officers to move in two files on opposite sides of the road. …eally, this technique works best with two teams of four or more officers. By moving on each side of the road, …ficers can both maintain cross coverage on alleys and intersections and they can also keep an eye on upper …ory windows on each side of the street to protect each other from an adversary who chooses to emerge …m a window and fire downwards.

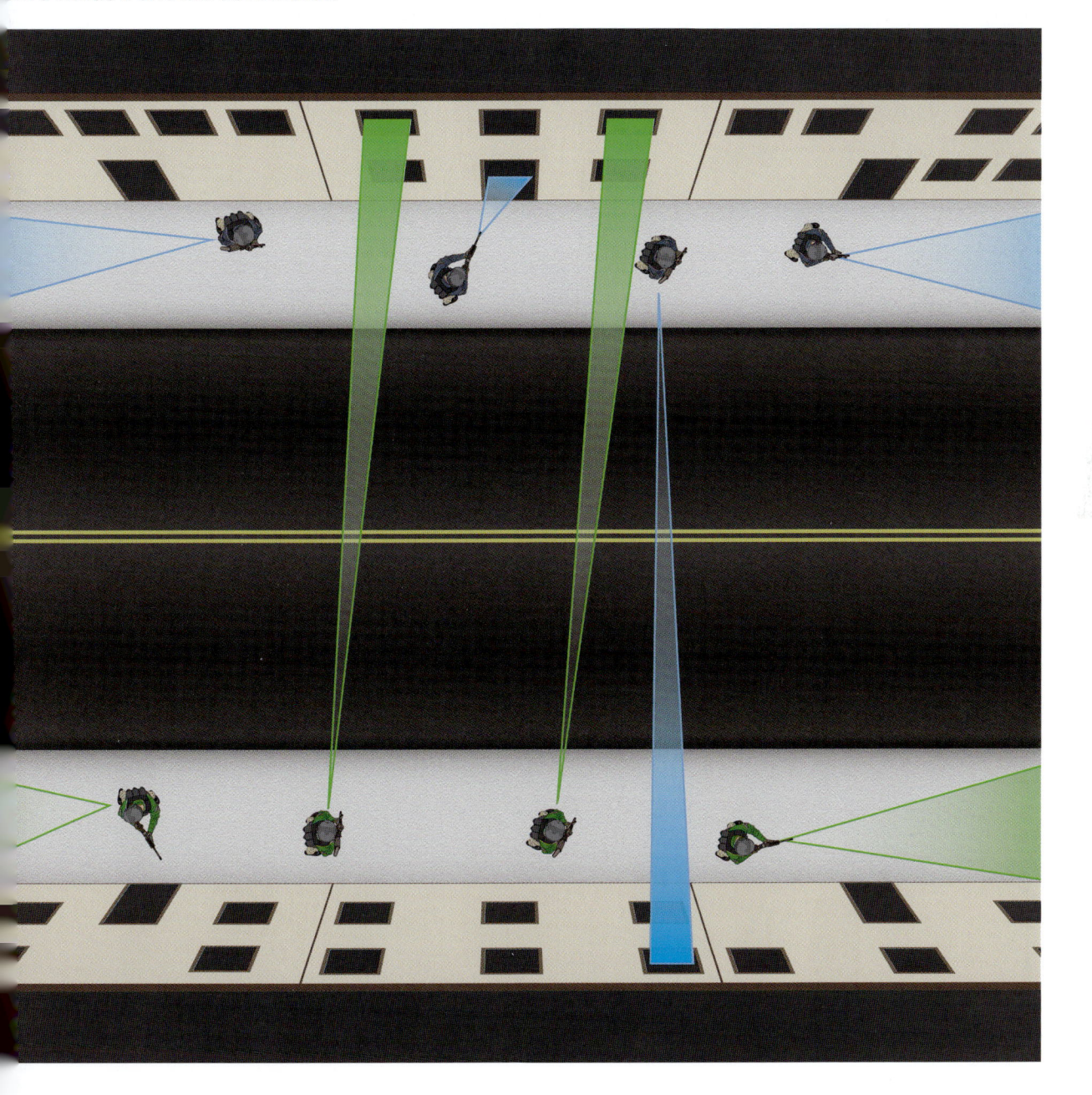

CROSSING ALLEYS OR NARROW STREETS

STEP 1 - Establish Near Side Security

If officers are taking fire from an alley but have to cross it, the lead officer will move around the corner and ta[ke] up a covered firing position to provide cover down the alley.

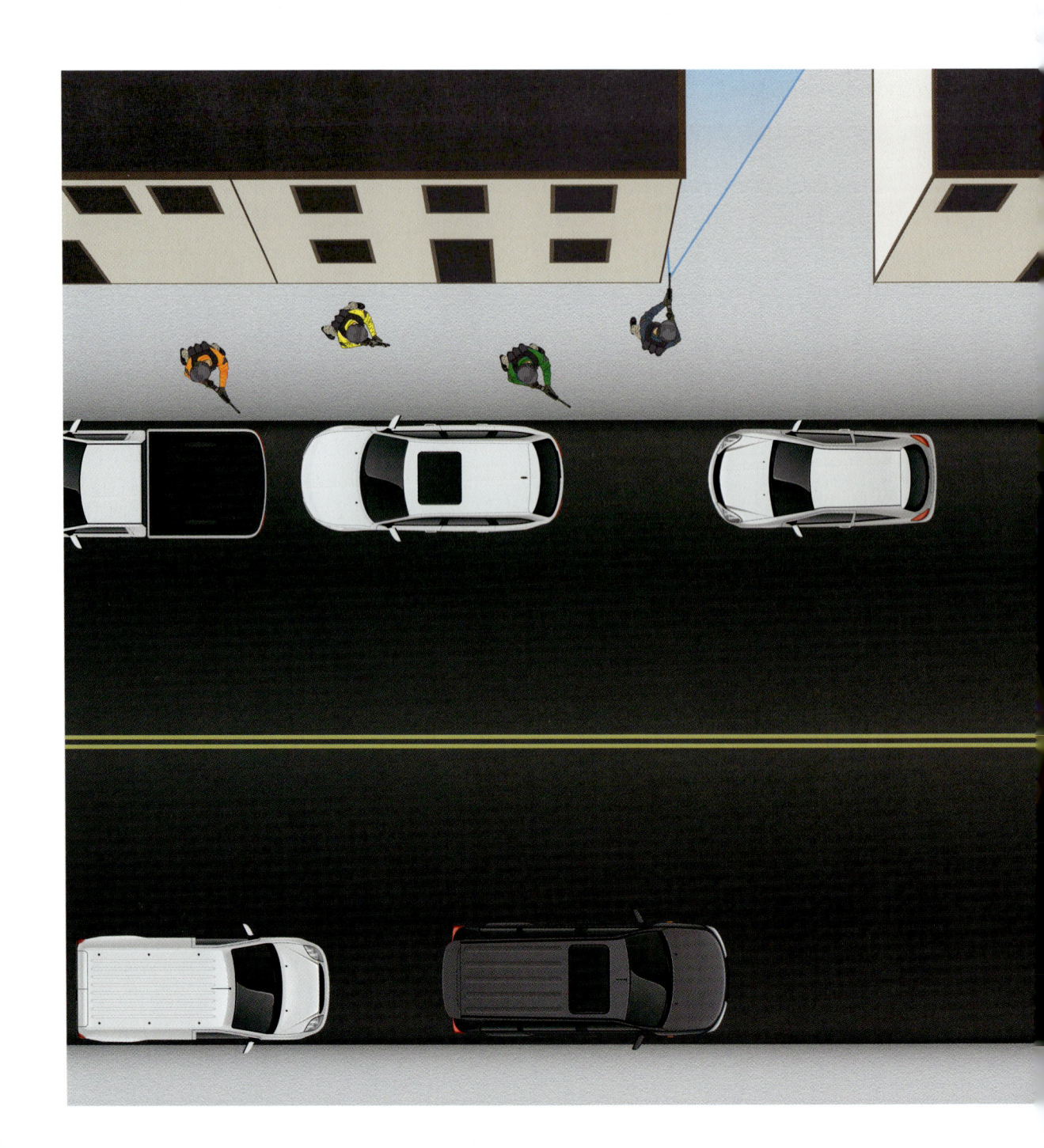

Exterior Movement 439

CROSSING ALLEYS OR NARROW STREETS

STEP 2 - Sprint Across

Once near side security is established, the remaining officers will sprint across the alley, maintaining spacing (5-10 yards between officers) as much as possible. When the last officer passes the officer providing near side security, the passing officer will call out "last man" (or use an arm squeeze) and the covering officer will join the rear of the formation.

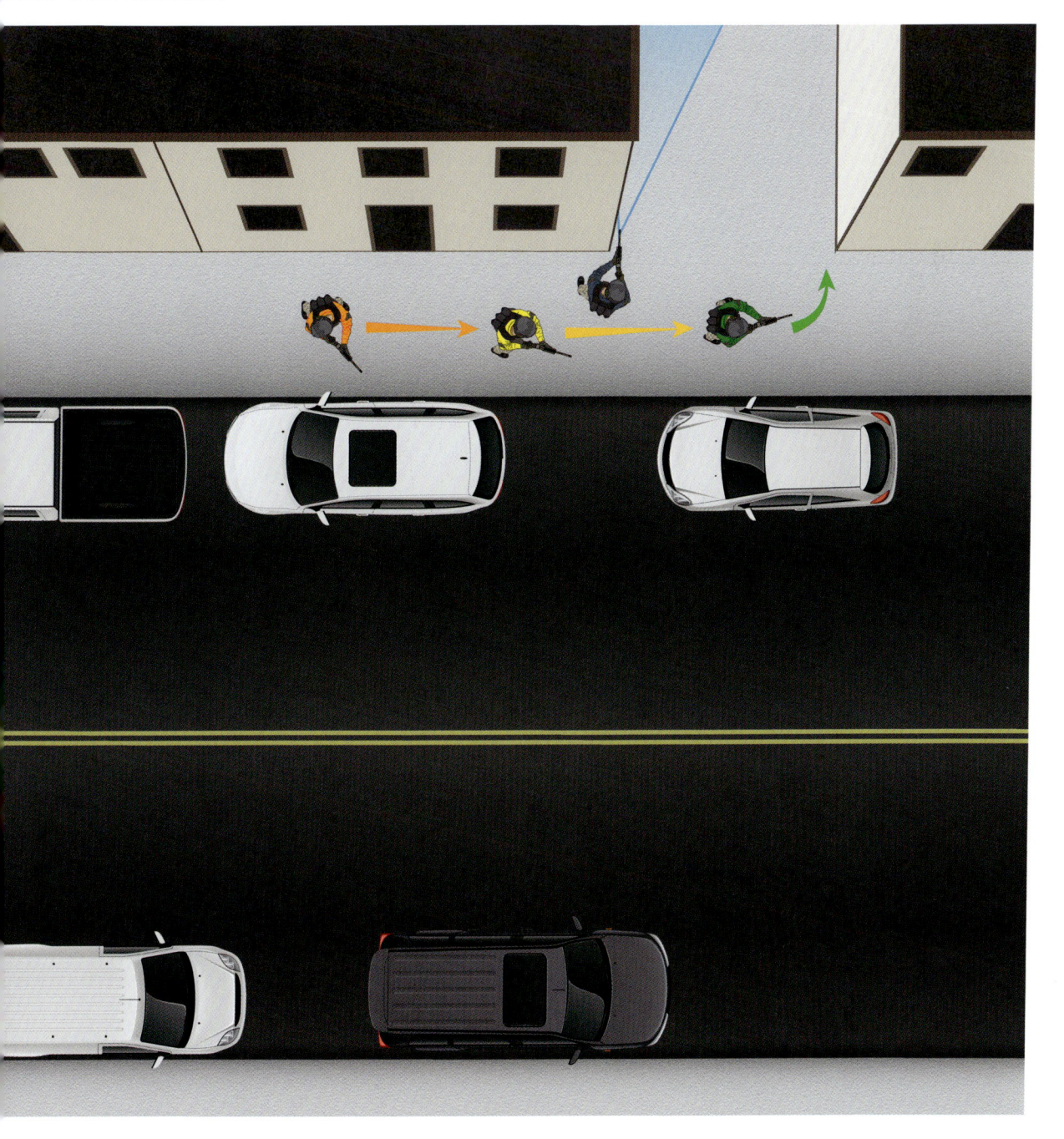

CROSSING ALLEYS OR NARROW STREETS

STEP 3 - Establish Far Side Security

When the first officer reaches the far side, he/she will stop at the corner and take up a covered firing positi[on] to provide cover down the alley. The rest of the officers will pass by and continue moving down the stre[et]. When the last officer passes the officer providing far side security, the passing officer will call out "last ma[n]" and the covering officer will join the rear of the formation.

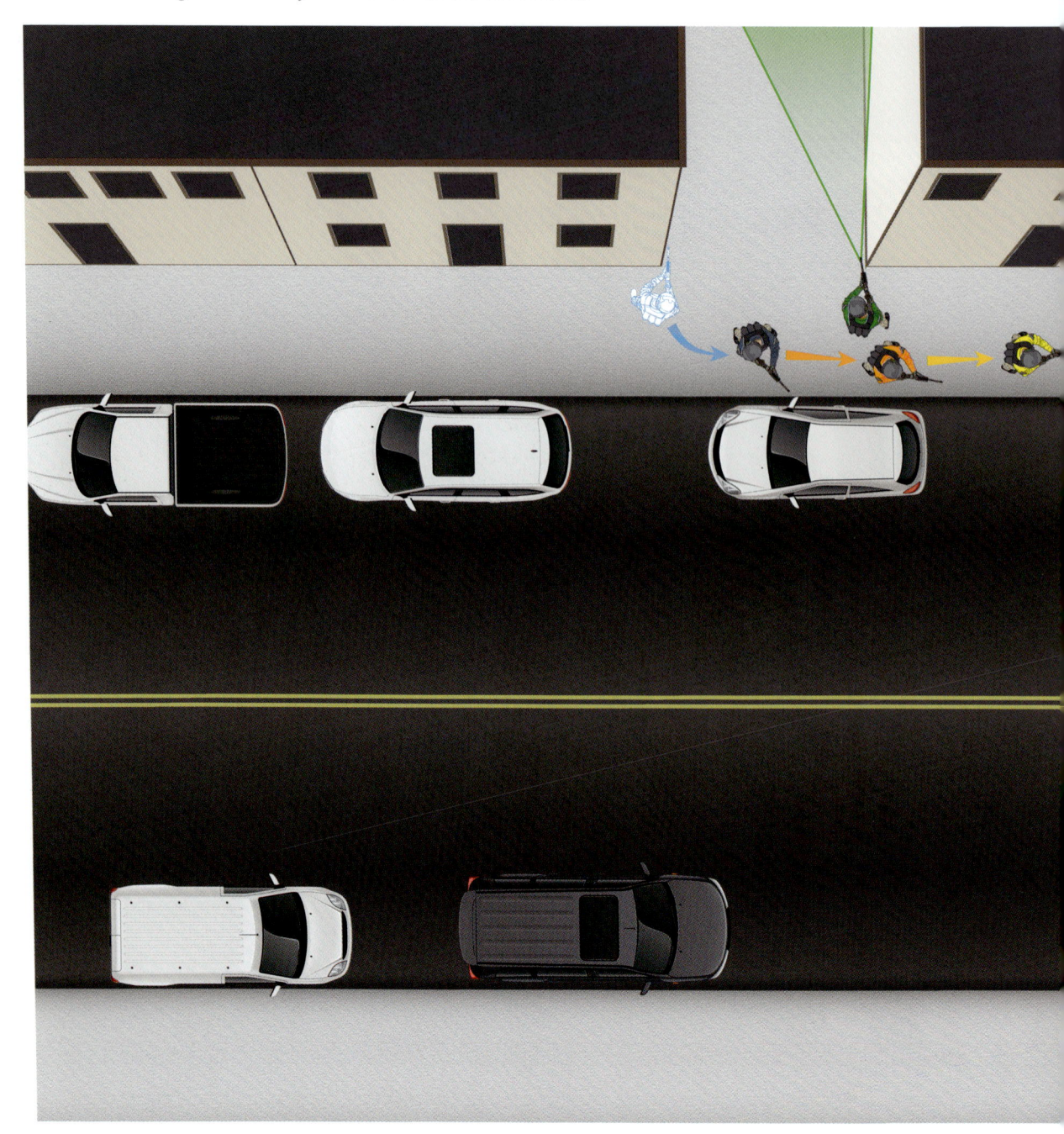

CROSSING WIDE STREETS

STEP 1 - Establish Near Side Security

Crossing a wide street under fire is the same as crossing an alley except it is sometimes advisable to place two officers providing cover at each corner. As the officers approach the street, the lead officer will take a knee and the second officer will move behind the lead officer. Both officers will execute a "high-low" clearing technique around the corner and cover down the street. Officers should only cross under fire if absolutely necessary.

CROSSING WIDE STREETS

STEP 2 - Establish Far Side Security

Once near side security is established, the next two officers will sprint as quickly as possible across the street maintaining spacing (5-10 yards between officers) as much as possible. When the two officers reach the opposite side of the street they will stop and provide far side security. They can either execute another high low technique or one officer can cover down street while the other covers to the front.

EXTERIOR MOVEMENT   443

CROSSING WIDE STREETS

STEP 3 - Sprint Across

Once both near side security and far side security are established, the rest of the team can sprint across the street. As the team passes each security element they will call out "last man" and the covering officers will join the rear of the formation. If there are only four officers in the team, once near and far side security is established, the near side security team will pick up and sprint across the street.

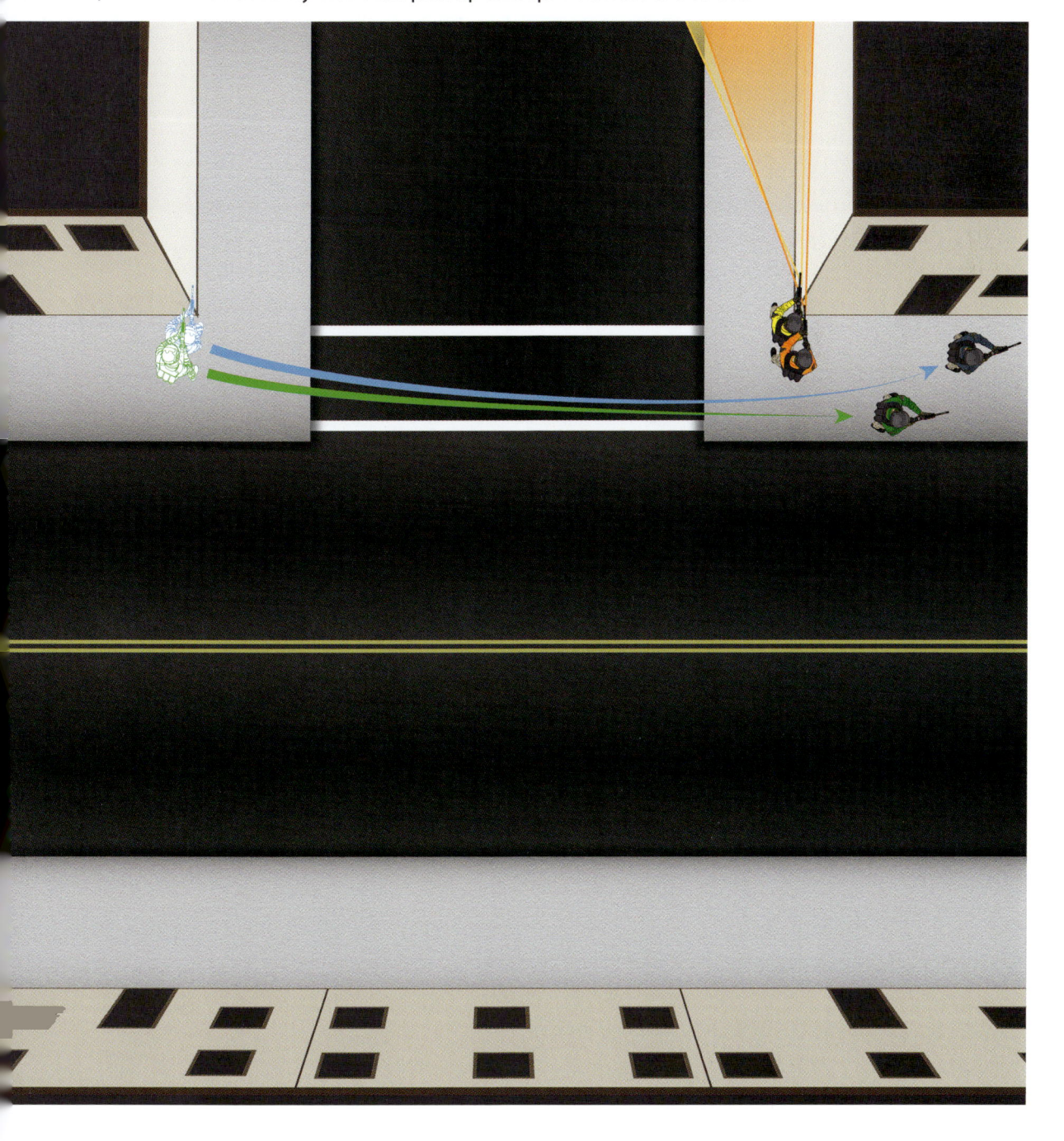

CROSSING WINDOWS

STEP 1 - First Officer Covers the Near Side

There are some situations when a team will be moving along the side of a building and will encounter window It is best for the team not just to walk in front of the windows since adversaries inside the building might s the team or shoot at the team through the windows. Instead, when the first officer identifies the window, h she will step out, away from the wall and raise the weapon to cover the windows.

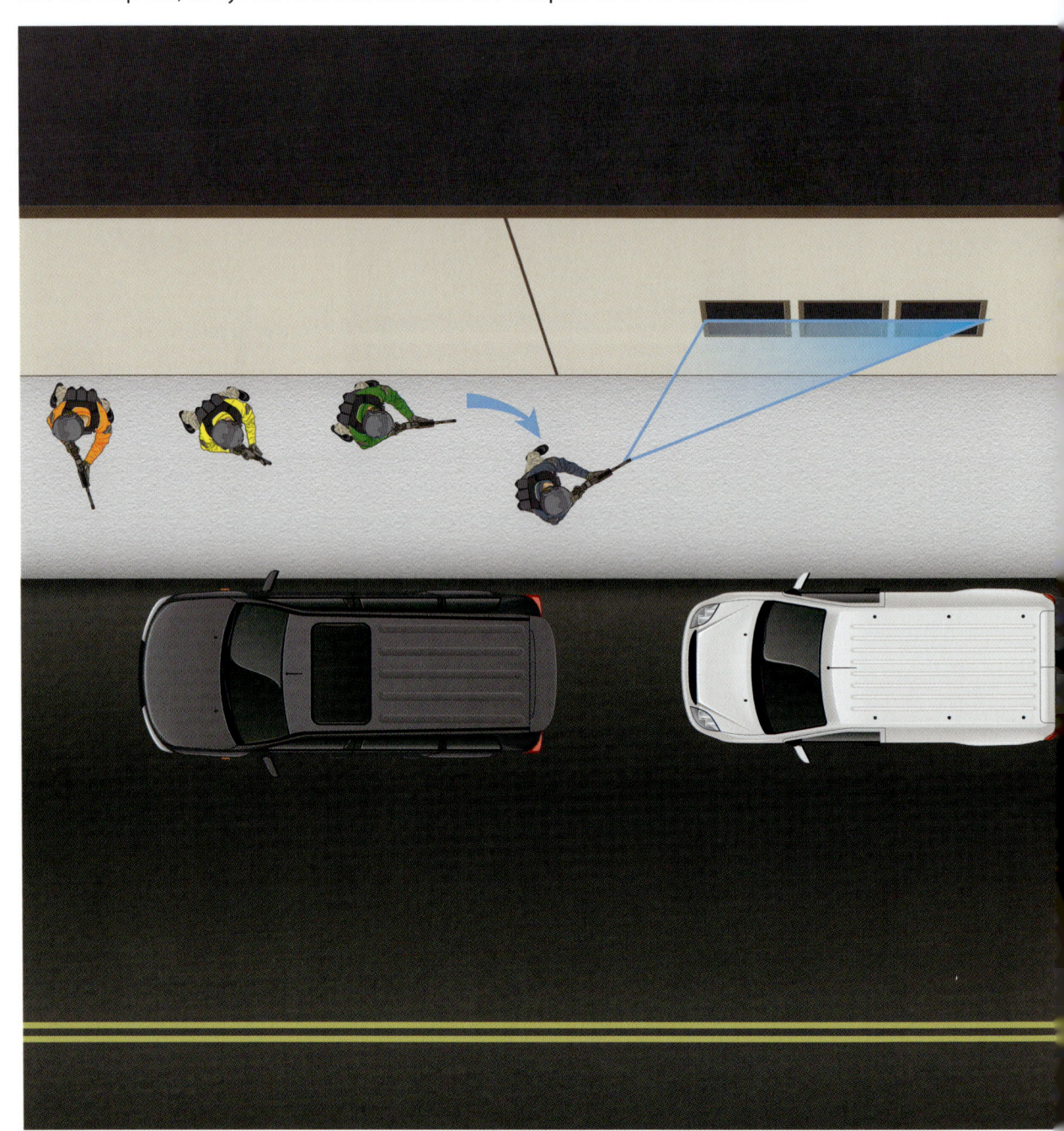

EXTERIOR MOVEMENT   445

CROSSING WINDOWS

STEP 2 - Team Crouches and Moves Past

As the lead officer steps out and raises the weapon, this is an automatic signal to the next officer that there are windows ahead. The next officer will crouch as low as possible and move forward, passing under the windows. The rest of the team will crouch and follow right behind. By stepping out, the lead officer creates a space for the rest of the team to move through, staying low and close to the wall.

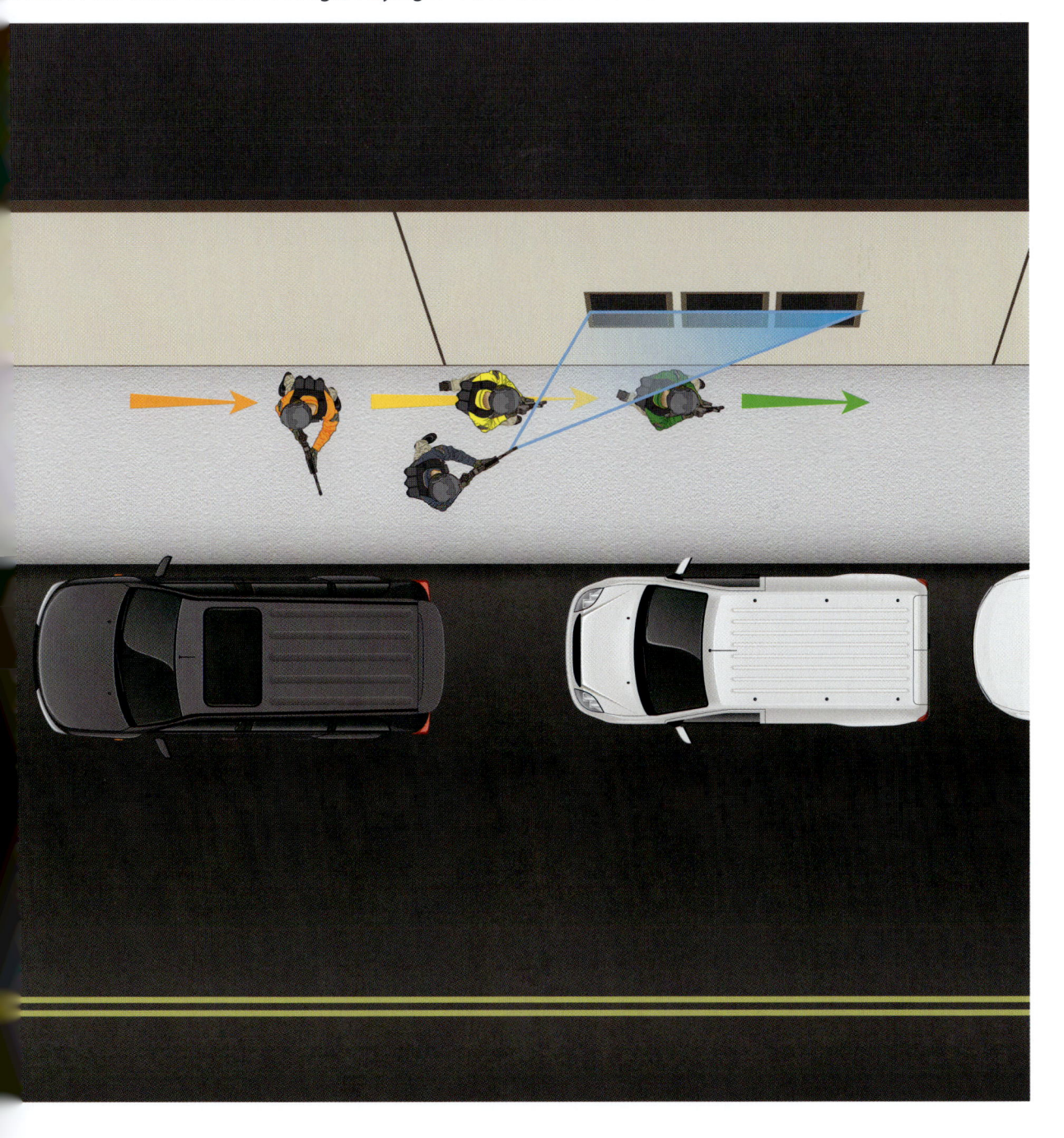

CROSSING WINDOWS

STEP 3 - Establish Cover on the Far Side

The first officer to move safely past the windows will step away from the wall and turn outward away from the building to cover the windows from the opposite side. It is important that the officer turn outward because otherwise he/she runs the risk of hitting the next officer in the face with the weapon.

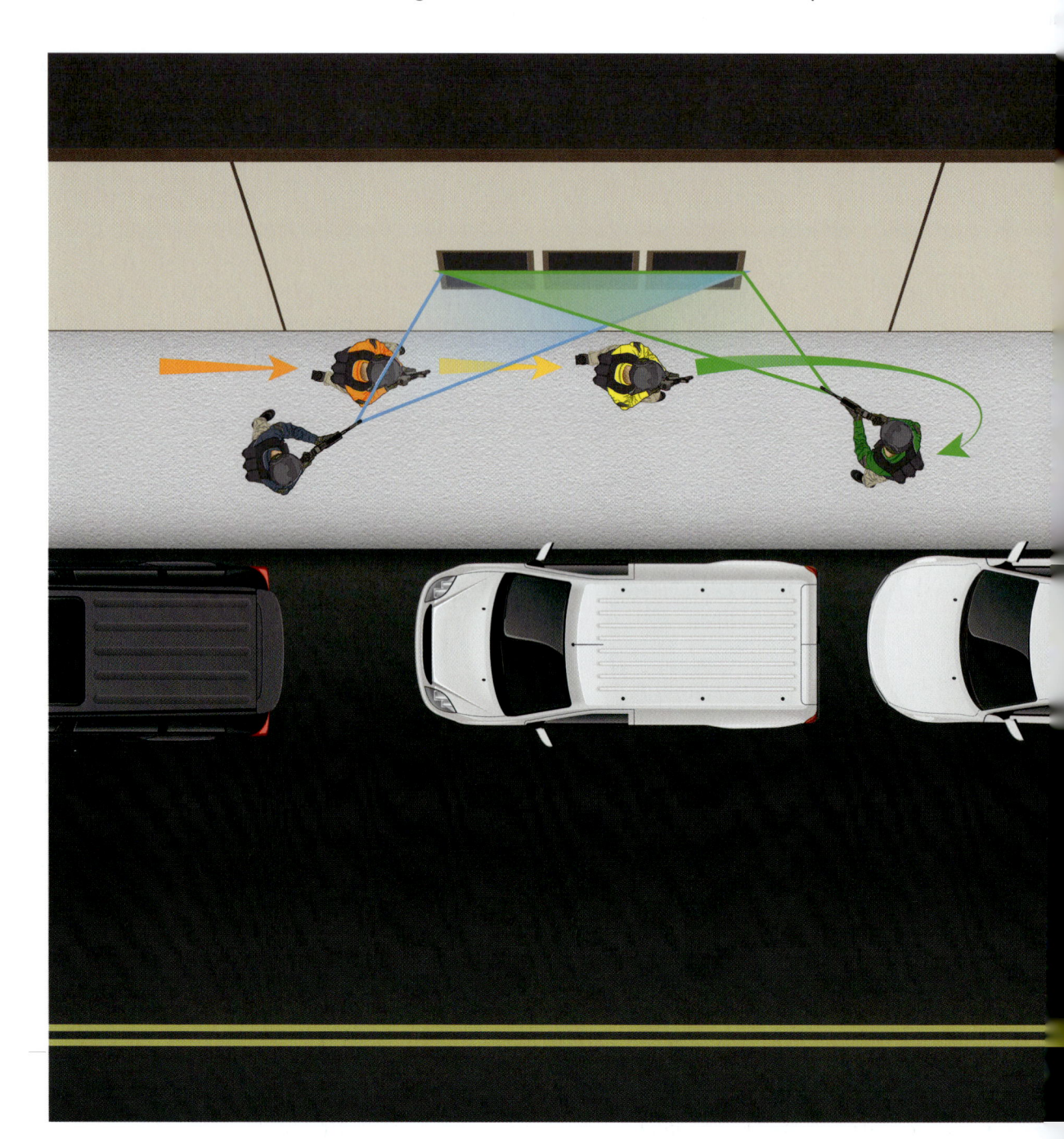

EXTERIOR MOVEMENT | 447

CROSSING WINDOWS

STEP 4 - Team Passes Through

By this time, the last officer in the team will have passed the officer covering the near side. As last officer passes the covering officer, he/she will call out "last man" to ensure no officer is left behind. The officer covering the near side will rejoin the rear of the formation. When the team passes the officer covering the far side, the same thing will happen and that covering officer will rejoin the formation as well.

SECTION 7

TACTICAL CONTINGENCIES

TACTICAL CONTINGENCIES
Prisoner Handling

Controlling occupants in a room can be one of the most challenging and distracting contingencies officers will encounter in a CQB scenario. Unarmed adversaries may resist arrest or attempt to flee, causing problems for the team. If there are innocent civilians in a target room, they must also be controlled and restrained until they can be properly searched. It can be very difficult to control civilians while also engaging threats in a room. If officers are not alert and highly trained there is a significant risk that they will accidentally shoot innocent people.

Civilian behavior can be very unpredictable in high-stress situations. Civilians may curl up on the ground. Some might cling to officers' arms and refuse to let go. Others might freeze and become entirely unresponsive. One of the most dangerous scenarios is when an armed civilian draws his/her weapon and attempts to fight back. While this sort of heroic action can save lives, it can also make it very difficult for LEOs to distinguish between threats and civilians. Officers must be prepared for all of these possibilities when entering a room. One of the best ways to prepare is to watch many videos of civilians reacting to crisis situations.

While civilians present a challenge and potential danger to the team, controlling suspects or hostile subjects is even more challenging. If subjects decide to resist arrest and tangle with an officer in physical confrontation, it can be difficult for other officers to get a clear shot. If several officers pile on the subject, they will be distracted and vulnerable to attack from adjacent rooms.

To control subjects and civilians in a room, officers will use three elements of control: dominating presence, verbal commands and physical contact. Officers will often have to use all three of these elements in conjunction in order to control the situation in a room. Once the occupants are under control, officers must carefully search and restrain each occupant. Officer should then do their best to segregate the occupants, placing potential threats along one wall and innocent civilians along the opposite wall. The "5 S's" can be a useful memory aid for dealing with prisoners: *Search*, *Segregate*, *Silence*, *Safeguard* and *Speed* to the next stage of processing. However, each department will have its own specific SOPs for prisoner handling.

If there are enough officers present on the scene, it is also possible to use a trail team or arrest team to handle prisoners while the entry team continues to clear the building. This is one of the most effective ways to handle prisoners without disrupting the momentum of the operation.

CONTROLLING SUBJECTS IN A ROOM

STEP 1 - Dominate the Room

The first step to controlling occupants in a room is to dominate the room. Ideally officers should not g[et] drawn into the middle of the room and engage in physical combat with the occupants. The officer's prima[ry] weapon is the best way to control occupants in a room. If officers get bogged down in physical combat wi[th] occupants, they will not be prepared to deal with lethal threats using their primary weapons.

PRISONER HANDLING

CONTROLLING SUBJECTS IN A ROOM

STEP 2 - Use All Three Elements of Control

To control occupants in a room, officers can use three elements: dominating presence, verbal commands and physical contact. The mere presence of armed officers in the room will help impose control on the people inside. If this is not enough and occupants continue to move or resist, officers can use aggressive verbal commands to force compliance. Each department will have their own preferences for which commands to use, however, it is important that commands are standardized. Three officers should not be yelling at a detainee to do three different things. If verbal commands are not enough, officers might have to use physical contact to control an occupant. For physical contact, at least one officer will provide coverage as the other grabs the occupant and moves the occupant to the desired position or location.

SHOW ME YOUR HANDS!

CONTROLLING SUBJECTS IN A ROOM

STEP 3 - Restrain and Search the Occupants

Using verbal and physical control as needed, the officers will line up the occupants along the wall of the roo[m] and assign at least one officer to cover them. In some cases, the officer will want to flex cuff or handcuff t[he] occupants before moving them. In other cases the officer will restrain the occupants once they are lined u[p] along the wall. Once the occupants are lined up facing the wall, another officer will go through and carefu[lly] search each occupant, checking every pocket for weapons or evidence. It can be useful to ask each occupa[nt] if he/she is carrying any weapons or dangerous materials before conducting a search.

CONTROLLING SUBJECTS IN A ROOM

STEP 4 - Segregate the Occupants

As more information is gathered on the occupants, the team will want to segregate occupants. It is best to separate the occupants into two groups. Creating more groups will cause confusion. One group can line up facing one wall and the other group can line up facing another wall. Exactly how to segregate the occupants is up to the individual department or officer in charge. Whichever officer is responsible for searching and segregating the occupants should ensure that they remain silent and do not talk to each other. Once the occupants are restrained, searched, segregated, lined up facing the wall and watched by at least one officer, they are ready to be moved off the premises.

USING AN ARREST TEAM FOR PRISONER HANDLING

STEP 1 - Blue (Entry) Team Dominates the Room

Blue team will enter and dominate the room, using the three elements of control to immobilize all occupan

PRISONER HANDLING

USING AN ARREST TEAM FOR PRISONER HANDLING

STEP 2 - Blue Team Calls in Green (Arrest) Team

At this point the blue team leader will call green team into the room and assign green team to finish controlling the occupants. Blue team must be sure green team has firm control before blue team moves on to continue clearing.

USING AN ARREST TEAM FOR PRISONER HANDLING

STEP 3 - Blue Team Continues Clearing

Once green team is in control of the situation, blue team can continue clearing the rest of the building officers expect to take many prisoners in one building, leaders might want to add personnel to the trail tea in order to have the manpower to handle all of the prisoners. When leaving officers in a room to contro prisoner, there should always be a minimum of two officers left in the room together.

TACTICAL CONTINGENCIES
Casualty Evacuation and Carry

Dealing with civilian casualties or injured officers is one of the most challenging scenarios an LEO can face. Evacuating a casualty is particularly difficult for the lone patrol officer, who may have to rescue his/her injured partner or a wounded civilian with no support. While other manuals will cover tactical medical skills in more detail, this section provides the basic fundamentals for how to get an injured person to safety in an emergency situation.

If a tactical team suffers a casualty, the first priority is to win the fight and secure the area. If all officers drop their coverage and focus on the casualty, there is an increased chance of taking another casualty. The critical concern for the tactical team is making sure the casualty is safe. In many cases, this can be accomplished without moving the casualty. Officers can simply lock down the room and call in emergency medical support. This is generally the best option since moving a casualty with a c-spine injury can be dangerous or fatal.

However, if there is no emergency medical support available and the casualty is in imminent danger, an officer may need to drag the casualty to a safer location where it is possible to administer medical aid. In this situation, the officer should first call for assistance over the radio. If possible, an officer should not attempt to provide medical aid under direct hostile fire. There is also no need to lift or carry the casualty. This can be difficult and dangerous, especially in the dark. All the officer needs to do is drag the casualty behind the nearest cover. This can be accomplished from a crouching position if necessary.

The officer can drag the casualty from under the arms or under the knees. If there are two officers present, one of the most effective techniques is to use a two-person carry, grabbing the casualty under both the arms and knees at the same time. Once the casualty is behind cover the officer can begin to provide medical assistance, while remaining alert for threats in the area.

EVACUATING A CASUALTY UNDER FIRE

STEP 1 - Dominate the Room

If the team enters a room and takes a casualty, it is critical that the team not stop fighting. The primary objecti must be to eliminate the threat and prevent more casualties. Once the room is dominated, the team lead must immediately communicate that an officer is down and needs medical assistance. If there are trail tear available, the lead team can continue to clear while the trail teams take care of the casualties. If no trail tear are available, the team will have to evacuate its own casualty.

CASUALTY EVACUATION AND CARRY | 461

EVACUATING A CASUALTY UNDER FIRE

STEP 2 - Provide Cover for the Evacuation

As soon as the team identifies the casualty, at least one or two officers will move to a good position to protect the casualty from enemy fire. These covering officers will face out and cover doors and danger areas.

OFFICER DOWN!

EVACUATING A CASUALTY UNDER FIRE

STEP 3 - Drag the Casualty to Safety

Once cover is established, at least one (preferably two) officers will drag the casualty to a safer location. T
could mean dragging the casualty out of the building, back to another room, or even into the corner of t
room or behind a piece of furniture. The objective is not to drag the casualty far but to simply get the casua
out of the line of fire. If there is no incoming hostile fire, it is best to leave the casualty in place and form
perimeter or defensive position around the casualty.

CASUALTY CARRY TECHNIQUES

One-Person Under Arm Drag

For this technique, the rescuing officer will approach the casualty from behind and reach under the casualty's arms, securing a firm grip. The rescuing officer will attempt to support the casualty's head and neck as much as possible by letting the head rest on the rescuing officer's chest. The officer will then move backwards, dragging the casualty to safety. This movement can be performed either from the standing position or kneeling position.

CASUALTY CARRY TECHNIQUES

Two-Person Carry

This technique is much faster and is the preferred technique if two officers are available. One officer will grab the casualty under the arms and the other officer will grab the casualty under the knees. The two officers will then quickly move the casualty to a safe location.

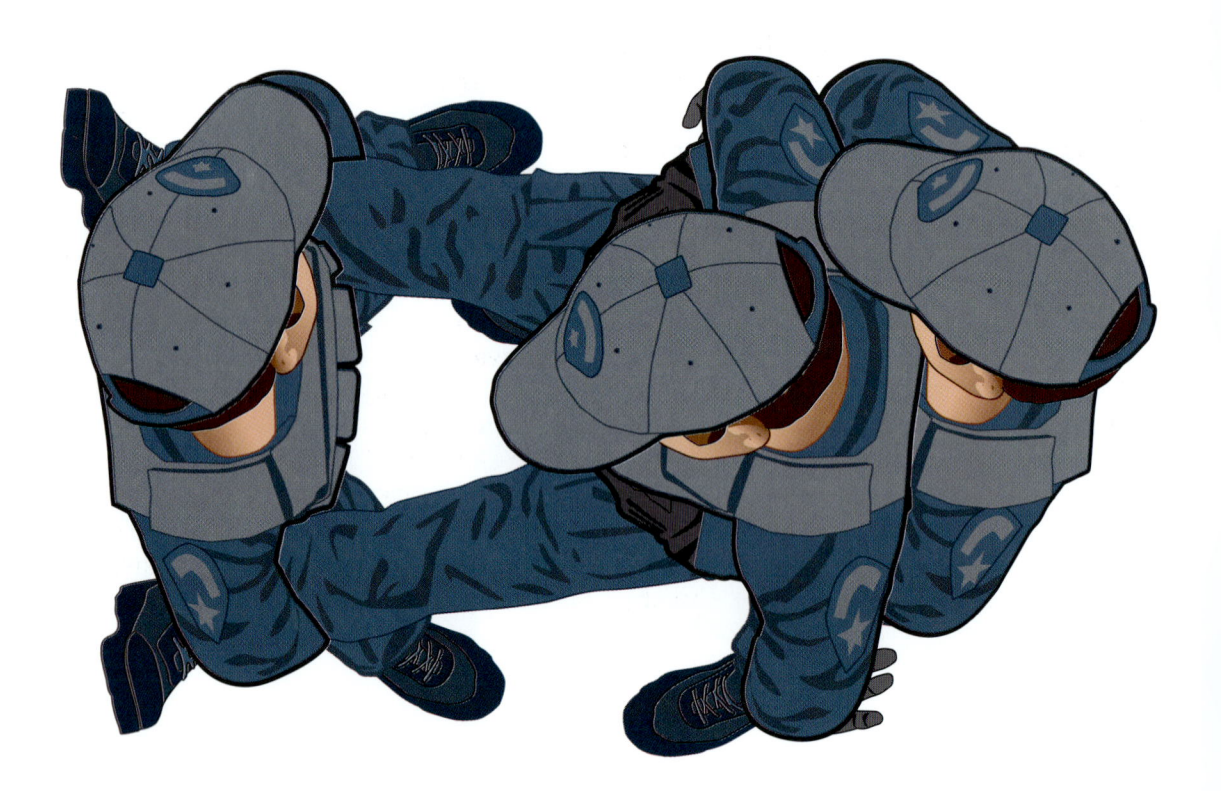

FURTHER TRAINING
Courses and Resources

This manual provides an overview of Close Quarter Battle tactics for law enforcement officers. However, the manual leaves many areas unexplored. There are a variety of other Special Tactics manuals, both current and in production, that are designed to compliment this manual. For more information on these additional manuals, visit **www.specialtactics.me**. Current and upcoming manuals will cover a variety of topics including: high-risk warrant, hostage rescue, CQB contingencies, sniper employment and breaching.

The *CQB Contingencies* manual is a particularly useful companion to this book. While this book focuses on the basics and mechanics of CQB techniques, the *CQB Contingencies* manual goes into more detail on how to deal with unexpected problems and variables including: mass casualty situations, fires, bomb threats, hostile attack dogs, barricade situations and suicide attacks as well as more detailed discussion of prisoner handling and casualty evacuation.

In addition to printed materials, Special Tactics offers in-person lectures and training courses for law enforcement units and organizations. Each course is custom tailored to customer specifications and can cover a variety of topics. For additional information on in-person training programs, visit the Special Tactics website.

If you have any questions, comments or suggestions regarding this manual, the Special Tactics staff welcomes you to contact us on our website at **www.specialtactics.me**. We look forward to hearing from you and hope you found this manual worthwhile. Thank you for keeping our communities safe.